Sponsorship for Sport Managers

Titles in the Sport Management Library

Sponsorship for Sport Managers

John L. Crompton, PhD
Texas A&M University

A Division of the International Center
for Performance Excellence
West Virginia University
262 Coliseum, WVU-CPASS
PO Box 6116
Morgantown, WV 26506-6116

Library of Congress Card Catalog Number: 2013946096

ISBN: 978-1-935412-54-0

Cover Design: Bellerophon Productions

Cover Photos: Cardiff City Stadium courtesy © Jon Candy/Flickr; Ashley Cole courtesy © sportsphotographer.eu, BigStockPhoto.com

Typesetter: Bellerophon Productions

Production Editor: Matt Brann

Copyeditor: Mark Slider

Proofreader: Maria denBoer

Indexer: David denBoer

Printed by Data Reproductions Corp.

10 9 8 7 6 5 4 3 2 1

FiT Publishing
A Division of the International Center for Performance Excellence
West Virginia University
262 Coliseum, WVU-CPASS
PO Box 6116
Morgantown, WV 26506-6116
800.477.4348 (toll free)
304.293.6888 (phone)
304.293.6658 (fax)
Email: fitcustomerservice@mail.wvu.edu
Website: www.fitpublishing.com

This book is dedicated to Bethany, Sherwood, Keira, Laura Jo and Dean.
May your futures be as enjoyable and satisfying as my life has been.

Contents

Detailed Contents

Preface

When Dennis Howard and I developed the third edition of our *Financing Sport* text, it quickly became obvious that in the 10 years since our second edition the array of strategies, techniques, vehicles, and tools used to finance sport had expanded considerably. It was apparent there was now too much material to incorporate comprehensive and in-depth coverage of all dimensions of the topic in a single text. There were two options: either reduce the depth of the coverage or extend the material to two volumes. Equivocating on the depth of coverage was dismissed because, selfishly, we regard the challenge of researching and discussing nuances of the material as being both personally satisfying and an integral part of our professional growth and development.

Selecting the sponsorship material as the topic of this second text reflects the extraordinary growth in investments on sport sponsorship during the past decade or so. Concomitantly, there has been much wider interest in studying it among the academic community, which has had two major results: An expansion of the literature both describing and analyzing sport sponsorship, and the emergence of specialist courses on the topic in sport management curricula.

Work on the two volumes proceeded simultaneously. Since I had led the sponsorship chapters in the two previous editions of *Financing Sport*, I continued in that role with this new volume while Dennis took the leadership role in the new third edition of the text. Ultimately, he found this role to be all-consuming and generously insisted that I should be the sole author of this sponsorship book. Nevertheless, Dennis' persuasion, encouragement, and facilitation of access to materials have been crucial to bringing this project to fruition. Indeed, the central reason for my involvement with these sport financing texts is the opportunity to work with him. The first book we wrote together was published in 1980 and the periodical renewal of our writing partnership has been important to retaining our close friendship over the past 35 years.

I am very appreciative of the assistance provided by Dr. Bob Madrigal and Dr. Bettina Cornwell, Dennis' colleagues at the University of Oregon. Both of them teach courses in sponsorship, as well as being leading scholars in researching the phenomenon. They generously offered access to materials, their course readings and class notes, and gave valuable counsel.

My mechanical writing tools consist of pen, yellow pad, scissors, and staples, which means that others have the onerous task of transcribing my difficult handwriting into typed form and safely securing the manuscript in the memory of a computer. Thus, special thanks go to Ms. Mary Burger, who exhibited both inordinate patience in interpreting my handwriting and cheerfully undertaking multiple edits of the material, and consummate skill in organizing the material into its final form.

The book is written from the perspective of sport managers. Securing additional financial resources through sponsorships is a prominent element in the job descriptions of many sport managers. For the most part, they do not seek sponsorship for the purpose of selling their product to a target audience (media tie-ins may be exceptions to this generalizations). Rather, it is companies that seek to increase their sales by linking with a sport event or facility through sponsorship. The sport manager's role is to understand how companies use sponsorship in their marketing programs, to be responsive to their needs, to charge an equitable fee for providing them with these leveraging opportunities, to be an active partner with the sponsors to help them meet their objectives, and to measure the extent to which these objectives were accomplished.

1

The Changing Role of Sport Sponsorship

DIFFERENTIATING SPONSORSHIPS FROM DONATIONS

In the context of this book, sponsorship is defined as a business relationship in which a cash and/or in-kind fee is paid to a sport organization or event in return for access to the exploitable commercial potential associated with that organization or event.[1] The distinctive terms in this definition which differentiate sponsorship from donations are *business relationship* and *exploitable commercial potential*. Both sponsorship and philanthropy provide funds, resources, and in-kind services to sport organizations, but the benefits sought in an exchange are different. The central benefit sought from philanthropy is the satisfaction of knowing that good is being done with the donated resources. Donations are altruistic and there is no expectation of a more tangible return. In contrast, the explicit rationale for investing in a sponsorship is that it will yield a commercial return on the investment.

While this conceptual distinction is clear, it is sometimes difficult to ascertain in a specific context. The effective operational determination of whether an investment is classified as a donation or a sponsorship is made by the IRS. If the IRS rules that a company receives a tangible, measurable, economic benefit from the contribution, then it is classified as a sponsorship investment undertaken for commercial advantage and is not eligible for a tax deduction. In contrast, if the benefits are perceived to be intangible, emotional, and not measurable, then the contribution qualifies as a gift and is eligible for a tax deduction. Thus, when an agreement requires that a property provides promotional benefits (e.g., media coverage or endorsements) these tangible benefits are treated as a business expense by the sponsor and as taxable income for the property. If the company does not require benefit from the property, then the sponsorship is treated as a donation so the revenue to the property is not taxable and it becomes a tax "write-off" for the company.

Corporate philanthropy is an oxymoron. Even though some corporate investments may be positioned and technically accepted by the IRS as donations, they are not altruistic. The officers of a corporation have no mandate to give away their shareholders' money. Their charge is to invest company resources in a way that optimizes the return to shareholders on their investment. Thus, a business should only make "donations" when it believes it is in its selfish interest to do so.

Potential company motives for donations become apparent in the following discussion of the three hybrid strategies shown along the continuum in Figure 1.1, which is anchored by unequivocal sponsorship and strategic philanthropy. This text focuses on the unequivocal sponsorship anchor, but it is recognized that these three hybrid strategies incorporate attributes of both sponsorship and philanthropy.

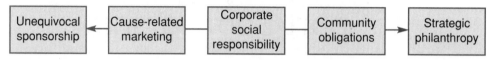

Figure 1.1. The Sponsorship-Philanthropy Continuum of Alternate Investment Vehicles.

Cause-related marketing strives to improve corporate performance through helping worthy causes, by linking donations to a cause with the purchase of a company's products or services. It aligns the commercial goal of increasing sales and revenues with corporate social responsibility. Companies contribute a specified amount to a designated cause when a customer purchases a company's product. The "specified amount" is effectively a "donation." However, the corporate contribution to the cause is conditional on consumers engaging in revenue producing transactions. Thus, even though corporations proclaim and position their donations to be acts of altruism, a company's reason for engaging in the partnership explicitly meets the definition of sponsorship in that a cash amount is paid to an organization and it is a business relationship exploited for commercial purposes.

Corporate social responsibility occupies a central position in the continuum. Frequent revelations of corporate shenanigans and accounting scandals have created an aura of public mistrust. The contagion effect extends this mistrust even to companies that are innocent of malfeasance. For a business to operate effectively, it must have a robust "license to operate." Hence, companies' engagements with sport properties may be driven by a perception that there is a need to improve this license and their image by demonstrating they are good corporate citizens. Thus, there is a business rationale in that the company seeks to enhance goodwill for its brands in the market place among potential customers, which it anticipates will lead to enhanced sales.

Community obligations are a localized form of corporate social responsibility with a similar rationale, which is sometimes characterized as "corporate paternalism." This is exemplified by, for example, a corporation headquartered in a community seeking "hometown hero" status. It has been suggested that this explains Federal Express Corporation's commitment of $100 million in naming rights to build an arena as part of the community's quest to attract an NBA franchise to Memphis, which is where the company's world headquarters is located.[2] The local focus means that the company's benefits are likely to be limited to enhancing the morale of employees, rather than seeking additional sales in the market place. Community obligation was the rationale offered by a large retailer for investing in a sporting festival: "Because we are based in

{name of city}, and that is one of its biggest events; we have to be involved" (p. 127).[3]
This theme was elaborated upon by another manager:

> [Name of city] is a unique place where corporations have built this city and so it's
> hard to say what you get if you do sponsor, but I think it's more clear what you
> don't get if you don't participate. . . . I don't think that we should take the view
> that you're forced to contribute money, but the quality of life in [Name of city] is
> directly related to the fact that corporations are committed to enhancing this
> quality . . . I would think that there's some subtle pressure applied by other corpo-
> rations . . . no one says, "Because company X spends it over here, it means we
> have to ante up." It's much deeper than that: It goes back a number of years when
> there was a recognition that participation in the community was something that,
> as a major employer, we had to take a leadership role in. And because we still
> retain our leadership position in the community along with the [other oil compa-
> nies], you cannot leave it, nor would we expect to—it's no longer something that
> we are pressured into. I think it is just an understanding that there is a role for
> companies who are large and are major employers and who, to some degree,
> access community services in a disproportionate amount that we need to return
> something. (p. 127)[3]

Again, while these community obligation partnerships lie towards the benefactor end of
the continuum, they do have a business element. For example, many businesses sponsor the local Special Olympics, an event that encourages the participation of those with
intellectual and developmental disabilities in sports. The intent of such sponsorships is
twofold: (1) to associate the company with a good cause and suggest that the business
is fulfilling a societal obligation to the community from which it draws customers,
employees, and investors and (2) to generate goodwill and enhance the image of the
business.[4] In some instances, the sponsor may be perceived as central to making the
event possible, which will heighten the goodwill that accrues. This is most likely to
occur for small events which often have difficulty securing financial support.[5]

Companies often seek to blur the distinction between sponsorship and philanthropy
in the public eye. While decisions may be based on the imperative to receive a return on
the sponsorship investment, businesses may seek to enhance public goodwill by con-
structing and communicating their support as altruistic. Clearly, it is advantageous to
sponsors if they can characterize their financial commitment as being philanthropic or
paternalistic, rather than being exploitative and profit motive driven. This is evidenced
by the term "sponsor" being replaced with synonyms such as "partners," "supporters,"
and "members" of the sport organization's "team" or "family," in order to convey an aura
of patronage rather than commercial interest.

In its early days, sponsorship often was not differentiated from philanthropy. Decisions to support a particular sport or sporting event frequently were made at the CEO's
whim, reflecting the personal interests of senior management rather than a careful
assessment of the benefits that were likely to accrue to the company from its investment. Today, decisions made in this way are unusual, but they are not unknown:

The world of sports is incredibly seductive to graying executives, who often would like nothing better than to recapture the days when they were jocks or dreamed of being jocks. The theory behind golf as a sponsorship is that you use it to reach a limited, but upscale audience of consumers, or if you are a business-to-business brand, to entertain your best clients. What's surprising, however, is the number of golf sponsorships purchased by consumer-product brands that are not particularly upscale and not striving to be. Let's be honest here. Many companies are in the sport primarily because the CEO is dying to be in the Pro-Am with Tiger Woods. That can quickly become on expensive round of golf. (p. 75)[6]

When senior managers' egos or personal preferences influence sponsorship decisions, they are putting their own interests above those of shareholders. At no cost to themselves, they are investing corporate funds in a sport event that yields, for example, season box seats for their own use.[7] However, as a result of the scandals in recent years that have focused attention on the integrity of corporate governance, there is now much more pressure on senior managers to demonstrate accountability for sponsorship investments by demonstrating how they are likely to increase a company's profitability.

Nevertheless, like many other corporate actions, sponsorship of a sport event is more likely to come to fruition if it is championed by a senior level decision-maker, and the champion's commitment may be stimulated by personal interest. A manager of event marketing commenting on a proposal observed that, "The chairman wanted it so you had to write it in a way that you should do it, and that was against our better judgment . . . He wanted it, so we did it." (p. 131).[3] At another company, a marketing communications manager observed, "If you can get to the heart of the CEO there are certain things that you can do" (p. 131).[3] While politics and relationships may still play some role in decisions, they are much less prevalent now that sponsorship has become an integral element in establishing a firm's overall strategic position.

Company executives and directors of sport properties are likely to have strong social networks and there is evidence to show that in some instances these may play a role in sponsorship decisions. Interlocking directorships and high ranking personal friendships among senior managers may be influential because decision makers are likely to invest in those ventures managed by people whom they know and trust. A public relations manager observed that if the president knows someone who sends a proposal "It'll get a lot more attention than it would at our level if it had come to us" (p. 131).[3] In the context of sponsorship, friendship and trust are key resources because it may take several years for a sponsorship to generate the returns a company seeks. If these resources exist from previous interactions, then this likely will expedite a sponsorship's effectiveness.

EXCHANGE THEORY

Sponsorship involves two main activities: (i) an exchange between a sport property and a company; (ii) the marketing of this linkage, which is primarily a sponsor responsibility, but a sport property has a central partnering role in facilitating it.[8] Thus, the central concept underlying sponsorship and donation/fundraising is exchange theory. This

Exhibit 1.1

Benefits That May Be Sought by Businesses From Sponsorship

Increased Brand Awareness

(i) Create awareness of a new brand

(ii) Create awareness of an existing brand in new target markets

(iii) Increase awareness of a unifying corporate brand being superimposed on multiple local brands acquired through corporate purchases

Brand Image Transfer

(i) Create a brand image when a brand enters a market for the first time

(ii) Reinforce the image of an existing brand

(iii) Reposition an existing brand

(iv) Increase "clout" through associating with a major sport property and with other companies sponsoring it which have a much higher profile

(v) Counter negative publicity

Demonstration Platform

(i) Showcase a brand's technical capabilities

(ii) Reinforce perceptions of the attributes of an existing brand

Hospitality

(i) Cultivate a relationship with key customers, distributors, retailers, and employees

Product Trial or Sales Opportunities

(i) Offer product trial to potential new customers

(ii) Generate sales leads

(iii) Induce sales increases through promotions tied to the sponsorship

(iv) Create on-site sales opportunities

theory is one of the most prominent theoretical perspectives in the social sciences and has been used to explain a wide range of phenomena. It has two main precepts: (i) two or more parties exchange resources; (ii) the resources offered by each party must be equally valued by the reciprocating parties.

In response to the first precept of exchange theory, sport organizations have a large number of relatively narrowly focused attributes that they may use as "currency" to facilitate an exchange with businesses. They are listed in Exhibit 1.1, but they can be classified into six broad categories that are shown in Figure 1.2: increased brand aware-

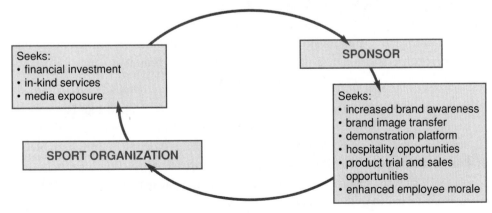

Figure 1.2. The Sponsorship Exchange Relationship.

ness, brand image transfer, demonstration platform, hospitality opportunities, product trial or sales opportunities, and enhanced employee morale.

In exchange for offering these benefits to companies, a sport manager may seek three types of benefits from them: financial, media, and in-kind. Often, the first question asked by a potential sponsor relates to how much media promotion will be forthcoming. Sponsors seek to maximize their "reach" (i.e., to access a larger number in their target markets than those who are on-site at an event). Thus, if media sponsorship is secured early, it is likely to make it easier to attract other sponsors. Alternatively, the sport organization can ask its major sponsor with which media the company would prefer to be associated, or with whom it has worked effectively in the past, and then it can approach those media. The downside of having a prominent media sponsor is that its competitors are unlikely to give the event significant coverage. This was illustrated by the fate of *Today* when it sponsored English soccer:

- *Today* was a new daily newspaper launched in the UK. It became title sponsor of the Football League to achieve brand awareness. This is a major reporting area for all media, but they boycotted the use of the official new sponsorship title of the League, because rival media did not want to give an advantage to a competitor. Not surprisingly, the "*Today* Football League" sponsorship lasted only one year and the newspaper itself subsequently soon went out of business.[9]

There are five types of in-kind benefits that a business sponsor may provide: (i) product support, which could include equipment, and food and beverages, for example, during MLB All-Star Game week Chevrolet provides automobiles for use by MLB executives, players, and VIPs, while at PGA tour events Cadillac or other automobile sponsors provide vehicles for use by players and PGA executives[10] (ii) personnel support, for example, assistance from staff who may have computing expertise that the sport property needs; (iii) prizes such as merchandise and gift certificates that can be used for promotion purposes by both the event property and by its cosponsors; (iv) website exposure that provides exposure to the sport organization and its event; and (v) communication resources and expertise to aid the sport property in increasing awareness and interest.

With regard to this latter in-kind benefit, when a sponsor invests in extending the promotion accompanying a sport event because of a desire to increase awareness of the sponsor's linkage to it, this obviously benefits the property owner. It has been noted that sponsoring corporations sometimes have more expertise and funds available for promotion than the sport property responsible for an event:

Every sports property, no matter how large, is in the midst of a ferocious battle for the attention of consumers. If the properties are honest, most will tell you they don't have the marketing expertise or dollars to make themselves unforgettable. But we sponsors do have those dollars, and unfortunately most event organizers—*most*—don't want sponsors to behave like marketing partners, regardless of what their agents tell us in the sales pitch.

If event organizers were smart they would end up in a situation where it doesn't cost them money to promote their property. Instead, other people—the sponsors—would actually pay to promote it. MLB leverages it sponsors' dollars by requiring them to promote the game. Sponsors have to build sweepstakes and promotions around baseball, they have to buy commercial time in national games, and a certain percentage of that commercial time must be spent on baseball-themed ads. When you add up these commitments, baseball has an extra advertising budget of millions of dollars that we sponsors are paying for (p. 5).[11]

It is easier for companies to invest in in-kind sponsorship rather than to use cash because it can be "hidden" from shareholders or employees who may be skeptical of the value of the sponsorship. Thus, an executive from Target commenting on his company's sponsorship of the NBA Minnesota Timberwolves' basketball arena observed: "We were concerned about negative reaction from the press, public, and employees. Try telling your employees you can afford to put the company's name on the arena when they are receiving only minimal raises" (p. 4).[12]

Few organizations are self-sufficient with respect to critical resources needed to augment an entity's strengths or ameliorate its weaknesses, so partnerships are endemic in contemporary society. Thus, sponsorships are viewed as strategic businesses alliances by both corporations and sport properties. These alliances involve pooling skills and resources to better achieve the objectives of both parties, enabling both entities to strengthen their positions in their respective marketplaces. These objectives may be *strategic* (e.g., a company entering a new market, or a sport property seeking enhanced prestige from associating with a major corporation) or *operational* (e.g., providing a platform that unifies a company's communications effort, or reducing costs to a sport property from in-kind I.T. assistance).

The second precept of exchange theory suggests that a corporate partner will ask two questions, "What's in it for us?" and "How much will it cost us?" The trade-off is weighed between what will be gained and what will have to be given up. A decision to invest will only be forthcoming if the trade-off is perceived to be positive and if the benefits accruing cannot be secured more effectively or efficiently through the use of another vehicle. A key feature of this second precept is that the exchange is perceived to be fair by both sides. Fairness is judged by two criteria: (i) the level of benefits received compared to those that were expected; and (ii) the level of benefits received compared to those received by other sponsors.[13] If these two criteria are not met, then a sponsor is likely to be dissatisfied. In such situations, "rainchecks" or future discounts will be required to restore balance to the exchange and remove the sponsor's dissatisfaction, or the sponsor will be unlikely to reinvest in the future.

EVOLUTION OF SPORT SPONSORSHIP

Chronological Evolution

The first businesses in the United States to be associated with, and invest in, sport events were in the transportation industry.[14] In 1852, a New England railroad transported the Harvard and Yale teams to a crew competition and vigorously promoted it. The company profited from the rail tickets sold to thousands of fans who traveled to the site. By the late 1890s, a similar strategy had been adopted by streetcar and rail companies in many cities by developing close links with baseball teams which generated traffic from downtown areas to the ballparks which tended to be on the periphery of cities.

Albert G. Spalding appears to be the first major corporate CEO to perceive the advantage of establishing a "business relationship" and the "exploitable commercial potential" from aligning with sport teams and events. Over a period of two or three decades, Spalding created the world's first dominant sporting-goods company, predating Nike, adidas and others by almost a century. As Exhibit 1.2 indicates, his companies were not always required to reciprocate with a "cash and/or in-kind fee to a sport organization" so some of the alignments may not qualify as sponsorships as defined in this text.[15] Nevertheless, he pioneered the potential of associating with sports to enhance brand equity; demonstrated the power of "official supplier status"; engaged in team sponsorships; and contracted for celebrity endorsements. All of these are prominent features of contemporary sport sponsorship.

Following Spalding, Harvey Firestone, the founder of Firestone tires, put his tires on a car driven by Barney Oldfield in the Indianapolis 300 in 1909. Oldfield told spectators, "My only life insurance is Firestone tires." Firestone contracted with him to paint this phrase on the side of his racecar, and he toured the country with it, "performing amazing feats of speed." He developed the Oldfield tire brand with Firestone which was widely popular. The racecar tires were identical to those sold for everyday use on roads in those early days, so the public saw how well they performed on the track and wanted them for their own vehicles. The race track as a demonstration platform was effective and gave rise to the adage "Race on Sunday, Sell on Monday."[16]

Similar pioneering sponsorship arrangements were instigated elsewhere, For example, two expatriate Englishmen, Felix Spiers and Christopher Pond, who had established a substantial catering business in supplying refreshments to the Melbourne and Ballarate Railway in Australia, underwrote the cost of the first tour of an English cricket team to Australia in 1861. Consistent with the goals of contemporary corporate sponsors who increasingly seek direct sales and revenues from their investment, Spiers and Pond netted a profit of $11,000 from their sponsorsip.[17] They also capitalized on the publicity they received from this very successful venture by returning to Britain to establish a famous catering company, Similarly, in France the magazine *Velocipide* sponsored an early automobile race in 1887.[18]

Despite these early beginnings, sponsorship investments remained relatively small and infrequent until the mid-1980s. Since then, their emergence as a primary strategic vehicle for many thousands of corporations has been remarkable. In 1987 sponsorship spending in North America amounted to $1.35 billion, increasing to $10.5 billion in 2003, and by 2012 it was almost $19 billion. Elsewhere, sponsorship of soccer in the UK in 1982 amounted to approximately $20 million per year.[19] Three decades later in 2012 one source of soccer sponsorship alone, shirt sponsorship of English Premier League teams, exceeded $235 million annually.[20] Given that these teams have multiple other sponsors (Manchester United, for example, has 32 other major sponsors)[21] it seems likely that annual sponsorship funds flowing into English soccer probably now approach $1 billion.

Exhibit 1.2

AG Spalding's Pioneering Use of Sponsorship: Brand Equity, "Official" Supplier Status, Team Sponsorship, and Celebrity Endorsements

The legendary Albert G. Spalding was the dominant pitcher in baseball in the 1870s. He parlayed his fame to transition into being the president and primary owner of the Chicago White Stockings in the 1880s. From this position he was the National League's chief promoter, spokesman, and enforcer of all matters related to the professional game. He was widely acknowledged to be "the brains of the National League" and was the key figure in establishing the white world of professional baseball as a viable commercial enterprise in the 1880s and 1890s.

He capitalized on his fame and positions by opening a sporting goods store in Chicago in the 1870s. By the end of the nineteenth century, from this base he developed a vast network of retail outlets, distribution channels, and manufacturing factories. Effectively, he creatively nurtured a new industry in sporting goods and he dominated that industry. Elements of sponsorship played a key role in building this empire.

In 1876, the National League gave Spalding an exclusive contract to publish the "official League Book" which served as a catalyst for his business expansion. He almost immediately supplemented publication of the league book with an annual volume, *Spalding's Official Baseball Guide*. Although this was *not* an official league publication its inside cover reprinted a letter from the League's secretary confirming the company's exclusive right to the book, not the guide, but Spalding did not make that distinction clear to the guide's audience! These publications, especially the guide, were powerful vehicles for promoting and selling Spalding's athletic products and for creating in the public mind the inseparability of the Spalding name from interest in baseball and sport in general. This appears to be the first major example of a corporate entity using sport to build its brand equity. (This term is explained in Chapter 2).

Parallel to the publication's relationship, Spalding contracted with the National League to provide its teams with baseballs for all league games in exchange for the exclusive designation as the maker of the league's official ball. In his *Guide* publication, Spalding unilaterally extended this mandate to also include non-league games stating, "Spalding's official League ball . . . *must* be used in *all* games played by League clubs, whether with League, professional, or amateur clubs."

By the end of the 1890's, Spalding was widely recognized as the leading figure in American sports. This resulted in his central involvement with the nascent U.S. Olympic Games movement. He led the U.S. contingent at the 1900 Paris Games and was the dominant force in the 1904 Games held in St. Louis where his companies designed the stadium, organized the track and field competition, provided the athletic equipment, and won awards for the quality of their products at the associated Exposition. The company's advertisements capitalized on these achievements saying Olympic officials "selected Spalding Athletic implements for exclusive official use . . . because of their acknowledged superiority, reliability, and official standings" (p. 88).

Spalding pioneered celebrity endorsements to promote his products. Thus, King Kelly and John "Monte" Ward, the most well-known baseball players of their era lauded the company's bats and baseballs. Similarly, professional road racers like Fred Titus, Walter Sanger, and L.D. Cabanne pronounced on the high quality of their Spalding bicycles and urged the public to purchase what the professionals rode. These three riders were signed to contracts requiring them to use Spalding equipment whenever they raced. Wearing racing shirts with the words *The Spalding Team* emblazoned across the front, the trio dominated the League of American Wheelman's circuit in 1894, ensuring that the Spalding company's sponsorship generated additional business.

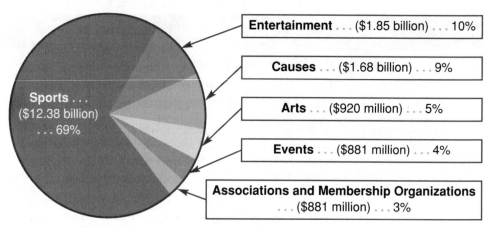

Figure 1.3. Shares of the North American Sponsorship Market.

Worldwide spending on sponsorship exceeds $51 billion.[22] While these increases are dramatic, remarkably, they underestimate the impact of sponsorship because they represent only the direct sponsorship fee and do not include the leverage and activation costs that accompany sponsorship investments. As sponsorship has grown, so has the supporting infrastructure with companies, their agents, and properties all having designated units to manage it.

Over two-thirds of sponsorship spending ($12.38 billion) is invested in sports (Figure 1.3). The four major U.S. professional leagues and their teams account for $2.46 billion of this: NFL, $946 million; MLB $585 million; NBA, $572 million; and NHL $356 million.[23]

There are 77 companies that spend over $15 million a year on sponsorship, and of these 11 spend over $100 million. They are listed in Table 1.1.[24]

The evolution of sponsorship in sport is vividly exemplified in Exhibit 1.3, which shows its dramatic growth in the Olympic movement in the past three decades.[25] In 1976 when Montreal hosted the Olympic Games, the Quebec separatist movement was prominent in political consciousness. The Canadian government did not provide financial assistance to Montreal because it feared the rest of the country would view this as support for the separatists and be outraged. Nevertheless, the city proceeded with its bid. Its popular mayor who led the effort to secure the Games assured his residents it would not require a sub-

Table 1.1. The Largest U.S. Company Investors in Sponsorship	
Company	**Amount ($ million)**
PepsiCo, Inc.	340–345
The Coca-Cola Co.	265–270
Anheuser-Busch Cos.	255–260
Nike, Inc.	215–220
AT&T, Inc.	175–180
General Motors Co.	170–175
Toyota Motor Sales U.S.A., Inc.	150–155
MillerCoors LLC	135–140
Ford Motor Co.	135–140
Adidas North America, Inc.	135–140
Verizon Communications, Inc.	105–110

Exhibit 1.3

The Evolution of Sponsorship at the Olympic Games

At the first modern Olympic Games in Athens, in 1896, financial pressures caused the Organizing Committee to raise money by selling souvenir stamps and medals, as well as advertising in the souvenir program. Those first Games also had an official travel agent in Thomas Cook. Thus, from the beginning, the Olympics had a commercial presence. In 1912 at the Stockholm Games, the IOC commenced selling broader commercial rights to corporations: several Swedish companies were permitted to take photographs and sell memorabilia. At the 1924 Games, two advertising signs appeared inside the Olympic Stadium adjacent to the scoreboard. This created such a furor that the IOC established a new rule in the Olympic Charter: "Commercial installations and advertising signs shall not be allowed in the stadia, nor in the other sports grounds."

However, the Olympics had to be paid for, so at the 1928 Amsterdam Games on-site concessions were solicited and one of the first vendors was Coca-Cola, which claimed the title of Official Olympic Supplier as a consequence of the company's contribution of 1000 cases of the soft drink to the American Team.

The Oslo Winter Olympics introduced licensing in 1952 when 135 agreements were signed mostly for decorative souvenirs; value-in-kind arrangements with corporations supported the Helsinki Games that summer and delivered food to athletes. The first full showing of sponsorship surfaced eight years later in Rome, when 46 companies paid to become "official sponsors/suppliers" of non-sports related products. This was the start of a flood of commercial support that reached its crest in Montreal with 628 sponsors.

The IOC created the TOP program in 1985 in order to develop a diversified revenue base for the Olympic Games and to establish long-term corporate partnerships that would benefit the Olympic Movement as a whole. The TOP program operates on a four-year term—the Olympic quadrennium. The TOP program generates support for the Organizing Committees of the Olympic Games (OCOGs) and the Olympic Winter Games, the National Olympic Committees (NOCs), and the IOC.

The TOP program provides each Worldwide Olympic Partner with exclusive global rights and opportunities within a designated product or service category. The global marketing rights include partnerships with the IOC, all active NOCs and their Olympic teams, and the two OCOGs and the Games of each quadrennium. The TOP companies may exercise these rights worldwide and may activate marketing initiatives with all the members of the Olympic Movement that participate in the TOP program. Thus. TOP partners are:

- Worldwide partners of the Olympic Games
- Partners of the International Olympic Committee
- Partners of the Olympic Winter Games
- Partners of the Olympic Summer Games
- Partners of all National Olympic Committees
- Partners of all Olympic teams competing in the Winter and Summer Games

The number of TOP partners and the revenues produced by the sponsorship program are listed below:

(Exhibit continues on next page)

Quadrennium	Games	Partners	Revenue (millions USD)	Average Per Partner (millions USD)
1985–1988	Calgary/Seoul	9	$96	$10.66
1989–1992	Albertville/ Barcelona	12	$172	$11.33
1993–1996	Lillehammer/Atlanta	10	$279	$27.90
1997–2000	Nagano/Sydney	11	$579	$52.64
2001–2004	Salt Lake/Athens	11	$663	$60.27
2005–2008	Torino/Beijing	12	$866	$72.16
2009–2012	Vancouver/London	11	$957	$87.00

Exhibit 1.3 *(Continued)*

The Evolution of Sponsorship at the Olympic Games

The Olympic Movement generates revenue through several programs. The IOC manages broadcast partnerships, the TOP worldwide sponsorship program, and the IOC supplier and licensing program, while the OCOGs manage domestic sponsorship, ticketing and licensing programs within the host country, under the direction of the IOC. In addition, NOCs generate revenue through their own domestic commercial programs.

The following chart provides details of the total revenue (in millions of dollars) generated from each major program managed by the IOC and the OCOGs during the past five Olympic quadrenniums.

The IOC retains approximately 10 percent of the revenues it receives from its programs to pay for the operational and administrative costs of governing the Olympic movement. 50 percent of its revenues go to the OCOGs to help pay their costs for the Summer and Winter Games, while the remaining 40 percent of revenues are allocated to all 205 participating NOCs to support the training and development of Olympic athletes and teams.

Source	1993–1996	1997–2000	2001–2004	2005–2008	2009–2012
Broadcast	$1,251	$1,845	$2,232	$2,570	$3,914
TOP Program	$279	$579	$663	$866	$957
OCOG Domestic Sponsorship	$534	$655	$796	$1,555	TBD
Ticketing	$451	$625	$411	$274	TBD
Licensing	$115	$66	$87	$185	TBD
Total	$2,630	$3,770	$4,186	$5,450	TBD

*Revenues shown in millions USD

stantial subsidy proclaiming: "The Olympics can no more have a deficit than a man can have a baby."[26] A member of the Montreal city council soon after prophetically stated: "It was an unqualified disaster. We're going to pay every day of our lives for a two-week party most of us couldn't attend" (PR3).[26] The Montreal Games vigorously pursued sponsors and 628 of them provided US $7 million in revenues. Nevertheless, the Games were a financial catastrophe for the city of Montreal which incurred a debt of $2.8 billion (approximately $10 billion in 2010 dollars) that was finally paid off in 2005.[27]

The 1980 Olympic Games were held in Moscow. Cost was not a concern because the Russian government hosted and funded them at great expense, regarded the Games as a significant propaganda opportunity and were focused on their political value. However, by 1980, the immense cost of the preceding Games led to a widespread perception that there was not a business model which could make the Olympic Games viable. Consequently, there was no interest by governments in hosting them. Indeed, there was serious discussion as to whether a UN or UNESCO-type organization should take over the Olympics as a sort of cultural heritage project in order for the event to survive.[28]

This was the crisis situation that prevailed when a group from Los Angeles came forward with the only bid for the 1984 Games offering an unprecedented and extraordinarily radical proposal. Their bid was contingent on the revolutionary precept that no public funds would be available. In the absence of any alternative bids, the International Olympic Committee (IOC) had no option but to waive Rule 4 of the Olympic Charter which requires the host city to be financially responsible for producing the Games. Instead, the IOC contracted with the Los Angeles Olympic Organizing Committee (LAOOC) which was incorporated as a private entity to produce the Games. There were many who philosophically opposed this commercialization arguing it was counter to Olympic mores, but pragmatically nobody presented a viable alternative to this approach.

It was the first Olympics to be privately funded as most of the funds were raised from sponsorships. The LAOOC persuaded 34 companies to each pay between $4 million and $13 million in cash, goods, or services. It pioneered the ideas of creating product categories, granting each category designated rights, and giving each sponsor product category exclusivity. This event is considered by many to represent the birth of contemporary sponsorship. It resulted in the Games producing a net profit of $222 million.

However, it also demonstrated the revenue potential of sponsorship to the IOC. As a result, after the Los Angeles Games the IOC established The Olympic Partners (TOP), which was modeled on the LAOOC's principle of assuring global exclusivity in each product category. The revenue from TOP sponsors subsequently accrued directly to the IOC, not to the host Olympic organizing committees. Under TOP, companies sign on for a four-year period embracing both the Summer and Winter Games. As Exhibit 1.3 reports, they gain the right to promote their Olympic affiliation in every country that participates in the Games and have worldwide exclusivity within their product category.

There have been exponential increases in the fee for TOP sponsorships. The $4 million to $13 million range in Los Angeles in 1984 soared to an average of $87 million per company in the 2009–2012 quadrennial period (Exhibit 1.3).[25] However, the IOC have added value for the partner companies by substantially reducing "clutter" through having fewer sponsors. Whereas there were 34 in Los Angeles, the number of subsequent TOP sponsorships has ranged from 9 to 12.

Evolution of the Conceptualization of Sponsorship's Role

Sponsorship's growth has been fuelled by an expansion in awareness of its potential power. This awareness has passed through three "eras," which are shown in Figure 1.4. Each advance builds upon the foundation of the previous era's understanding of sponsorship. During the initial "learning" stage in the 1980s and early 1990s sponsorship was perceived as a communication vehicle. As such, it was incorporated into companies' integrated communication strategies. The marketing director of a TOP sponsor explained the strategic impact of using sponsorship as a communications platform on his company:

> At the time, we had no company-wide marketing. Instead, we had dozens of departments going off in different directions. One person was doing a program about the heritage and tradition of the company, while another person's program

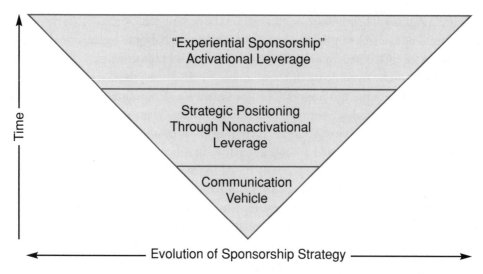

Figure 1.4. The Expansion of Sponsorship Strategy Through Three "Eras."

emphasized how modern we were. One person's marketing efforts touted the features of our products, while another person's emphasized the importance of our distributors. The print advertising was naturally very different from the television advertising. Not only were these individual marketing efforts sending out messages that competed with each other, the individual marketing budgets were too tiny to produce very much besides a lot of incremental waste.

Then we signed on as a worldwide sponsor of the Olympic Games, and, for the first time, we were able to convince our individual department managers to design their marketing materials around a single theme. Suddenly, we were able to get tremendous leverage out of our spending. A lot of small marketing budgets that used to be spent on efforts that cancelled each other out were behaving like one big marketing budget spent in a very focused and disciplined manner. The advantages for our brand were enormous. For the first time, there was a discernable consistency and style in all our communications, and it was easier for consumers to figure out who we were (p. 102).[6]

In the mid-1990s, there was a realization that its role could be much broader than communication. It morphed from a communication tool to a marketing platform and became a central component in the strategic positioning of a company's brands to differentiate them from the brands of competitors whose products are essentially similar. This stage was termed "sponsorship-linked marketing"[29] This movement to a marketing platform had two dimensions. First, as shown in Figure 1.5, there was integration of all the vehicles described in Figure 1.1 through which a company invested in sports properties. By ensuring they coalesced to focus on a coherent marketing platform, there were economies of scale and the impact on accomplishing marketing objectives was greater than the previous independent, piecemeal use of these funds. There was a realization that the whole was greater than the sum of the parts.

Figure 1.5. Integration of Sponsorship Investment Vehicles.

The second integration dimension that characterized arrival of the sponsorship-linked marketing era was a recognition that the central theme platform which sponsorships created became the focus that all elements of the marketing mix could use to leverage a sponsorship investment. As Figure 1.4 shows, initially this leveraging was nonactivational meaning that marketing activities supporting the sponsorship were likely to be passively processed by a targeted audience. Such activities may include public relations, paid advertising, on-site signage and T-shirt identification.

In the last decade, there has been an awareness that maximizing return on an investment requires that sponsorship leverage be "activated" rather than merely passive. This involves associating the brand with additional experiences linked with the sport event in which customers feel, think, act, or relate to it. This has been termed "experiential sponsorship" (p. 42).[30] Thus, for example, Coca-Cola's activation seeks "to create an unforgettable moment, i.e., a unique experience in connection with the brand" at the sponsored event.[30] Nonactivational and activational leveraging are discussed in detail in Chapter 5.

Accelerating Ubiquity

In recent years there has been a widespread expansion in the contexts of sponsorship from professional and elite sport to collegiate and high school sport. In a 1989 article in *The Chronicle of Higher Education*, corporate sponsorship was characterized as having made "relatively limited inroads into college athletics" (p. A37).[31] That has changed! Almost all NCAA Division I and II colleges and universities now have some form of corporate sponsorship. Historically, college sports sponsorship was fragmented. Each college operated independently making it difficult for major companies to develop integrated national marketing platforms. This is evolving. For example, IMG have created an extensive portfolio of schools which offers companies a national sponsorship platform that spans 49 states.[32] Companies can now have a presence in all of the states, or some subset of them, with one sponsorship investment. This is a more extensive reach then any of the major professional leagues can offer, since none of them have a presence in more than 30 states. In addition to offering a national platform, IMG can offer regional platforms. Thus, for example, there may be regional companies that might wish to target the 14 schools in each of the Southeast and Atlantic Coast Conferences.

One of the early companies to take advantage of these new platforms was Aaron's which operates at over 1,900 locations in 48 states and in Canada. Its business is sales and lease ownership and specialty retailing of residential furniture, consumer electronics, home appliances, and accessories. Since students and recent graduates are a primary target market, Aaron's became a sponsor of both basketball and football teams at 30 major universities across the country. The company explained its rationale:

> Our customers are fans of college sports, and this agreement provides us with a platform to reach millions of existing and potential Aaron's shoppers through 30 premier college athletic programs across the United States. The university audience is an important target for Aaron's on several levels. For example, current students and recent graduates on their own for the first time can gain independence when they sign a lease agreement with Aaron's. We never check credit and offer an affordable payment plan, which allows young adults to learn the responsibility of making monthly payments without the risk of ruining their fragile credit. Additionally, Aaron's are one of the few retailers in the country that is rapidly expanding and hiring new employees in a tough economy. Our more than 1,900 locations across the country offer a multitude of both managerial and entrepreneurial opportunities.[33]

Sponsorship is now percolating down from varsity level to intramural sports on campus. The corporate goal is to raise brand awareness among college students who are an influential, but relatively difficult to access, consumer group. While only 2% of college students are varsity athletes, it is claimed that 80% of them participate in recreational sports.[34] An illustration of intramural sponsorship is given in Exhibit 1.4.[34]

There are more than 18,000 high school athletic programs in the U.S., engaging over 6.5 million students in sport activities. However, an increasing number of school districts are unable to provide the funds needed to offer a full range of high school athletic programs. More high schools are moving to a "pay to play" system in which student athletes pay a fee for each sport they play. Approximately one-fourth of all high schools now collect such participation fees.[35] Typically, pay-to-play fees range from around $50 to several hundred dollars, but at the high end of the range being a student on multiple high school varsity teams can cost over $2,000. Sponsors have moved into this funding vacuum, especially soft-drink companies seeking to place vending machines in schools in return for their sponsorship.

Exhibit 1.4

Sponsorship of Intramural Flag Football

Flag football is a popular intramural program that has attracted sponsorship. Recent sponsors were Target (title sponsor), Nestlé Crunch (presenting sponsor) and Mentadent (presenting sponsor). The sponsors enjoy near year-round visibility on campuses that offer intramural flag football. Their banners encircle playing fields. Their names appear on cones that mark boundaries, and on flag belts. They distribute product samples and award prizes to the winners of sideline competitions. And they award expenses-paid trips to New Orleans to regional-winning teams in men's, women's, and co-ed divisions.

Regional hosts have welcomed as many as 58 teams to their campuses for three days of competition. "It is quite a sight," noted the intramural director at a regional tournament host institution, "If you drive by the fields during that weekend, you know who the sponsors are. It's very visible, almost a party atmosphere."

Another regional tournament host director observed that the advent of corporate sponsorship generated more interest in the tournament from local media, the campus community, and visiting participants. He said, "With corporate sponsorship, you have things like windbreakers, and you can do a lot of the niceties that you normally wouldn't have the money to do."

The director of marketing at Nestlé said that students surveyed three months after participating in the flag football tournament were twice as likely to list Nestlé Crunch among their five favorite brands of candy bars as they were upon their tournament registration. "What the sponsorship program allows us to do is to have continued brand presence throughout the year, via the websites that students access to look at calendars and the standings and via the message boards that are in the intramural facilities. Most important, we have a chance to participate in a relevant way in the consumers' lives by sponsoring an activity that is very near and dear to them."

State high school associations have similarly found it more difficult to organize statewide tournaments. They have become more expensive to develop as expectations of quality have risen, and gate receipts in many sports are insufficient to cover tournament costs. Thus, almost all high school state associations now have sponsors to support their regional and state athletic championship tournaments. Typical of these arrangements is that of the North Carolina High School Athletic Federation:

The federation serves 375 North Carolina high schools and has 26 sponsors invested in one of the four sponsorship levels offered: Presenting Partners

Courtesy of BigStockPhoto.com

(American Automobile Association [AAA], Time Warner, Wells Fargo); Official Sponsors (Wilson, Farm Bureau Insurance, Huddle High Schools, Musco, Max Preps); Event Sponsors (six companies); and Host City Sponsors (eleven companies). The levels of sponsorship range from a minimum of $1000 through $100,000.

Farmers Insurance is perhaps the most pervasive sponsor of high school sports. The company has arrangements with 18 state high school associations. Its typical investments are $250,000–$500,000 for statewide exclusive arrangements and $30,000–$50,000 for sport-specific partnerships. In a relationship-driven business like insurance, high school sports offer a vehicle for making connections. The key to making the initiative work for Farmers Insurance is the involvement of their network of independent local agents. The state association agreements provide access for these agents to partner with their local high schools. Typically, agents will invest $2,000–$3,000 per athletic season for banners and PA announcements, but many of them activate the sponsorship by prominently engaging as volunteers on the site at the games.[36]

Another emerging trend in the evolution of sponsorship in sports is affinity cards which is a form of cause-related marketing. These are used both by colleges and professional teams. The team links with a bank that issues credit cards. Each time someone uses the card, the team receives a contribution—typically 1%—of the amount charged. A team challenges its supporters to ask the question, "Why use a bank card that just gives money to the bank, when you can use one that gives money to the team you support?" By tapping people's loyalty to a team in this way, banks have an opportunity to encourage card-switching and to increase their market share. The cost to the banks is relatively small because these payments reflect a small portion of what they earn from annual fees and the interest that they charge card holders. It is also a small part of the percentage they receive from each transaction, which ranges from 1.5% to 6%, that they charge their participating merchants:

> Barclay Card partnered with the NFL to offer fans of the NFL teams their Extra Points credit card. The card incorporates the fans' team colors and logos. Cardholders earn points for a loyalty program created for each team that can be redeemed for team experiences, game day tickets, memorabilia, and all the NFL licensed merchandise. Card users earned NFL Extra Points every time they used the card and received a 20% discount for purchases on NFLShop.com made with the card.
>
> To activate the launch, a team branded web site was created where fans could learn about product benefits, win authentic NFL prizes, watch NFL videos, play interactive games, test their trivia skills, and download team wallpaper and a digital widget. Prior to the launch on Extra Points "Football Friday" Sweepstakes was operated for four weeks by the NFL which awarded authentic jerseys, hats, and other merchandise.[37]

The affinity card is being expanded to other industries beyond credit cards, as the vignette in Exhibit 1.5 illustrates.[38]

Exhibit 1.5

Extending the Affinity Principle Beyond Credit Cards

In Texas, and in 14 other states, electricity has been deregulated and multiple companies compete fiercely in major metropolitan areas in those states. Like credit cards, it is difficult for consumers to differentiate among electricity providers.

The University of Texas (UT) affinity card program with Bank of America is one of the country's biggest, reflecting the passion of its 280,000 alumni in Texas, and 450,000 across the country. Given the success of its affinity credit card, UT expanded the hybrid licensing/sponsorship principle by signing a six-year agreement with Champion Energy Services. This licenses Champion to sell electricity that is 100 percent derived from renewable sources (mainly wind power) as Texas Longhorn Energy in deregulated electricity markets.

Every new account generates funds for UT and consumers receive Longhorns' merchandise, memorabilia, access to events, ticket discounts, and other benefits as incentives. The program is promoted by stadium signage program advertisements, and web, television and radio advertisements. The price is competitive with that of other providers. The expectation is that when passionate fans are given the opportunity to give something to the school and be "green" without incurring additional personal costs, this will be persuasive in them electing to prefer the new brand over its undifferentiated competitors.

SOURCES OF SPONSORSHIP MOMENTUM

In the past decade, the rate of growth in sponsorship has far outpaced that of investment in any other form of marketing vehicle. It was noted earlier that the 1984 Los Angeles Olympic Games was the watershed event which demonstrated to the corporate sector that sponsorship could be a highly effective promotional medium. It created substantial impetus. Eight factors have undergirded this impetus and continue to stimulate contemporary corporate involvement in sponsorship: Specificity of target audiences; proliferation of broadcast and digital media; increased acceptance of the commercialization of sport; company mergers; globalization; the banning of tobacco advertising; advertising "clutter"; and contagion attributable either to mimicry or proximate geographic location.

A strength of sponsorship is that it is able to *efficiently communicate with specific target audiences.* Thus, widespread acceptance of the concept of market segmentation which emerged in the 1970s and 1980s enhanced corporate interest in sponsorship. Market segmentation is the process of partitioning large markets into smaller homogeneous subsets of people with similar characteristics who are likely to exhibit similar purchasing behavior. In the 1960s, most companies engaged in mass marketing. By the 1980s successful companies recognized that a mass market did not exist, but rather the marketplace consisted of segments or clusters of potential customers with a different propensity to purchase particular products and services. Acceptance of segmentation was accelerated by the high profile documentation provided by demographers of the fragmentation of society into yuppies, single parent families, dual-income households with children, "empty nesters," generations X and Y, and so on. This fragmentation made a company's potential customer more elusive and difficult to reach with traditional advertising.

Sponsors can target specific audiences by their choice of sport. This has been reflected in the growth of narrowly focused outlets that cater to special interests both in the broadcast and print media. For example, 40 years ago sport magazines were dominated by generic publications such as *Sports Illustrated* and were relatively few in number. Today, there are likely to be between two and six magazines and multiple websites and television channels catering to individual sports such as golf, running, baseball, football, or whatever. Their readership and viewer profiles offer the potential for sponsors to reach a large proportion of their target market through association with events conveyed as news by these media. The extraordinarily expanded opportunities to reach people through a profusion of media channels created by the broadcast and digital media have enhanced the ability of sponsors to access tightly specified target audiences. It has been noted that, "Sponsorship works because it fulfills the most important criterion of a communications medium—it allows a particular audience to be targeted with a particular set of messages" (p. 42).[39]

The *proliferation of broadcast outlets* including subscription services via cable or satellite, pay-per-view special events, Internet broadband, digital and high definition broadcasting, text and picture messaging, mobile phones and other digital forms, has led to a substantial increase in the amount of televised sport produced. Sport occupies a relatively high percentage of broadcast time, since much of it is relatively inexpensive to produce and it is widely popular compared to shows, documentaries, et al. The increased availability of broadcast outlets made it easier to expand a sponsorship's impact beyond those attending an event, so it stimulated more sponsorship.

Indeed, broadcasting sponsorship has become a distinctive element in the spectrum of sponsorship milieus. In this role the media sell sponsorships of transmission of sport events to advertisers offering sponsors such benefits as promotional trailers before a broadcast, break bumpers, and mention of their logo during cracks in the action.[30]

The growth of sponsorship has been inextricably linked with *increasing acceptance of the commercialization of sport* by the public and by organizing bodies. The author recalls meeting with the chairman of a leading English Premier League club in the early 1970s, who was also chairman of the Football League which was professional soccer's ruling body in England. The chairman was genuinely outraged and scornful at the suggestion of sponsorship saying, "You'd have all our players running around with Chevron on their shirts?" Ten years later, all major British soccer clubs were doing just that! It was

noted earlier in this chapter that a similar "acceptance curve" of sport sponsorship in the United States has percolated down from professional sport organizations, through colleges, to the high school level.

The proliferation of products and services, and increased competition that have characterized the market place in the past decade, have been accompanied by a *consolidation of companies through mergers and takeovers*. Thus, in many industries fewer but larger companies exercise more control and influence in distribution channels. This has made it more critical for producers to enhance relations with distributors. Sponsorships offer communication opportunities to do this through sport entertainment and hospitality. A related stimulus has been the evolution of large national food and drug chains that stock their own "No Name" and house brands. This has persuaded some consumer goods companies to invest more heavily in sponsorship promotional tie-ins which offer incentives for the trade and "push" volume through trade channels to consumers.[40]

Globalization has meant that companies now operate in multiple national markets in which they have no heritage or tradition. The universal appeal of sport means that sponsoring it offers a medium through which companies can ingratiate themselves and engage new national markets. Vodafone is emblematic of this strategy. In 1985 it was an embryonic company establishing a cellular telephone network in the UK. Today it is the world's second largest telecommunications company with over 450 million subscribers. It owns and operates networks in over 30 countries and has partner networks in over 40 additional countries. Vodafone has invested in high visibility sport sponsorships in almost every country it has entered as a means of quickly establishing a local national identity. It has used literally hundreds of these sponsorships for this purpose embracing whatever sport resonates in a given culture. The sponsored sports have included: rugby league, cricket, soccer, beach volleyball, netball, Formula One and other motor sports, Paralympics, Gaelic Athletic Association, triathlons, and so on. Global sports properties offer multinational corporations both a common platform for firms operating in multiple countries, and an opportunity to introduce themselves to new national markets they are seeking to penetrate. Consider the following examples:

> A motivation for Telstra (Australia's largest telecommunications company) to invest in excess of A$100 million dollars as part of its Sydney Olympic sponsorship campaign was to showcase its technologies to other parts of the world in addition to Australia, particularly Southeast Asia, a rapidly emerging market for such services. Similarly, Qantas's and Foster's decisions to sponsor the Formula One Grand Prix in Australia is not because of domestic market opportunities (F1 Racing is not such a popular sport in Australia as compared to some other sports) but because the race is broadcast into Europe, particularly the UK, and South America, where it has a large and loyal following and where both companies compete. (p. 225)[41]

The influence of two other factors which provided initial impetus for sponsorship in the early 1980s and early 1990s has waned in recent years. In 1971, Congress passed legislation *banning tobacco advertisements* on television, so companies making these products sought alternative promotion avenues. Sponsorship partnerships with sports were appealing for three main reasons. First, the association gave these potentially harmful products an aura of public respectability. Second, the extensive television coverage of sport provided them with access to that medium from which they were technically banned, even though their messages had to be indirect. Third, it enabled them to access the youth market, and recruiting adolescents to smoke is critical to the future viability of the tobacco industry. However, legal restraints were imposed on tobacco. These are discussed in Chapter 7, but essentially they prohibit tobacco companies from engaging in sponsoring activities.

In the 1980s and early 1990s when the number of television channels increased exponentially, the number of advertising messages vying for attention made it difficult for a particular message to make an impact. The problem of *clutter arising from the proliferation of advertisements* was accentuated by an increase in growth of 15-second spots and in the amount of time for commercials inserted into programs by the television companies: "The constant clutter of traditional media is like a roomful of people talking. If you cannot separate your voice, then you are wasting your money" (p. 4).[42] The reduced ability to communicate effectively with a target audience was negatively reinforced by the introduction and widespread use of both the "zapper," which enabled people to tune-out commercials without leaving their arm chair, and of recording devices enabling them to fast-forward or remove commercials. In this environment, sponsorship was perceived to be a cost-efficient alternative means of communicating.

This initial sponsorship stimulus waned as the profusion of sponsorships associated with televised sport created its own clutter. For example, the marketing director of a company that did not renew a sponsorship agreement with the NFL observed: "The NFL went from selling just eight major sponsorships a few years ago to selling 30 or more today. It's very hard to stand out in that crowd. There are so many sponsors that your brand's presence there is simply ignored, and the millions you paid to be involved are thoroughly wasted." (p. 73)[6] The effort to avoid sponsorship clutter, however, has itself added to the momentum as companies search for lesser known or under-sponsored sport events or organizations so their name will stand out and be free of clutter.

Contagion may emanate from two sources: mimicry of other companies or proximate geographic location. Both of these contexts may persuade additional companies to engage in sponsorship. *Mimicry* is illustrated by the propensity of companies in certain industries to engage in sponsorship of the same sport. For example, English cricket has a different title sponsor for each of its competitions. They are:

- Brit Insurance (England cricket teams)
- Investec (Test matches, i.e., 5-day international games)
- NatWest (1-day international games)
- LV = (4-day county cricket games)
- Clydestate Bank (40-over county games)
- Friends Provident and AXA (20-over county games)

All of these sponsors are financial services firms. Some of this mimicry may be explainable by the fit between financial service products and cricket's target markets. However, there is little evidence to indicate that companies in this sector would gain a particular advantage from sponsoring this sport as opposed to any other.[3] A more likely explanation is that this mimicry reflects competitive pressures with companies feeling obliged to engage in the sponsorship of cricket fearing that if they do not they will be at a competitive disadvantage.

Another explanatory factor for mimicry may be the notorious difficulty of measuring the return on a sponsorship investment. Executives responsible for making those decisions may believe that the involvement of peer companies gives their investment face validity and a sense of legitimacy, reducing the likelihood of their investment being challenged or criticized.

There is evidence to suggest that *proximate geographic location* propels some sponsorship activity. In these cases, the momentum derives not from the actions of other companies in their industry, but rather from other major companies in the same community. One manager explained, "We do some things just because we're a big corporate citizen" (p. 127).[3] If some large companies within a community support a particular event, then other managers may feel an obligation to join them.

THE SPECIAL STRENGTH OF SPONSORSHIP

The defining strength of sponsorship is that it offers opportunities for a company to establish a more intimate and emotionally involved relationship with its target audiences than is feasible with traditional advertising. Unlike advertising, the sport activity in which a sponsor invests is not part of the company's central commercial function. Advertising is intrusive and it is clearly a paid message overtly attempting to persuade or change attitudes. Advertising asks consumers to pay attention to the company's message and to buy the products, but gives them nothing in return.[6] However, sponsorship offers a more balanced exchange in that in return for accepting a company's commercial presence, consumers are offered a sporting event in which they are interested and whose quality may have been lower without the resources supplied by the sponsor. This may secure their interest and respect.

A company's relationship with most of its audiences is usually rather distant and obviously commercial, whereas sponsorship enables a target market to be approached through activities in which they are personally interested. The intent is to connect with audiences through their interests and lifestyle activities and, thus, create an emotional attachment between the audience and the company. In an interview with the author, an executive of Southwest Airlines said: "We aim to connect with people's passion points. That's why we go to sports: NFL, college football, NBA, because people are passionate about their teams. If we can hook into those passions, it creates a strong connection with those people." An illustration of how effective sponsorship can be in establishing this emotional connection is given in Exhibit 1.6 which describes how Toyota created a bond with the target audiences for its FJ Cruiser 4 × 4 off-road vehicle.[42a]

The marketing director of a food service business observed in explaining his company's shift from advertising to sponsorship: "The food service business traditionally advertises to people via radio, TV, and coupons—things most of us are bombarded with

Exhibit 1.6

Toyota's Engagement Framework

The most widely used model of the decision-process through which customers pass is AIDAR:

Awareness that a brand exists;

Interest in its distinguishing features;

Desire to purchase, resulting from a positive evaluation of its advantages over competitors;

Action, which is the purchase decision;

Reinforcement, confirming that the purchase was a wise decision.

However, Toyota developed an alternative model to clarify the objectives it establishes for its sponsorships. This Engagement Framework was designed to explicitly focus on the ability of sponsorships to foster an emotional connection between a brand and its audience. The framework is shown below.

Each of Toyota's sponsorships is likely to focus on one or two of the framework stages. Impressions (Level I) may be the goal for an undifferentiated product with low awareness. If a Toyota vehicle had observable feature/benefit advantages over its competition, then the goal may be to create opportunities for an audience to interact with it (Level II). Educate/inform (Level III) may be the focus if the audience is logic-oriented with strong rational purchase motivation, or is skeptical with doubts about some of a vehicle's attributes.

When launching its FJ Cruiser, Toyota targeted a niche market interested in its off-road capabilities. Its goals were targeted at Levels IV and V of the Engagement Framework: To provide opportunities for influential off-roaders to prove to themselves that Toyota and FJ Cruiser "share my values" and "fit my lifestyle"; and to inspire off-roaders to share their passion about FJ Cruiser and unite in person or via a social network.

Accordingly, "influencers" within the off-roading community were targeted who were passionate about the activity. Their knowledge of vehicle capabilities meant they were

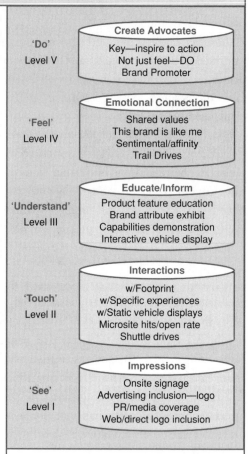

the most likely to be trusted by others as a credible word-of-mouth source about vehicle features. It was believed that if these true off-roaders became FJ believers, they would adopt the FJ as their own, and evangelize on behalf of Toyota for years to come.

Because the goal was advocacy, and not large-scale awareness, no television and little general market print were in the plan—the fate of the launch rested on the sponsorship program and the engagement marketing platform it created.

Many of the potential "influencers" were long-time Jeep-loyal off-roaders who needed to see and experience FJ Cruiser's capabilities. Thus, a grassroots sponsorship activation program was developed

---

Exhibit 1.6 *(Continued)*

Toyota's Engagement Framework

called Trail Teams. It was intended to win over this hardened community one trail at a time. Toyota also re-established its active sponsorship of the Toyota Land Cruiser Association. It sponsored and participated in local grassroots trail runs across the country. Key events were identified on nearly every major trail around the country, and Toyota sponsored or supported them all. Every aspect of the program was crafted to reinforce the belief that Toyota was an authentic partner in the off-road world; from the high-end, multi-tool premiums that were distributed to the technical trail-riding videos posted on the Internet.

Even the staffing process was reversed; rather than hiring traditional mobile marketing staff and training them in off-roading, the Trail Teams staff was recruited from existing off-road communities—and trained in mobile marketing. Throughout the program, FJ Trail Teams shared campgrounds with the community, giving away BBQ food and putting on free movie nights—all activations that were hyper-relevant to this target audience.

Once it reached the marketplace, FJ Trail Teams was everything new sponsorship marketing should strive for: credible word-of-mouth messages were flowing, authentic viral content was being generated, and communities were being created. An illustration of the impact of the sponsorship campaign was on display around a campfire in a remote town in the Colorado mountains. Every person there had spent hours on-line, communicating and planning this trip. Each had driven for hours or days to gather and celebrate their new passion. Four owners dedicated 11 months to organizing the event—with no corporate involvement. Five hundred enthusiastic fans, gathered together from 33 states and four countries united to celebrate one thing—a brand new product.

The sponsorship investment had evoked affinity and created a "their brand is like me" sentiment. It had inspired passion and loyalty, and created a sense of shared values that turned fans into brand advocates.

---

in our daily life. What feels right to us is a need to be more passionate and intimate because that's how we treat customers in our stores" (p. 1).[43] One of the pioneers of sponsorship stated:

> Sponsorship gives products value in the social and moral sense. It tells the consumer what a company believes, so the consumer may choose the product for its affinity with the realities of the consumer's life. Products don't borrow equity from sponsorship, they express equity through sponsorship. Companies that treat sponsorship simply as a channel for broadcasting messages, distributing products and processing transactions fail to gain the medium's real benefits. Sponsorship's power lies in its ability to draw an individual customer into conversation with the company. Sponsorship is not just a means to communicate a message. It is the message. (p. 2)[44]

The commercial intent of establishing an emotional relationship is to persuade consumers that "the sponsor supports sports events they care about, so they should patronize the sponsor."[45] Evidence of this reciprocity occurs when consumers make a conscious decision to go out of their way to support the brands that support the events which they care about.

Sport can convey strong images; it has a mass international audience; and it appeals to all classes. These attributes make it a natural vehicle for sponsorship.[46] However, its primary attribute is that sport matters to people. Many English Premier League soccer teams have RIP areas on their sites so fans can have their ashes scattered at the home of their beloved team. How many other businesses inspire such loyalty? Passionate followers of major college football teams do not go to games when it is convenient. Rather they arrange their lives around the football schedule. This degree of passion makes sport an invaluable conduit for any message that a company might wish to convey. Sport sponsorship enables a company to connect with potential purchasers who are relaxed, and in a state of mind and an environment that makes it likely they will be receptive. Sponsorship has the capacity to touch the hearts and minds of people. If it achieves this, then it is likely to facilitate potential purchasers spending quality time with a company and its products: "When you reach prospects who are interested in or are attending an event, they are yours. They are there because they want to be. They're part of the event and in a receptive mood" (p. 4).[11]

However, the pervasiveness of sponsorship has made the establishment of this emotional connection more difficult. In the 1980s and early 1990s, the novelty of companies investing in sporting events made audiences more receptive to emotionally bonding with them. Now the profusion of sponsorship partnerships has led many to take them for granted. The CEO of a prominent sponsor company noted, "We have to work a lot harder now to get consumers to transfer the warm feelings they have about a property to its sponsors" (p. 4).[11] He went on to articulate the importance of sponsorship's emotional relationship to his company's business:

I've been at John Hancock for 17 years. I have yet to meet the broker, financial advisor, or insurance agent who would ever admit that he or she wrote a piece of business because of our Olympic sponsorship. They, of course, believe it's the genius of their salesmanship that does the job. Yet we know the Olympics are a factor. In our business, where people are basically paying us to collect something they aren't going to live to collect, they are not about to give their money to a stranger. They entrust it to someone with whom they have a relationship, a company about which they feel strongly. If they associate your brand with an American winning a gold medal at an Olympic event, that goes a long way toward building that trust. When the sponsorship precedes the sales pitch, it softens that consumer and creates a certain receptivity that makes a sale more likely. (p. 4)[11]

SUMMARY

Exchange theory is the central concept underlying both sponsorship and donations, but the distinctive features which differentiate sponsorship from philanthropy are that it is a business relationship and it is seen by companies as a means by which they can exploit its commercial potential to aid their profitability. In its formative years, sponsorship decisions often reflected the personal interests of senior managers. This may still play a minor role in some decisions, but there is now an insistence on corporate accountability requiring that sponsorships demonstrate how they are likely to improve a company's profitability.

Sponsorship has grown exponentially in the past three decades. In 1987, sponsorship spending in North America amounted to $1.35 billion, but by 2012 it had escalated to almost $19 billion and over two-thirds of that was invested in sports. This surge was launched by the high profile success of sponsorship investments at the 1984 Los Angeles Olympic Games.

Since that beginning it has passed through three eras. The initial "learning" stage in which it was myopically viewed as a communication vehicle; through the "sponsorship-linked marketing" era when it was recognized as integral in market positioning and strategy, but leveraging was limited to nonactivational support activities; to the activation era of "experiential sponsorship" where it is used as a platform on which to develop meaningful experiences for customers. Initially, sponsorship was confined to professional and elite sport, but it has now percolated down to college and high school sport where it has become similarly ubiquitous.

Eight factors have undergirded this impetus and continue to stimulate contemporary corporate involvement in sponsorship: Specificity of target audiences; proliferation of broadcast and digital media; increased acceptance of the commercialization of sport; company mergers; globalization; the banning of tobacco advertising; advertising "clutter"; and contagion attribute either to mimicry or proximate geographic location.

The special strength of sponsorship is that it offers opportunities for a company to establish an intimate and emotionally involved relationship with its target audiences. Sport matters to people. This makes it an invaluable conduit through which to conduct business with them.

Endnotes

1. Cornwell T. B., Weeks C. S., & Roy D. P. (2005). Sponsorship-linked marketing: Opening the black box. *Journal of Advertising, 34*(2), 21–42.

2. Irwin, R. L., Irwin, C., & Drayer, J. (2010). Get fit with the Grizzlies: Application of entrepreneurship in sport sponsorship. In S. Chadwick & D. Ciletti (Eds.), *Sports entrepreneurship: Theory and practice* (pp. 35–50). Morgantown, WV: Fitness Information Technology.

3. Barrett, T., & Slack, T. (1999). An analysis of the influence of competitive institutional pressures on corporate sponsorship decisions. *Journal of Sport Management, 13*, 114–138.

4. Gwinner, K. (1997). A model of image creation and image transfer in event sponsorship. *International Marketing Review, 14*(3), 145–158.

5. Dean, D. H. (2002). Associating the corporation with a charitable event through sponsorship: Measuring the effects on corporate community relations. *Journal of Advertising, 31*(4), 77–87.

6. D'Alessandro, D. F. (2001). *Brand warfare: 10 rules for building the killer brand*. New York, NY: McGraw Hill.

7. Cornwell T. B. (2008). State of the art and science in sponsorship-linked marketing. *Journal of Advertising, 37*(3), 41–55.

8. Cornwell, T. B., & Maguan, I. (1998). An international review of sponsorship research. *Journal of Advertising, 27*(1), 1–21.

9. Masterman, G. (2007). *Sponsorship for a return on investment*. New York, NY: Elsevier.

10. Lynde, T. (2007). *Sponsorship 101*. Mableton, GA: Lynde and Associates.

11. IEG. (2001). Companies focus on sponsorship's core of genetic connection. *IEG Sponsorship Report, 20*(6), 1, 4, 5.

12. Eaton, R. (1991). Inside Target stores' sponsorship philosophy. *Special Events Report, 10*(17), 4–5.

13. McCarville, R. E., & Copeland, R. P. (1994). Understanding sport sponsorship through exchange theory. *Journal of Sport Management, 8*, 102–114.

14. Brooks, C. (1990, October). Sponsorship: Strictly business. *Athletic Business*, pp. 59–62.

15. Levine P. (1985) *A.G. Spalding and the rise of baseball: The promise of American sport*. New York, NY: Oxford University Press.

16. Firestone. (2012). Firestone racing: History of winning. firestonetire.com
17. Wilson, N. (1998). *The sports business*. London, UK: Piatkus.
18. International Advertising Association. (1998, September). *Sponsorship: Its roles and effects*. The Global Media Commission of the International Advertising Association, Madison Avenue, New York, NY.
19. Gratton, C. & Taylor, P. (1985, August). The economics of sport sponsorship. *National Westminster Bank Quarterly Review*, pp. 53–68.
20. fc business. (2012, July 24). Premier League shirt sponsorship deals top £100 m. Retrieved from http://www.fcbusiness.co.uk/news/article
21. BBC News. (2012, August 16). Manchester United in sponsorship deal with Bwin. Retrieved from www.bbc.co.uk/news/business
22. IEG. (2012, March 1). Economic uncertainty to slow sponsorship growth in 2012. *IEG Sponsorship Report*.
23. IEG. (2011, September 26). Major pro sports sponsorships to total 2.46 billion in 2011. *IEG Sponsorship Report*.
24. IEG. (2012, May 29). Following the money: Sponsorship's top spenders of 2011. *IEG Sponsorship Report*.
25. IOC. (2012). *Olympic marketing facts file*. Lausanne, Switzerland: International Olympic Committee.
26. Roughton B. (1990, September 23). Quebec, Montreal still owe $450 million in 1976 debt. *The Atlantic Journal and Constitution*.
27. Zimbalist, A. (2011). *Circling the bases*. Philadelphia, PA: Temple University Press.
28. Rines, S. (2007, January). Global marketing and no-name sponsorship: Interviews with Michael Payne, former International Olympic Committee Marketing and Broadcast Director. *International Journal of Sports Marketing and Sponsorship*, pp. 119–125.
29. Cornwell T. B. (1995). Sponsorship-linked marketing development. *Sport Marketing Quarterly*. 4(4), 15–24.
30. Ferrand, A., Torrigiani, L., & Camps i Povill, A. (2007). *Routledge handbook of sports sponsorship*. New York, NY: Routledge.
31. Leederman, D. (1989, February 22). 60 colleges that play big-time sports debate forming a consortium to lure corporate sponsors. *The Chronicle of Higher Education*, A37.
32. IEG. (2011, December 5). IMG gives sponsorship the old college try. *IEG Sponsorship Report*.
33. IEG. (2011, December 14). Aaron's, Inc. signs major deal with IMG College to partner with top universities across the nation. *IEG Sponsorship Report*.
34. Steinbach, P. (2000, January). Intramarketing. *Athletic Business*, pp. 26–28.
35. Kelly, D. (2000, December). Sponsors pay so students can play. *SportsBusiness Journal*.
36. Bourne, D. (2010, August 2). From media to stadiums, the dollars are flowing to youth sports. *SportsBusiness Journal*, p. 20.
37. IEG. (2010, September). NFL and Barclay Card launch new credit card program. *IEG Sponsorship Report*, p. 1.
38. Lefton, T. (2010, July 26). Are consumers ready for Texas Longhorns energy? *SportsBusiness Journal*, pp. 1, 28.
39. Sleight, S. (1989). *Sponsorship: What it is and how to use it*. Maidenhead, Berkshire, England: McGraw-Hill.
40. Cunningham, P., Taylor, S., & Reeder, C. (1992). *Event marketing: The evolution of sponsorship from philanthropy to strategic promotion*. Unpublished paper, School of Business, Queen's University, Kingston, Ontario, Canada.
41. Farrelly, F., & Quester. P. (2005). Examining international alliances through sponsorship. In J. Amis and T. B. Cornwell (Eds.), *Global sport sponsorship* (pp. 225–242). New York, NY: Berg.
42. Morse, J. (1989). Sponsorship from a small business perspective . . . or why a regional ice-cream company has high event content. *Special Events Report*, 8(14), 4–5.
42a. Savary, J. (2008). Advocacy marketing: Toyota's secrets for partnering with trend setters to create passionate brand advocates. *Journal of Sponsorship*, 1(3), 211–224.
43. IEG. (2000). Juice chain shifts spending from advertising to sponsorship. *Sponsorship Report*, 19(14), 1.
44. Ukman, L. (1996, May 6). Assertions. *Sponsorship Report*, p. 2.
45. Pracejus, J. W. (1998). *Seven psychological mechanisms through which sponsorship impacts consumers*. Paper presented at the 17th Annual Advertising and Consumer Psychology Conference, Portland, Oregon.
46. Gwinner, K., & Swanson, S. R. (2003). A model of fan identification: antecedents and sponsorship outcomes. *Journal of Services Marketing*, 17(3), 275–294.
47. McCabe, J. (1989). Integrating sponsorship into the advertising and marketing mix. *Special Events Report*, 8(7), 4–5.

2

Building Brand Equity: Increasing Brand Awareness and Enhancing Brand Image

The essence of successful sponsorship is the exchange of mutual benefits that occurs between a business and a sport property. Thus, for a sponsorship to be successful, the sport organization must be committed to working with its business partners to deliver the benefits they seek from it. Figure 1.2 showed there are six major categories of benefits that sponsors seek: increased brand awareness, brand image transfer, demonstration platform, hospitality, product trial and sales opportunities, and enhanced employee morale.

The first two categories, brand awareness and brand image, are the central components of brand equity and enhancing brand equity is an explicit objective that is common to almost all company rationales for engaging in sponsorship. This chapter focuses on that construct, while discussion of benefits associated with demonstration platform, hospitality, product trial and sales opportunities and employee morale, is deferred to Chapter 3.

THE BRAND EQUITY CONCEPT

A brand can be defined as the set of elements that differentiate the products of a seller from its competitors. Brand equity is the value premium realized from a brand name as compared to its generic equivalent. An alternate term sometimes used instead of brand equity is brand value. It is strategically crucial. In developed economies, companies have to compete for business in most product classes. The functionality of their offerings within a product class typically is similar. In such contexts, companies seek to have their product "stand out from the crowd" by creating strong brand equity. Brand equity is not an abstract concept. It is an asset that has substantial financial value to companies. Indeed, brand equity is sometimes a more valuable asset than a company's tangible assets. It can be calculated by measuring the revenues accruing from a product with a brand name compared to those perceived from the product if it did not have the brand name.[1] Strong brand equity should enable the brand to command higher profit margins and have more inelastic responses to price increases.

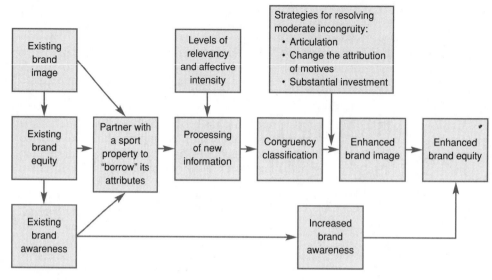

Figure 2.1. How Sponsorship Can Build Brand Equity.

The integrative framework shown in Figure 2.1 seeks to explain how sponsorships can enhance brand equity. Brand equity is dependent on consumers' knowledge of a brand (that is an understanding of what the brand does and what it stands for). The exhibit shows that knowledge is defined by two components, brand awareness and brand image.[1] A sponsorship's effectiveness in enhancing brand equity is evaluated by measuring the differences in brand equity before and after the sponsorship investment.

Brand image is defined as "perceptions about a brand as reflected by the brand associations held in consumer memory" (p. 3).[1] These associations may be tangible attributes such as experience with the product, price, design, or packaging, or intangible psychological attributes such as exciting, prestigious, energetic, edgy, or classic. Thus, brand image is a mental construct comprised of beliefs, ideas, and impressions residing in an individual's memory. It is an ordered whole built from scraps of information, much of which is inferred rather than directly experienced.

The sponsor partners with a sport property that possesses attributes it would like to appropriate or "borrow" and transfer to its brand. The stronger, more favorable, and more distinctive the sport property's attributes, the more potential there is for image transfer. If consumers have no familiarity with the sporting property's attributes, then there is nothing that can be transferred. An "image transfer" occurs when the attributes of a sport property are transferred to the sponsoring brand, because individuals connect information relating to a property's attributes, benefits, or attitudes toward it, with the brand's profile in their memory.

The flows illustrating this transfer process are shown in Figure 2.2. This shows a target audience has an emotionally passionate reciprocal relationship with a sport property. The property is the aggregate repository of all its fans' passions, but it reciprocates by returning experiences that nurture and sustain those passions. When a property signs an agreement with a sponsoring brand to invest in it, the sport organization authorizes

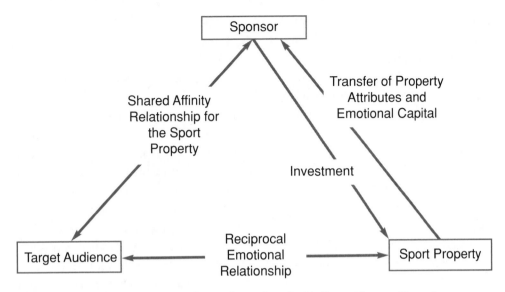

Figure 2.2. The Emotional Flows Associated with Brand Image Transfer.

some of its reservoir of both property attributes and emotional capital to be transferred to the sponsor. In crude terms the company says, "We want our brand to have this set of image attributes." The sport event says, "We will convey that set of image attributes to you for a price."

The acquisition of attributes and emotional capital enables the sponsor to "ride" on the borrowed equity. Both sponsor and fan have "skin in the game." They have become allies through their shared affinity relationship for the sport property and their mutual investment in it. This establishes a bond between them, rather than merely the potential for a business transaction. Optimally, the target audience may feel a sense of gratitude towards the company as well as an emotional affinity with it, believing that its support contributes to their enjoyment. Since people tend to buy brands toward which they have a favorable attitude, all else equal this affinity relationship is likely to lead to sales increases for the sponsor. NASCAR is renowned for the loyalty of its fans which has made it one of the most valued sponsorships in sport:

> The exceptional loyalty of NASCAR fans is a direct result of fan belief that without the sponsor, their favorite driver would have no ride. Fans view the sponsor as part of the team and transfer their loyalty to the sponsor's brand. Also, unlike viewers of a televised awards show or pro sports league championship, NASCAR fans see themselves as connected to other viewers and part of a larger community of interest. NASCAR fans define themselves against the market at large. They are members of a club and believe that supporting the sponsors is a behavior that shows you're part of the club.[1a]

This shared affinity was recognized by a leading sponsor of NASCAR who observed: "If you can find a way to transfer or borrow some of the loyalty fans feel toward NASCAR and its drivers—if you can attach some of that to your own brand, there's a very significant financial value to that" (p. 60).[2] This belief was reinforced by a research study undertaken by an independent third party which reported that 43 percent of NASCAR fans were influenced enough by NASCAR sponsorships to switch from their normal brand of a grocery store product to try a different brand, while 46 percent said they would purchase a brand costing as much as 10 percent more if it was associated with NASCAR over a less expensive brand that was not associated with NASCAR.[1a]

Similarly, the sponsorship marketing manager of Vodafone observed: "They see we're supporting what they love. So they in turn support us" (p. 1074).[3] The stronger people's emotional commitment is to a team or event, the more valuable that property is to a company. Committed fans are likely to have heightened sensitivity and positive affective feelings towards a company that helps their team or event—and by extension, themselves—accomplish their goals. It has been reported that intention to purchase increased as identification with a university's sports teams increased. That study concluded that high identifiers who had had an unfavorable attitude toward the sponsor, had significantly more positive intentions to purchase than did low identifiers without negative feelings about the sponsor. For high identifiers, it appeared that team identification acted as a heuristic that favorably disposed fans to want to buy products from a sponsor despite a pre-existing negative attitude toward the company.[3a]

PROCESSING NEW RELATIONSHIP INFORMATION

How Memory Works

A sponsor's success in accomplishing image transfer is strongly influenced by the way its targeted consumers process new information. The flows in Figure 2.2 show *what* occurs in brand image transfer. The intent of this section is to explain *how* it occurs.

Memory is a process of acquiring information and storing it over time, so it is available when needed. It cannot be observed, it has to be inferred, but there is general agreement that there are three elements in the memory process[4]: encoding, which refers to how information enters the system in a way that it will be recognized; storage, which is concerned with how the new knowledge will be integrated with what is already in memory and "warehoused" until it is needed; and retrieval which enables the desired information to be accessed.

The most widely accepted and influential conceptualization of memory is the node-link structure proposed by associative network models.[5] Associative networks posit that each unit of information in memory (brand, sport organization, name, idea, behavior, etc.) is represented as a node, and nodes that are related to each other are connected by links. Links are the vehicles which deliver new information to be encoded to related nodes, and which retrieve existing information from long-term memory.

The links connecting nodes together form a network of ideas organized on a set of relationships called schemas or knowledge structures. The schemas are cognitive frameworks developed through experiences which may derive both from direct interaction with a brand or sport property and from media sources. Schemas may be viewed as complex spider webs filled with pieces of data.[4] Incoming pieces of information are put

Courtesy of BigStockPhoto.com

into nodes. When information node categories are viewed as similar for some reasons, they are chunked together into schemas which are configurations that are familiar and can be thought about by an individual as a unit.

Schemas are an effective heuristic because creating categories of knowledge structure is much more efficient than individuals storing, retaining, and retrieving pieces of raw data one-by-one.[5] Also, categorizing causal relationships assists in making the huge amount of information in memory more comprehensible.

When new information about a brand or property is received, it is evaluated against existing schemas and this determines its perceived relevancy and value. It is more likely that incoming data will be retained if it is associated with other information already in memory. Information that is not consistent with a schema already established in memory is likely to be "filtered out." It has been suggested that schemas might also contain product categories that are typically part of fans' sport experience (e.g., beer and snack foods). Further, fans may also acquire sponsorship memory structures that they come to associate with traditional sponsors through repeated exposure to sponsorship-related promotions over time.[6]

Associative network models distinguish between long-term and short-term (or working) memory. Short-term memory is the information being actively processed at any given moment. It is limited in scope with a duration of less than 20 seconds, so few things can be held in it simultaneously. Long-term memory is the vast storage of information that can potentially be accessed. It is extremely durable, so once information is stored in long-term memory the strength of association is likely to decay very slowly. It has been concluded that, "The capacity of the overall network of long-term memory storage seems, practically speaking, to be limitless" (p. 79).[5]

The contents of short-term memory can be consolidated for storage in long-term memory through a process called elaborate rehearsal.[4] This involves thinking about the meaning of a stimulus and relating it to the schemas already in memory. Information is retrieved by activating the nodes in long-term memory, which occurs when consciousness of a cue reaches a certain threshold. The information is then brought up to short-term memory along the neural link pathways. Thus, ideas move in and out of short-term memory as they become activated and fade when the activation threshold is lowered.[5] The more a node is activated, the more likely it is to be used, that is, to be recalled and to be applied to incoming information.

This traditional social-psychological model of associative networks has been reinforced more recently by processes reported by cognitive neuroscientists who are exploring neural networks and the biological mechanisms underlying memory. Their work appears to confirm that memory is organized in terms of associative structures between items. It commenced in the 1990s and so is in its infancy, but it has been established that information is processed by specialist cells, called neurons, which communicate by sending electrical signals to one another.

Neurons are the nodes in the system. They receive signals from, and transmit signals to, other neurons by way of synapses that are attached to them and serve as the links. Thus, neurons form a highly interconnected network, and connections between neurons appear to play a crucial role in associative memory and recall. Complexity of the system can be gauged from the numbers—the human brain possesses approximately 100 billion neurons and 200 trillion connections![7]

Before a sponsor invests in a sport property, information about each of the two entities may reside in independent nodes in a consumer's long-term memory, but their partnership now establishes links between these nodes. Links vary in strength—some associations are stronger than others. An important feature of associative networks is that nodes are clarified and better labeled and links between them are strengthened each time they are activated. Thus, the more that individuals process a linkage between a sponsor's brand and a sport property, the stronger the association becomes.

Activation spreads from one node to another via the connecting links, so different stored units of information can evoke one another through the associative networks. Thus, if a piece of information activates a node, it will also activate other linked nodes, much as tapping a spider's web in one place sends movement reverberating across the web.[4] Thus, new information relating to attributes of a sport property will trigger amendments, either positive or negative, towards a sponsor's brand and vice-versa.

The Dual Roles of Brand Awareness

Brand awareness is related to the strength of the brand node in memory as reflected by people's ability to recognize or recall the brand.[1] Since nodes are clarified and links in associative networks are strengthened by repeated activation, repeated exposure to a brand is likely to increase awareness of it. Awareness has a dual role (Figure 2.1). First, in its direct role it can create two positive outcomes for sponsors: It may lead to increased sales in situations where customers think of one brand rather than its alternatives when confronted by multiple choices in a product class. Additionally, it has been suggested that repeated exposure to a brand often engenders an affective response (i.e., a liking for the brand).[8] Thus, brand awareness may directly influence brand equity (Figure 2.1) in situations where consumers adopt a decision rule to buy the brand with which they are most familiar. Further, high levels of familiarity with a brand have been found to result in more positive consumer reactions such as product satisfaction, word-of-mouth recommendations, and repurchase intentions.[8]

The context in which exposure to the brand occurs is critical. For example, a sign displayed prominently at a corner grocery store or side of a building is likely to be passively received and not register in the mind. The same sign displayed in a sports arena when spectators are cognitively involved and mentally alert is more likely to register. Thus, the organizer of the Clipper Round the World race observed: "Clipper sees sport and business welded together. We can't have one without the other. If we didn't have the yacht race we might as well be another trade delegation. The race gives us that something extra" (p. 37).[9]

These direct positive outcomes are especially likely to occur in low-involvement decisions where purchasers are indifferent to differences among brands, do not invest effort in trying to discriminate among them, and make their choices in a product category on the basis of name familiarity without a well-formed attitude towards the brand. Increased familiarity with a brand also makes it likely that when new information related to the brand is encountered, an existing strong schema will enable it to be effectively processed and absorbed.[8]

In addition to its direct role, brand awareness has a second function as a prerequisite for image transfer, since if there is no awareness of a brand, there is no node to which image information can attach to the brand in memory:[1] "Brand awareness is an important first step in building brand equity, but it usually is not sufficient. For most customers in most situations, the meaning or image of the brand also comes into play" (p. 79).[10] It is a cognitive action without the affective dimensions that characterize image. Whereas awareness is limited to cognitive recognition, a sport event's image has an affective dimension.

There are three situations in which investments in awareness are made for the purpose of establishing a memory node which can subsequently be used to develop a brand's image (Exhibit 1.1). The first is when a company is launching a new brand in the marketplace. This was illustrated by both the Showtime Channel and Qantas Airlines:

- Showtime launched its "Inside NASCAR" program which it perceived to be a "cornerstone of our sports programming." The channel was not a primary destination for NASCAR fans, so it needed to generate awareness among them. A primary tool for this was title-sponsoring the Showtime Southern 500 at Darlington Raceway, a historic track that has been hosting NASCAR for over 60 years. The sponsorship was activated with an online sweepstakes offering the winning fan a VIP trip for two to the race and an exact replica of the trophy given to the winning driver (including the same cost of $3,000). Also on the ground at the race, Showtime distributed promotional fliers, and DVDs of "Inside NASCAR."[11]
- For Qantas, Australia's hosting of the Rugby World Cup provided a platform to launch the $300 million redesign of its new business class as well as providing first access to it to the 40,000 overseas visitors who traveled to Australia to the event. The traditionally affluent rugby audience was a good fit for an airline relaunching its business class.[12]

The objective of creating brand awareness for a new product has been the rationale for some companies' investments in naming rights sponsorships because "You can't bypass the name on a stadium the way you zap a commercial—it's harder to ignore" (p. 14).[13]

The effectiveness of this strategy was demonstrated by Swedish telecommunications giant, Ericsson Inc.

- Ericsson was virtually unknown in the U.S. when it paid $20 million in 1995 for the naming rights to the NFL-Carolina Panthers new football stadium in Charlotte, North Carolina. From 1996 to 1998, the number of impressions Ericsson received in the national media increased by almost 400%, mostly in connection with the stadium. The effect of such exposure had a remarkable impact on Ericsson's brand awareness, both regionally and nationally. Market research conducted in 1998 found that in less than three years, the Ericsson brand grew from almost no public presence prior to signing the naming rights agreement to being recognized by 50% of adults in the Carolinas and by 44% nationally.[14] The owner of the Carolina Panthers observed that the naming rights deal has all but "eliminated the 'Who is Ericsson?' question." (p. 14).[13]

A second context in which awareness emerges as the dominant sponsorship benefit sought occurs when existing brands are expanding into new markets that have never heard of them. Exhibit 2.1 reports how the island of Malta used soccer to create aware-

---

Exhibit 2.1

Using Sport Sponsorship to Build Awareness for a Tourism Destination

Malta is an island country in the Mediterranean whose economy relies heavily on tourism. The Malta Tourism Authority (MTA) signed a sponsorship agreement with Sheffield United Football Club (SUFC) which is a second tier professional soccer club in the North of England with a large fan following. MTAs goal was to use the popularity of soccer and specifically SUFC to raise awareness of Malta to potential vacationers from the North of England. Malta offers a warm Mediterranean winter climate that contrasts markedly with the cold, windy, wet winter days in Sheffield. They had three supplementary goals: (i) to lobby UK airlines in the area to operate more flights to Malta; (ii) forge relationships with regional travel agents; and (iii) to forge relationships with the regional business community.

MTA received prominent branding on all shirts and team clothing, high-visibility stadium branding including naming rights to the largest stand, articles in matchday programs, and links through the SUFC websites, e-newsletters, and club publications. In addition, the team visited Malta for warm weather training camps and pre-season tours. These attracted fans to the island.

The sponsorship was activated by a competition to win a Malta vacation staged at all home games; hospitality to nurture airlines, tour operations, travel agencies, and media; an exchange trip between Malta and Sheffield children; and staged events with players to showcase Malta in exciting and fun locations on the island to provide media publicity.

The sponsorship was successful in that more direct flights to Malta from regional airports were scheduled; UK outward bound passengers to Malta increased more than the overall market; and Malta's brand awareness increased following far-reaching coverage of the partnership in regional and national newspapers and television.

ness of its potential as a vacation destination among residents in the North of England.[15] A similar strategy was used by Cape Breton Island:

- Cape Breton Island (CBI) on Canada's Atlantic seaboard sponsored one of the ten
  identical yachts which competed in the Clipper Round the World Race which
  covers 40,000 miles over approximately 10 months stopping at multiple ports
  around the globe. CBI with a population of 150,000 had little visibility. The
  Island's spokesperson noted: "Nobody knew where Cape Breton was and it was
  our job to market Cape Breton to the world. We managed to make our mark."
  The boat hulls and sails are branded. Since awareness is dependent on television
  and press photographic coverage, Clipper Ventures commissions and distributes
  its own television series of one-hour programs shown both locally and internationally on outlets such as the Discovery Channel in the U.S., the Sky network in
  Europe, and stations contracted to deliver the programming in South Africa,
  South-East Asia, and India. It also commissions on-the-water photography shots
  for its publicity efforts. Further, Clipper organizes hospitality events for its sponsors at each port on the race route. As a result, new companies came to CBI,
  including a sea cucumber plant. The CBI spokesperson reported that in return for
  their $2.1 million investment, "CBI received media value of $9.8 million, public
  relations valued at $2.4 million, and over $1 million economic impact on CBI as
  a result of the race stopping there. In addition, we made connections with influential people around the world. It really opened doors for us" (p. 37).[9]

Building awareness in new markets similarly was the primary rationale for Sony Ericsson's investment in the WTA tour and Lenovo's involvement in both the NBA and as a
TOP Olympic sponsor:

- When Sony Ericsson first became title sponsor for the Women's Tennis Association (WTA) tour it was a young brand. Rather than compete in the clutter of
  sponsorships in sports such as soccer and motor racing, it looked for a property
  that was global in scope but would allow it to build awareness free of clutter.
  Although the WTA tour was global in reach, there were opportunities to "local-
  ize" it since the 60 WTA events are held in 34 countries. This enables the company to link with local mobile phone operations to tailor campaigns to each of its
  markets. As the tour moved into more countries, Sony Ericsson moved with it.
  The company emerged as a global competitor using the WTA title sponsorship as
  its major marketing platform.[16]
- Lenovo is the dominant computer provider in China, but was unknown outside
  that country. To fuel its plans to expand into other markets, it invested $80 mil-
  lion as a TOP sponsor for the Beijing Olympic Games. In the US it sought to
  compete directly with Dell and HP and so became an NBA sponsor. It provided
  teams with PC notebooks and information systems, and co-branded with the
  NBA digital products such as flash drives and mobile hard drives. A Lenovo spokesperson said, "Our aim is to introduce the Lenovo brand and our products into the
  US market by working with the best sports marketing channel available" (p. 61).[17]

Cricket is the world's second most popular sport. In recent years a shortened, action-packed version of the game called Twenty 20 (T20) has emerged as a "made for television" product. Although the game does not have widespread visibility in the USA, a major effort to launch a T20 tournament there is being explored by Cricket Holdings America (CHA) backed by international support. CHA's CEO explained that the business model was to use cricket as a vehicle to introduce American companies to the subcontinent, one of the world's largest emerging markets whose populations are passionate about cricket:

> The franchises will have an appeal to a number of US corporations looking to expose themselves and build a profile in the subcontinent. We call it a commercial and cultural bridge between the USA and the cricket world. It is an inexpensive marketing platform to engage with a new, large audience. We have intense interest from a number of agencies and broadcasters.[17a]

A third context that causes companies to focus on awareness is the desire by multinational corporations to replace national or regional brands they have purchased with their own international brand. Exhibit 2.2 describes the Santander Bank's approach to this.[18] A similar rationale explained Aon's $32 million a year shirt sponsorship agreement with Manchester United:

- Aon is one of the world's largest insurance brokerages with an annual turnover exceeding $10 billion. It acquired 445 companies over a period of 20 years. Its

Exhibit 2.2

Using Sport Sponsorship to Create Awareness of a Single Brand Across Multiple Countries

Santander is the fourth largest banking group in the world with 90 million clients and 170,000 employees. A spokesperson noted, "Over the last 15 years we did a lot of acquisitions, and the priority during this period was to integrate banks, our technology platforms, operating procedures, and so on." However, Santander realized that their name was unknown in many of the countries in which they now owned banks, because the original names had been retained. The spokesperson went on, "We realized that it was very important to develop our brand because it is vital in terms of business. I would like to stress this. For us, branding is equal to strength. It is important to transmit and persuade people about our branding. The single brand makes life easier at an operational level as well as an awareness level. If there is a common approach to marketing, branding, and publicity it creates a lot of synergy."

The imperative to establish its branding in countries where it was unknown led to Santander becoming a major sponsor of the Ferrari Formula One racing team, which many believe to be the leading Formula One brand. In addition to becoming a single-brand bank, Santander needed to be recognized as a truly international brand and they believed, "If you are with Ferrari, then it is evident you have global capabilities." Santander pointed to the worldwide appeal of Formula One racing. "In Brazil there are 50 million fans of Formula One. These are passionate not casual fans. The same is true in Germany, Spain, the UK, and many other countries. With Ferrari we can develop an affinity between the audience and our bank."

over 36,000 employees are spread across 500 offices in 120 countries. The company's name, Aon, is a Gaelic word meaning "oneness." It was selected in an attempt to establish a unifying corporate identity. It failed. Indeed there was confusion with other major companies such as Aeon and Eon, and especially with Aegon which is also a large international insurance firm. The agreement with Manchester *United* was designed to accomplish unity and coalesce these disparate companies to establish a global identity for the company. Their spokesperson confirmed that awareness of the corporate brand was the rationale for the sponsorship: "Foremost is the notion of unifying our brand."[19]

Because they have a global reach, agreements such as Aon's sponsorship of Manchester United invariably are major investments. However, "amortizing" them across multiple markets makes them among the most cost effective types of sport sponsorship.

The Mediating Influence of Relevancy and Affective Intensity

It seems probable that in most situations the schemas of those who strongly identify with a property and brand are more likely to incorporate new information and embrace the linkage, than those who are less invested. If there is minimal engagement, then new information is less likely to be processed into long-term memory so no image transfer will occur. Strength of identity is a function of relevancy and affective intensity. The *relevance* of a brand to those engaged with a sport property may be assessed by how positively they respond to questions such as: Is the brand a member of a product class in which they have an interest? Do they currently use it or are they considering using it? If the sponsor has chosen its sport property wisely, then the target market's responses to these questions will align toward the positive end of a negative—disinterested—positive continuum.

Affective intensity or passion will be similarly influential in whether or not the sponsor-sport property link is processed.[20] This refers to the intensity of feelings, either positive (liking) or negative (disliking), towards each of the two entities. The extent to which there is connectedness with a sport property and brand will not be equal among members of a target market. Some will have no or minimal interest, others will be interested but be relatively passive and not emotionally invested, while still others will be rabid enthusiasts. Their level of passion and emotional engagement likely will influence the extent to which a sport property/brand linkage is processed. Strong passion and relevancy also are likely to be accompanied by a high level of previous knowledge in memory and high interest in the sport property's behaviors and actions.

There are two caveats to the general principle of high relevancy and strong passion leading to a higher degree of information processing. First, in the context of those sport events where passion is more ephemeral than enduring, there may be circumstances in which affective intensity is too high so it inhibits information processing. The dichotomous potential of high arousal contexts has been summarized in the following terms:

If a person experiences increased arousal, processing of stimulus-related information increases, and in turn, increased attention to processing results in greater acquisition and storage of information. This is called the processing efficiency principle. In contrast, the intensity principle suggests that increased arousal focuses so much attention on the arousal-inducing stimulus that processing of peripheral information is inhibited. Studies of television viewing support this perspective. In a study of advertisement recall for Super Bowl XXXIV, a game in which the outcome was not decided until the last play, recall was greater during the first half than during the more intense second half. It is argued that the intensity created during the second half led viewers to attend more to the game and less to the embedded commercials . . . Presenting individuals with marketing messages when they are in an aroused state could therefore either distract from communication goals, or it could result in an assimilation effect. (p. 31)[8]

A second caveat to the general rule recognizes that the potential of passion to be either positive or negative may create a conundrum for some sponsors. For example, associating with the New York Yankees may result in enhanced brand equity among Yankees' fans, but there may be a concomitant reduction in brand equity among passionate fans of the Boston Red Sox, some proportion of whom have strong negative feelings toward their traditional Yankee rivals.[20] The potential for negative impact has some empirical basis since it has long been known that unpleasant experiences produce more intense (negative) feelings and are more vividly recalled than pleasant experiences.[21]

CONGRUENCY CLASSIFICATION

The Role of Balance Theory

When new material is compared to an existing schema, a judgment is made as to its consistency with that schema. This comparison process is explained by balance theory whose principles were described by its originator: "By a balanced state is meant a situation in which the relations among entities fit together harmoniously . . . A basic assumption is that . . . relations tend toward a balanced state . . . if a balanced state does not exist, then forces toward the state will arise. If a change is not possible, the state of imbalance will produce tension" (p. 201).[22] The principle suggests that people react aversively to inconsistency and positively to harmony, consistency, and the expected, so they act in ways that further these latter outcomes rather than their antitheses. Imbalanced relationships are under some pressure to change towards balance, and that is how the theory predicts the likelihood of image transfer.

Balanced relationships are likely to result in strong image transfer because they are stored in memory as a single unit. Thus, positive attitudes by potential consumers towards both a sport property and a brand sponsor make a compact chunk in memory and cement image transfer. In contrast, imbalanced relationships are stored less efficiently in pieces.[5]

Exhibit 2.3 shows the eight possible outcomes of balance status[23] among the triad of potential consumers (PC), sport property (SP) and brand (Brand) sponsors. Balance can be restored by seeking either positive or negative consistency among the entities. Perceptions summarized by negative and positive signs in the triad relationships range

Exhibit 2.3

The Eight Possible Outcomes of Balance States Among the Triad of Potential Consumers, Sport Property, and Brand Sponsor, From a Consumer's Perspective

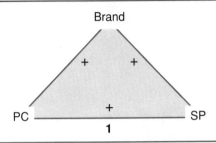

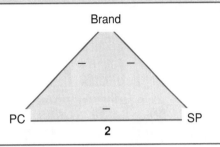

Triad 1 shows a balanced state among all three actors which is an optimum sponsorship scenario in that PCs' existing positive perceptions of a brand are reinforced.

Triad 2 shows no positive relationships among the actors. In this scenario, the sponsorship is perceived as irrelevant, is ignored, and does not create any balanced or unbalanced states.

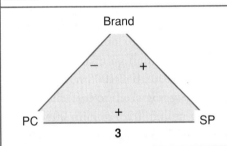

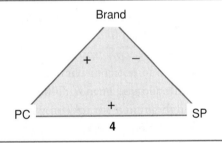

Triad 3 shows positive associations between PC and SP, and SP and Brand. To seek harmony PCs may re-evaluate their negative or ambivalent perceptions of the brand and shift it to positive.

Triad 4 shows the PC has positive association with both the SP and Brand, which suggests the PC will be seeking information that supports image transfer between SP and Brand.

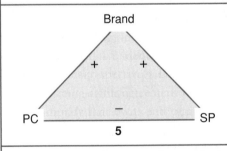

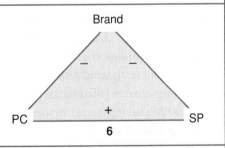

Triad 5 shows the PC has no interest in the SP, but has a positive perception of the Brand and views the SP/Brand association as positive. Given these strengths, the PC is likely to change his/her negative or ambivalent view of SP to restore harmony.

Triad 6 is unbalanced, but the positive link between PC and SP may provide a platform for restoring harmony by conveying information that establishes the SP/Brand image transfer and consequent positive view of Brand.

(Exhibit continues on next page)

Exhibit 2.3 *(Continued)*

The Eight Possible Outcomes of Balance States Among the Triad of Potential Consumers, Sport Property, and Brand Sponsor, From a Consumer's Perspective

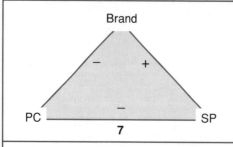

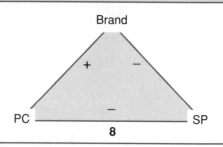

Triad 7 shows that PCs see the association between SP and Brand, but care about neither the SP nor the Brand. In this case, balance would likely be restored by ignoring the SP/Brand relationship, viewing it as irrelevant.

Triad 8 shows the PC is positive to the Brand, but has no passionate involvement with SP and sees no image transfer between SP and Brand. Balance would most easily be restored by changing the PC/Brand association to a negative by, for example, disapproving of the Brand, investing in SP, or by regarding the triad as being irrelevant and discarding any consideration of it.

along a continuum from mild to extreme. Thus, in imbalanced situations, whether balance will be restored by moving towards positive or negative congruence will be determined by the relative strength of the sources of incompatibility recognizing that affective intensity can be positive or negative and that relevancy may be high or low. The suggested outcomes for each of the triads offered in Exhibit 2.3 are only illustrative. If assumptions about the relative strength of feelings and relevancy towards the entities that are made in the interpretations of the triads are changed, then the balance outcomes may be contrary to those suggested in the exhibit.

For example, in Triad 6 if the positive attitude towards the sport property is mild, reflecting passive disinterest rather than committed emotional engagement, and the negative perceptions of the brand are strong, then consumers are likely to rethink their attitude toward the sport property so negative congruency rather than the positive congruency outcome suggested in Triad 6, would be the most probable outcome. When this thinking is personified so the illustration in Triad 6 moves from the general model of balance theory to thought processing by a consumer,[8] the hypothetical internal conversation might be as follows:

"As a Houston resident I am pleased when the Astros win. I read their team news on the sports page, take the grandchildren to a game a couple of times a year, and occasionally watch some of their games on television."

"I get angry at the massive amount of advertising of sugary soda drinks done by companies when they know these drinks are detrimental to people's health."

Balance can be restored by adopting either more positive perceptions of sugar soda drinks, or more negative perceptions of the Astros. The likely response to this imbalance given the relatively tentative support for the Astros and the strong negative attitude towards sugar sodas, would be a negative balance: "I am disgusted that the Astros have partnered with a sugary soda brand and will have nothing more to do with them."

Exhibit 2.3 shows both Triads 1 and 2 are in balance. Among the remaining six triad outcomes, the illustrative interpretations are that sponsorship could restore positive balance in Triads 3,4,5, and 6, while in Triads 7 and 8 balance among consumers is posited to be restored by them discarding or ignoring the sponsorship.

There are situations in which imbalance can exist without any tension being created to drive efforts for balanced congruency. For example, in Triad 3, it is assumed there is passionate engagement with a sport property, and support for linkage with the brand and the resources it generates. There is dislike for the brand, but this may not result in tension and harmony-restoring action if the sport property is not perceived to be harmed by the relationship.

Balance theory deals in absolutes, that is, relationships are either positive or negative. However, both sport properties and brands are multidimensional—that is, they are comprised of multiple attributes. This means that judgments against schemas are likely to be gradated rather than absolute, that is, they will show varying degrees of consistency[24] reflecting the number and strength of congruent attributes. Further, restorative actions that are taken are likely to ameliorate imbalance in increments rather than fully restore it.[25] This more nuanced approach incorporating *extent* to which consistency is met is captured by defining congruence as "the extent to which a brand association shares content and meaning with another brand association" (p. 6).[1]

Types of Sport Property/Brand Congruency

The originator of balance theory identified two independent types of associations between entities that were grounded in cognition and affection.[22] This early insight has remained a central tenet of image transfer suggesting that sport property/brand congruency is evaluated on two dimensions, function (cognitive) and image (affection).[26]

Direct functional congruency occurs when a sponsoring company's brand could be used directly in the event. Thus, for example, a golf equipment or accessory manufacturer will have obvious associations with a golf tournament. The level of investment needed by a company to establish the association between the brand and the sport property is likely to be small, because the similarities are likely to be self-evident to a target audience. Shoe, clothing, and equipment products often fall into this category. Examples include companies which:

- design and construct sport venues—architects, engineers, contractors, and subcontractors.
- develop, fabricate, and install sport lighting systems, indoors and out.
- make and market sports medical supplies—tape, wraps, ice packs, taping tables, whirlpools, and so on.

- manufacture and install sport surfaces—gym floors, tracks, aerobic floors, weight room floors, and rinks.
- develop and install equipment for heating, ventilating, dehumidifying, air conditioning, and acoustically treating sport venues.
- install timing, computing, and other technical operating systems.
- design and print tickets, programs, and other visual materials.
- manufacture and install the seats to accommodate spectators.
- make, distribute, and service sport equipment—the balls, sticks, bats, pucks, and nets[27]

Indirect functional congruency means there is a logical functional link between use of a product when spectating or participating, but the product is not an essential ingredient for the sport event to take place. It is likely to require more investment to establish a desired level of association than products which have a direct role in production of the event. The most pervasive sport sponsors of this type are beverage and fast food suppliers. Indeed, nonalcoholic beverages are the product category that is most active in sponsorship[25] (Table 1.1).

Image based congruency means that a target audience perceives a natural and "comfortable" relationship between the brand and sport event's images. The following examples illustrate brand and sport event image congruence:

- Lady Speed Stick Antiperspirant/Deodorant became title sponsor of the women's national half-marathon series. Their CEO noted, "Our brands work well together as we both appeal to confident, active, and empowered women." In addition to the image match, there is also a strong functional fit.[29]
- Passion Growers sells more than 200 million roses a year and 50 of their store outlets are within 13 miles of the Rose Bowl's Pasadena home. They are sponsors of the Rose Bowl whose CEO observed, "We have a passion for roses like no one else, so we are a great marketing platform for them."[30]
- The Hawaii Tourism Authority (HTA) sponsored the first two PGA tour events of the year. The islands have 70 golf courses and tourism is their major industry. The personality of golf with attributes such as leisurely, calm, clean, slow, civilized, and orderly is consistent with the image HTA seeks to convey. Their spokesperson commented, "There will be warm weather and beautiful views on TV at a time when many of our key markets are blanketed with snow."[31]
- Jimmy White was one of the world's finest players on the professional snooker tour. He signed a $160,000 sponsorship agreement with HPSauce, which is a leading brand of brown sauce. With the full backing of the sport's governing body he then invested $60 to legally change his name to Jimmy Brown! In addition, he swapped the traditional black tuxedo dinner jacket in which he usually played for an all brown outfit topped off with a light blue bow tie and white cap. The intent was that he would resemble a bottle of the sponsor's product. HP also sponsored the brown ball in tournaments—which scores four in snooker's color sequence—so the ball sported its Houses of Parliament logo.[32]

- Wellstone Communities is a national home building company that develops "lifestyle focused communities." It invested $1 million to be title sponsor of the long-established Dallas White Rock marathon. It used this to showcase its Cooper Life at Craig Ranch development of homes ranging from $400,000 to $2 million. The development was created in conjunction with Kenneth Cooper—the physician who coined the term aerobics in 1968 and whose clinic was located in Dallas—to offer residents direct access to fitness and healthcare facilities and services, including a 75,000-square-foot aerobics center. Other amenities included health seminars, and customized nutritional and vitamin supplement plans. While those benefits came standard with ownership, Wellstone also offered upgrades such as family medical care—including house calls—and access to dieticians and personal trainers.[33]

Does Congruency Facilitate the Most Effective Image Transfer?

It is widely recognized, accepted, and supported by the empirical evidence that the memorability of new information and image transfer is most likely when there is congruity or "plausibility" between a sport property and brand, because people favor associations that conform to expectations and allow predictability. A rich pattern of associations in existing schema will enhance the assimilation of new information. Thus, sport property/brand partnerships that are congruent should result in associations that are more easily learned *and* remembered than incongruent relationships.[34] However, schema congruent associations are not very noteworthy. New visual and contextual information pertaining to the association is predictable, which means it is unlikely to prompt elaborate processing. Hence, the positive response they generate typically is mild rather than extreme.[34]

In contrast, in his articulation of balance theory, its originator observed, "Unbalanced situations stimulate us to further thinking; they have the character of interesting puzzles, problems which make us suspect a depth of interesting background" (p. 180).[22] Thus, it is suggested that a different scenario unfolds when there is schema incongruity. The novelty of the association arouses curiosity because it violates expectations and individuals engage in more effortful and elaborate processing in seeking to resolve the incongruity. This additional elaborative effort increases the number of associative neural pathways stored in memory, which subsequently enhances recall of the incongruent relationship. Again, this effort will only be made if the relevancy and affective intensity criteria are met, because people have to be motivated to reconcile the incongruency.

The principle of congruity suggests that changes in evaluation of associations are always in the direction of increased congruity with the existing schema,[24] but the responses to moderate and extreme incongruity are likely to differ reflecting differences in the ease with which anomalies can be resolved. *Moderate* incongruities are those that can be successfully resolved and they are regarded as "interesting and positively valued" (p. 21).[35] This may lead to stronger associations than those elicited by schema congruity. Indeed, it is argued that the very process of resolving the incongruity is thought to be rewarding and thus may contribute to the resulting positive affect.[36]

In contrast, *extreme* incongruity is defined as incongruity that cannot be resolved or can be resolved only if radical changes can be made in the existing schema.[35] For example, 7-Eleven owns 5,300 convenience stores in the US and the company sponsored professional cycling. However, there was no schema congruency between the stores and cycling in consumers' minds, and their customers had no passion for cycling: "They never figured out a way to use it to get people in the stores" (p. 33).[37] The incongruity was so great that it could not be resolved and no image transfer or brand equity gains accrued.

Extreme incongruities may generate substantial cognitive elaboration, but the effort required to undertake this elaboration may lead more to frustration than to resolution, and to greater resistance to the positive sponsorship message. This may result in an unfavorable view of the association, confusion about the meaning of the brand, and perhaps a negative view of the sponsor. When the US Postal Service invested $36.8 million in sponsoring the professional cycling team led by Lance Armstrong over a six-year period, the relationship to many appeared to be extremely incongruent. The Postal Service's inspector general released an audit contending the agency could not justify the costs. The audit verified "only $698,000 of the $18 million claimed by the Postal Service over a four-year period as revenue generated" by the sponsorship. The extreme incongruity led to a barrage of public criticism. A typical comment was, "They should not be sponsoring sports, they are in the business of delivering the mail."[38]

The Elaboration Likelihood Model (ELM) of persuasion reinforces the contention that both congruency and incongruency could result in image transfer.[39] Where there is congruity, this transfer may occur through the "peripheral route" to persuasion. This relies on cues rather than cognitive processing, and explains why brand awareness may directly contribute to brand equity in addition to being a prerequisite for brand image (Figure 2.1). In contrast, image transfer in moderate incongruent associations occurs via the "central route." In this case people are thinking about and elaborating incoming information, so they engage in in-depth processing and consideration of information. Changes induced by this route are likely to be relatively enduring. Thus, in moderate incongruency situations "people are avid seekers of information", while when congruency prevails "they are best described as 'cognitive misers' who eschew any difficult intellectual activity" (p. 136).[39]

Another implication of the ELM may be that non-activational leveraging (passive communication) using the peripheral route may be effective in congruent contexts since they provide cues. However, activational leveraging (incorporating interactive experiences with customers) using the central route may be required in associations that are incongruent. These leveraging concepts are discussed in Chapter 5.

In summary, in most situations schema congruency is likely to result in image transfer because the task of encoding and linking the meanings of both sport property and brand will be easier for individuals to accomplish.[40] Image transfer is unlikely where there is extreme schema incongruity, but there are some contexts in which moderate incongruity may lead to equal or stronger image transfer than congruity. The primary mechanisms available to a company for resolving moderate incongruity are discussed in the following section.

PRIMARY STRATEGIES FOR
RESOLVING MODERATE INCONGRUITY

When the fit between sponsor and sport property is not obvious to consumers' schemas, then much more marketing effort has to be invested to explain the linked relationship. There are three primary strategies a sponsor may use to resolve moderate incongruity and, thus, fully exploit potential image transfer. They are articulation, change the attribution of motives, and commit substantial investment (Figure 2.1).

Articulation

Articulation is defined as the act of explaining the relationship between the brand and sport property to support the development of a congruent association in the mind of an individual. The concept is captured by the term "created fit."[41] Congruency is established on the basis of function or image. However, there may be "hidden" or latent congruent relationship meanings between the two entities that are not captured by function or image and only become apparent when they are verbally described through articulation. This added element can strengthen an already congruent association by adding other dimensions to it. Perhaps more importantly, it has been shown that making latent meanings explicit can be effective in ameliorating moderate incongruency by enhancing favorable attitudes to both a brand and property and enhancing recall of the association.[42]

Instead of relying on individuals' pre-existing schemas, articulation may activate a memory pathway that would not otherwise be activated.[8] Thus, in the example given below of Image Solar and a soccer club, the notion of "sustainable energy" may not have been activated when the association was related to existing schemas. By introducing and emphasizing that phrase, a memory pathway may be activated that would otherwise have remained dormant. The following examples are illustrative of sponsors' efforts to use articulation to remove incongruency:

- Image Solar sponsored Belgium's most successful soccer team RSC Anderlecht. The link? "Sustainability in player development and sporting performance is what characterizes our club. Sustainability in energy solutions is what represents our new partner. We consider this partnership an excellent fit."[43]
- Texas Instruments is one of the world's largest semiconductor and computer technology companies. For many, its investment of $20 million in a NASCAR sponsorship lacked congruency of image or function, but it became more apparent when it was explained, "These cars are very high-tech and very fast which is the image TI wants for its products."[44]
- FedEx is a NASCAR sponsor because, "After all, they both share the same values: speed, technology, precision, and reliability. And like the champion drivers themselves, FedEx offers expert handling, shipping everything from car parts to the cars themselves" (p. 3).[45] FedEx used similar articulation to explain its investment as the official delivery service sponsor for the NFL, the Super Bowl, and the Pro Bowl: "We have partnered together because we share key attributes of leadership, excellence, speed, precision, reliability, and global reach" (p. 130)[46]. Elsewhere the

company elaborated on this: "Is it possible to have a better game plan? FedEx and the NFL think so. That's why FedEx and NFL teams work so hard to improve the plays that will get them to their destination. Both the air and ground game plans must be coordinated. Through the air, Minnesota Vikings had the leading passer of last season with 4,717 yards, while on the ground, the New York Jets had the leading rusher with 1,697 yards. As the FedEx leader in the air, FedEx Express now has a powerful new ground game in FedEx Ground to serve you better" (p. 132).[46]

- Xchanging is an international business outsourcing solutions company. When it invested in the title sponsorship of the most historic event in the British sporting calendar, the annual Boat Race on the River Thames between Oxford and Cambridge Universities, the association fit was not obvious. Their CEO explained, "The event makes a very good business metaphor. If one person in that boat isn't pulling his weight then the whole team will suffer. Margins between success and failure can come down to one foot over a 4.25 mile course, so it really is a brutal event where 'winner-takes-all." There are no prizes for coming second" (p. 15).[47] That was the link!

- L'Oréal is a fashion company whose main brands are L'Oréal Men Expert and Garnier. It became the official lifestyle partner and supplier to the World Snowboarding Championships which is held every four years and attracts the best snowboarders from around the world. The fit may not be obvious but the Director of the Championships explained, "You can't win the World Snowboarding Championships without style—neither at day nor night. Style is crucial to impress the judges in daytime. At night, L'Oréal makes all look good as the lifestyle partner of WSC. They bring fun to the event.[48]

For articulation to be effective, it has to be perceived as cogent, credible, and meaningful. If it is specious and non-credible, consumer reaction is likely to be cynical and skeptical, and it will be discarded. Its effectiveness in the above illustrations likely will be variable because (i) some of the schema incongruity appears to be extreme rather than moderate; and (ii) some of the articulation claims appear to stretch credibility.

Articulation may evolve into the more elaborate form of storytelling. This is a more holistic approach to explaining the related concepts and motivations that undergird an association, offering a more comprehensive understanding of the entire relationship.[23]

Change the Atribution of Motives

One of the dimensions of a sponsoring brand's "personality" is consumers' perceptions of the sincerity of its involvement with "their" sport property. Attribution theory addresses how people make causal interpretations. It posits that members of a target market will cognitively infer a motive for a sponsor's investment in an attempt to understand the rationale for it. It recognizes that people interpret behavior in terms of its causes, and that these interpretations are important in determining how to react to the behavior. Thus, "Causal attributions play an important role in providing the impetus to actions and decisions among alternative courses of actions" (p. 125).[49]

The general model of attribution theory states that *antecedents* which comprise consumers' beliefs towards a sponsor and their suppositions about its motives; lead to *attributions* as to whether the sponsor is a loyal, empathetic, supporter of the sport property or is unreasonably exploiting it; which lead to *consequences* that result in consumers embracing or distaining the relationship.[50]

A central precept of exchange theory (Chapter 1) is that the relationship has to be fair to both sides. There will be an understanding that companies need to secure a return on their investment. However, the company's sponsorship will be perceived to have both extrinsic motives (commercial considerations) *and* internal motives (loyalty, support, belief in the property). If the company is explicitly mercenary and perceived to lack genuine, sincere support for the property, then its investment will be discounted, imbalance will not be positively restored, and image transfer will not occur.

It has been found that sponsor credibility is stronger in congruent then in incongruent associations, suggesting that in incongruent situations the onus is on companies to take steps to affirm their sincerity.[25] If a sponsorship is packaged as an act of social responsibility, corporate altruism, or benevolence, then motive attribution could enhance sponsor credibility which could contribute to the resolution of moderate incongruity.

Substantial Investment

The magnitude of investment influences the status of a sponsorship (e.g., title sponsor, presenting sponsor, official sponsor, official supplier), frequency of exposure, and extent of complementary leveraging and activation activity. Clearly, the larger the investment, the more likely it is that schema incongruency can be resolved.

This is well illustrated by the potential incongruency between a sport property and sponsors of brands in the product categories of tobacco, alcohol, gambling, and HFSS (products high in fat, salt or sugar). All of these products are widely condemned by the health community as being detrimental to people's well-being. Certainly, regular use of them is likely to detract from athletic performance. Nevertheless, sponsors use sport to counter these negative perceptions by seeking image transfer suggesting that use of these products is associated with vibrant health and athleticism. Indeed, Table 1.1 reported that the three largest corporate sponsors of sport in the US are in the HFSS and alcohol categories.

The ethical conundrum confronting sport properties on these issues is discussed in Chapter 7, but it is clear that large investments have been effective in resolving not only moderate incongruity, but in some cases extreme incongruity. Tobacco sponsorship offered perhaps the most egregious illustration. It is now effectively banned in the US, but for decades tobacco companies used the positive images of sport to obscure the potential hazards of their products. For almost 20 years, for example, Philip Morris's Virginia Slims brand was the title sponsor of the women's professional tennis tour. The target audiences were compatible. The images were extremely non-congruent, but through a large investment over a long period of time the Virginia Slims title sponsorship effectively transferred to the brand the positive image of female tennis players, "Quick speak the words 'Virginia Slims' and what do you see? A) Chris Evert or B) the cancer ward? If you answered A)—and most people do—then Philip Morris has you right where he wants you" (p. 36).[51] There is a link between the word "slim" and the activity of tennis as a means of becoming slim. Tennis champions are in peak physical condition, and since endurance is important, their hearts and lungs are particularly strong and healthy. The obvious implications of the linkage are that sport and smoking are both acceptable activities, and that smoking is acceptable, not harmful, and even desirable for women. A former Secretary of Health and Human Services observed, "When the tobacco industry sponsors an event in order to push their deadly product, they are trading on the health, the prestige, and the image of the athlete to barter a product that will kill the user." Another commentator stated, "When the pitchmen of Philip Morris say, 'You've come a long way baby,' [the catch phrase used to promote Virginia Slims cigarettes] they could very well be congratulating themselves; their success in co-opting the nation's health elite to promote a product that leads to an array of fatal diseases is extraordinary" (p. 35).[51]

CONTEXTS IN WHICH BRAND IMAGE IS A PRIORITY

There are five contexts in which companies may make brand image transfer the primary objective of their sponsorship to strengthen brand equity (Exhibit 1.1). The first is when *a brand enters a market for the first time* so the challenge is to create, rather than to change, its image. An illustration of how this can be done is provided in Exhibit 2.4 which describes Vodafone New Zealand's experience.[3] Exhibit 2.5 describes how Abu Dhabi sought to establish its national brand by creating "the world's biggest soccer club."[52,53,54] Red Bull energy drink, whose annual revenues now exceed $5.5 billion was launched in the early 1980s with the youth market as its target. It adopted a strategy of connecting with the lifestyles of its target consumers by adopting the theme "Red Bull

Exhibit 2.4

Creating Vodaphone's Image in New Zealand

When Vodafone entered the New Zealand mobile telecommunications market, it was dominated by a well-established New Zealand monopoly, Telecom New Zealand. Vodafone recognized that a strong and differentiated local brand was essential to their success and employed sponsorship as its central vehicle for achieving this. The company's theme was "youthful spontaneity." Hence, they partnered with sport properties that were "spontaneous, cool, and edgy," and sought a brand personality that would create links to youth. Their sponsorship portfolio manager explained that they build brand personality:

"Through association with events like Vodafone Xtreme Air, the Tony Hawk event in Aotea Square last year, where we were supporting a leading edge, youth-type activity, and in the form of freestyle BMX, skateboarding, freestyle motocross . . . I think that has helped shape some of what the brand is. It goes back to that brand personality at the core of it . . . the youthful spontaneity . . . so what I think that does for Vodafone is show us 'walking the talk' and delivering on our brand promise."

Subsequently, focus group interviews were done with consumers to identify their perceptions of the Vodafone brand and its sponsorship activities. The following table compares the image Vodafone desired in the left column with the consumer focus groups' perceptions of the company's image. There is a high de-gree of correspondence between the two columns, suggesting that Vodafone successfully accomplished brand transfer from its sport sponsorships. Indeed, 10 years after entering New Zealand, Vodafone had over 2.5 million customers, representing 53 percent of the country's mobile phone market.

Comparison of Vodafone's Desired Image with Consumers' Actual Perceptions of its Brand Image	
Vodafone Desired Image	Brand Image
Youthfulness	Youthfulness
Mischievousness	Fun
Cool	Relaxed
Spontaneous	Edgy
Risk-taking	Spontaneous
Strong	Pushing the boundaries
Underdog	Arrogant
Competitive	Energetic
Business savvy	Underdog
Forward thinking	Strong
Innovative	Innovative
	Text Messaging

gives you wings," then pursued it by investing heavily in "edgy" extreme sports such as motor sports, air races, BMX, skateboarding, cliff diving, mountain biking, and snowboarding. Their experience is described in more detail in Chapter 4 in Exhibit 4.1.

The second and perhaps the most common context is companies seeking to *reinforce a brand's existing image*, to give existing purchasers good feelings about purchasing it, and to encourage their loyalty towards it. Cadillac, for example, has an established image so the company's sponsorship objective is "to reinforce and enhance Cadillac's image among the general public—to use our name as a metaphor for excellence: 'The Cadillac of its class'" (p. 4).[55] Many brands explicitly state that they are leaders in their product class, but such self-promotion is awkward and ineffectual. To boast, "I am a leader" in a paid advertisement has a hollow ring to it. The effect is more likely to resonate through image transfer by associating with events that have a well established image of being the best or most prestigious—the Masters, Wimbledon, the Kentucky Derby, the Indy 500, or the Olympics. Citigroup's reinforcement strategy was articulated by their executive in charge of sponsorship who said:

Exhibit 2.5

Brand Transfer to a Principality?

In 2008, Sheik Mansour bin Zayed Al-Nahyan bought the English Premier League team, Manchester City, for approximately $300 million. The Sheik is a member of the Abu Dhabi royal family. His personal wealth is estimated at $37 billion, while the family's assets are approximately $1 trillion. Manchester City is a long-established Premier League team. Typically, they finished in the lower half of the league and they last won it 40 years previously. In the three years after Sheik Mansour acquired the team, they spent $1.5 billion buying the best players in the world from other clubs, and paying them the highest salaries in the world. Of this amount, only $600 million was generated by the team's revenues, and the remaining $900 million came from Sheik Mansour. Indeed, the team's salary bill alone exceeded the revenues it generated.[52]

The Sheik confessed to having little knowledge of soccer and that he did not expect to attend more than 10 games in the 60 game season. His intent was for "Manchester City to become the biggest club in the world." His purposes were awareness and brand transfer—to raise the profile of Abu Dhabi by it becoming the driving force and owner of the "biggest soccer club in the world." His spokesperson explained: "The purchase is to reinforce Abu Dhabi's position as a capital of both sport and economic development through supporting the Emirate's sports and attracting the world's attention to the United Arab Emirates through this purchase of one of the oldest English clubs."[53] As one commentator noted: "How better to guarantee headlines from Manchester to Madras than buying a football club and then launching raids for the world's greatest players."[54]

Citi doesn't need awareness. We're well known around the world, especially in the U.S. What is important to us is how we leverage partnerships to build and reinforce the attributes and values of our brand. We sponsor the Mets to support an iconic team and let our customers and clients experience Citi Field's iconic location. Sponsorship is all about connecting with the community. The same is true with our Olympic Games sponsorship. It's not about awareness but connecting with U.S. customers. It's all about connecting with consumers and building the brand values.[56]

Periodic outbreaks of racism have bedeviled professional soccer in Europe. A series of high visibility incidents have involved both fans directing racist chants and actions at players, and players using racist epithets directed at other players:

- Hublet is a Swiss watchmaker. The company became the first luxury watch brand to become a sponsor at the UEFA European Championships. This is the premier tournament for national teams in Europe held every four years. The company believed its existing reputation for integrity would be reinforced by allocating all its perimeter board and stadium signage at the tournament to promote the message, "No to Racism," instead of its own branding. The company's CEO thought this demonstration of corporate social responsibility would be financially advantageous. He explained, "Awareness of us is nothing compared to making a meaningful statement. We were one of the tournament's smallest sponsors, but by doing this we

Exhibit 2.6

Using Sport Sponsorship to Reposition a Brand

The classic image-transfer sponsor case study is the caffeinated, citrus-flavored soft drink Mountain Dew. Its beginnings can be traced back to the hills of Tennessee in the 1940s. Its name was a euphemism used in Southern culture for moonshine. It was promoted as a drink that would "tickle your innards" and until 1992 Mountain Dew was positioned as a drink beloved by hillbillies with the non-conformist lifestyle that connoted. That changed when the "Do the Dew" marketing campaign was launched targeted at young people who were doing things their own way and carving out their own lifestyle niches. The campaign showed them involved in extreme sports. Mountain Dew was a major sponsor of the first X Games in 1995 and has retained that involvement with both the Summer and Winter X Games. The X Games target a youth market with an "in-your-face" attitude.

This commitment was reinforced by the company's title sponsorship of the Dew Tour. The summer Dew Tour features various forms of skateboarding, BMX, and motocross, and is held at five venues across the country. The winter version comprises snowboarding and snow skiing competitions at three different ski resorts. A cumulative points system is used to allocate the purse ($2.5 million for the summer tour) among the professional athletes. The events are broadcast live on NBC Sports and are also featured on MTV in the US, and the broadcasts are distributed widely to many other countries.

This new genre emanating from Generation X was used to completely redefine Mountain Dew's image as cool, edgy, and exciting. In the company's terms Mountain Dew is about "individuality, some irreverence, and living life to the fullest." It has transitioned from being merely a soft drink, to becoming a cultural icon in the eyes of many in its target market. "Doing the Dew" has become a tagline for high-energy activity embraced by youth.

The resultant image change yielded dramatic results. Mountain Dew was the fastest growing soft drink in the 1990s. Furthermore, there was a 10% increase from 1998 to 2001 of teenagers saying. "Mountain Dew is a brand for someone like me."

made the biggest noise. We believe this action will stay with soccer fans even if they are not in the market for a luxury watch for another 10 years. It still will be a powerful differentiator when they are ready to select a brand to purchase."[57]

A third situation which may stimulate a focus on image transfer is *repositioning a brand*. Once people develop a set of beliefs and impressions about a brand it is difficult to change them. This relative permanency exists because once people have an established schema, they tend to selectively perceive additional data and to "filter out" any information that is inconsistent with it. However, sponsorship has proven to be a vehicle with the potential to facilitate repositioning, as the Mountain Dew vignette in Exhibit 2.6 illustrates.[26,58] Indeed, it has been observed:

No examples of potential image transfer could be more pronounced than those sought by sponsors of the X Games developed by ESPN. Combining new, perhaps once outlawed sports such as snowboarding, sky surfing, cliff diving, skateboarding, and mountain biking, the X Games target a youth market with an "in-your-face-attitude." The list of sponsors seeking an image transfer effect from such action sports include Taco Bell, Disneyland, Burger King, Levi Strauss, PepsiCo/

Table 2.1. Adjectives Illustrating Differences in Sports' "Personalities"	
Professional Golf	**Motor Sports**
Calm	Fast
Mature	Dangerous
Leisurely	Exciting
Clean	Aggressive
Formal	Masculine
Civilized	Wild
Accurate	Historic
Pressure	Tactical
Orderly	Tough
Slow	Thrilling

Mountain Dew, Coca-Cola, Kellog's, Gatorade, Schick, Reebok, and Activision (p. 28).[8]

When Gatorade repositioned itself from a sports drink provider to a sport performance and nutrition brand, it relied on brand transfer from its sponsorships in the four major U.S. sports leagues to give credibility to its new products and new direction.[58a]

The pioneers of brand positioning emphasized that the power of a brand resides in the minds of potential customers. They argued that it has nothing to do with what is done to a product, rather it relates to what a company is able to do with the minds of its potential customers.[10] Enhancing brand image involves creating additional brand meaning by better defining what the brand stands for in customers' minds. The function of brand positioning is to emphasize attributes of a brand that give it a sustainable competitive advantage or "unique selling proposition" which offers customers a compelling reason for buying that particular brand.[1] It is its intangible attributes that most frequently define and differentiate a brand. These can be effectively fostered through sponsorship, since it focuses on shaping consumers' feelings towards the brand by establishing associations with desired attributes of a sport property in their minds. Indeed, one of the most powerful image dimensions of sports is that most of them have distinctive "personalities." For example, consider the contrasting personalities of the US Open Golf Championships and the Indianapolis 500 Auto Race events listed in Table 2.1.[40]

In a product class where competing brands are essentially similar, associating with a sport's personality attributes provides a vehicle through which companies can differentiate their brands from those of competitors and strengthen brand equity. Image transfer may be facilitated by managers listing a set of descriptors which best describe their brand, then seeking sport properties whose image fits with those descriptors. Typical words may include:

accuracy	health	masculinity
strength	aggression	uniqueness
perseverance	thirst	reliability
speed	femininity	softness
risk	excellence	creativity
danger	co-operation	versatility
problem solving	teamwork	innovation

The following process has been suggested for distilling descriptors which best describe a sport event:

> On a whiteboard or large piece of paper, draw a circle in the center of it. In the area outside of the circle, write down every word that describes the personality of the event or property (fun, youthful, challenging, etc.). From brainstorming this with a team, the sponsor seeker will arrive at the point where it is able to distil the personality of the event or property into two or three words that truly encompass what the property or event is all about, what it stands for to the target audience, and how it makes them feel. Write this in the inner circle. It really is that easy! (p. 26)[59]

A fourth rationale for image transfer is to *build a perception of size, strength, and clout* through "running with the big dogs." It is an implied heuristic suggesting through peer association that by being in the sponsorship company of other firms that have a much bigger public profile, a company is equal to them in strength and size. This was illustrated by the CEO of John Hancock who stated: "What we sell is trust. People give us money for a policy and someday we give their loved ones more money back. The credibility of the Olympics is very important to a company like ours" (p. 103). He explained how the company used the Olympics to reinforce a brand image of size, strength, and credibility:

> The Olympic rings help John Hancock reinforce certain essential things about our brand over and over, in every line of business and in every market: that we are willing to support something our customers consider a good cause and that we are a big player. In truth, the rings suggest that we are a much bigger player than we actually are, given the company they put us in. The 10 other TOP Olympic sponsors include corporations like Coca-Cola and McDonald's, whose market capitalization dwarfs ours (p. 103).[60]

The message to prospective consumers was that the company could not afford to sponsor the Olympics unless it was a large, stable company.

The Annexus Group is a company that designs annuities and other financial products. The company became a sponsor of the NBA Phoenix Suns who play in the US Airlines center. Their director of national sales explained:

> The entire purpose of this partnership was for brand transference between Annexus and the Phoenix Suns organization. Annexus hosts a dozen events a year at the US Airways Center for brokers who sell their products. When brokers walk into the Center and see Annexus next to brands like Verizon, McDonalds, and Toyota it provides instant credibility.

The group sponsored the Suns' practice court because it connected the Suns' and Annexus' commitment to training. When Annexus brought brokers to the US Airways Center for meetings each month, training on their products was a large focus. Annexus had placed itself front and center in a facility that was used by some of the world's top basketball players.[60a]

Similarly, Emirates Airline moved aggressively to build a public perspective that it is a global carrier, rather than a regional Middle East or Gulf States airline. Sponsorship was central to this effort and explained the company's decision to invest as a major sponsor of the Soccer World Cup. Their spokesperson said: "When you see the FIFA World Cup there are six major partners including Emirates. Suddenly we are now one of six up there with the big boys. It's the way we want to be"(p. 18).[61] The other five partners were Coca-Cola, VISA, adidas, Sony, and Hyundai. At least, the first four of these were well-established as global companies, and Emirates was anticipating some image transfer to come from associating with them.

A final context that drives image transfer goals is to create a sense of corporate social responsibility in response to perceptions of corporate malfeasance. The intent is to borrow the imagery of integrity and authenticity that many sport properties enjoy:

- Waste Management is the biggest trash collector in the U.S. with an annual turnover of $13 billion. It endured a very public accounting scandal for which it paid $457 million to settle a civil suit and a $7 million fine levied by the Securities and Exchange Commission. A major challenge for the new management team who were appointed after the scandal was to create a new public image. Part of the strategy involved sponsoring events on the PGA tour, recognizing that golf has a reputation for integrity, and sponsoring NASCAR teams because of the sport's large and loyal fan base.[62]
- BP suffered a devastating demise in its brand image following the Gulf of Mexico oil spill disaster in 2010. Soon after, it became the official oil and gas partner for the London Olympic Games. A year later a survey sampling 3,192 UK adults revealed: Only 18% were not aware of BP's Olympic sponsorship; and among those who were aware of it, 38% believed BP was "getting better at working for a cleaner planet." The research company reporting the results stated: "These results provide persuasive evidence that sponsoring the Olympic Games can make a real difference in how people perceive a brand."[63]
- When the NBA's New Orleans Hornets were looking for a naming rights sponsor for the New Orleans Arena, they were approached by Louisiana Seafood Promotion and Marketing Board to name it "The Louisiana Seafood Arena." Much of the money for this was provided by BP as part of its effort to promote Louisiana seafood as safe after the oil spill.[64]

It is possible that the directionality of image transfer could move from brand to event rather than from event to brand; sometimes this "reverse association" is deliberately sought from a sponsor. This is most likely to occur when the sport property is perceived to be a potential "top performer" and, hence, an attractive proposition for a top performing brand. For example, a few years ago professional soccer in England was engulfed by a continuous flow of bad publicity caused by hooligans and gangs fighting at the games. The Premier Soccer League attracted sponsorship from Barclays Bank, one of the country's premier companies and at that time a symbol of propriety. The intent was to transfer "stability and order" from Barclays, without transferring "rowdiness" to

Barclays. Barclays felt that the sponsorship had a high profile and was closely connected to the British fabric, as well as a link to a young audience. Sponsorship research revealed that soccer fans felt that Barclays had taken risks by its commitment and that its sponsorship was critical to the health of the sport. In fact, the endorsement of a national financial institution was found to help the league's image—which, of course, then made the sponsorship more valuable.[65]

Fortuitous Image Transfer From Juxtapositon of Sponsors

The clutter of concurrent sponsorship partnerships associated with some sport teams and events suggests there may be some fortuitous and unanticipated brand image transfer side effects which occur through the juxtaposition of multiple brands.[66] In this situation, there is some likelihood that a brand will not only borrow attributes of the sport property, but also that consumers will associate one sponsoring brand with their perceptions of others.

It seems possible that when consumers see two or more brands with which they are familiar sponsoring the same sport property, their associative networks will link those nodes together. This could lead to attributes of the brands' images being transferred among each other. If they are not familiar with the brands, then such transfers will not occur because the associative network nodes and links will be weak or non-existent.

If one sponsor is a tobacco, alcohol, gambling, sugar soda drink, or fast food brand, other sponsors may be concerned that their reputation for being socially responsible companies may be damaged, given the increasingly critical and strident concerns regarding such product categories. Alternatively, concurrent sponsorships may offer possibilities for cooperating to positively develop or modify their brands' images and positioning. This was illustrated in the previous section of this chapter by John Hancock's and Emirates' concurrent sponsorships with much bigger companies to borrow their images of size and strength. The following hypothetical case illustrates the potential:

> Presume that Gatorade needs to strengthen consumers' perception of its "competitiveness" dimension, on which Nike is highly rated, while Nike wants to cultivate the "fun" dimension of its brand image, which is a salient perception of Gatorade. If Gatorade and Nike become concurrent sponsors of the same event, they could achieve their mutual goals. For instance, they could control the *side effect* of concurrent sponsorships by negotiating together with the event to ensure they benefit from each other's image transfer. (p. 121)[66]

It has been suggested that concurrent sponsoring brands becoming associated in consumers' minds is akin to co-branding. However, unlike co-branding, the association between the brands does not have to be formal to lead to a transfer of image between them.

SUMMARY

In most product classes, different companies' offerings are functionally similar. To differentiate their product from those of others, companies seek to create strong brand equity. Brand equity is defined by two components, brand awareness and brand image.

When they partner with a sport property, sponsors seek brand image transfer. This involves "borrowing" some of the property's attributes and transferring them to the companies' brands. Their success in accomplishing this is determined by the way consumers process information related to the partnership.

The information is processed in memory by associative networks comprised of nodes, which represent units of information, and links which connect those pieces of information. An organized set of related nodes and links forms a schema or knowledge structure. New information initially is processed by short-term memory. It is assessed against existing schemas and if it does not relate, or is not consistent with them, it is likely to be "filtered out." If it does relate, then the information passes through the neural pathways from short-term to long-term memory where it reinforces or amends the existing schemas.

Brand awareness and brand image have complementary roles enhancing brand equity. Brand awareness may enhance brand equity directly, or through its role as a prerequisite for enhancing image. Its direct influence stems from repeated exposure increasing customers' familiarity with a brand, and their proclivity to purchase brands with which they are most familiar. It is also a necessary condition for brand image, since if there is no awareness of a brand, there is no node to which image information can attach to the brand in memory. There are three contexts in which brand awareness may act as a prerequisite for image transfer: where a company is launching a new brand in the market place; where an existing brand is expanding into a new market that has never heard of it; and where multinational corporations are replacing national or regional brands they have purchased with their own international brand.

Enhancing brand equity involves creating additional brand meaning, by better defining what the brand stands for in customers' minds. One of the most powerful marketing assets of sports is their distinctive "personalities." Hence, aligning with a sport and appropriating its personality provides a mechanism though which companies can differentiate their brands from their competitors. The relevance of both the brand and sport property to consumers and their affective intensity for them will influence the likelihood of them absorbing new information. Relevancy refers to consumers' levels of interest or use, while affective intensity describes their degree of passion or feelings, either positive or negative, toward both partnering entities.

When new material is compared to existing schemas, a judgment is made as to its consistency with those schemas. This comparison process is explained by balance theory which suggests that people react positively to consistency, and if it does not exist, will act to restore it. Thus, if consumers have positive feelings toward a brand and negative feelings toward the sport property by adopting either more negative perceptions of the brand or more positive perceptions of the property (or vice-versa), they would take action to reconcile the inconsistency. Balance theory was subsequently extended by the principle of congruity. This recognized that congruency and incongruency were not absolute states because both sport properties and brands are multidimensional, comprised of multiple attributes. Thus, judgments against schemas are likely to be gradated rather than absolute, that is, they will show varying degrees of consistency reflecting the number and strength of congruent attributes.

Sport property/brand congruency is evaluated on two dimensions, function (cognitive) and image (affective). Direct functional congruency occurs when a sponsoring brand could be used directly in the event, so congruency is likely to be self-evident to the target audience. Shoe, clothing, and equipment products often fall into this category. Indirect functional congruency means there is a logical functional link with the sport event, but the product is not an essential ingredient for the event to take place. Beverage and fast food products are the most pervasive examples. Image based congruency means that an audience perceives a natural and comfortable relationship between the brand and the sport event's images.

It is widely accepted that image transfer is most likely when there is congruency between a sport property and brand. However, differences in processing perceived congruent and incongruent partnerships may lead to differences in image transfer and there are some contexts in which moderate incongruity may lead to equal or stronger image transfer than congruity. However, image transfer is unlikely where the incongruity is so extreme that it can be resolved only if radical changes are made in the existing schema.

There are three primary strategies available to companies for resolving moderate incongruity: articulation, which describes and explains the functional or image relationship between the sport property and brand when it might otherwise not be apparent, to support the development of an association in consumers' minds; change the attribution of motives so the sponsorship is packaged as an act of social responsibility or corporate altruism to enhance a sponsor's credibility; and substantial investment which is designed to remove incongruency by long-term and frequent reiteration of the association with complementary messages and activation.

There are five contexts in which companies may make brand image transfer a primary objective of their sponsorship: when a brand enters a market for the first time so the challenge is to create, rather than to change, its image; reinforcement of a brand's existing image; repositioning a brand; building a perception of size, strength, and "clout" for a brand; and demonstrating corporate social responsibility in response to corporate malfeasance. When sport properties have multiple sponsors, it is possible that a brand will not only borrow attributes of the sport property, but also those of its other sponsors. Such image transfers have the potential to be either negative or positive, and they may emerge as either unplanned side effects or carefully nurtured alliances.

Endnotes

1. Keller, K. L. (1993). Conceptualizing, measuring and managing customer-based brand equity. *Journal of Marketing, 57*(1), 1–22.

1a. Ukman, L. (2007). *How to measure, justify and maximize your return on sponsorships and partnerships.* Chicago, IL: IEG.

2. Warren, C. (2005, March). What to expect. *American Way*, pp. 58–62.

3. Cliffe, S. J., & Motsion, J. (2005). Building contemporary brands: A sponsorship-based strategy. *Journal of Business Research, 58*, 1068–1077.

3a. Madrigal, R. (2001). Social Identity effects in a belief-attitude-intentions hierarchy: Implications for corporate sponsorship. *Psychology & Marketing, 18*(2), 145–165.

4. Solomon, M. R. (2009). *Consumer behavior: Buying, having and being* (8th ed.). Upper Saddle River, NJ: Prentice Hall.

5. Fiske, S. T., & Taylor, S. E. (2007). *Social cognition: From brains to culture*. Boston, MA: McGraw-Hill.

6. McDaniel, S. R. (1999). An investigation of match-up effects in sport sponsorship advertising: The implications of consumer advertising schemas. *Psychology & Marketing, 16*(2), 163–184.

7. Kahana, M. J. (2012). *Foundations of human memory*. Cary, NC: Oxford University Press.

8. Cornwell, T. B., Weeks, C. S., & Roy, D. P. (2005). Sponsorship-linked marketing: Opening the black box. *Journal of Advertising, 34*(2), 21–42.

9. Hill, A. (2011, January). The people's race. *SportsBusiness International*, 33–38.

10. Ries, A., & Trout, J. (2001). *Positioning: The battle for your mind. Twentieth anniversary edition*. New York: McGraw Hill.

11. Smith, M. (2010, March 29). Showtime title-sponsors Darlington race. *SportsBusiness Journal*, p. 3.

12. Brook, S., & McGuire, M. (2003, July 24). A cup full of dollars. *The Australian*, pp. 4–6.

13. Zoghby, J. (1999, November 1–7). Ericsson makes name with NC stadium. *SportsBusiness Journal*, p. 14.

14. Friedman, A. (1997). *Naming rights deals*. Chicago, IL: Team Marketing Report.

15. SBI. (2010, April). Visit Malta and Sheffield United. *SportsBusiness International*, pp. 16–17.

16. Fry, A. (2008, June). Proving the power of partnership. *SportsBusiness International*, pp. 44–45.

17. Dan, Z. (2007, August). A tale of two brands. *SportsBusiness International*, pp. 60–61.

17a. Hoult, N. (2012, October 16). American dream of T20 league could hit English game. *The Telegraph*. Retrieved from http://www.telegraph.co.uk/sport/cricket/9616182/American-dream-of-T20-league-could-hit-English-game.html

18. SportsPro. (2010). Motorsport feature. *ProSport*, pp. 93–96.

19. Lefton, T. (2010, July 12). Far flung Aon unites with ManU. *SportsBusiness Journal*. Retrieved from http://www.sportsbusinessdaily.com/Journal/Issues/2010/07/20100712/This-Weeks-News/Far-Flung-Aon-Unites-With-Manu.aspx

20. Wakefield, K. L., & Bennett, G. (2010). Affective intensity and sponsor identification. *Journal of Advertising, 39*(3), 99–111.

21. Cason, H. (1932). The learning and retention of pleasant and unpleasant activities. *Archives of Psychology, 134*, 1–96.

22. Heider, F. (1958). *The psychology of interpersonal relations*. New York, NY: Wiley.

23. Woodside, A. G., & Chebar, J. C. (2001). Updating Heider's balance theory in consumer behavior: A Jewish couple buys a German car and additional buying-consumer transformation stories. *Psychology and Marketing, 18*(5), 475–495.

24. Osgood, C. R., & Tannenbaum, P. H. (1955). The principle of congruity in the prediction of attitude change. *Psychological Review, 62*(1), 42–55.

25. Dean, D. H. (2002). Associating the corporation with a charitable event through sponsorship: Measuring the effects on corporate community relations. *Journal of Advertising, 31*(4), 77–87.

26. Gwimmer, K. (2005). Image transfer in global sport sponsorship. In J. Amis & T. B. Cornwell (Eds.), *Global sport sponsorship* (pp. 163–178). New York, NY: Berg.

27. Meagher, J. W. (1992, May 14). And now a word from our sponsor. *Athletic Business*.

28. IEG. (2011, December 5). IEG property survey reveals deepening sponsor pool. *IEG Sponsorship Report*. Retrieved from http://www.sponsorship.com/IEGSR/2011/12/05/IEG-Property-Survey-Reveals-Deepening-Sponsor-Pool.aspx

29. IEG. (2012, January 11). Lady Speed Stick named title sponsor of the women's half marathon series. *IEG Sponsorship Report*. Retrieved from http://www.sponsorship.com

30. Lefton, T. (2010, May 24). Rose producer counting on this sponsorship to deliver. *SportsBusiness Journal*, p. 8.

31. Smith, M. (2011, January 3). Hawaii tourism group renews PGA Tour deal. *SportsBusiness Journal*, p. 4.

32. Buckley, W. (2005, February 12). Saucy, but future's Brown. *The Observer*. Retrieved from http://www.guardian.co.uk/sport/2005/feb/13/comment.willbuckley

33. IEG. (2006, November 6). Developer builds brand and lifestyle positioning through sponsorships. *IEG Sponsorship Report*. Retrieved from http://www.sponsorship.com/iegsr/2006/11/06/Developer-Builds-Brand-And-Lifestyle-Positioning-T.aspx

34. Cornwell, T. B. (2008). State of the art and science in a sponsorship-linked marketing. *Journal of Advertising, 37*(3), 41–55.

35. Mandler, G. (1982). The structure of value:

Accounting for taste. In M. S. Clark & S. T. Fisko (Eds.), *17th Annual Carnegie symposium on cognition* (pp. 3–36). Hillsdale, NS, Canada: Lawrence Tribune Associates.

36. Meyers-Levy, J., & Tybout, A. M. (1989). Schema congruity as a basis for product evaluation. *Journal of Consumer Research, 16*, 39–54.

37. Lowenstein, R., & Lancaster, H. (1986, June 25). Nation's businesses are scrambling to sponsor the nation's pastimes. *Wall Street Journal.*

38. Sandomir, R. (2004, April 24). Postal Service to end sponsorship of the team led by Armstrong. *New York Times*, p. D7.

39. Petty, R. E., Cacioppo, J. T., & Schumann, D. (1983). Central and peripheral routes to advertising effectiveness: The moderating role of involvement. *Journal of Consumer Research, 10*(Summer), 135–146.

40. Gwinner, K. P., & Eaton, J. (1999). Building brand image through event sponsorship: The role of image transfer. *Journal of Advertising, 28*(4), 47–57.

41. Cornwell, T. B., Humphreys, M. S., Mayina, A. M., Weeks, C. S., & Tellegen, C. L. (2006). Sponsorship-linked marketing: The role of articulation in memory. *Journal of Consumer Research, 33*, 312–321.

42. Weeks, C. S., Cornwell, T. B., & Drennan, J. C. (2008). Leveraging sponsorships on the internet: Activation, congruence, and articulation. *Psychology &Marketing, 25*(7), 637–654.

43. IEG. (2012, January 16). MAGE SOLAR to sponsor Belgian football club RSC Anderlecht. *IEG Sponsorship Report.*

44. Koeing, D. (2006, April 11). Winning the hearts of race-goers. *Houston Chronicle*, p. D4.

45. CART. (1999). *Man + machine: A look inside champ car racing.* Chicago, IL: CART.

46. Miloch, K. S. (2010). FedEx: Access to the world. In J. W. Lee (Ed.), *Branded: Branding in the sports business* (pp. 127–136). Durham, NC: Carolina Academic Press.

47. Roberts, K. (2008, May). The Blues Story. *SportBusiness International*, p. 15.

48. IEG. (2011, October 13). L'Oréal to become the official lifestyle partner and supplier to the World Snowboarding Championships 2012. *IEG Sponsorship Report.*

49. Kelly, H. H. (1973, February). The process of causal attribution. *American Psychologist*, pp. 107–128.

50. Kelly, H. H., & Michela, J. L. (1980). Attribution theory and research. *Annual Review of Psychology, 31*, 457–501.

51. DeParle, J. (1989, September). Warning: Sports stars may be hazardous to your health. *The Washington Monthly*, pp. 34–48.

52. Scott, M. (2012, May 10). Manchester City's £930 million spending spree to turn club into Premier League title contenders. *The Telegraph.* Retrieved from http://www.telegraph.co.uk

53. Conn, D. (2008, September 2). How City became a trophy brand for greater glory of Abu Dhabi. *The Guardian.* Retrieved from http://www.guardian.co.uk/sport/blog/2008/sep/02/aneweraforfootballhowcit

54. Dickinson, M. (2008, September 2). City's Arabs want promotion—for themselves. *The Times.* Retrieved from http://www.joinmust.org/forum/showthread.php?t=51043

55. Perelli, S., & Levin, P. (1988). Getting results from sponsorship. *Special Events Report, 7*(22), 4–5.

56. IEG. (2011, December 19). Citigroup's new sponsorship strategy: Less is more. *IEG Sponsorship Report.* Retrieved from http://www.sponsorship.com/iegsr/2011/12/19/Citigroup-s-New-Sponsorship-Strategy--Less-Is-More.aspx

57. IEG. (2009, February 9). Fab five: Sponsorship programs you should know. *IEG Sponsorship Report.* Retrieved from http://www.sponsorship.com/iegsr/2009/02/09/Fab-Five--Sponsorship-Programs-You-Should-Know.aspx

58. Lee, J. W. (2010). Mountain Dew: Taking soft drinks to the extreme. In J. W. Lee (Ed.), *Branded: Branding in the sports business* (pp. 163–170). Durham, NC: Carolina Academic Press.

58a. IEG. (2011). *Invest, don't buy: A smarter way to sponsor.* Chicago, IL: IEG.

59. Kolah, A. (2001). *How to develop an effective sponsorship program.* London, England: Sport Business Information Resources.

60. D'Alessandro, D. F. (2001). *Brand warfare: 10 rules for building the killer brand.* New York, NY: McGraw-Hill.

60a. Horowitz, S. (2012). How jersey sponsorship can be an effective marketing tool. *Journal of Brand Strategy, 1*(2), 180–184.

61. Starling, M. (2007, October). Sporting air miles. *SportsBusiness International*, pp. 18–19.

62. Hensel, B. (2004, November 11). Waste Management steps on accelerator. *Houston Chronicle*, p. D1.

63. Reynolds, J. (2012, February 17). BP's brand image benefits from London 2012 sponsorship, claims research. *Marketing.* Retrieved

from http://www.marketingmagazine.co.uk
/article/1117665/bps-brand-image-benefits-lon
don-2012-sponsorship-claims-research

64. Miller, C. (2012, January 24). New Orleans
Arena could become 'Seafood Arena.' *WNL
AM 870*. Retrieved from http://www.wwl.com

65. Prasejus, J. W. (1998). *Seven psychological mechanisms through which sponsorship influences consumers*. Paper presented at the 17th Annual
Advertising and Consumer Psychology Conference, Portland, Oregon.

66. Carrillat, F. A., Harris, E. G., & Laffery, B. A.
(2010). Fortuitous brand image transfer:
Investigating the side effect of concurrent
sponsorships. *Journal of Advertising, 39*(2),
109–125.

3

Other Benefit Opportunities from a Sponsorship

A company is likely to seek multiple benefit opportunities from its sponsorship in order to optimize its return. Thus, in addition to enhancing brand equity, it might strengthen relationships and bonding by extending hospitality to existing key clients, potential clients, distributors, and decision-makers; use the sponsorship to demonstrate superior technology; use hospitality privileges to create staff and dealer incentives; provide on-site sampling opportunities to induce product trial by potential new customers or engage directly in on-site sales; and enhance employee morale.

As sponsorship has matured there has been a progression in the benefits many companies prioritize, moving from the top to the bottom of those listed in Figure 3.1. In the late 1980s and early 1990s, sponsorship was viewed primarily as an alternative to advertising and as a way of getting media exposure to increase brand awareness. The belief was that if a large enough number of people were exposed to a brand, some satisfactory percentage of them would make their way through the stages of the purchase adoption funnel and buy it. This naïve view was replaced by a focus on emotionally connecting with customers through image transfer so as to enhance brand equity. Brand equity remains almost endemic in sponsorship objectives, but an increasing number of companies now also insist that their investment be explicitly linked to sales and that on-site sales opportunities be provided. A Sony executive reported: "We can't afford to do awareness. Our sponsorships will be completely dealer-based, including a complete selling environment on site with dealer signage, a dealer's model mix, pricing, and cash registers. People are going to be scrutinizing proposals even further to look for those benefits" (p. 2).[1]

Since enhancing brand equity is a long-term strategy not designed to generate immediate short-term sales, this greater focus on the immediate bottom line has resulted in more attention being given to the other three sponsorship vehicles directed at external clienteles: Demonstration platform, hospitality opportunities, and product trial and sales. These constitute the main focus of this chapter. However, the chapter begins by recognizing that the elements of a sponsorship that a company prioritizes are likely to be influenced by the position in the AIDAR (awareness, interest, desire, action, and

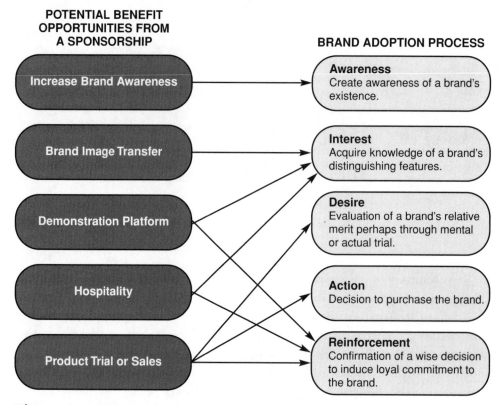

**POTENTIAL BENEFIT
OPPORTUNITIES FROM
A SPONSORSHIP**

BRAND ADOPTION PROCESS

Increase Brand Awareness

Awareness
Create awareness of a brand's
existence.

Brand Image Transfer

Interest
Acquire knowledge of a brand's
distinguishing features.

Demonstration Platform

Desire
Evaluation of a brand's relative
merit perhaps through mental
or actual trial.

Hospitality

Action
Decision to purchase the brand.

Product Trial or Sales

Reinforcement
Confirmation of a wise decision
to induce loyal commitment to
the brand.

Figure 3.1. The Potential Opportunities From a Sponsorship to Impact the Brand
Adoption Process.

reinforcement) decision process a brand occupies in a target audience's collective mind.
Although a primary sponsor's primary targets invariably are external clienteles, the final
section of the chapter points out that companies also seek to exploit a sponsorship's
potential for enhancing their employees' morale.

RELATING SPONSORSHIP OPPORTUNITIES
TO THE PURCHASE DECISION

A variety of decision-making paradigms which model the stages through which potential consumers pass before purchasing a brand have been proposed. The most widely
accepted of these models is AIDA. The acronym stands for Awareness-Interest-Desire-
Action. In the model of the brand adoption process shown in Figure 3.1 an additional
stage, Reinforcement, has been added to the end of the AIDA sequence because it has
been noted that: "What the company does to nurture the relationship with the customer, to build it, to strengthen it, is crucial to the company's marketing effectiveness
and efficiency. To work hard to attract new customers and then to be complacent in
strengthening the relationship makes little sense" (p. 132).[2] Hence, customer retention
as well as attraction of new customers is likely to be a primary objective of some businesses sponsoring sport. This involves reinforcing, reassuring, and confirming to customers that they made a wise decision in purchasing the company's product, and con-

tinuing to nurture the personal chemistry between key individuals which is so crucial in the selling dyad.

The brand adoption model shown on the right side of Figure 3.1 suggests that potential purchasers of a product pass through a process comprised of five stages from initial awareness to committed loyalty that constitutes a "purchasing funnel." They are defined as follows:

Awareness: An individual becomes aware of the existence of a particular brand and acquires some limited knowledge of its attributes.

Interest: More detailed knowledge of the brand's benefits is acquired. Interest in it and a preference for it develop as a favorable attitude emerges. A distinctive image of it evolves.

Desire: An appraisal of the brand's merit is made, if possible, through sampling it. If it is perceived to meet an individual's needs better than alternative offerings, then there is a desire or intent to purchase.

(Purchase) Action: This is the culmination of all that has gone before and the brand is purchased or rejected.

Reinforcement: Reassurance and confirmation to purchasers that a wise decision was made so as to consolidate loyalty to the brand.

The brand adoption model emphasizes that a purchase decision is usually the culmination of a process that starts long before an actual purchase takes place, and continues long after an initial purchase is made. A company's challenge is to design sponsorship benefits which will move potential customers from their present stage in the adoption process on to the next stage toward committed loyalty. For example, when Vodafone entered the New Zealand market, its initial objective was to create brand awareness quickly and the company believed sponsorship of sport was the most effective way to "cut-through" the clutter. When that was accomplished, the objective moved to the interest stage in the adoption process to use "sponsorship as a key driver of the brand . . . to capture the hearts and minds of New Zealanders in a way that's meaningful to them and gives them an experience that makes them feel the Vodafone brand values" (p. 1071).[3]

The biggest challenge with the adoption model from the perspective of sponsors is that it is a relatively long-term "drip-feed" association process which focuses on creating strong brand equity, leading to desire and ultimately to purchase. The most common breakdown point in the progression is between the desire and purchase stages. What frequently has been missing is the ability of targeted audiences to act quickly when they reach the desire stage. For most brands and products, consumers have to be in a given location before they can make a purchase, which is a major constraint inhibiting the progression from desire to purchase. One of the rapid changes in information technology has been the mobile phone companies' success in replacing the personal computer as the main access point to the Internet. Now that this has occurred it provides a further boost for sponsorship activity because purchases can be made instantly, eroding the gap between the desire and purchase stages. A decade ago it was prophetically noted: "As people become more familiar with the new technology available and in particular as the mobile phone becomes more widely used as a means for all forms of communication, so the link in the chain where probably 80 percent of potential sales break down will be strengthened considerably" (p. 166).[4]

Figure 3.1 illustrates how the five main sponsorship benefits available to businesses may be used to facilitate accomplishment of each stage of the brand adoption process. The lines in Figure 3.1 indicate the stage in the adoption process at which each of the sponsorship benefits may be targeted. For example, the two lines emanating from hospitality indicate that this benefit may be targeted at two groups: to reinforce and consolidate links with existing customers and suppliers; and/or to nurture interest in the company and its brands of those individuals who have been identified as strong future prospects. The roles of awareness and brand image transfer were discussed in Chapter 2. In the following sections of this chapter, the roles of demonstration platform, hospitality, and product trial and sales opportunities are described and illustrated.

DEMONSTRATION PLATFORM

Some companies use sport properties as vehicles for demonstrating their technical prowess to both public and business audiences. Especially with new technology, potential clients may be reluctant to pioneer untested systems because either they fear technology will not perform as expected, or they are not convinced that the gain will be worth its cost. Setting up and running the logistical/technology/communications for a major sporting event is a way of addressing these concerns: "By inviting key contacts to the nerve centers and hospitality facilities at events such as Wimbledon, the Olympics, Formula 1, or the FIFA World Cup, firms can demonstrate their products in the most exclusive and sought-after environments with absolutely no worries about competitor activity. They can also ask the question: 'If it's good enough for the demands of this organization, will it be good enough for your business?'" (p. 451)[5] One of the benefits such companies invariably receive is that when viewers see a score, statistic, or graphic related to the sporting activity they are watching, they also see the name of the company whose technology provided the data.

Exhibit 3.1 illustrates how Seiko used sport as a demonstration platform.[6] Telecommunication companies and a cycle wheel manufacturer provide other examples:

- Ship-to-shore technology using satellite and wireless communications has led to a substantial increase in sponsorship of ocean yacht racing and enhanced public interest in it, because the sport can now be followed in real time via personal computers and mobile platforms. In major races crews post daily diaries and use webcams, while websites are linked to monitoring systems in the boats and even display human performance indicators such as crew members' heart rates. Yacht racing has proven to be a creative showcase for telecommunications companies and has resulted in them emerging as the most active sponsors of endurance sail-

---

Exhibit 3.1

Seiko's Use of Sport as a Demonstration Platform

Seiko's in-kind sponsorship of sport events was designed to showcase the excellence of its timing technology. The different sport federations set the standard for how exact the timing needed to be. Seiko developed and provided the equipment to meet those standards. Most sport events require an accuracy of one hundredth of a second, but some, like luge in the Winter Olympics, demand an accuracy of one thousandth of a second.

The company became sponsors with responsibility for timing at multiple Summer and Winter Olympics; all of the Track and Field World Championships in the past 25 years; European, Commonwealth and Asian Games; and many other world class events. Their Director of Marketing explained the company's rationale:

> We showed the world that, where split second timing and reliability were needed, Seiko was the choice of the top sports events. Our aim was to show that Seiko had the technical skills to time world-class sports. We did that by making enormous investments in the technical service that we delivered to timed events. There was a direct link between the demonstration of our excellence through sports timing and the increase of our sales. The more sports we timed, the more we sold.

---

ing. Thus, for example, Vodafone, British Telecom, Alcatei-Lucent, Alice, T-Systems, and Tele2 all have recent sponsorship partnerships with the America's Cup. It is a platform for them to demonstrate and promote their technical expertise, as well as to secure image transfer through association with the prestige, lifestyle, and technology attributes of the sport.[7]

- Zipp Speed Weaponry is a bicycle wheel maker in Indianapolis. The company was founded in 1988 and has become the world's leader in high tech bicycle wheels. It was competing against long-established European and Japanese wheel makers in this market. To demonstrate its technical prowess, Zipp sponsored professional cycling, triathlon, and cyclecross teams. The success of its teams in high profile events such as World Championships, Olympic Games, and the Tour de France is attributed in part to the technical superiority of Zipp's equipment. As a result, the company has grown dramatically and now employs over 150 people with more than 50 percent of its sales coming from overseas. Their CEO said, "There's no question that racing exposure pays off internationally.[8]

There is an implied endorsement by sport properties of these sponsors' products. The message is "this brand must be excellent or it would not be allowed to be a sponsor of our team or event." The consumer is likely to infer that the event or team is endorsing the quality of the brand. The official status of a sponsor implies some measure of quality.

In addition to being a showcase for its existing technology, a company's involvement may stimulate it to improve on that technology. Manufacturers that sponsor cars in Formula 1 motor racing report it extends their research and development work. Lessons learned in the extreme environment of Formula 1 can help them with their road going automobiles. A sponsor of tires for these cars said, "Our engineers have really pushed

Exhibit 3.2

The Olympic Games as Fashion Show

Roots is a Canadian-based apparel company with a full line of clothing based on the outdoors. Established in 1973 as a small specialist footwear company, its annual turnover now exceeds $100 million. In 1998 the company became the exclusive outfitter for the Canadian Olympic Team and subsequently expanded this role to embrace the US and UK Olympic Teams also. Those sponsorships resulted in exponential growth in sales and profits.

Roots has used the opening and closing ceremonies of the Games as a demonstration platform to display its styles to a worldwide audience. The athletes are on television wearing their fashionable and trendy clothes with no visual obstruction during the most visible moments of the Games. That is a scenario that could not be replicated at any cost by traditional advertising. At the Salt Lake City Games' opening ceremony, the US team's uniforms attracted extraordinary attention. The company's CEO reported:

The Olympics were incredible. Literally, the day after the opening ceremonies Roots garments were on TV everywhere and we were in magazines and newspapers. The products just started to fly out of the stores . . . We had waiting lists of tens of thousands of people who signed up just to get a hat (p. 54).

The US team's red, white and blue berries were especially eye-catching. The company sold over a million of them as they transitioned from being a simple accessory to becoming a pop culture phenomenon. Roots sold over $40 million of Olympic merchandise associated with the Salt Lake City Games. When outstanding athletes are perceived to endorse a product *en masse* as a team in a "feel good" atmosphere like the Olympic Games, it enhances the probability that emotional ties to the brand will be established.

their knowledge of rubber and compounds in conditions that only the pressure of Formula 1 can create"(p. C9).[9]

A sponsorship can be a lever to elevate the news value of a new technology being demonstrated, especially if it is novel and interesting. This expanded reach will further enhance a company's brand-building goals, because publicity is not only more cost-effective than advertising, it is also more credible. Even if media coverage is not forthcoming, the sponsorship provides a context to make a demonstration more interesting and vivid for the company to use in its own promotional efforts.[10] This is illustrated in Exhibit 3.2 which describes how the Olympic Games opening ceremony was used by a company to launch eye-catching clothing styles whose visibility was leveraged by the media.[11]

HOSPITALITY

Relationship marketing is a central facet of many companies' marketing strategies. It is defined as attracting, developing, and retaining customer relationships. Its central tenet is:

The creation of "true customers"—customers who are glad they selected a firm, who perceived they are receiving value and feel valued, who are likely to buy additional services from the firm, and who are unlikely to defect to a competitor. True customers are the most profitable of all customers. They spend more money with the firm on a per-year basis and they stay with the firm for more years. They

Courtesy of BigStockPhoto.com

spread favorable word-of-mouth information about the firm, and they may even be willing to pay a premium price for the benefits the service offers (p. 133).[2]

Establishing this kind of relationship requires the building of social bonds with customers, "staying in touch with them, learning about their wants and needs, customizing the relationships based on what is learned, and continually reselling the benefits of the relationship" (p. 138)[2]

Hospitality at sport events facilitates this bonding and client cultivation: "Guest hospitality refers to those opportunities whereby the company can make face-to-face contact with select publics in a prestigious social context, thereby strengthening and personalizing relationships with decision makers, trade channels, and business associates" (p. 37).[6] Investments in hospitality recognize that decisions on whether to choose supplier A or B are rarely made only on price. Often it comes down to level of comfort with the people involved; the confidence that service suppliers can deliver on their contractual commitments.[12] Professional relationships are forged through networks and hospitality is a networking mechanism. Business built on transactions will come and go, but business built on relationships is durable. Hospitality, also enables a sponsor to thank existing clients—and holding on to them is less expensive and time-consuming than finding new ones. It gives companies a face-to-face opportunity to listen to their clients' current priorities or concerns in a leisurely, relaxed environment.

The objective of offering hospitality to existing or prospective customers at a sport event is not to conduct business, but rather to use a relaxed informal context outside the normal business environment to create a personal interactive chemistry which will be conducive to doing business later. Indeed, a crucial tenet of hospitality is not to do anything that makes guests feel uncomfortable or that makes them feel that they are being sold to. It offers access to valued stakeholders that would not be possible without the event as a backdrop. The role of hospitality opportunities at the interest stage of the brand adoption process (Figure 3.1) in facilitating sales has been articulated in these terms:

> An invitation to discuss trade is often counter-productive because the target audience is wary that acceptance of the invitation to discuss trade will be interpreted as a commitment to actually trade. Moreover, in the case of a meeting which has as its sole objective the investigation of opportunities for trade, embarrassment is the only result where one party wishes to trade but the other does not. This contrasts with a situation where any non-professional common interest—stamp collecting, social drinking, or sporting event—is either the pretext for a meeting, the real object of which is to investigate opportunities for trade, or is the main attraction where trade is discussed only incidentally. In these cases both parties can avoid loss of dignity in the event that they are unable to reach agreement about prospects for trade, and can meet again in the future to discuss other projects without rancor (p. 176).[13]

Gauging the value of hospitality is challenging because its main role of relationship building is not quantifiable. There may be anecdotal evidence that hospitality produces results, but this is unlikely to impress an internal auditor charged with evaluating the merit of a sponsorship. The difficulty of quantifying a return on hospitality investments makes it imperative that they adopt an explicit strategic approach with deliberate intent beyond: "Let's invite friends, and existing and prospective customers to a big party." This strategic type of approach is illustrated in Exhibit 3.3.

In the US, the Sarbanes-Oxley Act of 2002 tightened accounting requirements for public companies so they became much more restrictive as to what qualified as a business expense, whether they are acting as hosts or guests. Paying the transportation, lodging, tickets, and other related expenses of sending or inviting executives subsequently came under much closer scrutiny. The itineraries have to demonstrate that they are a true business expense and not merely a perquisite.

Hospitality is often a prominent justification used by leaders in host communities for spending large amounts to attract mega events. They highlight their potential for bringing new business to the host area. The aspirational rhetoric is convincing to many, but results invariably are disappointing because no intentional organizational vehicle is put in place to facilitate realization of the aspiration. Without such a vehicle any positive business outcomes are serendipitous, relying on unplanned ad hoc interactions among executives in attendance, or private meetings between interested parties who were already networked. A watershed arrangement implemented at the Sydney Olympic Games changed this mindset. The host organization established the Business Club Australia (BCA) which is described in Exhibit 3.4.[14] This model was subsequently adopted by almost all host communities of mega events.

Hospitality can be facilitated without sponsorship and this occurs at most major sport events through the sale of boxes, suites, and similar options. However, guests are likely to be more impressed and feel more important if they are invited to a sporting

Exhibit 3.3

A Systematic Six-Stage Approach to Hospitality

Stage 1: Set clear objectives for each customer up front.

If the intent is to host opinion formers, then it must be decided up front how their good opinions will be manifested. This means establishing objectives that are SMART—specific, measurable, achievable, relevant, and time bound. (SMART objectives are discussed in detail in Chapter 5). Examples are:

- Winning new business (five new contracts for $30,000 each) within three months of entertainment).
- Maintaining current business under threat from competitors (ensure no erosion of current business at 100k units per annum, representing 80 per cent of all customers' requirements for this type of item, within three months of entertainment).
- Thanking customers and maintaining support (post-evaluation of number of referrals generated by the entertained customer in the six months following entertainment).
- Providing a backdrop for a new business initiative (ensure customer has agreed to formal business meeting to discuss the initiative within 30 days).

Stage 2: Identify the key invitees from the customer organization.

This will involve identifying who in a company is best placed to deliver on the desired objective or at least influence a positive outcome, and ascertaining whether entertaining those people at this sport event will favorably influence them.

Stage 3: Select an appropriate entertainment opportunity.

It is not enough simply to entertain the right people at a sport event that interests them. The following factors should be applied to determine if a particular event is the most appropriate option.

Type of client. The level of investment in the hospitality should be linked to the seniority of the invitees. As a general rule, the more senior the client, the greater the investment should be. However, there has to be sensitivity to their organization's policies so, for example, public officials will sometimes be precluded from accepting high priced hospitality.

Mix of clients. The hospitality is likely to be more memorable and powerful if the invitees are of interest to each other.

Appropriate group hosting. In general, the more senior the guests, the more hosts should attend. The highest ratio required is normally one host to three guests, but for less senior clients this could extend to a 1:9 ratio. Lower ratios make it difficult to interact effectively with guests, while if there are too many hosts in relation to guests, then guests may not feel the event has been arranged primarily for them.

Partners. Some invitees' partners may have low interest in the sport event and bored people rapidly communicate their lack of interest to the wider group. In these instances, alternative programs may be offered to partners while the event is taking place.

Stage 4: Select the relevant hosts to complement the clients.

In most cultures, the more senior the guest, the more senior the host must be, except where, for example, a middle manager has a long-standing and fruitful relationship with a senior manager in a client company. It is also important to guard against a senior group from the host company accompanying a party largely made up of junior/middle managers from clients and prospects. Resentment on one side and self-consciousness on the other will not make for a positive experience.

Stage 5: Take steps to avoid last-minute cancellations.

Late cancellations are costly because they prevent the host company from optimizing the use of its hospitality asset. These can be minimized by confirming and re-confirming dates with clients, their assistants and, if invited, partners; engaging clients by providing regular updates on the event; and ensuring clients are well-briefed to eliminate uncertainty around attendance, itinerary, directions, parking, availability, dress code, etc.

Stage 6: Evaluate hospitality outcomes.

It is not enough for guests to have had a good time if this does not achieve some specific, desired result for the host company. Effective measurement enables patterns to be derived over time and lessons learned and applied to future entertainment. (Methods for doing this are discussed in Chapter 10)

Exhibit 3.4

Business Club Australia: Initiating a New Approach to Maximizing Return on Investment in Hospitality at Mega Events

The genesis of the idea for Business Club Australia (BCA) sprang from representatives from the Sydney Organizing Committee for the Olympic Games (SOCOG) who attended the preceding Atlanta Olympics. They observed that while a large number of international business decision-makers were there, there was no established vehicle through which the hosts could relate to them. One of those representatives commented:

> The origin of the club actually lies in learnings out of Atlanta. There were all these business people floating around—we wondered how we could actually make a connection. How could we question them? What sort of vehicle could we use? And the concept of a "club" seemed like a good vehicle because of the nature of the networking venture. (p. 246)

The BCA was comprised of representatives from the federal government, state governments, major corporations, industry trade associations, and from SOCOG and the IOC. Official sanction from the SOCOG and IOC allowed the BCA to use the Olympic Rings in its promotional materials which bestowed legitimacy on the initiative, and it brought the network of Olympic sponsors into its membership. This bundling of BCA memberships with Olympic sponsors and suppliers served to increase the numbers of people present in the BCA Center which added to its euphoria, sense of excitement, and general atmospherics. The downside of this was that it precluded some companies from participating because they were competitors of Olympic sponsors.

The BCA was positioned as a "club" since it was designed to develop interpersonal relationships among members. It was launched at 90 Australian Consulates around the globe, two years before the Games commenced. They identified international business leaders who intended to visit Sydney for the Games. Membership was on an individual rather than an organizational basis, and members were linked online in a database called the BCA "Virtual Club." Over 1,000 members from the Australian business community and over 10,000 internationals were signed up.

During the Games, the BCA was centrally located in a building on Sydney Harbour and included a 98-meter catamaran berthed alongside the wharf. Facilities inside the center included venues for meetings and informal networking, computer terminals, office equipment, and multilingual trade assistance from Austrade. The catamaran had a large function room for hosting breakfasts, lunches, dinners, and cocktail receptions, as well as a VIP suite for more private meetings. BCA was designed as "kind of like a dating agency for business" where, using specifically programmed networking functions, visiting internationals were "matched" with potential Australian business partners.

The BCA Center drew over 17,000 attendees during the Games. By one month after the Games it had generated $260 million in committed investments and was "well on track" to achieve its target of $577 million. The sophistication and effectiveness of the BCA model has subsequently led to it becoming an integral ingredient of host community programs at mega events.

occasion for which their host is a sponsor. Hence, a feature of naming rights sponsorships is not only that key clients can be hosted in luxury suites and premium seats but, importantly, this is done in the sponsor's "own building."

Care has to be taken to ensure that companies who have invested in sponsorship do not see their presence ambushed or diluted by hospitality buyers. Effective hospitality revolves around exciting and/or interactive activities conducive to networking and socialization. Hospitality linked with sponsorship is differentiating because it gives access to additional perks such as behind-the-scenes tours and appearances by coaches and players. Many fans are hero worshippers and the opportunity to meet with their sporting idols is a memorable lifetime event. One sponsor noted, "Anyone can throw tickets at buyers, but not everyone can give them time with the team and a behind-the-scenes tour (p. 8):[15]

- FedEx Corp. leverages its NBA sponsorship in part by hosting clients and prospects at the league's All-Star Game. Taking advantage of the international makeup of the league, the company uses the event to build business for its overseas shipping services by pairing up players with representatives of companies who do significant business in the players' home countries. "They have the opportunity to meet the athletes, participate in basketball clinics, and go out for dinner," said the NBA's senior vice president of marketing partnerships.[16]
- The Bay Area has two MLB teams, two NFL teams, an NBA franchise, and an NHL team. To separate itself from these sporting entities and from Stanford University across the Bay, the University of California invited its sponsors to barbecues at the athletic director's house and had its coaches there. They also invited them to tailgate parties with key alumni and business leaders.[17]
- Hospitality was built into the iShares Cup series of sailing races in that during each race each yacht carried a VIP guest on board "for an adrenaline pumping race" giving iShares and companies sponsoring the individual boats, an exceptional opportunity to offer exciting client entertainment experiences. Their CEO stated: "It is simply the best hospitality platform we could hope for" (p. 19).[18]

This kind of access provided to sponsors enables a company to differentiate itself from other companies offering hospitality by conferring on the business the added value of being seen to be part of the event.

Some companies, especially technology firms, use hospitality to showcase their offerings. Thus, for example, a motorsports sponsor reports, "All of the guests who come to a race are given a tour of the paddock and one of the engineers addresses what we have done to incorporate our technology into the car."[16]

- Similarly, IBM Corp. leverages its sponsorship of tennis's U.S. Open, PGA Tour, Wimbledon, and other high-profile sports properties to demonstrate products and services ranging from servers to software to IT solutions. "It's a thrill for (guests) to walk into the bowels of a stadium and pass athletes and people with the media. We then engage them in a discussion of how the event's business needs relate to their needs," said IBM's director of worldwide sponsorship marketing.

  IBM tries to engage their clients and prospects on their "pain points," using the property's pain as an example, the director said. At the U.S. Open, for instance, IBM and the U.S. Tennis Association representatives spoke about the need for the event to reduce costs while facing a growing infrastructure, and how IBM was able to provide virtualization technology that helped reduce the number of servers it needed from sixty to nine.[16]

Exhibit 3.5

Hospitality at the Sydney Olympics

Hospitality opportunities were a central benefit received by the Olympic TOP sponsors, but in addition to their $50 million sponsorship commitment to the IOC these companies had to pay for the hospitality of their guests. The average business-class air ticket to Sydney from the United States cost $7,000. Additional costs for event tickets, hotel rooms, food and beverage, excursions et al., increased the total cost to approximately $30,000 per guest. Since the TOP sponsors each brought between 1,000 and 1,500 guests to the Games, their hospitality bills typically ranged from $30 million to $45 million. Given the magnitude of cost incurred, "Companies are far more deliberate because there is a lot more accountability. It's not any longer for the chairman and 50 of his closest family and friends."

The Olympic hospitality programs typically are organized into four or five "waves." For example, VISA flew in 1,200 guests in four waves of 300 to Sydney for the Games. Each wave is likely to be of between 3 and 5 days' duration with transition days occurring when one group of guests departed and the next group arrived. Some guests were regarded as being more important than others in terms of benefits that accrued to a sponsor as a result of a long-term relationship between the sponsor and the guest. The more important guests received invitations to take part in either the first wave, that coincided with the Opening Ceremony, or the final wave, that included many of the gold medal events and the Closing Ceremony.

The sponsor hospitality department of the Sydney Organizing Committee of the Olympic Games was responsible for meeting the needs of approximately 40,000 guests. Priority room allocations in the city's leading hotels were made available as part of the contractual agreement signed with each sponsor.

The uniqueness of the hospitality opportunity is becoming more important. One sport marketer observed: "The average trade manager now receives five invitations to NASCAR events. Five years ago, he would only get one. Obviously, he will look for the best package, the one that takes care of his kids and spouse . . . People want to do more than just attend an event, it has to be made special" (p.4).[18] Given the plethora of invitations, the decision to give up an evening or a weekend will be based on how "hot" is the ticket or the quality of the sport event experience being offered. This has resulted in higher expectations for hospitality activism. A specialist firm in this area reported: "In every RFP we respond to companies use the term: 'unique one-of-a-kind experience'."[20] Participation is also more likely if the invitation is extended to the family. This, for example, could involve providing sport instruction clinics for children which was reflected in the activism efforts of Aon and Sony Ericsson:

- As part of its sponsorship with Manchester United, Aon sponsored Skills and Drills, a five-city U.S. tour that featured coaches and players from the Manchester United soccer school. The events were used to host top clients and their children, who participated in a half-day soccer clinic. The company accommodated 40–50 families at each event. A spokesperson confirmed, "It was a very compelling opportunity for an Aon broker or account manager to spend time with his or her clients in a unique setting."[20]

Exhibit 3.6

The Pay-Off from Hospitality at the Olympic Games for the John Hancock Company

Part of John Hancock's platform for leveraging its Winter Olympics sponsorship was to generate additional sales by using hospitality as an incentive for staff and to generate new business from potential clients. During the Games, Hancock rented a luxurious 15th century estate and guest house close to the Games' city. There it entertained its top sales people and pitched group insurance and pension plans to corporate clients. In all, John Hancock brought 650 people to the Games. "Our program incorporated a number of different groups" said a spokesperson. "Over 50% were our top salespeople, what we call our 'President's Cabinet.' About 35% were the guests of a couple of divisions that brought over top prospects for a seminar wrapped around the Olympics. The rest were non-sales employees who had done well the previous year. We had a little business and had a little fun. It was basically used for incentive delivery, client entertainment, and client prospecting."

Did John Hancock's Olympic mega-dollars pay off? While the company spent $1.4 million on its internal incentive program, several hundred thousand dollars more than normal, their spokesperson said that over 128 agents qualified for the trip, compared to the usual 50 or 60. Better yet, the Olympic program generated approximately $50 million in revenue from new policies, a 20% increase over last year. "We've already closed some deals with prospective clients we brought into the Games," he said.

- Sony Ericsson as part of its sponsorship of the women's pro tennis tour offers clients and prospects the opportunity to participate in tennis clinics led by pro tennis players. The company noted: "It's one thing to go to Wimbledon, but it's another thing to meet athletes and participate in these functions. That helps differentiate the event from a regular tennis tournament, and people talk about the experience."[20]

The magnitude of investment in hospitality at the Olympic Games is illustrated in Exhibits 3.5[21,21a] and 3.6.[22] It adds substantially to the cost of a sponsorship but, as the John Hancock vignette in Exhibit 3.6 illustrates, the pay-offs are potentially high.

PRODUCT TRIAL AND SALES OPPORTUNITIES

Product trial or sales opportunities relate to the desire, purchase action, or reinforcement stages of the adoption process (Figure 3.1). Product trial opportunities are particularly valuable because moving people from interest in a brand to the desire stage, which involves seriously evaluating its merits to determine whether a purchase should be made, is a difficult task. Individuals may have an interest and be favorably disposed towards a brand, but they may have never tried it. This is especially likely to occur among products for which the cost of trial is high in terms of money, time, potential embarrassment, or whatever. Sponsorship offers a vehicle for encouraging trial which is the most effective method by which potential customers can assess a brand's merits:

- PopSecret is a NASCAR sponsor. The brand sets up microwave ovens at every track entrance, treating fans to free samples.

- Lowe's sponsors auto racing and BASS fishing events. At each site the company creates Lowe's How-To Village, where visitors can test tools and other products sold at the chain. The village also invites the product manufacturers to participate.[23]

- The Tough Mudder endurance races consist of a 14-event series across the country of 12–14 mile races over rugged terrain with military-like obstacles. Degree Men Everest is an antiperspirant and deodorant that releases extra bursts of fragrance when you sweat. The company provides samples to all competitors "arming them with the odor and wetness protection necessary to stay fresh during the race." Their spokesperson explained, "Guys want the latest and greatest products used by the pros to reassure them they can meet any challenge with confidence."[24]

Courtesy of BigStockPhoto.com

- Clif and Luna Bars are energy bars that have historically eschewed traditional media in favor of sponsoring grassroots endurance events at which they can induce product trial. Their spokesperson said, "Our category is largely driven by trial, conversion, and driving customers to retail." Hence, PowerBar, which is a competing Nestle brand, similarly sponsors national and international running and triathlon events as a platform to have athletes sample the bars and to build credibility for their energy attributes.[25]

Product distribution may also be used to reinforce the favorable feelings that existing users have towards a brand (Figure 3.1). When Coca-Cola or Pepsi-Cola or their distributors sponsor sport events, the availability of complimentary beverages at the end is intended to remind participants of their refreshing, recuperative qualities and to consolidate loyalty towards them.

The ultimate goal of a company's sponsorship is to increase sales of its products. Hence, sponsors increasingly are seeking the right to engage in on-site sales at sport events. It has been noted: "While naming rights partners enjoyed the many tangible elements provided in the newer agreements, the critical addition was the opportunity for the naming rights partner to derive 'business-back" (p. 40).[26] Sponsors want a large number of distribution points; the vending and pouring locations to be as inviting as possible; and properties to provide promotions that will drive on-site sales. This should include emails sent to participants in advance of the event and signage alerting people to the on-site transaction opportunities.

- Given that 98% of entrants to the New York marathon register on-line, the marathon offers its sponsors a chance to use the site for e-commerce. It also sells a co-branded watch from sponsor Timex Corp. and training gear and apparel from ASICS.[27]

Properties have to liaise closely with their existing concessioners in developing on-site opportunities that work for all three parties. Concessioners identify the items they want to sell, then the property finds sponsor partners to provide those items. Thus, sponsors often sign two agreements: A marketing agreement with the property and a vending rights agreement with the concessioner.[28]

The most widespread sales vehicle at sport events is pouring rights. In return for its sponsorship a company receives exclusive rights to sell its beverages at the facility or event. A property may sell pouring rights for alcoholic and non-alcoholic beverages. The following example illustrates these types of partnerships:

- Pepsi is the "Official soft drink of Comerica Park," home of the MLB's Detroit Tigers. In addition to exclusive pouring rights, the Pepsi Picnic Park is a 250-seat section with a dedicated concessions area for fans who receive outfield box seats and a pre-game buffet. Pepsi also sponsors a "Family Values Section" which provides up to 1,700 tickets to selected games for charitable organizations. Pepsi receives signage throughout the stadium; the right to display its Aquafina and All Sport logos on cups, squeeze bottles, coolers, and towels

Exhibit 3.7
The US Army On-site Sponsorship "Sales"

The US Army sponsors NASCAR and NHRB teams and brings its Strength in Action Tour to each race site. Its goal is to generate quality "sales" leads among 17–24 year olds who are uncertain about a career path. The Tour features opportunities for individuals to engage in an Apache helicopter flight simulator, a rock climbing wall, and a robotics exercise in which participants guide a "droid" through an obstacle course. To gain entrance, participants must provide information and scan a driver's license, after which they get radio-frequency ID tags. That arms approaching recruiters (sometimes as many as 20 are on-site) with plenty of information as they try to sell an Army career, while escorting potential recruits through the exercises.

Equipped with tablet PCs, the recruiters can approach someone who has already indicated an interest in technology when registering and whet his or her appetite by dropping, "Did you knows?" like "the average U.S. army soldier has $17,000 worth of equipment with him when he's in the field" or "there are 150 different career-path opportunities within the Army." If they want to learn more about career paths, in-depth orientations are given and if they so wish they can complete a preliminary enlistment screening interview.

The races not only deliver the desired demographic, but as a spokesperson noted, "The drivers are great athletes and a big draw, but they also allow us to show that the team-orientation of what they do is very similar to the teamwork that makes the Army work."

in both the Tigers and visiting team's dugouts during games; and the right to use the Tiger logo on Pepsi packaging, vending machines, and delivery trucks in the Michigan marketplace.[29]

Exhibit 3.8

State Farm Generates Sales Leads from Hispanics

State Farm Insurance used its sponsorship of the MLB to target 25–54 year old Hispanics by developing a traveling baseball show that included a 60 x 60 feet miniature baseball diamond and a museum dedicated to great Hispanic baseball players. The tribute trailer displayed player memorabilia and video footage of great Latino players such as Roberto Clemente, Juan Marichal, and David Ortiz. An interactive display showed the hometowns of famous Hispanic players and replayed broadcasts of famous homeruns in Spanish. An enormous, 65-foot monitor showed ongoing baseball games. The show also included a miniature homerun derby on the baseball diamond, where children and adults could try to belt out a dinger using soft, rubberized balls.

At each stop, State Farm invited famous Hispanic baseball players to make celebrity appearances and sign autographs, such as retired Los Angeles Dodgers and St. Louis Cardinals player Pedro Guerrero, former Houston and Colorado star Willy Taveras, and Hall of Famer Orlando Cepeda.

Visitors to the exhibit provided contact and personal information on an electronic tablet to receive State Farm paraphernalia or baseball tickets. About a dozen people staffed the exhibit. State Farm representatives followed up with the potential customers via phone or e-mail.

The trailer toured the country from late April through September, stopping at various Hispanic celebrations such as the Fiesta Broadway in Los Angeles, which annually attracts 500,000 visitors. The campaign targeted the top-10 Hispanic markets, including Los Angeles, Chicago, and Miami. It visited MLB games, including the All-Star Game. The campaign engaged 225,000 people and generated more than 70,000 surveys in one year. Approximately 30,000 people requested follow-up information from State Farm on insurance packages.

On-site selling is no longer confined to categories like soft drinks, alcoholic drinks, and bottled water. For example, banks can negotiate ATM placements in their agreements, while retailers might erect temporary sales outlets.[30]

Mizuno is the official footwear and apparel sponsor of USA Volleyball. This gives it exclusive rights to sell these items on-site at major tournaments. Their representative reports, "Our dealers will make between $30,000 and $60,000 in product sales at these events."[31] Exhibit 3.7 reports the US Army's "sales" efforts that emanate from its car racing team sponsorships.[32]

In some cases where on-site sales are not possible, the sponsors' activities are designed to drive traffic into their stores or to generate leads for subsequent selling efforts. The following two vignettes illustrate the former strategy, while State Farm Insurance's strategy for generating sales leads from Hispanics based on its MLB sponsorship is described in Exhibit 3.8.[33]

- The salesman was sitting in his John Hancock booth at a gymnastics championship, and young children were dragging their parents over to meet him. *To talk to the life-insurance salesman!* The attraction was the Olympic rings embellishing his booth and the Olympic pins and paraphernalia he was handing out. He collected a list of 700 appreciative families who might need a whole-life-policy. By the time he finished his follow-up calls he had made 35 sales. He observed, "The Olympic rings break down barriers that are naturally there in our business." John Hancock believes the five-ring symbol is more valuable than the intangible symbols of its rivals: Prudential's rock or Met Life's Snoopy. The CEO said, "In an industry with a fair amount of scandal and shakeout, we're looking for market insulation."[34]

- Leslie's Swimming Pool Supplies is the world's largest retailer of pool and spa supplies. They are a sponsor of the PGA Phoenix Open, and have 54 retail stores in the greater Phoenix area. During the weeks prior to the event, Leslie drives sales in its stores by offering a free ticket to the event with any purchase over $100.[35]

Some of a sponsor's investment is likely to be directed at "pushing" its products through a distribution channel by using incentives associated with the sponsorship. For example:

> Event tickets, VIP invitations, or hospitality can be used as rewards for reaching sales targets and can therefore act as incentives for distributors. The sponsor can also allocate tickets to distributors for them to pass on to their customers via competitions and loyalty schemes, for similar results. In both cases the distributor is being provided with incentives to perform better and the sponsorship vehicle is the catalyst. T-Mobile, the mobile telecommunications company, devised both push and pull strategies for the UK in order to exploit its rights as an 'official partner' for the European Soccer Championships. The end user 'pull' promotions involved free downloads, texting, free call minutes, and exclusive event content packages, whilst the incentives for its key retail partner. Carphone Warehouse, consisted of event ticketing (p. 52).[36]

ENHANCING EMPLOYEE MORALE

While a sponsor's primary objectives are likely to be directed at increasing sales from customers, they are also likely to exploit a sponsorship's potential for enhancing employee morale. Exhibit 3.9 describes how UPS used its Olympic sponsorship to do this.[36a] If employees identify with, or better still become emotionally involved with, a sponsorship then it may create a sense of pride and commitment to the company. There is an expectation that this employee pride will not only enhance their positive feelings towards the company, but will also spread positive messages to others regarding both the company and its role in sponsoring sport:

- Home Depot has 200,000 employees. The company's vice president of marketing and communication noted that a goal of all their sponsorships, whether it was the Olympics, NASCAR, or a community event, was to enhance employee morale. "At the end of the day, it's the person in that orange apron who smiles and walks you to your product who will be the difference . . . There aren't a lot of companies where you can wear an apron with Olympic team emblems . . . It's a real powerful emotional platform . . . They get used to it and feel good about it. The company takes the association with the Olympics one step further by hiring Olympic

Exhibit 3.9

Selected Measures of the Effectiveness of UPS's Olympic Games Sponsorship

One of the United Parcel Service's (UPS) goals for its Olympic Games sponsorship was to link the Games to employee incentive programs. Winners of these programs were divided into gold, silver, and bronze categories. Gold winners received tickets to the Games, including travel and accommodations. Silver winners were flown to IOC headquarters in Lausanne, Switzerland, for a special awards ceremony at the Olympic Museum, while bronze winners received a variety of Olympic memorabilia. Among the programs developed were:

- *Triple Jump*, which was an incentive program for sales staff tied to individual goals. It resulted in 40% of UPS' sales force significantly exceeding their individual targets.

- *Going the Distance* was a lead generation program targeted at non-sales staff designed to build business for UPS. It resulted in non-sales staff opening over 1,200 new high-volume accounts.

For drivers of delivery vans, UPS organized *Gold Medal Driving*, an incentive scheme to maintain a zero-avoidable accident rate. *The Decathlon* was a company-wide quiz designed to reinforce and extend employees' knowledge of the company, and 70% of those taking the test recorded a score of 100%.

contenders through its Olympic Job Opportunity Program. A spokesperson said, "It's our piece of the Olympics; we have Olympic hopefuls working side by side with our associates. They're great role models, goal oriented, dedicated, and have a great work ethic." (p. 1)[37]

A program designed to improve customer service is more exciting when it is themed with a major sport team or event. Involving the athletes in visits to a company's plants to sign autographs or making tickets available to staff may help build a bond with them. The margarine brand, Flora, sought similar benefits from its sponsorship of the London Marathon:

- Flora used its sponsorship as a theme for employee team-building activities and provided opportunities for involving employees' families. It encouraged employees to participate and guaranteed their entry into the race; encouraged other personnel to become involved as race stewards; hosted parties for its staff who were involved in any way with the race; and used it as a platform to promote fitness and health within the company.[36]

The Bank of Ireland wanted to know the impact on its staff of the bank's flagship sponsorship of the Bank of Ireland Gaelic Football Championship. They found that 80 percent of all employees—from senior managers to bank assistants—expressed pride in the bank's sponsorship of the event. Similarly, a firm sponsoring a race car reported that its employees followed the successes and failures of the car closely and were enormously proud of their association with it.[10]

When Toyota became title sponsor for the Toyota Tundra 200, a NASCAR Truck Series Race in Nashville, one of its primary goals was to thank employees at five nearby factories. A company spokesperson reported, "We have had what we think was the largest NASCAR hospitality venue of any event. There were between 8,000 and 9,000 people in our 10 acres of hospitality tents. It was a huge success."[38]

Vodafone believes sponsorship has enabled the company to build emotional connections with its employees by partnering with activities they are passionate about, as well as cultivating a favorable corporate culture by leveraging internal competitions and providing staff with sponsorship-related incentives. This aspiration appeared to be validated by a Vodafone customer service representative who said: "When a sponsorship event is coming up, Vodafone always involve us in it. Yeah, it is clever but it's good because at least they make us feel involved and give us a little passion for Vodafone." (p. 1071)[3]

When Aon signed its shirt sponsorship agreement with Manchester United, it gave a replica shirt retailing at $80, to each of the company's more than 36,000 employees around the globe. This may represent only a small proportion of the 6 million Manchester United shirts sold annually (a number greater than all NFL teams combined!) but it was viewed as a means of giving a sense of corporate identity to employees at disparate firms that Aon had acquired.[39]

SUMMARY

A company's external marketing goals for a sponsorship will be guided by a brand's position in the minds of its target audience. Its intent will be to progress that position through the AIDAR sequence of a customer's decision process—awareness, interest, desire, action, and reinforcement. While enhancing brand equity remains the most pervasive objective, that long-term strategy is accompanied by a growing concomitant focus on exploiting sales and profitability. This greater attention to the latter stages of the AIDAR sequence is manifested by seeking more opportunities to use a sponsorship as a demonstration platform, for hospitality, or for product trial and on-site sales.

Companies use sport properties as a demonstration platform to showcase a brand's technical capabilities, or to reinforce positive perceptions of its attributes, to both public and business audiences. The objective in creating hospitality opportunities is not to conduct business, rather the intent is client cultivation. A relaxed informal atmosphere associated with a sport event is used to create a personal interactive chemistry which will be conducive to doing business later. Hospitality can be used to cultivate relationships not only with customers, but also with other important publics such as distributors, retailers, and employees. Sponsorship may offer a vehicle for offering product trial to new customers, or generating sales leads. This is particularly valuable because until individuals try a product they are unlikely to purchase it, especially if it is a relatively expensive product. The ultimate goal of sponsorship is to increase sales. This might be accomplished by inducing sales through promotions associated with the sponsorship, or from creating on-site sales opportunities. An ancillary goal is to enhance employee morale by seeking ways to emotionally involve personnel with the sponsorship. The intent is to create a sense of pride and commitment to the company.

Endnotes

1. IEG. (1996, May 6). Trends: New models for sponsorship profits. *IEG Sponsorship Report*, pp. 2–4.

2. Berry, L. L., & Parasuraman, A. (1991). *Marketing services: Competing through quality*, New York, NY: The Free Press.

3. Cliffe, S. J., & Motsion, J. (2005). Building contemporary brands: A sponsorship-based strategy. *Journal of Business Research*, *58*, 1068–1077.

4. Currie, N. (2000, June/July). Maximizing sport sponsorship investments: A perspective on new and existing opportunities. *Sports Marketing & Sponsorship*, pp. 159–166.

5. Rines, S. (2002, December/January). Guinness Rugby World Cup sponsorship: A global platform for meeting business objectives. *International Journal of Sports Marketing & Sponsorship*, pp. 399–464.

6. Meenaghan, J. A. (1983). Commercial sponsorship. *European Journal of Marketing, 17*(7), 5–73.

7. Why Seiko went sailing. (2008, December 13). *YachtSponsorship*. Retrieved from http://www.yachtsponsorship.com/2008/12/why-seiko-went-sailing/

8. Associated Press. (2003, August 8). It's so easy to pedal this product. *Houston Chronicle*, 3C.

9. Stiener, R. (2001, July 15). Corporate fear that drives the F1 circus. *The Sunday Times*, C9.

10. Aaker, D. A., & Joachimsthaler, E. (2000). *Brand leadership*. New York, NY: The Free Press.

11. Kraft, P. (2010). Roots: Branding to the world, one beret at a time. In J. W. Lee (Ed.), *Branded: Branding in the sports business*. Durham, NC: Caroline Academic Press.

12. IEG. (2006, November 6). Three steps to ensuring your hospitality programs will work. *IEG Sponsorship Report*. Retrieved from http://www.sponsorship.com/iegsr/2006/11/06/Three-Steps-To-Ensuring-Your-Hospitality-Programs-.aspx

13a. Collett, P. (2008). Sponsorship-related hospitality: Planning for measurable success. *Journal of Sponsorship, 1*(3), 286–296.

13. Bentick, B. L. (1986). The role of the Grand Prix in promoting South Australian entrepreneurship; exports and the terms of trade. In J. P. A. Burns, J. H. Hatch, & T. J. Mules (Eds.), *The Adelaide Grand Prix: The impact of a special event* (pp. 169–185). Adelaide: The Centre for South Australian Economic Studies.

14. O'Brien, D. (2006). Event business leveraging: The Sydney 2000 Olympic Games. *Annals of Tourism Research, 33*(1), 240–261.

15. IEG. (2002). DeWalt strategy ensures eight-figure motorsports team title pays for itself. *IEG Sponsorship Report, 21*(20), 8.

16. Fry, A. (2008, January). Come dive with me. *SportBusiness International*, pp. 38–41.

17. Skinner, B. E., & Rukavina, V. (2003). *Event sponsorship*. New York, NY: John Wiley.

18. SBI. (2007, August). Sharing brand values. *SportBusiness International*, pp. 18–19.

19. The changing role of hospitality in sponsorship. (1990). *Special Events Report, 9*(14), 4–5.

20. IEG. (2010, October 12). Corporate hospitality sheds recession-related stigma renews focus on ROI. *IEG Sponsorship Report*. Retrieved from http://www.sponsorship.com/IEGSR/2010/10/12/Corporate-Hospitality-Sheds-Recession-related-Stig.aspx

21. Woodward, S. (2000, September 11–17). Going for the corporate gold. *SportBusiness*, pp. 1, 54.

21a. Brown, G. (2000). Taking the pulse of Olympic sponsorship. *Event Management, 7*, 187–196.

22. Alonzo, V. (1994). The wide world of sport marketing. *Incentive, 168*(5), 44–50.

23. IEG. (2000). Lowe's test waters with title of new angling series. *IEG Sponsorship Report, 19*(12), 7.

24. IEG. (2011, September 7). Degree Men gets tough on sweat and odor at Tough Mudder events. *IEG Sponsorship Report*.

25. IEG. (2011, September 6). Snack on this: nutrition bars, increase sponsorship activity. *IEG Sponsorship Report*.

26. Wallace, R., & Vogel, J. (2000). The proliferation of naming rights and escalation of fees. In D. Gruen & M. Freedman (Eds.), *2000. Inside the ownership of professional sports teams* (pp. 40–43). Chicago, IL: Team Marketing Report.

27. IEG. (2009, April 27). Ten ways properties can add value to their sponsorship efforts. *IEG Sponsorship Report*.

28. IEG. (2008, August 11). Making concessions: The growing importance of on-site sales rights to properties and sponsors. *IEG Sponsorship Report*.

29. SportBusiness. (2001, September 27). Major League Baseball's Detroit Tigers have named Pepsi the "official soft drink of Comerica Park" as part of a new multiyear agreement. *SportBusiness Journal*.

30. IEG. (1998). Integrating sales rights into sponsorship. *IEG Sponsorship Report*, *17*(9), 4–5.

31. Manahan, T. (2010, March 29). Youth sports still in good shape as girls volleyball qualifiers show. *SportBusiness Journal*, p. 8.

32. Lefton, T. (2010, November 22). Events become front line for recruiting. *SportsBusiness Journal*, p. 18.

33. Dreier, F. (2010, November 20). Travelling baseball show targets Hispanics. *SportsBusiness Journal*, p. 20.

34. Starr, M., & Springen, K. (1996, January 15). A piece of the Olympic action. *Newsweek*, pp. 58–59.

35. IEG. (2012, January 13). Leslie's Swimming Pool Supplies sponsors Waste Management Phoenix Open—PGA tour event—Free tournament tickets available at Leslie's stores. *IEG Sponsorship Report*.

36. Masterman, G. (2007). *Sponsorship for a return on investment*, Boston, MA: Elsevier.

36a. Kolah, A. (2001). *How to develop an effective sponsorship program*. London, UK: Sport Business Group.

37. IEG. (2000). Companies tap sponsorship to retain employees. *IEG Sponsorship Report*, *19*(7), 1.

38. Warren, C. (2005, March). What to expect. *American Way*, pp. 58–62.

39. Lefton, T. (2010, July 12). Far-flung Aon unites with ManU. *SportsBusiness Journal*.

4

Naming Rights Sponsorships*

W
hile corporations were alerted to the benefits and value of sport sponsorship by its role in the 1984 Los Angeles Olympic Games, the potential of
naming rights as a sponsorship vehicle was not widely recognized until a
decade after that watershed event. There were isolated examples of facilities that were
endowed with corporate names, but they did not meet the central two conditions of
sponsorship, that is, they were not conceived as being manifestations of a business relationship between the corporation and facility owners, and they were not exploited for
commercial ends.

For example, Chicago Cubs' Wrigley Field has had a corporate name since 1926.
However, it was named to honor the team's owner, rather than being conceived as a business relationship with the chewing gum company that his family also owned, and no
payments for the naming rights were made. A similar situation characterized Busch Stadium—home of the MLB St. Louis Cardinals team. The stadium first received this name
in 1954 and it was intended to honor the team owner, Gussie Busch. A new stadium was
constructed in 1966 and it retained the name, but it was not until the 1970s that there
was gradual recognition of its commercial potential exemplified by signs for the beer
products, appearances by the Budweiser Clydesdales, and an organist's frequent rendering of the Budweiser advertising anthem—*Here Comes the King*—to rev up the crowd.[1]

These early glimmerings from Busch suggesting that naming rights could have commercial potential were reinforced in 1971 when Schaefer Brewing Company paid
$150,000 to name the New England Patriots stadium, Schaefer Field. This first naming
rights agreement was followed two years later, by the Buffalo Bills renaming War Memorial Stadium, Rich Stadium, after signing a $1.5 million, 20-year agreement with Rich
Products, a local frozen food supplier.[2]

These early naming rights agreements did not stimulate a widespread trend. From
the early 1970s through the mid-1980s, few sports facilities were corporately named.
During this period, major sports venues, all of which were publicly financed, typically
maintained the tradition of being named either for prominent civic leaders such as the

*This chapter is adapted from material included in *Financing Sport: 3rd Edition*, a companion volume to this text,
authored by Dennis R. Howard and John L. Crompton.

Hubert H. Humphrey Dome in Minneapolis (1982) and Brandon Bryne Arena (1981) in New Jersey, or to provide local or civic identity such as the Louisiana Superdome (1975) and Pontiac Stadium (1978).

The naming rights of the Los Angeles Forum were sold to Great Western Bank in 1987, Arco Arena was named in Sacramento in 1988, and the Target Center in Minneapolis in 1990, but it was not until the last half of the 1990s that naming rights agreements became widespread. From 1995 through 2000, the number and financial magnitude of venue sponsorships grew significantly. By 1997, one-third (41 of 113) of the venues used by teams in the four major leagues had been named for corporations.[2] Within five years, that percentage doubled. By 2002 the proportion of corporately-named venues had increased to almost 70%, with 80 of 121 teams playing in facilities named after major companies.[3] In part, this growth was stimulated by the large number of new sport facilities that were constructed in the late 1990s. The availability of these new facilities created an unprecedented inventory of titling opportunities for corporations seeking to exploit the commercial benefit of placing their names on prominent sports venues. In 2012, over three-fourths, or 94 of 122 professional teams in the "big four" major leagues in North America, played in corporately-named venues. At the start of the 2012 season, 13 of 19 Major League Soccer teams also were playing in stadiums named for a company or brand.

WHY COMPANIES BUY NAMING RIGHTS

Initially, the principal reason companies found naming rights appealing was the exposure opportunities provided by taking the name of a conspicuous public attraction. From an exposure perspective, naming rights, like many other sponsorship vehicles, offer companies advantages over traditional advertising:

> You can't bypass a name on a stadium the way you zap through a commercial— it's tougher to ignore. While each sponsorship needs to be measured for its effectiveness, a lot of marketers are looking for a less cluttered, high impact way to get a brand in front of the public eye. Associating with marquee properties is one great way to accomplish this (p. 14).[4]

The scarcity of supply enhances the chances of escaping clutter. Because there are only a limited number of such opportunities, competitors find it more difficult to duplicate a naming rights communication platform.

The unique "24–7" exposure afforded by naming rights agreements is an appealing benefit, particularly for companies with little or no brand recognition. Swedish telecommunications giant Ericsson, Inc. was virtually unknown in the United States before it paid $20 million in 1995 for the naming rights to the NFL Carolina Panthers' new stadium in Charlotte, North Carolina. Market research conducted in 1998 found that in less than three years the Ericsson brand grew from almost no public presence to being recognized by 50% of the adults in the Carolinas and by 44% nationally. The owner of the Carolina Panthers observed that "the naming rights deal all but eliminated the 'Who is Ericsson?' question" (p. 14).[4]

Established companies have been attracted to naming rights sponsorships because of the long-term, national exposure benefits they offer. Why was Farmers Insurance willing to commit over $20 million a year for 30 years to name the proposed NFL stadium in Los Angeles? According to Farmers chief marketing officer, the answer was simple: "You go to where the people are." During the year they signed the agreement with the Anschultz Entertainment Group (AEG), 18 of the 20 most watched television shows in the U.S. were NFL broadcasts.[5]

While enhancing a company's awareness is the driving rationale for naming rights agreements for some companies, for many others it is the company's desire to use the facility as a platform for increasing sales. Indeed, the amount of a rights fee increasingly is based on a company's estimate of the amount of incremental sales that will be realized from the sponsorship. The incremental sales benefits are most apparent in naming rights transactions that convey exclusive selling rights to the entitled company. For example, the Pepsi Center in Denver, Colorado, home to the NBA Nuggets and NHL Avalanche, provides Pepsi USA with exclusive pouring rights in the building, allowing the company to recapture a significant portion of the $3.4 million they pay in rights fees annually. Philips Electronics paid $185 million for the naming rights to Atlanta's 20,000-seat arena which is home to the NBA Hawks and NHL Thrashers. The 20-year agreement provides Philips with a 10,000 square foot consumer products display area, The Philips Experience, where the company can showcase its latest consumer entertainment products. In addition, the agreement required the venue to be fitted exclusively with Philips equipment and products from the state-of-the-art turnstiles to the hundreds of big screen monitors located throughout the arena.[6] Banks may place their ATMs in a building and airlines their ticket booths. Companies also use their affiliation with a popular sports team to create traffic-driving promotions, such as player appearances at retail outlets, to derive tangible benefits from their naming rights agreements.

The final benefit, closely related to increasing sales, is the hospitality opportunities provided to companies through naming rights partnerships. An almost universal element of every naming rights contract is that the corporate partner receives access to at least one luxury suite in the sports venue. This allows the company to create indirect selling opportunities with key customers by hosting them in premium surroundings at games or concerts. As was noted in Chapter 3, the goodwill engendered through these kinds of hospitality efforts is intended to strengthen business relationships that translate into increased or renewed sales opportunities. Some naming rights agreements have extended hospitality benefits to corporate partners beyond the venue itself. These extended benefits may include: providing the company with the right to designate a number of guests to travel on the team charter to away games during the regular season, making retired players or "legends" available for company events, and making "star" players available for personal appearances at company events on non-game days.

The summary of benefits received by Scotiabank in its agreement with the NHL Ottawa Senators illustrates the range of tangible rights commonly extended as part of naming sponsor's deal (see Figure 4.1). Scotiabank, Canada's third largest bank, signed a 15-year, $26 million contract for exclusive entitlement rights to the arena. In addition

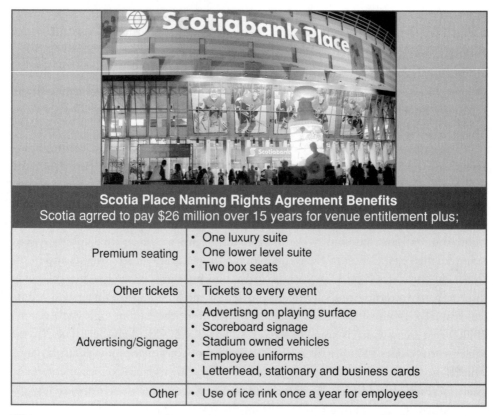

Figure 4.1. Benefits received by Scotiabank from Naming Rights Agreement.

to the arena being named Scotiabank Place, the bank also received premium seating inventory (two suites and two box seats), and exclusive access to the facility for an annual trade show, and a day on the ice for company employees.

Ultimately, all of these corporate rationales for investing in naming rights are expected to increase companies' profitability. If investors believed naming rights contributed to this end, then there should be a boost in a company's stock price when such agreements are announced. A study of the naming rights holders at 49 stadiums and arenas reported that on average the companies' stock prices increased 1.65% at the time the agreements were first announced. This was a 'net-of-market' increase; it was strongly statistically significant; and was considerably in excess of the returns associated with other major marketing programs such as the signing of Olympic sponsorships or celebrity endorsers.[7]

THE GROWING VALUE OF NAMING RIGHTS AGREEMENTS

There have been substantial increases in the amounts paid by corporations for these rights over the past two decades. In 1998, Staples office products company set a record by agreeing to pay $100 million for the rights to the new downtown arena in Los Angeles. Within a year, FedEx eclipsed the $200 million barrier when the package delivery company paid $205 million ($7.6 million per year on average for 25 years) to the Wash-

Courtesy of BigStockPhoto.com

ington Redskins to name the NFL team's new football stadium FedEx Field. Shortly thereafter, the $300 million barrier was broken when Reliant Energy purchased the rights to the Houston Texans new football stadium in 2000 at $10 million per year.

Substantial naming rights activity occurred until the Great Recession occurred in 2008. Between 2001 and 2007, 13 naming rights contracts in excess of $100 million were signed. Two of the largest were signed in early 2007. When Citigroup, Inc. agreed to pay $400 million ($20 million per year over 20 years) for the naming rights to the new New York Mets ballpark, it was the most expensive sports-stadium rights sponsorship ever, superseding the previous record agreement at Reliant Stadium by a substantial margin. The Citi Field fee reflects the size of the New York City market, but it was enhanced by the sign's visibility to automobile traffic on the adjacent New York Grand Central Parkway and its visibility from La Guardia Airport. Shortly after the Citi Field announcement, Barclays Bank announced it would become the new naming rights partner with the Brooklyn Nets and would pay between $300 and $400 million over 20 years for the naming rights to a new arena which opened in 2012.*

Tables 4.1 and 4.2 identify the 20 largest stadium and arena naming rights deals in North America, respectively. Leading the way by a substantial margin is the Farmers Insurance naming-rights agreement worth $600 million. Early in 2011, AEG, an entertainment company that owns and manages many prominent venues including the Staples Center, announced a 30-year agreement with Farmers which would name a proposed stadium in Los Angeles, Farmers Field. The deal is unique in that it is speculative. At the time of the signing there was no stadium—a site had not even been approved—and no team! There has not been an NFL franchise in Los Angeles since the Rams aban-

---

*In 2011, *Sports Business Journal* reported the actual worth of the Barclays Center naming rights agreement at $200 million. The authoritative publication reduced the original value announced by the Nets after reviewing the official prospectus for the issuance of the arena bonds.

Table 4.1. 20 Largest *Stadium* Naming Rights Deals

Name, City, Team (League)	Total Price (millions)	Length (Years)	Avg. Annual Payment (millions)	Expiration Year
Farmers Field, Los Angeles, (NFL)	$600–$700	30	$20–$23	TBD
MetLife Field, New York, Giants/Jets (NFL)	$425–$625	25	$17–$20	2036
Citi Field, New York, Mets (MLB)	$400	20	$20.0	2028
Reliant Stadium, Houston, Texans (NFL)	$310	31	$10	2032
Gillette Stadium, New England, Patriots (NFL)	$240	15	$8.0	2031
FedEx Field, Washington D.C., Redskins (NFL)	$205	27	$7.59	2025
Minute Maid Park, Houston, Astros (MLB)	$178	28	$6.36	2029
University of Phoenix, Arizona, Cardinals (NFL)	$154.5	20	$7.72	2026
Bank of America Stadium, Charlotte, Panthers (NFL)	$140	20	$7.0	2023
Lincoln Financial Field,, Philadelphia, Eagles (NFL)	$139.6	20	$6.98	2022
Lucas Oil Stadium, Indianapolis, Colts (NFL)	$121.5	20	$6.07	2027
Citizens Bank Park, Philadelphia, Phillies (MLB)	$95	25	$3.8	2029
M&T Bank, Baltimore, Ravens (NFL)	$79	15	$5.0	2017
Great American Ball Park, Cincinnati, Reds (MLB)	$75	30	$2.5	2032
Home Depot Center, Los Angeles, Galaxy (MLS)	$70	10	$7.0	2013
U.S. Cellular Field, Chicago, White Sox (MLB)	$68	23	$2.96	2025
Chase Field, Arizona, Diamondbacks (MLB)	$66.4	30	$2.2	2028
Comerica Park, Detroit, Tigers (MLB)	$66	30	$2.2	2030
Petco Park, San Diego, Padres (MLB)	$60	22	$2.73	2025
Sports Authority Field at Mile High Stadium, Denve,r Broncos (NFL)	$60	10	$6.0	2021
CenturyLink Field, Seattle, Seahawks (NFL)	$60– $100	15–20	$4.0–$5.0	2019–2024

Source: *SportsBusiness Journal*, In-Depth: Naming Rights, September 19–25, 2011

Table 4.2. 20 Largest Arena Naming Rights Deals				
Name, City Team (League)	Total Price (millions)	Length (Years)	Avg. Annual Payment (millions)	Expiration Year
Barclays Center Brooklyn Nets (NBA)	$200	20	$10.0	2032
American Airlines Center Dallas Stars (NHL), Mavericks (NBA)	$195	30	$6.5	2030
Philips Arena Atlanta Hawks (NBA)	$185	20	$9.25	2019
Nationwide Arena Columbus Blue Jackets (NHL)	$135	Indef.	NA	Indef.
TD Garden Boston Bruins (NHL), Celtics (NBA)	$119.1	20	$5.95	2025
Staples Center Los Angeles Kings (NHL), Lakers (NBA), Clippers (NBA)	$116	20	$5.8	NA
Prudential Center New Jersey Devils (NHL)	$105.3	20	$5.26	2027
Toyota Center Houston Rockets (NBA)	$95	20	$4.75	2023
FedExForum Memphis Grizzlies (NBA)	$90	22	$4.09	2024
Consol Energy Center Pittsburgh Penguins (NHL)	$84–105	21	$4.0–$5.0	2031
RBC Center Carolina Hurricanes (NHL)	$80	20	$4.0	2022
Excel Center Minnesota Wild (NHL)	$75	25	$3.0	2024
Pepsi Center Denver Avalanche (NHL), Nuggets (NBA)	$68	20	$3.4	2019
Bell Center Montreal Canadiens (NHL)	$63.94	20	$3.2	2023
Honda Center Anaheim Ducks (NHL)	$60.45	15	$4.03	2020
HP Pavilion at San Jose San Jose Sharks (NHL)	$47	15	$3.13	2016
Verizon Center Washington Capitols (NHL), Wizards (NBA)	$44	20	$2.2	2017
American Airlines Center Miami Heat (NBA)	$42	20	$2.1	2019
AT&T Center San Antonio Spurs (NBA)	$41	20	$2.05	2022
Amway Center Orlando Magic	$40	10	$4.0	2020

doned the market for a new stadium in St. Louis in 1994. Crucial to the return of the NFL to Los Angeles was the construction of a modern, fully-loaded stadium. For more than a decade, a number of alternatives were proposed including the renovation of both the LA Coliseum and Rose Bowl sites, building new state-of-the-art venues in suburban communities, and AEG's most recent proposal to build a new stadium as part of their existing downtown entertainment district, L.A. Live. While Los Angeles was working on building a new stadium, the NFL Commissioner in his 2012 State of the League address, reiterated the league's intent to bring NFL football back to the city.[8] The intent of the AEG-Farmers partnership was to provide momentum for AEG's plan to build a new $1-billion stadium. AEG believed the announcement of the record-breaking naming rights sponsorship with Farmers would expedite approval by the city for its stadium proposal. AEG's President stated it ". . . doesn't mean football is back (in L.A.) tomorrow. But it means we took probably the most significant step in the last 15 years to getting football back here soon."[8] The naming rights agreement between AEG and Farmers is conditional on the new downtown stadium being built and occupied by an NFL franchise. At that point, the conditional agreement would be activated and Farmers would start making payments of no less than $20 million per year, providing AEG with a crucial source of contractually obligated income for 30 years.

While by far the largest, the Farmers contract was one of several major naming rights agreements announced in 2011. In August 2011, another insurance company, MetLife, became the naming rights partner for the new $1.6 billion stadium jointly occupied by the New York Giants and Jets. The total value of MetLife's commitment was estimated at between $425 to $625 million,* with the company making annual payments of between $17 and $20 million over 25 years.

From the beginning of construction of its new stadium in 2006, the Dallas Cowboys had identified AT&T as their preferred naming rights partner. However, when the two sides were close to agreement in 2008, the onset of the Great Recession resulted in AT&T having to lay-off 12,000 employees so negotiations were halted. The agreement was finally consummated when economic conditions improved in 2013 at a reported fee of $17–19 million per year. A novel aspect of this agreement was that approximately $500,000 per year went to the city of Arlington to assist in servicing the $325 million bond package it issued to partially fund the stadium.

These agreements appeared to signal the re-emergence of corporate interest in naming rights. During the difficult economic climate of 2008 and 2009, most companies were reluctant to commit millions of dollars to naming rights sponsorships. In 2009, when the economy was at its lowest point, the only major agreement completed was at Orlando Magic's new arena. The $40-million, 10-year sponsorship to name the venue the Amway Center was signed by the team owner, who was also the co-owner of Amway Global. The fact that he had a controlling interest in both the team and the

---

*Estimates of the value of the MetLife naming rights deal have ranged from a high of $23 million to a low of $17 million per year. The most commonly reported annual payout is a range between $17 and $20 million over 25 years. Using these figures, the total value of the MetLife Stadium deal would range between $500 million and $425 million.

company buying the rights was a significant factor in consummating the arrangement. The otherwise depressed market prompted a leading sports economist to declare the recession period of 2008–2010 as "the worst time in the last 20 years to sell naming rights."[10]

CHALLENGES AHEAD

While there are signs that corporate interest is rebounding, many teams are still having a difficult time finding naming rights partners. Exhibit 4.1 (next page) describes the saga of the MLB Washington Nationals' unsuccessful effort to sell the naming rights to "Nationals Park"—five years *after* the team opened the new ballpark—illustrating the challenges facing teams in the post recession-economy. Prior to moving into the $693 million venue to start the 2008 season, the Nationals had hoped to create a naming relationship with a national brand worth $8 to $12 million annually for 10 to 20 years. The Nationals were still seeking a naming rights partner when this book went to press in late 2013.

Part of the challenge is the limited prospect pool. With more than three-fourths of major league teams playing in corporately-named buildings, a substantial share of major companies with national brands have already entered into long-term naming sponsorships with existing facilities. As shown in Table 4.3, some of the largest companies in a wide range of consumer product and service categories have committed millions of dollars annually to place their company name or brand on a sports facility. A few prominent consumer service firms have purchased the naming rights to multiple venues (e.g., American Airlines, AT&T, and Wells Fargo). The result is that many of the major national brands, owned by companies with both the capability and willingness to invest the substantial financial resources necessary to buy and sustain naming rights sponsorships, are no longer available as potential prospects.

Table 4.3. National Brands with Sports Facility Naming Rights by Product or Service Category	
Product or Service	**Major Companies**
Airlines	Air Canada, American, United, US Airways
Automobile	Ford, Honda, Toyota
Banking	Bank of America, Citizens, Wells Fargo
Energy	Consol Energy, Chesapeake Energy, Reliant, Xcel
Financial Services	Citi, Edward Jones, PNC, Raymond James, Scottrade
Insurance	Farmers, MetLife, Progressive, Prudential, Safeco
Telecommunications	AT&T, Bell Centre, U.S. Cellular, Verizon

Exhibit 4.1

Marquee Opportunity—or Missed Opportunity? Washington Nationals' Naming Rights are Still Marketable

Whatever happened to [Insert Corporate Name Here] Park? When the Washington Nationals opened their new stadium on the Anacostia River four years ago, "Nationals Park" was widely understood to be a placeholder, to be used only until the team sold naming rights to some corporate brand for upward of $10 million a year.

But on April 12, the Nationals started their fifth season in none other than Nationals Park. And to experts in the sports marketing world, the stadium remains one of the great unrealized marketing assets in America.

"It's sort of a mystery why it's not sold yet," said Dean Bonham, CEO of French sports marketing firm Bonham/Wills & Associates and negotiator of 12 major stadium naming rights deals. "It's a prominent market. The team—it's not a World Series team, but it's an interesting team. I can't see any reason why that deal hasn't been done."

The Nationals aren't talking. There's little outward evidence of an active sales effort, industry insiders say. One potential deal bubbled up late last year, but that was the only activity since the ballpark's earliest days, said Lisa Delpy Neirotti, a sports management and tourism professor at George Washington University who speaks with club sources regularly.

But that doesn't mean a deal isn't out there, waiting for the right blend of creativity, opportunity, salesmanship and shrewd strategizing to take hold. While it might have been much easier to strike a deal before the recession hit corporate America, experts say the market hasn't dried up entirely, as evidenced by recent deals in Los Angeles and New York. Major stadiums in Dallas, Miami, and Kansas City, however, remain without a sponsor.

To be sure, some experts acknowledge the Nationals' best chance to make a deal may have been before the stadium opened. According to one industry analyst, "They were in the marketplace at a time when you would have thought it would have been a good window of opportunity to sell. But, by the middle of 2008, we realized we were in serious trouble economically and the markets just shut down."

Experts say the naming rights' value has eroded only modestly—perhaps justifying a conservative approach from team owner Ted Lerner and his son, Mark Lerner. The closest avatar for Washington might be the Philadelphia Phillies,

which have a $57.5 million, 25-year deal with Citizens Bank, along with a $37.5 million advertising package—less than $4 million a year. But unrealistic expectations may be to blame for the lack of a deal prior to 2008. Before the recession, Rob Prazmark, CEO of 21 Sports and Entertainment Marketing Group, Inc. said, "Everybody involved believed the Nationals could lure top dollar in the heyday of naming rights." Dean Bonham also felt the Nationals' expectations exceeded market reality, "If I had to offer a guess on why it hasn't been sold, I would guess it's related to an inaccurate analysis of the value of the property as opposed to the lack of marketability." Skepticism rests in a widely-held belief that in a struggling economy there simply aren't many companies with the wherewithal, political freedom, and positive brand identity to strike a deal amenable to the Nationals.

By far, the industry best represented on the marquees of major venues are financial services providers, followed by the automobile industry. Since the federal bailouts and Troubled Asset Relief Program, however, those companies have been closely scrutinized by lawmakers and regulators. Citibank, for instance, drew ire from several on Capitol Hill when it struck a $400 million, 20-year deal to name the New York Mets' new stadium in 2008. Others may hesitate to follow in their footsteps, particularly in Congress's backyard.

Local corporate partners have emerged as trendy buyers of naming rights now, case in point being Baltimore's M&T Bank Stadium or San Diego's PetCo Park. But one obvious local candidate, Capital One Financial Corp., is working on an acquisition of ING Direct's U.S. business, and companies with major strategic moves in play often don't agree to such ancillary, high-dollar deals.

Multiple experts said the buyer could be a complete dark horse, a company that wouldn't generally consider a naming rights deal, but could be swayed with the right package of unique benefits only offered by the Nationals—for instance, signs literally visible from the U.S. House offices or the U.S. Department of Transportation. Prazmark said the Nationals may find the most promise in expanding a relationship with an existing marketing partner.

For now, the Lerners appear to be willing to sit on that potential value, just as Dallas Cowboys owner Jerry Jones has done with the crown jewel of stadium naming rights, Cowboys Stadium.

Source: This article written by Ben Fisher, Staff Reporter, appeared in the *Washington Business Journal* on April 13, 2012.

Consequently, most of the recent agreements have been with companies which have a more "local" association or connection to the market or city in which they purchase the naming rights. Teams seeking venue naming partners have found a more receptive client pool within their own region or market area, so a significant number of naming sponsorships established over the last decade have been with firms whose company headquarters are located in the same city or metropolitan area as the venue they name. Examples include: Farmers Insurance (Farmers Field, Los Angeles), Petco Animal Supplies (Petco Park, San Diego Padres), Sports Authority (Sports Authority Field at Mile High, Denver Broncos), H.J. Heinz (Heinz Field, Pittsburgh Steelers), Target Corporation (Target Field, Minnesota Twins), Consol Energy, Inc. (Consol Energy Center, Pittsburgh Penguins), FedEx Corporation (FedEx Forum, Memphis Grizzlies), Ever-Bank (EverBank Field, Jacksonville Panthers), and BMHO Harris Bank (BMHO Harris Bradley Center, Milwaukee Bucks). The executive vice-president of BMHO Harris, in explaining his bank's decision to purchase the naming rights to the Bradley Center in downtown Milwaukee stated, "Sponsorship of a community treasure like the Bradley Center is a great opportunity for us to deepen our local commitment and strengthen our relationship with customers in Milwaukee and across Wisconsin."[11] Expanding the firm's visibility and connection to the local and regional market is a common theme, as expressed by Sports Authority's chief marketing director in announcing the sporting goods firm's decision to purchase the naming rights to the Denver Broncos stadium: "We're the third largest private company in Colorado, yet people don't know that our headquarters are in Colorado. We don't look at this as a corporate partnership. We look at this as a Colorado sponsorship."[12]

While the shift from national to more local or regional companies has allowed teams and venues, in smaller markets, to sell naming rights sponsorships, it has meant that those teams often have had to settle for less money and for shorter-length partnerships. The limited prospect pool and poor economy have made it difficult for teams to negotiate sponsorship fees comparable to those established prior to the 2008 Great Recession. Two recent naming rights sponsorships illustrate this broadening trend. The Miami Dolphins and Sun Life Financial signed a five-year, $25 million partnership in 2012, and the Jacksonville Jaguars reached a 5-year, $16.6 million agreement with Ever-Bank in 2010. After signing the agreement, the Jaguars Chief Financial Officer confirmed that the terms were as good as the team could negotiate in the current market, commenting, "From our standpoint, the term was shorter than we would have liked, [and] the dollars were less than we would have liked."[13] Other teams or venues signing shorter-term agreements include: Oakland Raiders ($7.6 million for 6 years with Overstock.com), New Orleans Saints ($100–$120 million for 10 years with Mercedes-Benz USA), and the Denver Broncos ($60 million for 10 years with Sports Authority).

A primary reason companies are increasingly reluctant to enter into extended naming rights contracts is that the uncertain economic climate makes it difficult to justify long-term sponsorships of 20 years or more. Firms have become more cautious and circumspect. As one experienced naming rights negotiator asserted:

In a world that's changing so rapidly as the one we live in, does it make sense to commit that much money for that much time? It's a tactic that limits your flexibility to move dollars from one investment area to another because they are committed for years. So here's the thing: Companies need to be nimble. They need to be able to change direction quickly. If they conduct any media mix modeling, they can evaluate pulling the plug on less effective marketing investments in favor of new tactics or current tactics proving to be more effective.[9]

While there are challenges to professional teams and venues attempting to find naming rights sponsors, the market remains viable. The Farmers Stadium, AT&T Stadium, and Mercedes-Benz Superdome agreements are recent examples of successful transactions. However, the reality for many teams playing in smaller markets or in older venues is that there are not as many available prospects who will be willing to commit as much money for as many years as in the past.

SHIRT AND TEAM NAMING RIGHTS

Shirt and facility naming sponsorships offer different types of exposure. Companies whose names appear on facilities benefit from their association being routinely referenced in external media. This benefit does not accrue to companies that appear on team jerseys. But those jerseys become the focus of fans throughout the event, whether viewed live or on television. Given the active focus of fans on the players and their shirts, it seems likely that this association will resonate more strongly than facility naming rights.

While facility naming sponsorships are widely accepted by the four major U.S. professional leagues, this has not been extended to shirt or apparel naming rights. There is a belief that fans see their teams' shirts as sacred real estate. The NFL does permit the manufacturer's name or logo to be discretely featured on footwear, apparel, and helmets. Similarly, an NBA uniform has the maker's insignia on it. Their regulations require manufacturers to pay the leagues a fee for the right to display these logos. The NCAA uniform rules limit the size and number of manufacturers' logos on game jerseys to "a single manufacturer's logo not to exceed 2¼ inches square." A similar limitation is imposed on socks, headbands, and wristbands.

Major League Soccer (MLS) teams do sell shirt ("kit") sponsorships. The back of club jerseys are reserved for league-wide sponsors, but the front is available for individual club shirt sponsors. The league established a floor of $500,000 per year for this. Unlike the English Premier League, MLS prohibits online gambling companies from jersey sponsorships. The MLS shirt sponsors are listed in Table 4.4. The amount companies are willing to pay to use MLS teams as a platform for connecting their brands to team supporters has increased substantially in recent years. Vitamin manufacturer, Herbalife, paid the Los Angeles Galaxy $4.4 million for shirt and team naming rights for the 2012 season, which is the highest value MLS jersey sponsorship to this point.

The reticence of the American major leagues to embrace shirt sponsorship was shared by the European soccer leagues a few decades ago. Club uniforms were perceived to be

Table 4.4. MLS Club Shirt Naming Rights		
Team	Sponsor	Annual Value
Chicago Fire	Quaker	Undisclosed
Chivas USA	Corona	Undisclosed
Columbus Crew	Barbasol	Undisclosed
FC Dallas	AdvoCare	Undisclosed
D.C. United	Volkswagon	$3.1 million–$3.7 million
Houston Dynamo	Greenstar Recycling	$2.54 million
Los Angeles Galaxy	Herbalife	$4.4 million
Montreal Impact	Bank of Montreal	Undisclosed
New England Revolution	UnitedHealthcare	Undisclosed
Philadelphia Union	Bimbo	$3 million
Portland Timbers	Alaska Airlines	Undisclosed
Real Salt Lake	XanGo	$1 million
Seattle Sounders FC	Xbox	$4 million
Toronto FC	Bank of Montreal	C$4 million+
Vancouver Whitecaps FC	Bell Canada	C$4 million+
The New York Red Bull jersey sponsor is Red Bull, which owns the club. Teams without jersey sponsor: Colorado, Kansas City, San Jose.		

an integral part of a team's heritage and of the heritage of the sport. Thus, shirt sponsorship was banned by the English soccer authorities until 1977. Liverpool became the first club to endorse shirt sponsorship when they signed an agreement with Japanese electronics giant Hitachi. Others quickly followed, so within a decade it had become an accepted non-controversial practice. As global interest in the English Premier League (EPL) and foreign media coverage have grown exponentially, they have driven huge increases in shirt naming right fees.

Foreign broadcast rates for EPL games increased by over 400% between 2006 and 2011 which led to commensurate increases in shirt sponsorship fees. Apparel sponsorships for preeminent EPL teams are now extraordinarily lucrative. In 2012, Manchester United reached an agreement with U.S. automobile manufacturer, General Motors, to put the Chevrolet brand on its shirt. Starting in 2014, the record rights sponsorship will cost General Motors $420 to $490 million over the seven-year contract period.[14] In effect, General Motors is paying $60 to $70 million per year for the Chevrolet brand to receive 90 minutes of guaranteed exposure in matches that attract huge global audiences. Manchester United is reputed to be the most popular sports team in the world with over 650 million followers.

While Manchester United is the pre-eminent brand in the EPL, other teams also have impressive shirt sponsorship arrangements. United's cross-town rivals, Manchester City, negotiated a 10-year agreement with Abu Dhabi's Etihad Airways for $56 million a year, which includes naming rights to the team's stadium and practice ground as well as shirt sponsorship. Similarly, Arsenal signed a five-year extension of their sponsorship partnership with Emirates Airline to cover the 2013/14 to 2018/19 seasons at $48 million per year for both shirt sponsorship rights and naming rights to their stadium. Liverpool signed a six-year agreement with Warrior Sports, owned by New Balance, to sponsor the club's shirts at $40 million a year. Liverpool's replica shirt sales reach nearly 900,000 a year, making it the fourth largest selling kit in the world behind Manchester United, Barcelona, and Real Madrid. Top European soccer clubs in other countries have negotiated similar amounts. For example, the Qatar Foundation's logo will appear on the front of Barcelona's shirts in return for $200 million over five years from the nonprofit.

The escalation in EPL shirt naming sponsorship fees was vividly illustrated by Chelsea. The club had signed a deal with Umbro, a sport apparel supplier, in 2001 for $8 million a year for 10 years. In a move which is perhaps unprecedented in professional sports, five years later the club paid Umbro almost $40 million to terminate the contract (which resulted in Umbro's shares falling by 6% when it was announced).[15] This freed the club to sign a shirt naming rights sponsorship with Samsung at $30 million a year for 10 years.

From a corporate sponsor's perspective, shirt naming rights are likely to be preferable to facility naming rights, because they have the added value not only of appearing in front of live crowds but also on television and in press action photographs. In addition, they appear on the replica uniforms purchased and worn by fans of the teams. Thus, shirt sponsorship creates thousands of "mobile billboards" displaying a company's name in every park and open space in countries where children seek to emulate the skills of their team idols, and these shirts are also worn by older people as casual leisure wear.

In their ongoing search for new revenue sources, it seems likely that the U.S. major leagues ultimately will follow the European soccer precedent and embrace shirt naming rights. Indeed, the WNBA perhaps began to pave the way for this to occur when the Phoenix Mercury signed a three-year sponsorship worth $1 million annually with an identity theft protection company, and other WNBA teams quickly followed this precedent. The minor league arm of the NBA, the NBA Development League, has also moved into uniform sponsorship. In 2012, the NBA owners discussed the potential of jersey sponsorship and the deputy commissioner stated: "If we add sponsor logos to jerseys, we recognize that some of our fans will think we've lost our minds. But the NBA is a global business and logos on jerseys are well established in other sports and commonplace outside the U.S."[15a] Similarly, the NFL revised its rules to edge into jersey sponsorship by authorizing practice team jerseys to carry the name of a sponsor on a $3\frac{1}{2}-4\frac{1}{2}$ inch patch.

Perhaps the ultimate naming rights agreement from a corporate perspective is to have the franchise branded with the corporate name. Red Bull pioneered this strategy and subsequently the company has continued to exploit it extensively. Their success is described in Exhibit 4.2.

Exhibit 4.2

Red Bull Creates Its Own Sport Properties

Red Bull, a company that essentially created the energy drink market and continues to dominate it with a 70% market share, has specialized in creating its own sport properties. One of the company's fundamental tenets has been that a successful sport property can be built and not simply bought. Typically, it has invested in comparatively small sport properties before building them and molding them to fit the Red Bull image. The Red Bull sport empire now comprises soccer teams around the world, Formula One (F1) racing teams, stadia and arenas around the globe and perhaps most distinctively, an unparalleled portfolio of extreme games and action sports properties.

Red Bull's slogan is "Gives you wings." From its launch in 1987 in Austria, it built a brand based on extreme sports and fast living. The company's first involvement in sport in 1991 was the creation of the Red Bull Flugtag event, first hosted in Vienna, Austria, which aligned perfectly with its slogan. The Flugtag requires participants to design and build flying contraptions to be launched off a 9.1 meter high ramp. It signaled Red Bull's intention to seek brand transfer by linking with extreme sports. Since the advent of the Flugtag event, Red Bull has been ever-present in adventure and 'new-age' sports, including sponsoring and heavily branding over 500 action sports events and athletes, such as free-runners, snow boarders and sky-divers, and further solidifying its reputation as a counter-culture brand with new events dominating the adventure sports industry. Today, Red Bull has an arguably unrivalled international sporting empire, including, among others: EC Red Bull Salzburg (Erste Bank Hockey League, Austria), FC Red Bull Salzburg (Austrian Bundesliga), F1 teams Red Bull Racing and Scuderia Toro Rosso, Major League Soccer's New York Red Bulls, NASCAR's Team Red Bull, Red Bull Brasil FC (Segunda Divisão Paulista, Brazilian second division) and fifth division German football club SSV Markranstädt, to be renamed RB Leipzig.

Key among Red Bull's sporting properties, the creation and promotion of innovative, new sports events has reinforced the brand's image and reputation. Typical of the company's properties is Red Bull Crashed Ice, which was launched in 2000. It is a combination of hockey, downhill skiing, and boarder cross (also known as Snowboard Cross, a sport seen at the Winter Olympics), and represented the new breed of sporting events that Red Bull would seek to utilize as a means of reaching its target market and promoting the image of the brand. Creating a sport in its own right to promote

a brand was almost unheard of prior to Red Bull's exploits in extreme sports.

Each year, competitors from across the world take part in a series of 11 qualifying trials across North America with more than 100 skaters taking part in the sport's final event which has been held in cities in North America and Europe, including Stockholm, Duluth (Minnesota), Moscow, and Quebec. As the event was developed, Red Bull ensured that it was built on the ethos of the brand. While it is recognized that organizations such as Whitbread have established events for the promotion of their brands, including the Whitbread Round the World Race. Red Bull went one step further in establishing its own sports with Red Bull branding and Red Bull rules.

Before joining the ranks of F1, Red Bull recognized a potential niche market that had yet to be exploited: the idea of merging the speed and racing elements from F1 with flying. Thus, the concept of the Red Bull Air Race was launched in 2003 in the small Austrian town of Zeltweg.[17] Now it is a full-fledged motorsport series in its own right, attracting a global audience of 300 million from over 180 countries. The average on-site crowd at an air race is 400,000. Over 3.5 million people attend an air race event each year. It has become such a huge sports property that a separate, independent management company—Red Bull Air Race GmbH—now runs the series with Red Bull itself as the title sponsor. It is the fastest growing motorsport in the world. The sports company is a highly profitable venture, as well as a sponsorship vehicle for Red Bull, with revenues accruing from their sponsors such as Audi, Seat, and Breitling; licensing from gaming to television; ticketing and hospitality; and primarily from their host city fees. A Red Bull spokesperson explained:

> We build a temporary racing arena and race track, a big benefit to any city as there is no permanent infrastructure to build and be maintained. This allows us to deliver on the major objectives we hold in common interest with our host city partners: the track is laid out in a way that the city skyline forms the background and reference point; and the people who watch the race [on television] can immediately recognize the city in which the race is taking place. The spectators can enjoy the incredible view of the action whether they are at the back of the crowd or in the front. Not only are they right up close to the racing, but they can take in the entire scope of the race track.

(Exhibit continues on next page)

Exhibit 4.2 *(Continued)*

Red Bull Creates Its Own Sport Properties

The important thing in a partnership is to underline the win-win situation for both parties involved: we deliver a strong global recognition based on all the people following each stop of the championship plus the millions of spectators coming to a town for the race weekend and creating a strong economic impact. The return on investment for a hosting city is significant and this is also the basis for a growing number of cities actively applying to host a race. It is only natural that a huge demand on the market faces a limited number of available race dates. This leads to an increase in the hosting fee in combination with an increase in delivering on return on investment. (p. 61)[17]

Red Bull racing, the brand's first entry into F1, was established in 2004 when the company bought Jaguar racing from Ford. While this was the company's first foray into team ownership in F1, it was far from Red Bull's first involvement in the sport. The company had previously had a sponsorship agreement with the Sauber racing team and had established a successful Junior Driver program sponsoring promising young drivers across the world. Red Bull also sponsored a number of drivers in the GP2 series, seeing them as potential stars for the future.

In F1, Red Bull created a second team named Scuderia Toro Rosso to act as a developmental team for Red Bull Racing. By having two teams, engines could be tested in both teams' cars allowing the most powerful engines to be selected, and promising young drivers could be groomed. Red Bull's championships in F1 have shown that success can be built organically and not merely bought through sponsorship and manufacturer investment.

Red Bull's involvement in soccer commenced in 2005 with the purchase of struggling Austrian club SV Salzburg. A year later, the company solidified its growing market position in the US with the acquisition of the New York based MLS franchise then called the Metrostars. Subsequently it acquired Red Bull Brasil who play on the lower divisions of the Brazilian regional leagues, and RB Leipzig who play in the fifth tier of German soccer.[18]

Red Bull has strict criteria for any sports property it creates or buys. The team or event must bear the Red Bull name in some way and must be branded or re-branded to meet the company's color scheme and identity. With its soccer teams, however small, Red Bull insists on blanket exposure for the brand. Where possible the team's stadiums have all been renamed the 'Red Bull Arena.'

Playing in Red Bull-named arenas and stadia, hosting new and unrivalled sporting events, and branding everything with Red Bull's colors and logo, the company has succeeded in building one of the most visible sporting empires and one of the most prominent counter-culture brands in the world. Few sporting entities have enjoyed such visibility across the multitude of sports and platforms. Many owners are content to respect the traditions and history of sport, and the typically behind-the-scenes nature of sports ownership. Red Bull, however, has shown a new way in which to build a brand through sport, and it's evidence of the potential marketing and brand-building vehicle sport provides.

Red Bull has proven to be a pioneer in utilizing sport to develop and enhance its brand as an extension of the core product, rather than merely an associated property. Even though the company has sought to extend its sporting portfolio into more mainstream sports, it has chosen sports befitting the company's own brand image. Adventurous, at times dangerous, and generally ambitious, Red Bull's sports empire reflects the company's own interests and identity. Few companies can rival Red Bull's innovation and perseverance in utilizing sport as a key driver of business and extension of the core brand.

An alternative to owning the property is to purchase the right to change a property's name to the corporate name without owning the team. This was the strategy adopted by Tau Ceramica which is one of the best basketball teams in Europe, but is also one of Spain's top producers of floor and wall tile.[19] The company bought the team name in exchange for an infusion of money and changed the team's existing name to the corporate name. The company does not own the team. If it did so, then it would be unable to withdraw its name if the team were chronic losers and would have to invest company funds in players and basketball, which is not its business. The team's name resonates among the young, active, sports-minded consumers who make up the company's desired demographic target market. A similar sponsorship model was adopted by a Welsh company:

- Total Network Solutions (TNS) was a full-time professional soccer team playing in the Welsh Premier League based in the village of Llansantffraid. The company, TNS, was based in the area and agreed to provide the team $400,000 over four years in exchange for it changing from its village name to TNS. The company's managing director commented: "Immediately we had our name being read out on the national radio, then on Sky Television, then on the BBC. We reckon about 8 million people hear the name each Saturday when the football results are reported." The arrangement worked so well for TNS that the company increased its sponsorship to $800,000 a year which enabled the club to become more successful and generate additional visibility for TNS. The arrangement ended when TNS was taken over by British Telecom.[20]

There are other examples of this in Europe. For example, Caja San Fernando and Unicafa are named after Spanish banks. In the U.S., major league franchises have remained linked to geography not corporate entities. When Federal Express Corporation tried to buy the team name of the Vancouver Grizzlies franchise when it moved to Memphis, the NBA refused to allow it but it seems likely this will be revisited in the future since it is a potentially lucrative revenue source.

COLLEGE VENUE SPONSORSHIPS

Table 4.5 shows that a growing number of colleges and universities have sold naming rights to stadiums and arenas on their campuses. Most of the collegiate sponsorships are modest when compared to those negotiated by major league teams. However, the number and financial magnitude of sponsorships have grown substantially over the past ten years, with some approaching the values realized by big league professional venues. The single largest agreement was the $40 million agreement Pepsi signed with Fresno State University. After acquiring the naming rights to the university's proposed sports and entertainment center, the soft drink company "passed through" the naming opportunity to one of its key retail suppliers in central California, Save Mart Supermarkets. The joint sponsorship agreement resulted in the new facility being called the Save Mart Center, with PepsiCo retaining exclusive pouring rights across the entire Fresno State campus and receiving preferred aisle and shelf space placement for Pepsi products in all Save Mart outlets.

Colleges frequently name sports facilities after major donors. The requirement at most universities to qualify for naming status is that the lead donor contribute 50% of the cost of the construction or renovation.[21] However, this is not a rigid criterion and in some cases it may be as low as 30%. In addition, an increasing number of colleges are requiring a maintenance endowment to accompany the 30% to 50% capital contribution before they will offer a donor naming rights. The magnitude of the maintenance endowment varies, but an endowment sufficient to generate 30% of the total maintenance costs appears to be a fairly typical figure.

Table 4.5. Top 10 College Naming Rights Deals					
Facility	**School**	**Total Price (millions)**	**Length (Years)**	**Avg. Annual Value**	**Year Expires**
Save Mart Center	Fresno State	$40	20	$2,000,000	2023
TCF Bank	Minnesota	$35	25	$1,400,000	2034
Comcast Center	Maryland	$25	25	$1,000,000	2026
Apogee Center	North Texas	$20	20	$1,000,000	2030
AT&T Stadium	Texas Tech	$20	25	$800,000	2019
Chevy Chase Bank Field at Byrd Stadium	Maryland	$20	25	$800,000	2030
Bright House Stadium	Central Florida	$15	15	$1,000,000	2022
Summa Field at InfoCision Stadium	Akron	$15	20	$750,000	2029
TD Ameritrade Park	Creighton/ College World Series	$15	20	$750,000	2030
Papa John's Cardinal Stadium	Louisville	$15	32	$468,750	2040

Source: *SportsBusiness Journal*, In-Depth: Naming Rights, September 19–25, 2011

Naming rights extend beyond the building to particular facilities within the building.[22] These may include plazas, auditoriums, halls of fame, natatoriums, gymnasiums, weight rooms, and locker rooms. Thus, Ohio State University sold the naming rights to the gymnasium inside its event center to Value City Department Stores for $12.5 million, so the university's basketball and hockey teams play in the Value City Arena at the Jerome Schottenstein Center. The late Mr. Schottenstein was founder of Schottenstein Stores Corp, who at the time of the naming rights agreement owned Value City, a discount department store chain. The naming rights agreement pays tribute to his many contributions to the city of Columbus and Ohio State University and, at the same time, provides broad exposure for the Value City brand. Georgia Institute of Technology signed a six-year agreement with McDonald's restaurants. In return for $5.5 million and a percentage of gross revenues, McDonald's received the rights to operate restaurants at two campus locations and Georgia Tech agreed to rename a square-block area of the campus containing its basketball arena and other athletics facilities as the McDonald's Center at Alexander Memorial Coliseum.[23]

When dealing with donors, naming rights are made in perpetuity. This is an important difference from naming rights sponsorships at professional facilities which are in force only for as long as they are paid for or until the agreement terminates. When a college needs to renovate a facility 20 years after its construction, it cannot jettison the original owner's name and replace it with the name of the lead donor of the renovation. A way has to be found to incorporate both donors' names. For example, the original Smith Pool when renovated may become the Smith Pool in the Jones Natatorium to accommodate both the original and the renovation lead donors.

Although the number and value of agreements has increased, there is resistance among some schools that are wary of increasing commercialism on campuses. Some on college campuses view the selling of corporate exposure as "an invasion of the sacred realm of academe," arguing that educational programs "should not be in the business of promoting commercial products." (p. 13)[24]

Thus, the athletic department at Stanford University reacted to criticism of growing commercialism by removing all large corporate signs and banners from its football, basketball, and baseball venues. This corporate "cleansing" cost the athletic department approximately $2.5 million per year.[25] The Athletic Director at Stanford commented, "I see this as the right decision for Stanford, but I'm not sure we're a national model for anybody else. Only the rich can afford to be moral. If the choice had been either to have advertising or drop sports, we might have come to another decision." (p.3).[26] While few schools may follow Stanford's lead, it is clear that many will struggle with finding an appropriate balance between maintaining the ideals of amateurism and academic integrity and the ever-increasing expense of sustaining big-time collegiate athletic programs.

Perhaps the compromise reached by the University of Iowa offers a model for future collegiate naming rights agreements. To address both institutional concerns regarding academic mission and the athletic department's pragmatic need for financial support, Iowa named its campus arena, Carver-Hawkeye Arena. Roy J. Carver, chair and founder of a tire manufacturing company, gave $25 million to the university. The university "insisted that Hawkeye be part of the name so you'd know where the thing is." (p. C12).[27]

Given growing sensitivity about the commercialization of college sports, negotiations involving the sale of naming rights are especially complicated in the college sector. One experienced naming rights negotiator commented, "There are many more folks in the mix on the college-side than on the professional side. On the pro side, you're dealing with single ownership. But, on the college side you're dealing with an athletic director, a president, a board of regents or trustees, and then sometimes there's also a state public works division involved. There are just more hoops to go through." (p. 14).[26]

Despite these challenges, the potential financial benefits of selling naming rights sponsorships for stadium and arena development will continue to incent many colleges and universities to pursue corporate naming partnerships, because "The money available is hard to ignore."[27] With so many collegiate athletic programs facing severe budget pressures, it is likely that corporately-named sports venues will increasingly become common part of the collegiate sports landscape.

MUNICIPAL AND HIGH SCHOOL SPONSORSHIPS

It was noted in Chapter 1 that sport sponsorship has percolated down to the municipal and high school levels, so there are now numerous local entities that have sold facility naming rights. Like colleges, many municipalities and high schools are constrained in pursuing naming rights agreements because their stadiums are already named after prominent local residents. Attempts to replace those names would invariably result in community outrage. Thus, viable candidates for sponsorship are limited to facilities that bear generic names and new facilities. Among municipalities, one of the most prominent sponsorships was negotiated by the city of Medford in Oregon for its new $24 million 132-acre sports park:

- The sports park is located adjacent to an interstate highway and so receives substantial visibility from passing traffic. Medford signed a $650,000 naming rights agreement over six years with U.S. Cellular so it was named the "U.S. Cellular Community Park." In addition, the city negotiated a $350,000 naming-rights agreement with Charter Communications for the "Charter Field" baseball field at U.S. Cellular Community Park. Charter supplies in-kind advertising and production services to offset costs associated with promoting recreation programs and services. In return, the company receives premium outfield and scoreboard signage, as well as additional signage within the park and the Santo Community Center gymnasium.

- King County, Washington, Parks and Recreation Department had a five-year partnership with Seattle-based Group Health that provided over $600,000 for their velodrome. Group Health received exclusive naming rights for the velodrome and title sponsorship for their popular Friday Night Racing Series.

- The city of Costa Mesa, California, partnered with Volcom, a local skateboard apparel company, to sponsor the operation and maintenance of a skateboard park in the city. Volcom is paying the city $30,000 each year for 10 years for naming rights, logo placement on the skate park bowls, a shade shelter constructed in the shape of their logo, the right to use the park for two weekends a year for events, and a link on the city website.

- The YMCA in Pittsburgh, Pennsylvania, entered into a naming rights agreement with locally-based PNC Bank Foundation for a new facility, which will contain several additional named elements.
    - The Reed Smith LLP law firm has purchased the naming rights to the Y's new swimming pool, which will be known as the Reed Smith Aquatics Center.
    - Massaro Corp., the Y contractor, bought the rights to the lobby, which will be called the Massaro Welcome Center.
    - Highmark will have the rights to the main exercise space on the second floor, which will be known as the Highmark Wellness Center.[30]

Naming rights at municipal sport facilities remain the exception rather than the rule, but in the last few years this form of sponsorship has grown exponentially at high school facilities.

The movement is perhaps most prominent in Texas, where an early pioneer was Midland ISD. They partnered with Grande Communications to put the company's name on its stadium in return for $1.2 million over 25 years. This was quickly surpassed in 2003 by Forney ISD whose new $4.4 million stadium was named Citibank

Stadium, replacing the previous Jackrabbit Stadium named after the school's mascot. In return for the naming rights, Citibank agreed to purchase the bonds used to finance the stadium at a discounted interest rate that saved the ISD $1 million over the 15-year life of the bonds. The revenues escalated yet again in the state in 2004 when Tyler ISD partnered with Trinity Mother Frances Health System, renaming its 14,000 seat Rose Stadium, Trinity Mother Frances Rose Stadium in return for $1.92 million over 12 years. When the new 10,000-seat stadium in Conroe ISD serving three high schools was opened in 2008, it was named Woodforest Bank Stadium in return for $1 million paid over 10 years by the bank. Examples in other states include:

- In Worcester, Massachusetts, Commerce Bank and Trust paid $1 million to help renovate Foley Stadium, now "Commerce Bank Field at Foley Stadium," where the city's five high schools play football, soccer, and lacrosse.
- Vernon Hills, Illinois, negotiated a $100,000, 20-year naming rights sponsorship of a high school field with local paint manufacturer Rust-Oleum Corp. Funds were used for the field's scoreboard, refreshment stand, lights, and other amenities. The company's name was displayed on a plaque on a pillar near the entrance to the stadium and in the press room.
- In Brooklawn, New Jersey, the Alice Costillo School sold naming rights for 20 years for its gym to ShopRite, the town's only supermarket, for $100,000. The funds will help pay for maintenance and operations of the gym.[30]

The moral, civic, and legal issues described in the following paragraphs that surface in debates over naming rights at high school sport facilities, for the most part also arise in the municipal sport facility context. Invariably, there are critics of such agreements who are concerned about over-commercializing the schools. For example, The Commercial Alert, a non-profit activist group objected: "One after another, schools across America are dedicating themselves not to role models, but to corporations. It is a sign in the decline in our own values that we name things not after our heroes or history, but after corporations with the deepest pockets. Instead of promoting character and honor, they are pushing products, and the self-indulgence of the commercial culture."[31]

It is argued by some that selling naming rights to public school facilities privatizes civic responsibility and makes taxpayers less likely to vote for school funding measures. Further, they suggest that this practice may exacerbate inter-school inequities since schools with a more "marketable" student body—most probably those located in affluent areas—are likely to be most attractive to corporate sponsors.[32]

Legal scholars warn of potential First Amendment pitfalls that may arise when public high schools solicit naming rights agreements: "Specifically schools might find it increasingly hard to reject undesirable sponsors—"bad name" sponsors, or those marketing undesirable products—without running afoul of the First Amendment" (p. 3).[32] They point out that naming rights are undoubtedly a form of "speech" which may limit schools' ability to reject sponsors based on their identity or message. The potential for such undesirable outcomes was illustrated by the Ku Klux Klan's successful court challenge which won it the right to be included in Missouri's Adopt-A-Highway program, much to the chagrin of the program's administration.[32] Schools might be confronted with similar challenges if the group seeking naming rights is a church or a mosque, or the National Rifle Association, or the Gay & Lesbian Alliance Against Deformation, or some other group with a controversial identity or message that schools would rather avoid endorsing.[33] Among potential commercial sponsors, the situation could arise if alcohol, sugary drinks, or fatty snack food brands sought the naming rights.

To this point, there have not been any reported cases of sponsors suing schools to force their names on to school sport facilities. However, the potential of these sponsorships to generate revenue for high school varsity athletic programs that are being forced to move to "pay to play" funding; the perceived potential value of naming rights sponsorships to corporate entities; and the strength of opposition to such commercialization make it likely this issue will both remain on the agenda and be controversial. Further, the conflicting views make it likely that rejected sponsors will sue alleging impermissible viewpoint discrimination and a violation of their First Amendment rights:

> Unfortunately, simply saying "no" to these sponsors may be more difficult than school boards expect. The selection of named sponsors raises concerns that can lead straight from the schoolhouse to the courthouse: Once a school has one named sponsor, other would-be sponsors may be able to claim a First Amendment right to participate, just as would-be speakers have a constitutional right to participate in other government-created forums (p. 1).[33]

The primary defensive action that high schools can take against such potential suits is to develop, and then carefully follow, written policy statements which incorporate viewpoint-neutral reasons to exclude undesirable sponsors: "Although this may not be a perfect antidote to all First Amendment challenges, it does insulate school boards against charges of viewpoint discrimination, which are probably the strongest First Amendment charges they will face (p. 15).[32]

THE POTENTIAL FOR CONTROVERSY

What's in a name? that which we call a rose

By any other word would smell as sweet

With these words Juliet Capulet tells Romeo Montague that a name is an artificial and meaningless convention, and that she loves the person who is called "Montague" not the Montague name. In some contexts, however, Shakespeare got it wrong because names do matter. They have power and meaning. A name is not merely a label, it is a shorthand for describing who or what someone or something is. If the entity bearing the name is important to people, then it follows that the name matters.

Changing a name changes the relationship with the thing being renamed. When a facility has a long-established, beloved heritage name, it is likely to be associated with fond memories stretching back across generations. If it is changed, many will feel a loss of ownership, continuity, and history. As a result, those involved in making such a change are likely to be subject to opprobrium, ridicule, and regarded with contempt by many. When the storied New York Yankees moved to their new stadium in 2009, their management recognized the power of the stadium's cultural meaning. Consequently, they avoided upsetting fans by retaining the "Yankee Stadium" moniker at their new site and resisting the temptation to sell naming rights at it. However, they did sell rights for entrances and concourses. Others have not been so wise. Consider the case of Newcastle United which has one of the most renowned, largest, and most passionate fan bases in the English Premier League:

- When Newcastle United was purchased by a new owner, he changed the team stadium's 119-year-old name from St. James' Park to SportsDirect.com@St. James' Park so it incorporated the name of the new owner's sports equipment company. This was greeted with massive outrage from all sections of the city. While no additional revenue accrued to the club from this naming right, the owner's intent was to use his company's name to showcase the potential of the stadium naming rights to other companies that might purchase them. His expectation was that the naming rights would sell for about $15 million annually. There was no interest. Indeed, the name become fodder for comedians' jokes and was subjected to national ridicule. The owner persevered. He attributed the lack of interest to companies wanting the opportunity to fully rebrand the stadium, rather than only to attach their name to St. James' Park. Accordingly, he changed the showcase name to Sports Direct Arena. The fans were even more intensely affronted, and were scathing and unstinting in their criticism. The end result was fan alienation and contempt for the owner; extensive and extended national and local negative publicity for his company; and creation of a toxic environment which destroyed any interest among potential stadium naming rights purchasers.

While well intentioned, the decision to name the new stadium for the NFL Denver Broncos for an investment management firm touched off a strong public reaction. When the stadium authority announced that the new stadium would be called "Invesco Stadium," fans led by a prominent businessman threatened a lawsuit to prevent the corporate naming agreement. The intent was to preserve the name "Mile High Stadium," the name of the old stadium to which fans had formed a strong emotional attachment and sense of community identification. The largest daily newspaper in Denver declared that it made an editorial decision not to reference Invesco in any mention of the new venue, and would refer to it only by its historical name, Mile High Stadium. The protracted controversy eventually was resolved by a compromise in which an agreement was reached to officially call the stadium, "Invesco Field at Mile High."

In a reflection of the criticism that arises in debates about naming rights at municipal and high school sport facilities, opponents of selling naming rights to public facilities in which professional teams play have argued there is a civic cost to having a public building named after a corporation:

The airport doesn't have a corporate name. Parks don't have corporate names. Bridges don't have corporate names. If, as political leaders and sports boosters claim, stadiums and arenas are components of our social and cultural infrastructure, then why not honor public heroes and heroines by naming our sports venues after them? (p. 482).[34]

Nevertheless, public concern over naming facilities for companies at professional franchise stadiums has receded in recent years as they have become common. The change in public sentiment was reflected in the renaming of Mile High Stadium in which a locally-based company, Sports Authority Inc., succeeded Invesco as the new naming rights partner. The board of the Metropolitan Football Stadium Authority voted unanimously to rename the Broncos home field, "Sports Authority Field at Mile High Stadium." The $120 million, 10-year agreement provoked no public backlash. Acceptance has been aided by many naming rights agreements being linked to new facilities. If a facility is new the heritage associations with it and the relationships of fans and community with it are much weaker.

In addition to being sensitive to fan sentiments, companies considering naming rights also have to scan the broader political environment. The challenge was illustrated by Citigroup's conundrum relating to its $400 million investment of $20 million a year for 20 years for the naming rights to Citi Field which was intended to make the company's name synonymous with New York baseball.

- The agreement was signed in 2006, but when the Great Recession arrived in 2008 Citigroup received a $306 billion bailout loan from the US Treasury to insure loans and asset-backed securities, and laid off 52,000 employees. Many in the media and the US Congress urged the company to "Scrap the deal with the stadium" and make sure you take care of these folks who have mortgages."[35] It was pointed out, "Even in the flush times during which it was signed, the deal seemed questionable. With high name recognition and a place among the world's banking leaders, Citigroup hardly needed the Citi name plastered on a ballpark to enhance itself" (p. 3).[36] The company's rationale for retaining the naming rights agreement was that it "provides an incredible platform to promote our world-class brand, enhance our relationship with current clients, attract new clients, and expand our considerable community efforts" (p. 3).[36] It was pointed out that "for a company as big as Citigroup, $20 million a year for naming rights is pocket change. Still, the spending is symbolic. It's on a baseball stadium in a gloomy economy, an investment that seems to thumb its nose at laid off workers (p. 3)."[36] Despite the criticism the naming rights agreement remained in place.

SUMMARY

At this time, three-fourths of major league sports facilities in North America have been corporately named, with the aggregate investment in these sponsorships exceeding $6 billion. The escalation in their value was exponential in the decade before the Great Recession of 2008. It was arrested by the poor economic conditions of that period, but subsequently re-emerged with several major agreements, led by the record-breaking

Farmers Insurance company's $600 million, 30-year agreement with AEG to name a proposed football stadium in downtown Los Angeles.

Corporations seek three major benefits from becoming naming rights partners: (a) 24/7/365 exposure; (b) the ability to use the venue relationship as a marketing platform to increase sales; and (c) the entertainment and hospitality opportunities provided by the sponsorship. The visibility provided corporations through their alignment with prominent sport venues is attractive to companies with little or no brand recognition. Increasingly, however, corporations have been attracted to naming rights sponsorships because of the substantial business-building opportunities they provide. Many agreements now include provisions that guarantee corporate naming rights partners opportunities to sell their products inside "their" venues.

Although the brand equity and sales benefits emanating from naming rights sponsorships make them attractive investment opportunities, teams hoping to sell venue rights face challenges. With over 75% of major venues already corporately named, there is a diminished prospect pool because a significant share of companies with both the interest and financial capacity have already committed to such sponsorships. Consequently, in recent years teams have increasingly shifted their focus from national brands to finding naming partners with a more "local" association. This has meant that many have had to settle for less generous terms, with respect to both the financial value and the length of the agreement. Most venue sponsorships in recent years have been for much shorter duration than those prior to the Great Recession. The uncertain economic conditions since that time have resulted in companies being reluctant to enter into extended naming rights contracts. Instead of 20- or 30-year agreements, most naming rights sponsorships are now no longer than 10 years in length.

While the four major U.S. sport leagues have not yet authorized naming rights on team jerseys, these are sold by MLS teams and are widely used in other countries. In the EPL, for example, Manchester United, Manchester City, Liverpool, and Chelsea have multi-year jersey naming rights for annual amounts of $65 million, $56 million, $40 million, and $40 million, respectively.

Colleges have become active participants in selling naming rights sponsorships to their stadiums and arenas. Their opportunities for doing this are constrained by existing facilities being named in perpetuity in honor of lead donors and opposition to continued expansion of the commercialization of college sports. Nevertheless, while the financial terms are modest compared to those negotiated by major league franchises, the incremental revenues make selling naming rights increasingly attractive to cash-strapped collegiate programs.

Like other forms of sponsorship, facility naming rights is percolating down to municipalities and high schools. Just as there was resistance and criticism of professional and college naming rights sponsorships in their formative years, so such debates now often arise at these local level facilities. The criticisms usually revolve around over-commercialization of city and high school facilities; abdication of civic responsibility in favor of corporate values; and legal challenges associated with conforming to the First Amendment while excluding "undesirable" sponsors.

Naming rights can be controversial, especially if they are being imposed on a facility that has a long-established, beloved heritage name. The loss of such a name translates to a loss of emotional ownership, continuity, and history to many fans and is likely to alienate them. Naming rights sales are much less controversial when they are attached to new facilities.

Endnotes

1. Associated Press. (2004, August 4). Anheuser-Busch buys Cardinals stadium rights. *USA Today*. Retrieved from http://usatoday30.usatoday.com/sports/baseball/nl/cardinals/2004-08-04-busch-stadium_x.htm

2. Naming Rights Deals, *Team Marketing Report* (1997). Chicago: IL, p. 63.

3. Mahony, D., & Howard, D. (2001). Sports business in the next decade. *Journal of Sport Management, 15*(4), 275–296.

4. Zoghby, J. (1999, November 1–7). Ericsson makes name with N.C. stadium. *SportsBusiness Journal*, p. 14.

5. Bertoni, S. (2011, February 4). When did Farmers commit $700 million to an NFL team that doesn't exist? *Forbes.com*. Retrieved from http://www.forbes.com/sites/stevenbertoni/2011/02/04/why-did-farmers-commit-700-million-to-an-nfl-team-that-doesnt-exist/

6. Howard, D., & Crompton, J. (2004). *Financing sport* (2nd ed.), Morgantown, WV: Fitness Information Technology.

7. Clark, J. M., Cornwell, T. B., & Pruitt, S. W. (2002, November/December). Corporate stadium sponsorships, signaling theory, agency conflicts, and shareholder wealth. *Journal of Advertising Research*, pp. 16–32.

8. Farmer, S. (2011, January 31). AEG, Farmers Insurance in naming rights deal for proposed NFL stadium. *Latimes.com*. Retrieved from http://articles.latimes.com/2011/jan/31/sports/la-sp-0201–la-nfl-20110201

9. Levy, K. (2011, October 19). Mercedes-Benz Superdome—worth it? Or worthless? *Forbes.com*. Retrieved from http://www.forbes.com/sites/keithlevy/2001/10/19/mercedesbenz

10. Why Cowboys can't sell naming rights. *Fan Nation*. Retrieved from www.fannation.com/truth_and_rumors/view/102674-why-cowboys-cant-sell-naming-rights

11. Kass, M. (2012, May 21). BMO Harris secures Bradley Center naming rights. *The Business Journal*. http://www.bizjournals.com/milwaukee/news/2012/05/21/Bmo-harris-secures-bradley-center-naming-rights.hmtl?page=all

12. Kils, M. (2012, August 10). Sports Authority makes a play to have its name on Broncos Stadium. *Denverpost.com*. Retrieved from http://www.denverpost.com/broncos/cl_18658353

13. Mitchell, T. (2010, July 28). How the EverBank-Jaguars deal was reached. *The Florida Times-Union*. Retrieved from http://jacksonville.com/sports/football/jaguars/2010-07-28/story/city-hall-prepares-give-4-million-show-support-jaguars

14. Man Utd deal takes shirt sponsorships to new heights (2012, August 3). *IBN Live*. Retrieved from http://ibnlive.in.com/news/man-utd-deal-takes-shirt-sponsorships-to-new-heights/278195-5-21.html

15. Day, J. (2005, January 20). Chelsea pays £24 million to drop Umbro. *The Guardian*.

15a. Sandomir, R. (2012, April 17). NBA takes a look at jersey sponsorship. *New York Times*.

Retrieved from http://www.nytimes.com/20
12/04/18/sports/basketball/nba-takes-a-look-
at-jersey-sponsorship.html?_r=0

16. Gorse, S, Chadwick, S., & Barton, N. (2010).
Entrepreneurship through sports marketing: A
case analysis of Red Bull in sport. *Journal of
Sponsorship*, *3*(4), 348–357.

17. Cushman, D. (2000, December). Air to the
throne. *SportsPro*, pp. 60–61.

18. Emmett, J. (2009, December). The mainstream strategy. *SportsPro*, pp. 56–59.

19. Schoenfeld, B. (2001, May 28–June 3). No
city name, just a happy sponsor. *SportsBusiness
Journal*, pp. 1, 38.

20. Rae, R. (2003, August 14). Villagers go in unlikely search of big city solutions. *The Guardian*.
Retrieved from http://www.guardian.co.uk
/football/2003/aug/14/sport.comment

21. Cohen, A. (1999, July). The naming game.
Athletic Business, pp. 37–43.

22. Teams search and fund new avenues of revenue from the naming rights of stadiums and
arenas sections. (2001, January). *Team Marketing Report*, *13*(4), pp. 1–2.

23. Blumenstyk, G. (1995). Georgia Tech and
McDonald's sign $5.5 million deal. *Chronicle
of Higher Education*, *XLI*(21), A44.

24. Tucker, J. (2000, December 26). Schools for
sale? *Oakland Tribune*, pp. 1, 13.

25. Workman, B. (1998, February 20). Stanford
seeks way to reverse trend of commercial sponsors. *San Francisco Chronicle*. Retrieved from
http://www.sfgate.com/bayarea/article/BAY
-AREA-FOCUS-In-the-Corporate-Arena-3012
844.php

26. Post no billboards. (2000, September/Octo-
ber). *Stanford Magazine*, p. 3.

27. Miller, A. (1995, November 17). It pays to play
name game. *Columbus Dispatch*, p. C12.

28. Lee, J. (2001, August 8–13). Colleges feature
fewer chances, more hassle. *SportsBusiness Journal*, p. 14.

29. Tanner, J. (n.d.). Corporations go back to
school: Colleges attract naming rights deals.
Marquette National Sports Law Institute. Retrieved from https://law.marquette.edu/na
tional-sports-law-institute/corporations-go-back
-school-colleges-attract-naming-rights-deals

30. Octagon Inc. & Civic Entertainment Group
LLC. (2010). *Fairfax County Park Authority
sponsorship marketing plan*. Fairfax County VA:
County Park Authority.

31. Johnson, M. A. (2010). Branded! Public schools
court corporate sponsors. Retrieved from
http://www.msnbc.msn.com/id/38524061/ns
/us_news

32. Blocher, J. (2007). School naming rights and
the First Amendment's perfect storm. *The
Georgetown Law Journal*, *96*(1), 1–57.

33. Blocher, J. (2006, Fall). Selling the name on
the schoolhouse gate: The First Amendment
and the sale of public school naming rights.
School Law Bulletin, 1–15.

34. Weiner, J. (1999). *Stadium games: Fifty years of
big league greed and bush league boondoggles*. Minneapolis, MN: University of Minnesota Press.

35. Nasaw, D. (2008, November 25). Baseball stadium named for Citigroup faces scrutiny. *The
Guardian*. Retrieved from http://www.guar
dian.co.uk/world/2008/nov/25/citigroup-new
-york-mets-stadium

36. Sandomir, R. (2008, July 20). Citigroup puts
its money where its name will be. *The New
York Times*, p. 3.

5

Corporate Decisions Associated With Sponsorship Partnerships

Sport managers are most likely to succeed in soliciting sponsorship partners if a marketing approach is adopted, which means that they look at their sponsorship opportunities through the eyes of the companies from which they seek to attract investment. This approach is illustrated by the well-known marketing aphorism, "To sell Jack Jones what Jack Jones buys, you have to see Jack Jones through Jack Jones' eyes." The extent to which sport managers are able to see their opportunities through the eyes of potential sponsors, and tailor their sponsor opportunities to meet the needs of business, is likely to determine their success. For this reason, this chapter focuses on corporate decisions associated with sponsorship partnerships.

Companies are required to make four major decisions to optimize the effectiveness of their investments in sport sponsorships. If sport managers are cognizant of these decisions, then they will be better prepared to respond to them during the solicitation process which is discussed in Chapter 9. A company's first task is to frame the benefits it seeks (which were generically described in Chapter 1) in the operational form of specific objectives. The second task is to identify properties which are a good "fit" with the company in terms of both congruency of function or image, which was discussed in Chapter 2, and target markets. Third, a decision has to be made on length of the sponsorship commitment. The final requirement is to develop the leveraging activities that will be implemented using the sponsorship platform.

SPONSORSHIP OBJECTIVES

Too often there is a tendency by both companies and properties to overlook the need for specific objectives and go directly to address the fit and leveraging issues. This is a mistake. Frequently, answers to the question, "What are we trying to achieve?" are multifaceted and complex. Many people are likely to have responsibility for leveraging a sponsorship and their efforts will be diffused if there is not a small set of focused, measurable outcome objectives.

Specific objectives are the mechanism through which a sponsor clearly communicates its expectations to a property. These direct the property where to focus its efforts in assisting its business partner to succeed. Both partners need the clarity on what the company is seeking to accomplish, which specific objectives provide. Without them, there are no benchmarks against which performance can be measured to determine the extent to which investments are successful. The importance of specific objectives was expressed by one company's leading sponsorship executive in these terms:

> The relationship should operate as a partnership and for this to happen both parties must enter with clear sponsorship objectives. Both parties should come to the table with an understanding of how to forge a strong brand association, how this will contribute to these broader objectives, and how the relationship should function including roles and resource inputs. Without this you cannot generate the kind of synergies and collaboration the relationship offers and if you don't do it early on it can be difficult to rectify the situation. (p. 324)[1]

Establishing clear objectives enables sponsors to solicit specific commitments from properties on exactly what they will do and what resources they will commit to assist the sponsor in accomplishing its goals. Everyone knows and agrees what success will look like and how it should be measured. It places the onus on sport event managers to contribute their ideas on how the business platform might be leveraged. It has been found that the failure of sponsorship partnerships often can be traced to the failure of both parties (but in particular the sponsor) to clearly and formally articulate their expectations for the relationship and what they desired from their partner.[1]

Chapter 1 described the six major benefits that companies may seek and multiple dimensions of each of them were listed in Exhibit 1.1. However, these are only generalized goals and those which a company elects to pursue have to be operationalized in specific terms. The key criterion for effective objectives is that they should be S.M.A.R.T.—specific, measurable, achievable, results-oriented, and time-bounded. Most sponsors have a general idea of what they expect their investment to deliver. Unfortunately, relatively few express their expectations in S.M.A.R.T. terms, but this proportion is increasing as demands for accountability accentuate.

There is a big difference between, "The objective is to increase customer awareness of Brand K" and "The objective is to increase customer awareness in our target markets from 40% to 60% in the month immediately after the event." If the benefits sought are discussed in *specific* terms, then it removes fuzziness and the lack of operational focus that accompanies generalizations.

Measurable objectives facilitate evaluation and accountability since only if objectives are measurable can the outcome from a sponsorship be evaluated. Items that sponsors may seek to measure include:

- Sales figures
- Sales growth
- Quantity and quality of media coverage

- Propensity to purchase
- Number of events held
- Number of new names in the database

- Number of attendees
- Customer opinion and satisfaction
- Sponsorship awareness
- Brand awareness
- Brand image
- Prompted and unprompted brand recall

- Number of sales leads generated
- Target profit or revenue
- Advance ticket sales
- Wholesale ticket sales
- Number and quality of cross promotions
- Audience propensity to attend the next sponsored event[2]

The *achievable* and *results-oriented* criteria serve to crystallize executive thinking since managers are forced to consider the limitations of a sponsorship and examine carefully whether of not it is the best vehicle for achieving the specified objective. Finally, *time-boundedness* influences decisions relating to the optimum length of commitment for a sponsorship. Examples of the difference between S.M.A.R.T. and generic objectives are given in Table 5.1.

It was noted in Chapter 3 that sponsors' emphasis is extending beyond awareness, interest, and brand equity to an expectation that sponsorships will contribute more directly to immediate sales. If the goal is to increase sales, the development of S.M.A.R.T. objectives will require the following questions be addressed:

- What type of sales—new customers, incremental, loyalty, up selling?
- Through what distribution channels—retail, web, smartphone, tablet, social media?
- To which target markets?
- During what time frame—length of the sponsorship or further out?
- From what benchmark?
- How are the critical success factors to be measured and determined?[2]

Table 5.1. Non-SMART and SMART Objectives	
Non-SMART	**SMART**
Increase Sales	Create incremental sales of 12% over the benchmark of $400,000 per week during the 6-weeks promotional period as determined by retailer returns.
Develop database	Develop a database of no less than 2,000 qualified prospects as determined by salary level, age range, professional and family status, and current life insurance products held.
Gain media coverage	Achieve a minimum of 10 news announcements in national, local, and regional media. Awareness of the sponsors linkage to the event will increase by 15% when pre-event recall is compared to past-event recall measured 4 weeks after the event is over.
Demonstrate good corporate citizenship	Increase positive public opinion about the organization's commitment to the local community from 45% to over 65% as determined by an annual public opinion survey.

Sponsorship objectives have to fit within broader goals of a company's overall communications strategy. At Cadillac, for example, a sport sponsorship investment's objectives must specifically contribute to one of two broad goals:

> Two goals dominate our marketing strategy at Cadillac. A specific sport sponsorship investment's objectives must specifically contribute to one of these broad goals. One is to impact our narrow and demographically specific target market with direct product exposure that will result in immediate sales. The second goal, though more abstract, is equally important—to reinforce and enhance Cadillac's image among the general public—to use our name as a metaphor for excellence: "The Cadillac of its class." (p. 4).[3]

THE FIT BETWEEN A SPORT PROPERTY
AND A SPONSOR'S BRAND

A company will require that any property it considers be a good "fit" with its brand. The question of fit is primarily a company's responsibility rather than a sport property's because, obviously, the company has the best understanding of its investment objectives. Almost all companies engaging in sponsorship find it most efficient to seek a fit with an existing sport property. However, a few have concluded that the most effective vehicle for securing a good fit is to develop and own a new sport property. Creation and ownership of an event establishes a company's "authenticity" with event participants, making it easier to emotionally bond with them. That is, the company is perceived to be involved, engaged, committed and giving something back to the sport, rather than simply buying in as a sponsor to exploit it for commercial gain.

Creating an event is a much more demanding option, but it has the advantage that it can be specifically tailored to a company's needs. Red Bull pioneered this strategy and subsequently the company has continued to exploit it extensively. Their development of it described in Exhibit 4.1.[4] As a company's needs change, the company as owner and title sponsor is able to change the event to accommodate the changed needs. An example is given in Exhibit 5.1[7].

An intermediate position between sponsoring a well-established event and owning a newly created sport property is to seek out an unproven, low profile event that is potentially a good fit and invest substantially in it to boost its profile and status. If this strategy is adopted, then the company should structure its payment as a form of investment finance rather than a straight sponsorship fee. This will entail retaining some rights in the event either in perpetuity or for a long period of time. This will ensure that at the end of the first contract period, the property does not demand a price many times the original fee, reflecting the event's new high profile status, when it was the company's investment that created much of the added value.

A good fit between a company and a property is determined by two elements. First, the brand's functional or image congruity with the sport property which was discussed in Chapter 2. Second, the extent to which the target markets of the brand and the property are compatible.

Exhibit 5.1

iShares Develops and Owns an Event to Meet its Sponsorship Goals

The iShares Cup is an Extreme Sailing Series held at iconic venues close to shore. The "stadium" concept of racing accommodates tens of thousands of spectators. iShares is a financial management and investment company specializing in the fast growing Exchange Traded Funds (ETF) market. It has a strong retail presence in the US, but wanted to expand to Europe and other continents by focusing on professional investors. Their spokesperson confirmed: "We have been able to construct the event to meet our business needs. Our contract gives us real ownership of the circuit in terms of where it goes, the venues and identity of the competing teams, allowing us to really shape the property. It is easy to badge something, but you can really meet your business goals if you can choose the right partners and build some-

thing from the ground up. It has a strong appeal with the European markets we are currently targeting" (p. 19).

Reflecting its European thrust, a "grand prix of sailing" is hosted at a core of European venues, for example, in the UK, France, Germany, Switzerland, The Netherlands, Italy, and Portugal, but it is gradually expanding in accordance with iShares' business plan. So, one of the series' unique selling points is that during each race each boat will carry a VIP guest who will be on board for an adrenalin pumping race, giving iShares, and companies sponsoring the individual boats themselves, an exceptional opportunity to offer exciting client entertainment experiences. "It is simply the best hospitality platform we could have hoped for," the spokesperson said.

Figure 5.1 displays these two elements on vertical and horizontal axes which creates a grid, Those sport properties whose audiences are similar in demographic and lifestyle profile to the brand's target market *and* whose image or function is congruent with the brand are likely to be considered "Viable" (cell 1). Those with a dissimilar target profile

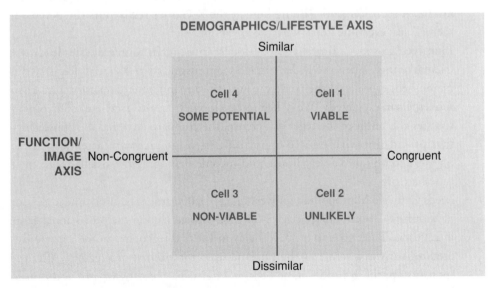

Figure 5.1. Grid of Outcomes Derived from Plotting the Sponsor's Brand and the Sport Property's Images with Audience Profiles.

and non-congruent image or function are "Non-Viable" (cell 3). If the brand's function or image is congruent with that of the property but the audience profile is not, then it is an "Unlikely" candidate (cell 2). In cell 4, the target audiences are compatible, but neither the function nor the image of the brand is obviously congruent. It was noted in Chapter 2 that sometimes articulating the non-obvious linkage between brand and property may be effective in creating a fit, so sponsors may see "Some Potential" in those situations.

Congruency of Target Markets

The target market of the company and target market of the sport event must match. It is important to be able to say to a company, "Your clients are our clients." When a company sponsors a property it is essentially buying an audience and it needs to know as much as possible about that audience. The emphasis placed on compatibility of target audiences makes it imperative for sport managers to undertake research which delineates the audience profile of their event. The most common type of match is on the basis of sociodemographics. For example, the U.S. women's soccer team successfully attracts sponsors which are seeking to establish a relationship with children and their mothers. A spokesperson for Toys'R'Us Inc. explained: "If you saw any of the World Cup games, it was substantially kids and families at the stadiums. When the event has that sort of appeal and we are the nation's top toy retailer, it's one of those things that makes way too much sense not to happen" (p. 7).[8] The following examples further illustrate sociodemographic fits:

- The U.S. Navy sponsored the summer X Games because it was an effective vehicle for targeting 17–24 year-old males. It had two recruiting booths and demonstration booths on site. They made contact with hundreds of potential future sailors. A recruiter said, "Being here at the X Games really puts the Navy out there. It lets everyone know what we are about."[9]
- Bluegreen Corp. is a timeshares developer whose main source of sales leads was telemarketing. When the Federal Trade Commission's Do Not Call Registry was established, this closed the company's access to many potential customers. Their spokesperson explained: "We've had to develop new face-to-face marketing opportunities as a result of the registry." Hence, the company invested in sponsorships that provided it with on-site opportunities to interact with attendees in the $50,000 to $85,000 a year household income demographic to talk about their timeshare projects.[10]
- Leeds Carnegie Metropolitan University has 41,000 students. It became a sponsor of Yorkshire Cricket Club, perhaps the most storied club in the professional game in England. Their ground at Headingley in Leeds is legendary in the sport and is used regularly as a venue by the England team for international games. After the sponsorship, the ground's name became "Carnegie Headingley". In addition to hosting cricket in the summer, the ground is used by two major league professional rugby teams in the winter. The city of Leeds has a large sub-population whose ethnic roots are in India and Pakistan. The university sought to attract

more international students, especially from Asia, Australia, and New Zealand. Their spokesman explained: "It gives us an 'in'. We do have a lot of students with Asian connections and obviously cricket is enormous in Pakistan and India. Our chances of attracting them to study at Carnegie can only be enhanced by the opportunities we can offer them, which will soon include the chance to study at Headingley itself.[11]

In some instances the demographic fit may be further qualified by the need for there to be a geographic fit:

- 7-Eleven has 5,300 retail stores within the US. It is headquartered in Dallas, but has over 400 and 250 stores in the Chicago and Miami areas, respectively. It wanted to connect with 18–44 year-old men and drive them into its stores, since they were the company's primary target market. Its research showed that the passion of these male customers was for pro sports. Accordingly, the company invested sponsorships in the MLB Chicago Clubs and White Sox, NBA Chicago Bulls, and the NFL Chicago Bears; in the NBA Miami Heat; and in the NBA Dallas Mavericks and the Texas Motor Speedway which is located in Fort Worth. These three geographic areas reflected those areas in which 7-Eleven had the most stores.[12]

An increasing number of companies are concluding that the availability of sociodemographic data relating to a sport event is not sufficient for them to make good decisions about the degree of fit. One respected commentator observed, "The information that sponsors generally gather—age, gender, marital status, education level, and income—is not what matters in determining what to sponsor. Does knowing your customer is a 32-year-old female tell you that she's passionate about skiing?" (p. 2).[14] Sponsors want to know the lifestyles and buying habits of those attending the event and those watching it on media. They seek evidence that there is a propensity by fans and viewers to purchase their products and services. Thus, for example, a consumer electronics manufacturer is more likely to be receptive to a sponsorship proposal if a property can demonstrate its audience purchases electronic gadgets much more frequently than the general public.

Global Brands' Strategy is the adidas group's division responsible for all the product and marketing functions of the adidas and Reebok brands. Its recognition of the importance of basing sponsorship on lifestyles is described in Exhibit 5.2.[15]

The basic premise of investigating lifestyles is the more that is known and understood about them, the more effectively a company can communicate with them. Lifestyle marketing targets consumers based upon their lifestyles and interests. The illustration in Exhibit 5.3 shows how lifestyle information relating to people's food and drink preferences was used by Bassing America to persuade new companies to become sponsors.[16] Lifestyle research seeks to draw more recognizable "live" human portraits of an audience than is possible with sociodemographics. A spokesperson for the Lincoln Financial Group which invested in a sponsorship of the America's Cup, the most prestigious yachting event, explained: "We look at sports as a key aspect of the 'lifestyle segment' of our marketing program, and we associate with shows and events that appeal to their interests. The marketing strategy is really a lifestyle-oriented strategic view where

Exhibit 5.2

Global Brands Strategy: Recognition of the Role of Lifestyles

Global Brands is a division of the adidas group, responsible for all the product and marketing functions and long-term development of the adidas and Reebok brands. Their strategic plan is based on five key global lifestyle trends.

"The consumer is at the heart of everything we do. This is the first and most important realization, and we must adhere to it to deliver long-term success. To be successful across consumer segments, we acknowledge that a strategy of mass production or mass marketing is no longer sufficient. Only by identifying and understanding consumers' buying habits, their fitness level, their motivations and goals for doing sport, and their individual lifestyles, can we create meaningful products, services, and experiences that build a lasting impression. In this respect, we have identified five key global trends which will be important to address with our brands and sub-brands over the next five years."

• **Fit for life:** Sport is no longer just about competing and winning. Sport is becoming more embedded in consumers' everyday lifestyles. Motivations and goals are becoming more holistic, relating to fun, socializing, and quality of life.	• **You are what you know and what you do:** Society is embracing a life-long learning attitude, and placing more emphasis on what we know and do versus what we have and where we come from.
• **Celebrating individuality:** Consumers increasingly fulfill their desire to differentiate from one another by being more creative—on the one hand mixing and matching products and services they need, and on the other hand seeking personalized offerings tailored for them.	• **Together is better:** There is an increasing need for meaningful social interaction, both online and offline, as consumers become more mobile, and the rise of digital technologies makes it easier for them to connect with like-minded people.

• **Back to basics:** For everyday life, products and services are desired to be simple and authentic, making consumers' lives easier, rather than more complicated. There is a growing interest in outdoor activities, reflecting the desire to reconnect and be in tune with nature.

you understand the lifestyle of your target audience" (p. 12).[17] Major companies are likely to know the lifestyle characteristics of their consumers. Before signing a sponsorship with a property, many of them will sample their consumers to ask what attribute they associate with the sport property to ensure the match is strong.

• An executive responsible for Toyota's luxury car model, Lexus, explained why they competed so strongly with Cadillac for title sponsorship of the Senior PGA Tour Series: "We did a lot of research on what our potential customers do in their leisure time. They go to art, they go to theaters, they play golf. We want Lexus to be there as part of their environment" (p. 16).[18]

• Subaru's research showed that primary passions of its buyers were winter sports, gardening, and motor sports, so the company invested in sponsorships in those areas. More recently it found that a threshold number of new buyers' interests were in running and yoga, so properties in these areas were added to its portfolio. Their spokeswoman stated: "Our strategy is to support activities that Subaru own-

Exhibit 5.3

How Bassing America Identified Potential Sponsors for Its Amateur Fishing Tournaments

Drawing from its 55,000 members, Bassing conducts an annual survey at its spring events. In a typical survey, 75% of participants in its amateur fishing tournaments completed the four-page questionnaire that included questions about product usage. Bassing used the results to target new sponsors.

They discovered, for example, that 67% drank liquor and 61% cited bourbon as their liquor of choice. After analyzing brand preference and researching the industry, Bassing targeted two bourbons for proposals. Neither brand was a category leader; they were brands that Bassing felt could gain market share by sponsoring their events.

Within a few weeks, favorable responses were received from both. Bassing met with one and held the other on the sidelines. After two successful meetings, they were thrown a curve. The company's management wanted to use the tournaments to promote their rye brand instead. Bassing reminded them that the research showed only 8% of their liquor-drinking members chose rye, but they were determined. Bassing declined the offer and broke off talks because

they believed the sponsorship was doomed to fail. They contacted the other bourbon brand, George Dickel Tennessee Sippin' Whiskey, and signed a contract and promotional package at the first meeting.

Another question on the survey that helped Bassing obtain a sponsor was, "Do you eat while fishing?" It was followed by: "If yes, what?" Seventy-eight percent of respondents said they ate while fishing and 38% wrote in Vienna sausage. Bassing researched Vienna sausage makers and found only one brand had ample distribution within their tournament territory. They made a presentation to that brand, Amour Star Canned Meats, but were turned down because they missed the company's budget cycle. The following year an agreement was signed.

This type of survey can be conducted by all sport organizations. They could conduct on-site interviews themselves or hire a research firm. After two or three surveys, a definite mainstream customer lifestyle is likely to emerge. The organization is then in a strong position to systematically approach a prospective sponsor with a niche or target for its product or service.

ers are passionate about. That won't change . . . one of the things we have found is that Subaru owners collect experiences over possessions. We want to be a part of as many of their experiences as we can."[19]

However, superficial lifestyle matches can be misleading as the following vignette illustrates:

- A premium whisky brand made a decision to sponsor motorsports based on research that showed a high percentage of whiskey drinkers among fans of the sport. When results from the sponsorship were disappointing, additional research into the purchasing habits and lifestyles of racing fans was commissioned. It revealed that they were much more likely to purchase non-premium brands and drank whisky only on special occasions. In direct opposition to the sponsor brand's positioning, they were more likely to drink whiskey as a shot or mixed with soft drinks. Thus, it should have targeted its racing sponsorship at building loyalty among the niche audience of its consumers to be found in the suites and skyboxes at race tracks instead of trying to convert the fans in the grandstands.[19a]

Length of Commitment

There is a general consensus that for sponsorship to be effective there should be a relatively long-term commitment with three years sometimes being advanced as the minimum desirable period. A thriving partnership depends on mutual trust between the parties. Real trust, beyond verbal platitudes, only comes from familiarity, chemistry, and actions accumulated over time as a result of working together. Short-term commitments do not provide adequate time to exploit and leverage a sponsorship. It usually takes longer to establish a linkage between the sport event and a sponsor's brand in a target market's mind, and this linkage is key to achieving the benefits being sought. As a sponsor's relationship with a property lengthens the cognitive association of brand awareness becomes more established, and the emphasis of the sponsor will shift from awareness building towards establishing an emotional connection with consumers which will strengthen brand equity.[20] A one-off or short-term commitment could hope to establish only a tentative linkage which is likely to dissipate quickly. It has been observed:

> If a link to a sponsored property has successfully been created, it is wasteful to walk away from that property. Long-lasting sponsorships will logically have a stronger link, require less investment to create, and have an impact over a longer time period. If a sponsorship is lost because there was nothing (legally or morally) that tied the property to the sponsor, the investment will be wasted. Worse, some of the sponsored property's sought-after associations might become owned by a competitor. As a result, it is very useful to obtain an agreement to have the right to return to the sponsorship in subsequent years. (p. 220)[21]

The typical evolution of a sponsorship has been described in the following terms:

> The first year will be spent learning about the event or activity, making contacts (and probably quite a few mistakes), and finding your way in this new area. The second will start to show the potential you are hoping for, while the third should, if you have done your work correctly, see the benefits accrue, the audience accept your presence and motives, and the media to be comfortable with linking you with the activity (p. 124)[22]

In contrast to a short-term linkage, a long-term commitment may leave an enduring legacy (i.e., create a value that extends beyond the actual sponsorship). In Chapter 2, it was noted that long-term memory is very durable, so the strength of association is likely to decay slowly. This means that when a long-term sponsor is replaced by another company, the replaced sponsor is likely to continue to be associated with the sport property in consumers' minds. This residual relationship confirms the value of committing to a long-term agreement.[23] Tracking studies have repeatedly reported instances where past long-term sponsors are credited as having an association with an event which they ceased to sponsor many years previously:

- Carling, a brand of beer, was a long-time sponsor of the English Premier League and it used the sponsorship as a platform for its entire promotional campaign.

Given the strong associative links it forged in the minds of the English population when it exited its sponsorship, it could still use football as its marketing platform without being the sponsor of the Premiership. This involved sponsorship agreements with individual teams, major media links with print and broadcast outlets, and public relations activities.[24]

A corollary is that some of the brand equity that incoming sponsors following long-term predecessors are seeking will not accrue. Implications of this are that (i) incoming sponsors should plan to establish a long-term sponsorship of their own with a view to accruing similar residual benefits and (ii) they should be prepared to spend considerable amounts in activation and leveraging the sponsorship to supplant the previous relationship in people's minds.

The enduring relationship is likely to be especially strong if the former and replacement sponsors are competitors in the same product class.[23] The similarity of the two sponsors makes it difficult for the replacement brand to dominate over the memory of the former sponsor. It has been suggested that in these cases, the key to creating a link that is distinct from the earlier sponsor will be to develop a unique articulation platform that strengthens a link between some characteristics that the replacement sponsor has that the former sponsor does not.[25]

There is considerable evidence that companies can cultivate a "first-mover" advantage in sponsorship.[26] That is, the first sponsor establishes a large amount of goodwill with a passionate sport audience and that audience continues to associate the company with the event, even after it has terminated the arrangement. Obviously, the longer the relationship endures, the stronger it is. It has been reported that "Once such an advantage had been established, it reduced the incentive for a competitor to become involved" (p. 125).[26] First-movers in sponsorship appear to be able to create barriers to entry for potential competitors who may subsequently seek the sponsorship. One manager reported:

> "I have a lot of respect for [the competitor]: They've stayed the course with [ice] hockey for years and years, and they own that sport, from minor hockey, all the way up to the NHL, on a very tangible basis." He also revealed that his company's attempts to become involved with the same sport had resulted in only a 4% awareness of association among consumers, despite "spending a lot of money on the program." (p. 125)[26]

Reasons for Ending the Relationship

Although long-term relationships have advantages, it is likely that companies initially will commit for three years, review the results, and then decide whether or not to renew. Partnerships between organizations end because of either predisposing factors or precipitating events.[27] *Predisposing factors* are inherent, pre-existing conditions that doom the partnership from the outset. They may emanate from such factors as poor interpersonal chemistry among the individuals responsible for operationalizing the sponsorship; lack of expertise, engagement, or commitment by one or both partners; or ambiguities in the contract that resulted in the parties having different expectations about actions or outcomes.

Thus, a primary reason for sponsors terminating their investments is the lack of effort and imagination shown by properties in leveraging the partnership. Too often their contributions are limited to facilitating or enabling sponsors to implement activation, and policing to protect them from on-site ambushing. Their definition of a cooperative alliance sometimes equates "joint effort" to efficient account servicing.[1] While companies' perspectives of sponsorship have evolved from viewing it as a communication vehicle to recognizing its potential as a strategic business platform, the perspective of many sport property managers has not similarly evolved. A senior executive of a sponsoring company expressed his frustration at this passiveness:

> We use sponsorship to build the brand and create sales over time and we came to the conclusion that there was much more that could be achieved and the relationship would work best if we made far better use of each others' unique resources and co-activated. For example, to conduct joint promotion to sell more merchandise, ours and theirs, using the strength of our distribution channels in capital cities where they wish to grow the game. We also saw great opportunity for joint product development and joint product launches. And this required much more planning and strategizing. There was collaboration but not on any substantive or systematic level, certainly not relative to the opportunities. In the end they were happy playing a very limited role and this placed us and the relationship in an untenable position. (p. 326)[1]

Another executive explaining why an agreement was terminated stated: "We really upped the ante, investing more, taking more risks, uncovering more opportunities and despite benefiting greatly from this [the property] did not really change their behavior." (p. 327)[1]

It has been suggested that a lack of reciprocation and responsiveness by sport properties sometimes is attributable to "the 'success breeds failure' syndrome in strategic management—[properties] continue to repeat practices that have been successful in the past (in this case sell and serve sponsorship) despite changes in the marketplace rendering the approach unsatisfactory" (p. 326).[1] The sponsors' desires for more active collaboration from properties requires more engagement from them in joint research, planning, promotion, activism, new business development, and the merging of relationship assets such as databases. If properties fail to respond in a substantive way, then sponsors are likely to go elsewhere.

Precipitating events are those that create pressures for a change in the relationship. There are four precipitating events that may lead to sponsorship agreements not being renewed, even if the results have met expectations. First, market conditions or a company's management may change leading to changes in its marketing strategy:

- Ford Motor Co. of Canada dropped its sponsorship of the MLB Toronto Blue Jays after 10 years because its corporate marketing objectives changed. While the property continued to deliver plenty of impressions, good awareness scores, and desirable hospitality opportunities, the company had shifted its overall marketing focus to women and younger buyers. A spokesman said, "There was value there, but with a more youthful skew to our models, and with women buying 52% of our cars, it no longer made sense to spend a lot of money on a property that speaks to older men" (p. 4).[28]

Vodafone was a UK-based business and its initial efforts were focused on developing the UK market. When its business expanded into other countries, then the change in target market emphasis resulted in a shift in its sponsorships. Vodafone's chief marketing executive explained:

> When we started with Manchester United, Vodafone was still largely a UK-based business with a growing set of international interests. Manchester United fitted very well at that point as a very big sporting brand, a UK-based team with quite a good international fan base. It fitted us at that point of time. However, because the business focus shifted we terminated the Manchester United deal with two years still to run, and signed a three-year deal to become a partner of the Champions League. The Champions League offered full European exposure and a wider global marketing platform. It is part of the evolution from a UK-based business to a multi-national one.[13]

A second reason why investment in a successful sponsorship may not be renewed is a reduction in the impact or loss of conscious association of a sponsor with the event. For example, long-term sponsors for whom hospitality is an important benefit often feel obligated to invite most of the same customers to avoid offending them, which reduces its impact and makes it difficult for a company to realize incremental benefits.

The third reason is the substantial costs of some sponsorships that have made it challenging for companies to establish enduring relationships. For example, NASCAR sponsorships now exceed $20 million for a year and with leveraging costs this figure becomes much higher, Hence, the days of race fans associating one driver with one sponsor and one car over the course of a season have withered away. Indeed, fewer than 20% of NASCAR teams now have the same sponsor for a whole season. Most sponsors now commit for only a few races and this fragmentation creates clutter. This reduced longevity also reflects the general shift in sponsorship emphasis away from brand awareness towards product trial and sales. Brands increasingly use the NASCAR platform to create excitement at point-of-sale stands and retailer based promotions. One executive explained:

> It's all about programming and ROI, not about awareness or consumer engagement. Sponsors get their one-off have a photo shoot with the driver and they've got their point-of-sale material. They're looking to get what they need for less money, so one or two rides might be all they want. There's no conversation with the consumer, it's all about the retailer. (p. 16)[29]

Finally, like all products and brands, it has to be recognized that sponsorships have a natural lifecycle, The only way to be certain when a sponsorship is no longer viable is to undertake continuous measurement to ascertain when it is no longer cost-effective in meeting the sponsorship's objectives. When a company decides to withdraw from a sponsorship, it should be morally, and preferably contractually, obligated to give the sport property ample time to find a replacement, in order to pre-empt any criticism that may be forthcoming from ending a relationship.

LEVERAGING THE SPONSORSHIP PLATFORM

The term *leverage* is used to describe "all sponsorship-linked marketing communications and activities collateral to the sponsorship investment" (p. 638).[30] The term *platform* means that sponsorship of a sport event provides a central theme around which a company can focus, and integrate an array of different elements that leverage its investment. The sponsorship payment gives a company the right to exploit the sport event (i.e., it buys the platform). Brands have to leverage their sponsorship, rather than simply announce it. Leveraging the platform involves developing and implementing a plan that will effectively accomplish the exploitation.

Unlike advertising, sponsorship does not deliver messages communicating *why* a brand should be purchased. If a large audience is aware of the name but lacks an understanding of the brand's distinctive qualities, then the sponsorship will be limited in what it can accomplish, It needs to be complemented by an array of elements that amplify the implied message. The purchase of property rights is the beginning of a sponsorship process, not the end. Unless a company invests in resources to leverage the sponsorship platform, it is likely to have wasted its investment. Indeed, as sponsorship has matured, there has been a tendency for companies to commit to fewer sponsorships, but to spend more in support activities that leverage those sponsorships.

Leveraging a sponsorship platform has cost implications. The sponsorship fee represents only part of a company's total investment. The associated leveraging costs incurred to optimize a sponsorship's impacts are likely to be substantial. The sponsorship literature is replete with recommendations on what should be the ratio of leverage spending to the sponsorship fee. The International Events Group (IEG) conducts an annual survey of over 100 properties and they report the average ratio over the past decade has fluctuated between $1.30 and $1.90 being spent on leverage for every $1 in sponsorship rights fees. These averages are derived from a fairly large number of sponsors, so they hide wide variations among them. Indeed, while 12% of the companies in IEG's survey reported a leverage ratio of 4:1 or more, 39% reported 1:1 or less.[31]

Ratios are based on the rights fee that is paid, but their use as benchmarks is conceptually flawed because there is no obvious relationship between the fee paid and the leveraging activities emanating from the sponsorship.[32] For example, if the fee increased by 50%, there is no reason why the cost of leveraging should increase 50% if it has been successful in achieving the company's objectives at its preciously budgeted figure. If rights fees rise substantially, then adherence to fixed ratios can result in leveraging costs that are unsustainable for no reason. Indeed, after experience with an array of leveraging elements, it is likely that some will be discarded as being ineffective. In this case, the leveraging budget may decrease without any adverse impact on accomplishing the sponsorship's objectives. Such a decrease in costs will lead to an increase in ROI. Thus, adopting a fixed ratio makes no sense. Instead, the question should be asked, "In what leveraging elements should the company invest to accomplish its sponsorship objectives?" and the budget should be based on responses to that question.

While the leveraging investment required to support a sponsorship may be substantial, it may not require a company to make additional investment. The sponsorship platform often provides an opportunity to refocus, redirect, and better integrate the use of existing resources, so sponsorship may be regarded as an expeditious vehicle for making more effective use of existing funds.

Leveraging elements can be classified into two categories: Nonactivational and activational (or activation for short). Nonactivational communications are defined as "communications that promote the sponsorship association, but that may be passively processed by the sponsorship audience." In contrast, activation is defined as "communications that promote the engagement, involvement, or participation of the sponsorship audience with the sponsor" (p. 639).[30] Both types of leveraging are discussed in the following sections.

Nonactivational Leveraging

Nonactivational leveraging includes such elements as onsite signage and banners, T-shirt identification, information about the sponsorship on the company and property websites, and sponsor name mentions in broadcasts. However, the major nonactivational leveraging vehicle has been the traditional media. IEG's survey of over 100 companies engaged in sponsorship noted, "Sponsors are letting go of some of the more traditional less engaging ways to communicate their partnerships." The survey found, for example, that only 51% used on-site signage, while the proportion buying media to leverage their sponsorship dropped from 86% in 2005 to 72% in 2012.[31] However, 72% is still substantial and their purchase of advertising was complemented by 77% of properties reporting they also leveraged through public relations.

One of the central issues in negotiations between a potential sponsor and a sport manager is likely to be the probable extent of the event's media coverage, since this remains a major component in the leverage of a sponsorship platform. If a sponsor is seeking increased brand awareness or image transfer benefits, then a key to receiving them is the extent, and the quality, of visibility in terms of its compatibility with the brand image that can be achieved with the target audience. Thus, it is likely that a sponsor will require an estimate of the extent of media coverage before committing to an investment.

A property's preferred media partners will be determined by the event's target markets, because different media appeal to different demographic and lifestyle segments. There are five avenues through which sport properties may pursue media exposure. The most traditional approach has been to negotiate in-kind trade-outs with a television station, radio station, or newspaper. The media provide some combination of advertising time or space that the property can use to promote the event and its other sponsors' roles in it; a commitment to an agreed amount of editorial coverage of the event; and provision of graphic, promotional, and production expertise for the property's promotion efforts. In return, the media receive some combination of identification; rights to transmit the event, event merchandise which they can give away as prizes to their audiences; tickets and VIP packages to give their advertisers; and a portion of the property's paid advertising. A common arrangement is for the amount of free space to be equal to the property's paid advertisement commitment to the medium.

Loosened legal restrictions on the ownership of multiple media outlets has resulted in major consolidations among media companies. For example, whereas a decade ago perhaps a dozen radio companies competed in a local market, now there may be only two or three. This has led to there being less interest among media companies in enhancing their visibility and image in a community. Thus, traditional trade-out agreements have become less appealing, and there is an insistence that sponsorships should lead directly to increasing a media company's revenues. Indeed, the first question media are likely to ask when approached to be a sponsor is: What do you have that we can sell?

Pressure from digital media and persistent ongoing declines in traditional media audiences have caused the traditional print and broadcast media to become more involved with sponsorships and to view them as a supplementary revenue source. Engaging with sport properties and sponsors provides the media with a platform to offer benefits to their advertisers that extend beyond the printed page or broadcast time. Further, if a media company is actively engaged as a sponsor of an event, then other companies involved as sponsors are more likely to use that medium for paid advertising which is part of their leveraging effort. Indeed, media that are sponsors may offer selected advertising space at reduced rates, which the sport property can incorporate into its packages with other sponsors. This may specify a minimum amount that sponsors must spend with the property as a media rights holder guaranteeing the media sponsors a revenue stream, and ensuring that the property receives a high fee for the media rights to the event.[33]

Thus, a second avenue for securing media exposure is for media to pay cash to sponsor an event in exchange for the right to sell sponsorships to others. The media have strong relationships with many advertisers and for this reason often are in a better position to attract them as sponsors than the property itself. This arrangement is a non-traditional source of revenue for the media which directly enhances their bottom line. Typically, if the arrangement is limited to selling sponsorships in designated categories, then the media will buy all the rights and retain all revenues. If they take responsibility for all sponsorship sales, then the fees are likely to be divided between the media and the property on a commission basis. An executive in charge of a radio company's sponsorship observed, "In general, the more properties want from their radio partners, the more they will have to give. You hire us to put a marketing plan together and sell sponsorships and we'll split that revenue 50/50. Or if you want a joint venture partner where we support the downside, then we'll need to share in gate revenues, booth sales, and concessions" (p. 4).[34] When the media are involved in selling sponsorships, they have a vested interest in the event being successful, which is likely to reinforce their efforts to effectively promote it.

Courtesy of iStockPhoto.com

The proliferating number of broadcast media opinions mean that properties can use multiple platforms: Facebook, mobile phones, tablets, consoles, etc. The emergence of cheap bandwidth, the proliferation of tablets and smart phones, new broadcast forms such as IPTV and web TV, and new distribution outlets as Google and Apple launch their own TV subsidiaries, have resulted in a substantial expansion in the demand for content material.[35]

Out of this dynamic environment, a third avenue for involvement with the media that has emerged is for sport properties to develop their own media. Brands that formerly sponsored content now create and distribute it. Red Bull has been one of the pioneers of this movement.

- Red Bull uses the content from the properties it owns, and the events and athletes it sponsors to feed its own media. It publishes *Red Bulletin* magazine and produces documentaries, movies, games, and apps. In addition, its content is streamed 24 hours a day on Red Bull Web TV and Red Bull Radio. Red Bull Facebook has 23 million likes. Upload views of Red Bull's YouTube channel are at 207 million, while upload views on Red Bull USA's YouTube channel are at 91 million.[35]

Among others who previously sold media rights but now distribute their own sport content though their own media channels are the University of Texas; the Pac-12 Conference; and Manchester United which is building its own branded global social network and media outlet that targets its international base of an estimated 350 million supporters.

A fourth mechanism is a "time buy" arrangement whereby the property essentially rents space to broadcast its event. It tries to recoup the cost of buying the air time by selling advertising during the broadcast. In these instances the media are not sponsors since the property is paying for the air time (unless the air time is discounted), but this is likely to make it easier to attract other sponsors since it extends the event's audience reach.

The final avenue for obtaining media involvement is to secure editorial coverage. Some sponsors think of the media only as a conduit to a wider audience. However, in addition to extending the audience coverage, the media have a second important dimension in that their coverage takes the form of news, which engenders greater credibility than exposure gained through advertising. Sport is a particularly valuable sponsorship vehicle because it is especially newsworthy. This is true even at the grassroots and amateur levels of sport, where the local and regional media may be the only source of exposure. Indeed in those situations where a sport property has a geographic monopoly in that it is the only major entity of its type in the area, its newsworthiness is heightened.

In the editorial context, there is no exchange of benefits and the media are interested in satisfying their audiences, not sponsors. Hence, sponsor visibility may be important to the sponsor, but it is not important to the media. To achieve exposure, the sponsor and sport manager have to start from a position of satisfying the media's needs by providing interesting and informative stories. This was illustrated by 7-Eleven's sponsorship of the Chicago White Sox. 7-Eleven negotiated with the White Sox that the team's weeknight games would start at 7:11 pm. News of this time change generated 128 TV mentions, exposure the company valued at $500,000. It also earned coverage in 107 newspaper articles.[12]

The media often are reluctant to accept and acknowledge the role of sponsors at a sport event. Many newspapers and television stations believe that to credit sponsors of sporting events in editorial coverage could potential harm their advertising revenue, since companies are spending their communications money on the sponsorship rather than on advertising. The philosophy is "When you are in the business of selling media time or space, you don't want to give away time or space." This explains why one company received so little television news coverage in its sponsorship of a major marathon: "In more than three hours of coverage, our logo never appeared recognizably, even though it was on runners' bibs, start and finish line banners, and signs along the route. In fact, although the pre-race interviews were conducted beneath the starting banner, shots were kept tight to frame our logo out of the picture."[36] One of the ways in which events responded was by renaming their events or venues so editors could not omit the title sponsor. For example, they could omit the sponsor's name for the Rose, Cotton, Fiesta, and Citrus Bowls but were forced to incorporate it in the Outback Bowl.

When title sponsorship first emerged, the most common reaction among media was not to credit title sponsors at all. However, there was a realization that some events wouldn't happen without sponsors which would remove a popular source of news for the media. Hence, a compromise position now appears to be the norm, whereby a majority of the print media (including The *Associated Press* wire service which feeds hundreds of newspapers nationwide) mention title sponsors in the first reference to an event but not in subsequent references or headlines.[37] This industry practice typically pertains only to title sponsors; most newspapers ignore presenting and lower level-sponsors.

As a general rule, broadcast media will not credit title sponsors unless the event or sponsor purchases advertising time during the broadcast. There are two approaches to formulating this type of agreement. First, properties can buy a block of time from the network—say 30 minutes—to broadcast an event. This fee includes the cost of the ten 30-second advertising spots that typically accompany a 30-minute show. In most cases, the property seeks to sell advertising space to recoup the cost of purchasing the airtime. The property can then produce the show itself or have the broadcaster do it. This approach enables the property to provide a fully integrated sponsorship/advertising package including pictures and mentions of the sponsor on the air, in graphics, and in advertisements. Many PGA tournaments use this approach. However, the risk is that properties may not be able to sell all the advertising spots and thus have to absorb the cost.[37]

The alternative approach is for a property to purchase advertising time from the network in return for receiving title credits in mentions in pre-promotion of the event, graphics, and on-the-air pictures and mentions. Contracts will often specify such details as the number of mentions a company receives on the air and when its sign is to be shown on camera. Typically, broadcasters require title sponsors to purchase between 15% and 25% of the total inventory.[37]

Activational Leveraging

When people are asked to recall or recognize the logos, banners, or advertisements they saw at an event they recently attended, the number of positive responses is usually disappointingly low. Nonactivational leverage elements stream one-way communications from an organization to an audience. The audience does not interact, they remain passive, and the message never makes it into most of their memories.

Activational leveraging (activation) recognizes that sport sponsorship should be conceptualized as a relationship-building tool rather than as an advertising or public relations vehicle. The traditional sponsorship model asked, "What can this property do for my company?" The activation model asks, "What can this property do for my target market?" It requires that sponsorships incorporate interactive, immersive customer experiences.

It is much more than a Facebook page, a tent in the event area, enthusiastic sales representatives, and free product. It is not merely putting a product in consumers' heads; it is about eliciting an emotional response from them. Activation is "experiential sponsorship." Winning hearts and minds and emotionally bonding with potential customers is done by knowing their passions and asking, "How do we connect with those passions in an engaging way." Coca Cola expresses the sponsorship activation goal well: "To create an unforgettable moment i.e. a unique experience in connection with the brand." This is exemplified in the context of sailing in Exhibit 5.4.[38] A corollary of creating that memorable moment is that people are likely to share it with others though social media, so its impact is leveraged.

If a target market is not engaged with the brand in an interactive way, then there is unlikely to be any memory association with it. Attitudes developed through direct

Exhibit 5.4

Activation of a Sailing Sponsorship

Sailing offers a particularly rich context for activation since guests can be centrally involved in the action. Indeed, it has been suggested: "Exclusive, emotional, and memorable are the keywords of a potentially unique experience where the added value can exceed that of any other corporate activity in the world of professional sports . . . It can certainly offer a guest/VIP an experience that will outlive that of any sport, both in terms of immediate impact and long-lasting effect" (pp. 73, 74).

The best examples are the "17th man" and "5th man" spots respectively reserved on deck on the America's Cup and the iShares Cup Extreme 40 Sailing Series. Guests, VIPs, and journalists are not taken out for an informal outing on the water, they actually get a taste of the competition by taking part in official races during which a place on the final leaderboard is at stake—and that makes all the difference. From that perspective, it is interesting to note that 93% of VIP guests surveyed placed the iShares Cup in the top three hospitality days they had ever attended. With a spot on boat during each race, a total of 170 guests were treated to that very special experience during the opening event of the iShares Cup in Venice. During corporate outings, VIPs can actually sail round-the-world races, take the helm of record-breaking machines that have made the headlines of the international press and have a taste of life on board in the most direct fashion.

The sense of freedom and escape one experiences upon boarding a boat, helps bring down barriers between individuals. CEOs, politicians, and other influential key players will interact much more naturally aboard a boat, where they are "locked together," than they would do ashore, with the added bonus of being miles away (or at least under that impression) from e-mails, meeting rooms, and daily constraints. Accessibility to even the greatest names in sailing is another point that differentiates it from other high-profile sports, where a simple handshake with a champion often proves problematic. Close proximity and interaction with sailing legends, world champions and record holders who share their experiences in their own words is bound to make the moment memorable, exclusive, and enthralling.

experiences are stronger, more enduring and more resistant to change than those developed indirectly from nonactivational leverage elements.[39]

The changing nature of technology and the way which fans consume sport has opened up a myriad of opportunities for activation. The availability of interactive media makes possible the creation of "co-produced brand environments,"[39] characterized by a real and shared sense of relationship between the brand and the customer. With smartphones and tablets, the relationship between brand and event can be reinforced all year-round by providing a continuous flow of entertainment, interactive games, and information about the athletes and the event. Information hungry fans can be provided with match highlights, player personality features, player diaries, and behind-the-scenes footage.

Since over 50% of Americans report playing a game every day,[40] the development of highly sophisticated interactive games has become a central activation component of most major sponsorships. The following examples from Heineken and Breitling are illustrative:

- Heineken sponsored the European Champions League. It created StarPlayer which is a real-time game that allows soccer fans to predict outcomes during actual games.

Playable through an iPhone app or Facebook page, it opens for play 10 minutes before the game starts. When the whistle blows to start the game, the game timer synchronizes with the TV time. Users can play individually or enter into a league with friends. Unlike ordinary TV, the game immerses fans in the action. There is a continuous array of interactive features. For example, players get eight attempts per game to predict if either team will score within the next 30 seconds. Scores for correct replies are based on how quickly the answer is registered. Free kicks and corners trigger a menu of options—goal, miss, save, clear—and the score reflects the outcome's likelihood. The site creates a platform for fans to extend and deepen their experience of the game, all the while keeping them involved with the brand. Thus, Heineken moves from being a brand message to being a relationship partner in experience creation.

- Breitling watches, sponsor of Reno's National Championship Air Races created Breitling Reno Air Races around the event for iPhone, iPad, and iPod Touch. Powered by a sophisticated graphics engine, the game immerses players into the Reno Air Race with a range of options using different types of aircraft. Players can customize their planes before joining the race to become the fastest pilot in the world.[40]

Games are likely to be only one element in a host of activation activities associated with large sponsorship investments. The comprehensive nature of these is illustrated in Exhibits 5.5 and 5.6 describing adidas's and Proctor & Gamble's activations around their London Olympic Games TOP sponsorship,[41,42] and by Guinness' leveraging of the Rugby World Cup sponsorship in Exhibit 5.7.[43]

Many sponsoring companies lack the resources to develop interactive games or to embrace the kind of comprehensive activation programs shown in the adidas, Proctor & Gamble and Guinness examples. However, the key to strong activation is creativity and ingenuity, rather than substantial resources. Creative activation can cut through the clutter at an event if it involves something distinctive and it does not have to be expensive as the following example illustrates:

- Managers of a sponsor of the PGA tour stop in Phoenix could not understand why one of the other sponsors consistently emerged as the number one sponsor in studies measuring unaided recall and passion. They assumed this company was spending considerable amounts to leverage its platform. However, they found its leverage was limited to $500! They put water coolers, with free water, at every hole. On them it said, "Refreshment provided by American West Airlines." They provided something meaningful for fans in the hot desert sun and people remembered. The event's major sponsors using added value events like long drive contests all had lower-recall.[44]

A number of vignettes that were used in earlier chapters to illustrate other points, serendipitously included examples of activational leverage. So they can be quickly referenced by the reader, they are listed in Table 5.2. Some of these are relatively pedantic, such as free samples to participants, but others are impressively creative.

Exhibit 5.5

Adidas Activation Around the London Olympic Games

Adidas activation revolved around seven main axis, and there were measurable objectives connected to each of the efforts.

1	Knowing that Nike would activate around the Games, albeit in an unofficial capacity, adidas launched its program in 2008. Reach and efficiency were achieved by tagging existing advertising with the London 2012 mark, including its massive "all in" campaign. Interest was built with athlete, musician, and community partnerships, while engagement was accomplished through adidas-branded fitness venues, touring events, and social media.
2	Its adiStars program was aimed at students, aged 13 and up. Broad objectives were to increase sports participation and the audience for its products; build brand equity; grow brand preference; garner a marketing database; and generate entertaining content for its YouTube channel. Tactics for increasing brand equity included co-branding with LOCOG. Tactics for building brand preference were designed to maximize engagement through participation. Users registered and created teams consisting of their own friends to complete a series of sporting challenges or missions. Teams practiced, including viewing videos with tips from adidas-sponsored UK athletes. When ready, the team performed and recorded a mash-up video of their effort, using the editing tools on the site. Teams that finished tasks and missions were rewarded with personal messages from athletes; top teams got live coaching from an adidas brand ambassador. Other rewards included badges for display on personal web pages and the chance to be a VIP on an adidas commercial shoot.
3	AdiStars aligned with earlier London 2012 efforts, including AdiZones which were free outdoor multi-purpose, youth fitness areas that adidas built in each of the five Olympic boroughs and additional sites across the UK. AdiZones had huge public approval ratings and were backed by the government's Department of Children, Schools, and Families.
4	The brand also activated its sponsorship through the adiTour roadshow. Housed in an inflatable, visitors could learn the best training methods, participate in a series of challenges, and get feedback (and gear and footwear advice) from coaches.
5	To reach young adults not interested in sport and borrow the cool of music, adidas designed "About to Blow" featuring emerging musicians and Olympic athletes. It was promoted with posters and a YouTube documentary in 2009.
6	Reaching an even broader audience and connecting its brand to civic pride were the objectives for the brand's November 2010 "We are London" campaign celebrating London's creative talent and featuring UK rap artists.
7	Adidas's official outfitter category included licensing, and with Team GB's uniforms designed by superstar Stella McCartney, adidas targeted fashionistas as well as sports fans. It promoted its kilt in the *Sunday Times'* "Style" magazine and posted a stylish video on its homepage and on Facebook.

Exhibit 5.6

Proctor & Gamble Activation Around the Olympic Games

P&G activated its TOP sponsorship at the London Games around the theme "Proud Sponsor of Moms" by providing services for athletes and their families as well as for fans. P&G Family House in central London, a home away from home for athletes and their families, was a tangible demonstration of thanking families of the athletes. Guests had access to the Ariel Express Laundry Service, Pampers Play Village and P&G Beauty Express Counter. More than 90% of P&G's allocation of 6,000 tickets was given away to the public through promotions.

An on-pack ticket giveaway around Mother's Day in 2011 generated $20 million of extra sales for P&G in the U.K. For 2012 Mother's Day, P&G entered anyone uploading a "Thank You Mum" video to a microsite into a draw to win a family ticket to an Olympic event. Olympic brand ambassadors, including star British runner Paula Radcliffe, were featured in an online video thanking their own mothers, and all print and PR activity drove traffic to the digital campaign.

P&G "Thank You Mom" spots garnered 10 million views on YouTube before airing on TV. The day before London 2012's opening ceremonies, views of P&G-posted Olympic content exceeded 53 million. During the Games, P&G linked its social activity to what people were seeing elsewhere to amplify the effect. For example, activity from P&G's 150 sponsored athletes appeared on the day the athlete competed. P&G believed its activated sponsorship increased sales by $500 million over the course of the Olympic Games year.

Table 5.2. Previous Vignettes that Illustrate Activational Leverage

Page	Sponsor	Property	Activation Elements
18	Barclaycard	NFL	Extra points credit card and interactive website
35	Showtime	NASCAR	Sweepstakes, DVDs
37	Cape Breton Island	Clipper Race	Meeting with business leaders at each Clipper stop
73	IBM	All properties	Backstage tours and visits with athletes
74/81	Aon	Manchester United	Touring Skills and Drills coaching clinic and replica shirts to all employees
75	Sony Erickson	WTA	Tennis clinics with pro players
75	PopSecret	NASCAR	Free samples from microwave ovens
76	Lowe's	BASS fishing	How-to Villages where tools and other products can be tested
76	Degree Men Everest	Tough Mudder	Free samples to competitors
76	Clif and Luna Bars	Running races and Triathlons	Free samples to competitors
77	U.S. Army	NASCAR and NHRB	Strength in Action Tour: flight simulators, rock climbing, robotic guiding
78	State Farm	NBA	Traveling basketball show with interactive features

Exhibit 5.7

Developing a Sponsorship Platform to Leverage an Investment

Guinness is the world's leading stout brand of beer and market leader in every major territory in the world. The company considered itself to have an 80/20 market in which 80% of sales are accounted for from 20 percent of customers. While there was room for growth within this section of the market, the company was keen to increase consumption within the 80% group of occasional stout drinkers as well as grow the stout market by attracting customers from drinkers of other types of beer.

Guinness has been a major sponsor of rugby tournaments and leagues around the world including the UK Rugby Premiership League, the Six Nations Cup, and the Rugby World Cup (RWC). This case discusses the company's sponsorship of the RWC.

There were several reasons for Guinness' sponsoring the RWC. The company wanted to reinforce its image as a "world-class brand" and felt that this could be achieved through an association with a world-class event. The market for the brand and the RWC also provided a good match. Guinness was available in 150 countries worldwide; the RWC is broadcast to 135 countries with a television audience of four billion. Priority markets for Guinness also had a keen playing interest in the RWC, providing a strong communication platform for the brand to its target audience. Guinness and rugby were a good fit with a similar target audience and image, and were inextricably linked through social drinking. Rugby was perceived as being good, clean, industrious, strong, virile, masculine, and exciting. These descriptors were consistent with the image the brand wanted to project.

Objectives

Guinness allowed individual markets to prioritize objectives, but the following were identified centrally:

- to increase consumption in priority markets (e.g., Great Britain, Ireland, France, Australia, New Zealand, South Africa, and Canada) in both on and off trade in the lead up to, and during, the RWC;
- to achieve top-of-mind awareness linked to the RWC in priority markets and to be perceived as the dominant sponsor;

- to use the sponsorship as a vehicle to reinforce and build on the Guinness "brand essence" and to inject energy, promote newsworthiness, and contemporize the brand;
- to create one consistent global identity in terms of message, image, and activity;
- to motivate and facilitate employees and business partners in all markets to exploit the sponsorship.

The Target Market

The external and internal target markets for the sponsorship program were clearly defined:

External
- current consumers
- young male beer drinkers (18 to 34)

- secondary—all male adults
- on and off trade retail partners

Internal
- employees
- joint venture partners
- agents

Broadcast Sponsorship

The total investment by Guinness was approximately $24 million. The sponsorship fee was $4 million, broadcast sponsorship in the UK was $7.5 million, and broadcast sponsorship was also acquired in Ireland, South Africa, Canada, and on the European cable/ satellite channel Eurosport. Television coverage in the UK included (i) a preview program; (ii) 41 live matches; and (iii) 16 highlight programs. For each live match, Guinness received one 15-second introduction; eight 5-second identification breaks; and one

Exhibit 5.7 *(Continued)*	
Developing a Sponsorship Platform to Leverage an Investment	
10-second exit break, in which the company was recognized as the sponsor. Over the entire tournament, this provided 512 slots.	The context of the recognition spots was varied to reflect elements of the contestants in each game and their linkage to Guinness.
Advertising	
Advertising was purchased in many of the broadcasts, and themed press and radio campaigns were organized. The press advertising campaign was initiated several months before the RWC and featured numbers on players' shirts as a countdown refer-	ence to the number of weeks before the competition began. The company purchased a one-page advertisement in the official souvenir brochure and in individual match day programs.
Promotions	
Guinness packs included a competition, and there were numbers on each pack. Numbers were featured on the broadcast sponsor spots, and those with winning numbers were awarded vacations to rugby playing nations and an array of different merchandise with RWC and Guinness logos. Merchandise was also offered for sale and as gifts with the purchase of a 24-can case of Guinness.	Over 5,000 pubs posted an exterior "Official Banner" to encourage traffic to those pubs. Pubs also offered three drinks for the price of two one hour before key home matches, which encouraged early arrival at the pubs and encouraged trade support. Distinctive hats in the shape of a Guinness glass were given free for every four pints purchased at pubs close to stadiums.
Public Relations	
Tickets were given to newspapers and radio stations to offer as prizes in competitions. Public relations coverage had to focus on fans and be fan based, because it would be inappropriate for an alcohol brand to focus on players. Streakers (fans who run on the pitch naked) have become a tradition, so a collapsible Streaker prevention tube of material was issued to all stewards. When placed over a streaker, the tube resembled a pint glass of Guinness. This generated substantial interest and front page stories and pictures when it was demonstrated to the national press. Several other public relations gimmicks of this nature were also developed. Journalists were invited to a briefing dinner at a London club and were given press packs, photographs, and merchandise. Key speakers at the function were legendary players. Diary columns were produced and sent regularly to journalists. They featured humorous stories and off-the-wall statistics such as the amount of Guinness consumed in pubs and stadia during the event. Picture	stories were created with the aim of placement in the news, rather than the sports pages of the press. One hundred thousand copies of the RWC Guide were produced and distributed by Guinness to journalists, employees, bars, and overseas markets for distribution. The guides were also used as premiums in Guinness promotions. Guinness hired double-decker buses painted in black and white corporate livery to attend matches. The highly-visible vehicles had teams of singers who handed out song sheets and encouraged the crowds to sing rugby songs and gave out vouchers for free pints of Guinness from bar facilities inside the grounds. The company produced 23 million limited edition cans worldwide that were RWC themed. Guinness worms were animated characters created to feature in the broadcast sponsorship. They were also featured in radio and press advertising and were brought to life on match days as "life-size" characters that took to the streets and mingled with the crowd.

(Exhibit continues on next page)

Exhibit 5.7 *(Continued)*

Developing a Sponsorship Platform to Leverage an Investment

Hospitality

Guinness used its hospitality rights to entertain key trade contacts, staff, and competition winners. There was, for example, access to ticket/hospitality packages for all markets for trade incentives as far as Spain,	South Africa, and Dubai. In Dubai, hospitality/ticket packages were used in pub promotions targeting ex-patriots. Similar promotions were organized in Malaysia, the Netherlands, and Argentina.

Guinness RWC Ambassadors

Guinness used the services of some of rugby's best-known ex-players to be RWC ambassadors during the tournament. The ambassadors were used for both internal and external purposes. Internal use included the ambassadors attending staff and trade	events. The ex-players attended various RWC campaign launches across the world. The ambassadors were present in Guinness hospitality suites during the tournament and mingled with the guests and employees of Guinness.

Trade Loaders

A series of incentives was produced for the trade to encourage increased Guinness stocking levels and upgrades to larger	packs. This included merchandise-based incentives as well as the opportunity to win match-day tickets.

Signage

The sponsorship arrangement with RWC gave Guinness perimeter boards at all matches, except those staged in France where the *Loi Evin* law prohibits alcohol sponsorship. Guinness was also able to ne-	gotiate additional signage opportunities, including first and second tier sites, concourses, official training grounds, media centers, press conferences, and official functions.

Website

Apart from the official RWC website, Guinness created its own site for the event. This was considered a success as the *Daily Star* newspaper voted it "Megasite of the Month,"	and it received a score of 72/100 in *New Media Age*. A survey suggested that 96% of visitors considered it to be "good fun."

Additional Rugby Sponsorship

Guinness sponsored minor rugby competitions in Italy, the Netherlands, Kenya, Malaysia, and Spain to enhance the relevance between the brand and the sport and to increase sampling opportunities. In the Netherlands, the company sponsored a series of coaching clinics for local teams and used a	famous player to launch the initiative. The training sponsorship was arranged in tandem with a campaign to ensure that all clubs promoted television viewing of the RWC in the rugby clubs, and this was, in turn, linked to Guinness promotional activity.

Activation through delivering personalized service to customers often is effective in establishing an emotional connection with them. Consider the following four examples:

- Spanish soccer club Seville partnered with insurance company Pont Grup to offer season-ticketholders who were laid-off from their jobs a free pass for the following season. The program responded to high unemployment in the area and generated extraordinary goodwill and emotional connection for both the sponsor and the property.[45]
- Arcadia Brewing Company sponsored the inaugural Kalamazoo Marathon and created a special-edition beer, called Finish Line Ale, specifically for the event. It was available to all at the end of the race. The company established an emotional and enduring bond by creating an imaginative souvenir that celebrated the runners' accomplishments of completing a marathon.[46]
- Coleman sponsored eight NASCAR events, selecting the tracks with the largest campgrounds. It created a mobile Coleman Cares repair and sales center which visited each of the sites, providing free repairs to campers. The company's spokesperson said, "People are bringing products their parents gave them, and we're bringing them back to life. They're walking away with a family heirloom. That's the ultimate one-on-one connection" (p. 6). The company received letters, calls, and emails thanking Coleman for the repairs.[47]
- Crocs partnered with 40 or so running races across the country and activated their sponsorship by setting up post-race "Comfort Zones" near the finish line. The comfort zones had masseuses, water, and ice baths where runners could sooth their aching feet. And after a dip in the ice bath—which was in a large container shaped like a shoe—staffers helped the runners put their tired feet into a pair of Crocs. While the brand was not originally targeted at runners, its success in the running demographic provided a base on which to grow general consumers: "We hit a passion point, and 89% of customers said they were more likely to consider buying a pair because of the experience," Their spokesperson said. "This was a campaign that was organic and authentic, and it added value to the experience."[48]

Engaging sports fans by providing them with the opportunity to become "stars" like the celebrity players they support is another widely used activation vehicle. The trophy tour is one mechanism for doing this and it is used by *Sports Illustrated* and Heineken. An especially imaginative activation using this theme was Samsung's "Win When You're Singing" experiential promotion. This capitalized on the propensity of British soccer fans to inspire their heroes to victory by serenading the team with creative songs written by fans:

- The *Sports Illustrated* Heisman Trophy Tour presented by Nissan stops at 10 major college football venues. Its 10,000 square foot tent features: the Heisman Trophy (which Nissan sponsors); former Heisman winners; a lineup of Nissan vehicles, and the opportunity to take a virtual test drive in them; and fans having a digital picture of themselves taken in which they appear on a dummy *SI* cover with the

Heisman Trophy. *SI* and Nissan both activate their association with football in an engaging way. *SI* owns the platform and can
thus customize it. The publisher has replicated this activation model with many of its
other properties, for example, its annual
swimsuit issue and its Sportsman of The
Year Award, offering activation sponsorships
to organizations wanting to align with them.
For instance, the Las Vegas Convention and
Visitors Authority are main sponsors of the
swimsuit activation which comprises over
two dozen events focused on Las Vegas.[49]

- Heineken sponsors the European Champions League. One of its activation elements is
a trophy tour similar to that of *Sports Illustrated*. It attracts considerable media attention at every stop. When it toured Africa,
over 50,000 people had their picture taken
with the trophy.[50]

- When the manager of Chelsea Football
Club in the English Premier League im-
plored the Chelsea fans to sing louder to inspire the team, his call to action was widely

Courtesy of BigStockPhoto.com

publicized in the UK media. As a result, Samsung, the club's major sponsor, decided to take action and created a match day experiential promotion that engages
with fans, adds value to their match-day experience, and demonstrates Samsung's
passion for football. Win When You're Singing offered supporters the opportunity
to sing their favorite Chelsea chant for the Samsung film crew before a game at
Stamford Bridge—their stadium—with the best entries picking up cutting edge
Samsung prizes. The top four performers enjoyed their fifteen minutes of fame
with their efforts being shown on the big screen at halftime. All of the chants were
then uploaded to the Samsung Win When You're Singing website, providing the
fans with entertaining user-generated content to watch and download. An overall
winner for the season was selected by a public vote via the promotional website.
The activity proved extremely popular and the fans enjoyed participating by
watching, singing, or writing new Chelsea songs. Hundreds of supporters participated and hundreds of thousands of fans visited the site to view the content.[51]

SUMMARY

Too frequently, sponsors' objectives are expressed only in general terms which results in
a lack of operational focus. Objectives should be SMART—specific, measurable, achievable, results-oriented, and time-bounded. These kinds of specific objectives remove fuzzi-

ness from what is being sought from a sponsorship and meet the increased pressures for demonstrating accountability.

The "fit" between a sport property and a company's brand is determined by compatibility of the images of the two entities and the congruency of their target markets. The most common target market match is on the basis of sociodemographics and geographic location. However, an increasing number of companies are concluding these are an insufficient basis for them to make good decisions about the degree of fit. They want to know about the lifestyles and buying habits of those attending and watching an event. Such lifestyle research draws more recognizable "live" human portraits of an audience than is possible with sociodemographics. There is a general consensus that for sponsorship to be effective there should be a relatively long-term commitment with three years often being advanced as the minimum desirable period. Long-term commitments frequently create a level of association that endures beyond the actual sponsorship.

Sponsorships terminate because of either predisposing factors which are inherent, pre-existing conditions that doom the partnership from the outset, or precipitating events which create pressure for a change in the relationship. There are four primary precipitating factors: changes in a company's marketing strategy; reduction in the impact or loss of conscious association of a sponsor with the event; increasing cost of a sponsorship; and end of a sponsorship's natural life cycle.

A sponsorship provides a platform that serves as a central theme around which a focused, integrated. consistent positioning strategy can be developed through an array of different conduits. The purchase of sponsorship rights is the beginning of a strategy, not the end. If a company does not invest resources to exploit the platform a sponsorship provides, it is likely to have wasted its investment.

Leveraging elements can be classified into two categories: nonactivational and activational. Nonactivational communications are those that promote the sponsorship association, but they are likely to be passively processed by the sponsorship audience. The major vehicle for this type of leveraging is the traditional media. There are five avenues through which sport properties may pursue media exposure. The traditional approach was to negotiate trade-outs, but most media now insist on opportunities to generate revenue if they are a sponsor. Thus, a second avenue is more common by which the media pay cash to sponsor an event in exchange for the right to sell sponsorship to other companies. An emergent third avenue is for properties to develop their own media outlets to distribute their sport content. A fourth arrangement with media is a "time buy" arrangement whereby a property essentially rents space to broadcast its event. The final avenue is to secure editorial coverage through a property becoming a news event, which engenders greater credibility than exposure gained through advertising.

Media are reluctant to acknowledge the role of sponsors in editorial coverage, because companies are spending their communications money on sponsoring the event rather than on advertising their brands in the media. The policy of most print media is to mention title sponsors in the first reference to an event, but not in subsequent references or headlines. As a general rule, broadcast media will not credit title sponsors unless the property or sponsor purchases advertising time during the broadcast.

Activational leveraging requires that sponsorships incorporate interactive immersive customer experiences that become unforgettable moments. This has been greatly facilitated by the evolution of technology which enables an association between a brand and event to be reinforced all year round with a continuous flow of entertainment, interactive games, and information about the event and its athletes. The key to effective activation is creativity and ingenuity, rather than substantial resources. It has to be distinctive, which does not necessarily mean it has to be expensive.

Endnotes

1. Farrelly, F. (2010). Not playing the game: Why sport sponsorship relationships break down. *Journal of Sport Management, 24*, 319–337.

2. Kolah, A. (2001). *How to develop an effective sponsorship programme.* London, England: Sport Business Information Resources.

3. Perelli, S., & Levin, P. (1998). Getting results from sponsorship. *Special Events Report, I*(22), 4–5.

4. Gorse, S., Chadwick, S., & Barton, N. (2010). Entrepreneurship through sports marketing: A case analysis of Red Bull in sport. *Journal of Sponsorship, 3*(4), 348–357.

5. Cushman, D. (2000, December). Air to the throne. *SportsPro*, pp. 60–61.

6. Emmett, J. (2009, December). The mainstream strategy. *SportsPro*, pp. 56–56.

7. SBI. (2007, August). Sharing brand values. *Sport Business International*, pp. 18–19.

8. Bernstein, A. (1999, August 9–15). Toys 'R' Us makes play for soccer kids. *SportsBusiness Journal*, p. 7.

9. Mendoza, T. (2011, August 2). *US Navy sponsors X games.* Press release US Navy. Story number NNS110802–26.

10. IEG. (2006, August 28). Time to sponsor for vacation ownership company. *IEG Sponsorship Report*. Retrieved from http://www.sponsorship.com/iegsr/2006/08/28/Time-To-Sponsor-For-Vacation-Ownership-Company.aspx

11. Wilson, A. (2006, April 6). From ivory tower to sporting cathedral. *The Guardian*. Retrieved from http://www.guardian.co.uk/sport/2006/apr/06/cricket.sport

12. IEG. (2007, January 15). Sports teams thank heaven for 7-Eleven's new deals. *IEG Sponsorship Report*. Retrieved from http://www.sponsorship.com/iegsr/2007/01/15/Sports-Teams-Thank-Heaven-For-7-Eleven-s-New-Deals.aspx

13. Culf, A. (2006, February 8). Vodafone rings changes without sentiment in quest for global power. *The Guardian*. Retrieved from http://www.guardian.co.uk/sport/2006/feb/09/marketingandpr.mediab

14. Ukman, L. (2002). Assertions. *IEG Sponsorship Report, 21*(16), 2.

15. Global Brands Strategy. (2012). *Annual report 2011. Adidas-group: Corporate Publications.* Retrieved from http://adidas-group.corperate-publications.com/2011

16. Brett, J. H. (1990). Evaluation: Measuring return on investment. *Special Events Report, 9*(7), 3–6.

17. Brockington, L. (1999, August 9). Lincoln's upscale drive leads to Cup. *SportsBusiness Journal*, p. 12.

18. Serafin, R. (1989, August 21). Caddy goes for golf: Luxury cars vie for sponsorship. *Advertising Age*, p. 16.

19. IEG. (2011, March 28). Increased sales plus new customers equals new sponsorships for Subaru. *IEG Sponsorship Report*. Retrieved from http://www.sponsorship.com/iegsr/2011/03/28/Increased-Sales-Plus-New-Customers-Equals-New-Spon.aspx

19a. Ukman, L., & Krasts, M. (2012). *A sponsorship measurement solution: Applying marketing science to evaluating performance.* Chicago, IL: IEG.

20. Nickell, D., Cornwell, T. B., & Johnston, W. J. (2011). Sponsorship-linked marketing: A set of research propositions. *Journal of Business and Industrial Marketing, 26*(8), 577–589.

21. Aaker, D. A., & Joachimsthaler, E. (2000). *Brand leadership.* New York, NY: The Free Press.

22. Sleight, S. (1989). *Sponsorship: What it is and how to use it.* Maidenhead, Berkshire, England: McGraw-Hill.

23. McAlister, A. R., Kelly, S. J., Humphreys, M. S., & Cornwell, T. B. (2012). Change in a sponsorship alliance and the communication implications of spontaneous recovery. *Journal of Advertising, 41*(1), 5–16.

24. Currie, N. (2000, June/July). Maximizing sport sponsorship investment: A perspective on new and existing opportunities. *Sports Marketing & Sponsorship*, 159–166.

25. Cornwell, T. B., Humphreys, M. S., Maguire, A., Weeks, C., & Tellegen, C. (2006). "Sponsorship-linked marketing: the role of articulation in memory." *Journal of Consumer Research*, *33*, 312–321.

26. Berrett, T., & Slack, T. (1999). An analysis of the influence of competitive and institutional pressures on corporate sponsorship decisions. *Journal of Sport Management*, *12*, 114–138.

27. Olkkonen, R., & Tuominen, P. (2006). Understanding relationship fading in cultural sponsorships. *Corporate Communications: An International Journal*, *11*(1), 64–77.

28. IEG. (2000). How to keep long-term sponsorships fresh and productive. *IEG Sponsorship Report*, *19*(20), 1, 4–5.

29. Smith, M. (2010, May 24). The changing look of NASCAR sponsorship. *SportsBusiness Journal*, pp. 14–17.

30. Weeks, C. S., Cornwell, T. B., & Drennan, J. C. (2008). Leveraging sponsorships on the Internet: Activation, congruence, and articulation. *Psychology & Marketing*, *25*(7) 637–654.

31. IEG. (2012, March 19). Old habits do die; sponsor survey sees less reliance on ads, signage. *IEG Sponsorship Report*. Retrieved from https://www.sponsorship.com/iegsr/2012/03/16/Old-Habits-Do-Die--Sponsor-Survey-Sees-Less-Relian.aspx

32. Mago, D., & Bishop, T. (2010). Fixed rights to activation ratios can harm sponsorship ROI. *Journal of Sponsorship*, *4*(1), 9–14.

33. IEG. (2008, June 2). Media partner overview: Industry wars means sponsorship grows. *IEG Sponsorship Report*.

34. IEG. (2002). Radio/event partnerships grow more sophisticated. *IEG Sponsorship Report*, *21*(17), 1, 4–5.

35. Ukman, L. (2011, November 2). Why content matters. *IEG Sponsorship Blog*. Retrieved from http://www.sponsorship.com/About-IEG/Sponsorship-Blogs/Lesa-Ukman/November-2011/Why-Content-Matters.aspx

36. Eaton, R. (1991). Inside Target stores' sponsorship philosophy. *Special Events Report*, *19*(17), 4–5.

37. IEG. (1998). Media standards for crediting title sponsors. *IEG Sponsorship Report*, *17*(5), 4–5.

38. Turner, M. (2009). Sailing opportunities: A sea of B2B opportunities. *Journal of Sponsorship*, *3*(1), 73–78.

39. Zwick, D., & Dieterre, O. (2005). The ebusiness of sport sponsorship. In J. Amis & T. B. Cornwell (Eds.), *Global sport sponsorship* (pp. 127–146). Oxford, England: Berg.

40. Ukman, L. (2011, August 22). Sponsorship activation meets gamification. *IEG Sponsorship Blog*. Retrieved from http://www.sponsorship.com/About-IEG/Sponsorship-Blogs/Lesa-Ukman/August-2011/Sponsorship-Activation-Meets-Gamification.aspx

41. Ukman, L. (2011, July 25). Sponsorship success depends on activation. *IEG Sponsorship Blog*. Retrieved from http://www.sponsorship.com/About-IEG/Sponsorship-Blogs/Lesa-Ukman/July-2011/Sponsorship-Success-Depends-on-Activation.aspx

42. Ukman, L. (2012, August 5). Olympic sponsorship winners and losers. *IEG Sponsorship Blog*. Retrieved from http://www.sponsorship.com/About-IEG/Sponsorship-Blogs/Lesa-Ukman/August-2012/Olympic-Sponsorship-Winners-And-Losers.aspx

43. Rines, S. (2002, December/January). Guinness Rugby World Cup sponsorship: A global platform for meeting objectives. *International Journal of Sports Marketing and Sponsorship*, pp. 449–464.

44. IEG. (1999). Sponsor loyalty: It's not just for NASCAR anymore. *IEG Sponsorship Report*, *18*(6), 3.

45. Andrews, J. (2011, June 30). Activation watch: Praiseworthy programs from Budweiser and Spanish insurer. *IEG Sponsorship Blog*. Retrieved from http://www.sponsorship.com/About-IEG/Sponsorship-Blogs/Jim-Andrews/June-2011/Activation-Watch--Praiseworthy-Programs-from-Budwe.aspx

46. Kander, J. (2011, May 2). Brewer makes special-edition ale for marathon sponsorship. *IEG Sponsorship Blog*. Retrieved from http://www.sponsorship.com

47. IEG. (2000). Coleman expands sponsorship portfolio, increases focus on sales overlays. *IEG Sponsorship Report*, *19*(12), 6.

48. Dreier, F. (2010, November 22–28). Engaging the crowd. *SportsBusiness Journal*, pp. 15–18.

49. Lefton, T. (2010, November 27). Nissan steers toward college football. *SportsBusiness Journal*, p. 16.

50. Emmett, J., & Cushman, D. (2008, December/January). If anyone can, Heineken. *Sports Pro*, pp. 62–65.

51. SBI. (2008, May). Activation, activation, activation. *SportsBusiness International*, p. 19.

6

Ambush Marketing

An ambushing company is an uninvited guest to a sponsored event.[1] Ambush marketing is defined as: "A planned effort by an organization to associate themselves indirectly with an event in order to gain at least some of the recognition and benefits that are associated with being an official sponsor" (p. 11).[2] It occurs when a company that has no formal rights as an official sponsor, associates its own brand with a sport property with the intent of communicating the false impression that it is a sponsor. A company is likely to engage in ambush marketing because either an official sponsorship is too expensive, or there are pre-existing commitments by the property to a competing company.

Ambushing has two complementary goals. The first is to weaken the public's perceptions of a competitor's official association with an event, so official sponsors derive less benefit from that association than might have been anticipated. The second goal is to associate indirectly with the sport event in order to gain some of the recognition and benefits that are associated with being an official sponsor.

The term appears to have emerged at the 1984 Olympic Games when Kodak announced itself as the proud sponsor of ABC's *broadcast* of the Games and became the provider of the *official film* of the U.S. track team. This strategy was aimed at undermining and reducing any gains that accrued to Fuji which had paid to be an official sponsor of the Games. It illustrated an axiom in ambushing in that the strategy's effect depends strongly on similarity. It is confined primarily to competitive brands in the same product class.

Kodak's success alerted other companies to the potential of ambushing for furthering their strategic marketing goals and its adoption grew rapidly. At the 1988 Winter Games in Calgary, Wendy's used the same strategy to ambush McDonald's which was the official sponsor. Like Kodak, Wendy's sponsored the broadcast of the Games on the ABC network. Wendy's reinforced this ploy by placing ski-racing posters in its stores with the caption "We'll Be There," printing stories about the Olympics on its tray liners, and inscribing a drawing that resembled Olympic rings on its napkins.[1]

American Express was another pioneer of ambushing in the 1990s when it sought to counter the positive impact accruing to its rival VISA which was an official Games sponsor. When the Winter Games were held in France, American Express ran a major advertising campaign that featured the French Alps with the caption "Winter Fun and

Games." For the Barcelona Summer Games, the slogan changed to "And remember, to visit Spain, you don't need a visa." At the following Winter Games in Norway the slogan became, "If you're traveling to Norway, you'll need a passport, but you don't need a visa."[1] The word "Olympic" was never used so the Games' intellectual property rights were not abrogated, but the allusions were effective in persuading many viewers that American Express was an official sponsor.

At the Atlanta Olympic Games in 1996, Nike organized what is still regarded as the epitome of ambushing:

> Nike's ambush of the 1996 Atlanta Olympics is still seen as the ambush of all ambushes. Saving the $50 million that an official sponsorship would have cost, Nike plastered the city with billboards, handed out swoosh banners to wave at the competitions and erected an enormous Nike center overlooking the stadium. The tactics devastated the International Olympic Committee's credibility and spooked other organizations such as FIFA into adopting more assertive anti-ambushing strategies.[3]

These ambushes resulted in the owners of major sport events developing the set of legal and marketing protection strategies discussed later in this chapter to counter ambushing that now make it much more difficult. The owners of sport properties had three goals in developing these defense mechanisms: (i) to protect the integrity and financial viability of the event; (ii) to build the event brand and goodwill in it for the future; and (iii) to fulfill contractual obligations to sponsors.[4]

The opportunity for ambush arises because there are usually multiple entities involved in the staging of a sport event. These may include a sport federation or league; individual countries or teams; individual athletes; the media; and merchandise licensees who are authorized to produce books, videos, records, toys, photographic collections, et al., all of which offer sponsorship opportunities. Each of these entities has the right to sell sponsorship. It is unlikely that one company would have sufficient resources to purchase the rights to all avenues for associating with a property. This makes it almost inevitable that there will be conflict between competing companies all of which have legitimately paid for sponsorship rights with one of these entities. The proliferation of entity sponsorships has been described as "the biggest challenge facing sponsorship as a medium, and indeed perhaps the major contributor to sponsor confusion, an environment in which ambush marketing is able to thrive." (p. 309)[5]

Two key points about ambush marketing should be emphasized. First, it is a well-planned effort, not a one-shot commercial or *ad-hoc* decision. It is likely to be costly to get people to perceive the ambushing company as being a sponsor, involving prime-time advertising and expensive activation. Indeed, it is possible that ambush marketers may end up spending more than their "official partner" competitors for the same result. Thus, the popular perception that ambushing may capture the benefits of a sponsor at a fraction of the official sponsor's costs often is fallacious. Second, the main objective is not exposure *per se* since this could be achieved by regular advertising independent of the sport event. Rather the intent is to become a "pseudo sponsor" by "gaining the benefits associated with being a sponsor or weakening the impact of a main competitor being the exclusive sponsor of an event." (p. 11)[2]

The fees paid by companies to sponsor major events continue to increase which suggests that ambush marketing has not adversely impacted the value of official sponsorship. Companies would not continue to invest large amounts of money in it if they doubted its effectiveness. This indicates that the sophisticated counter-ambush strategies enacted by properties and official sponsors that are discussed later in the chapter have been successful in protecting sponsorship value. However, there are still sufficient loopholes in their defenses that opportunities for ambushing remain, albeit they are now more expensive and more challenging to create.

IS AMBUSHING ETHICAL?

Is ambushing unethical, or is it an example of imaginative, creative, ethical marketing? The issue has been extensively discussed, with the debaters predictably espousing views that reflect their self-interest. The early definitions of ambush marketing were pejorative implying unethical business conduct, and among many property owners and official sponsors the belief remains that it is unethical. They perceive ambushers as appropriating something that does not belong to them, usurping benefits from a sport property for which they have not paid, and in so doing jeopardizing the financial standing of the property. Thus, a leading IOC Board member characterized ambush marketing as "non-creative, non-ethical, and non-professional" (p. 164).[6] The IOC suggested it should be

Courtesy of stock.xchng.com

described by the term "parasite marketing" to sensitize the public to the notion that ambushers are obtaining nourishment from the host event without giving anything in return.

The pejorative rhetoric of other property owners is similarly robust and emotionally charged: "Like leeches they suck the lifeblood and goodwill out of the institution" (p. 353);[7] "It is a form of theft practiced by corporate pariahs" (p. 356);[7] "Ambush marketers are thieves knowingly stealing something that does not belong to them . . . it breaches one of the fundamental tenets of business activity, namely truth in advertising and business communications" (p. 208);[8] or from the marketing director of Visa, "Ambush marketing implies a connection to an event for which you have not compensated the owner. There's another word for it: stealing" (p. 353).[7]

However, this perspective no longer prevails among impartial observers. It has been replaced by a recognition that while properties are obligated to protect their sponsors' contractual rights using all legal and marketing mechanisms available to them, nonsponsors have a similar obligation to their shareholders to engage in all legal commercial activities around the event that will enhance the profitability of their companies. This shift in perspective has been facilitated, at least in part, by the general public's ambivalence and disinterest in allegations of ambush marketing. It would not work if target audiences denounced it as being unethical and shunned companies that practiced it. For the most part, the public is unaware if it taking place, but when they are cognizant of it the typical reaction is benign. It is usually regarded as a trivial issue. Indeed, some are likely to smile and admire the chutzpah and creativity of the ambushing companies.

There are now dozens of advertising agencies who promote their expertise in ambush marketing. Those who engage in ambush marketing resent the suggestion that it is unethical and state that such charges represent only "self-serving pleading in the guise of intellectual commentary." (p. 4)[9] They point out that sponsors do not "buy the rights to the entire thematic space in which the purchased property is usually only one resident . . . When you own and license Kermit, you sell only the rights you own to one specific frog—not all frogs—and maybe not even all green ones." (p. 4)[9] Since sponsors have not bought and do not own the thematic space, they have no right to control it. Competitors which are not official sponsors have to ask the question, "What promotional efforts or programs can I do within this thematic space to get marketing benefits that are not part of the official sponsorship agreement?" (p. 4)[9] They consider it to be a healthy business practice consistent with the American tradition of encouraging competition in the market place. Indeed, it has been argued that such healthy competition has the long-range effect of "making sponsorship properties more valuable, not less, in that successful ambushes, over time, help weed out inferior sponsorship properties." (p. 4)[9] There is no doubt that ambushing has resulted in more extensive and creative use of the platform that sponsorship provides for strategic marketing, and to much tighter contracts between properties and sponsors.

Nevertheless, the unofficial nature of ambush campaigns means there is a risk of association with impropriety: "From a brand positioning perspective, ambush marketing can be tricky. If a brand relies heavily on values such as honesty and correctness, ambush marketing is not something I would necessarily recommend." (p. 18)[10]

The U.S. economic system is designed to encourage companies to compete vigorously, but honestly. Managers have a moral obligation to maximize returns to the stockholders for whom they work. Provided actions are lawful and in the company's best long-term interest, they should be pursued. Thus, "the argument that if I'm an inventive non-sponsor mining the sponsored thematic space in a clever way, the public may come to think of me as an Olympic sponsor is not an argument supporting non-pursuit of ambushing activities, but is rather a possible testament to the marketing skills of a non-sponsoring competitor." (p. 4)[9]

A sponsor's investment does not operate in a vacuum, free of the competitive pressures that are inherent in the economic system. Sponsors and properties have an obligation to identify the parameters of what they are purchasing, including an understanding of what they can and cannot control. These are key factors in determining the price/value of a sponsorship. Competitors have no ethical obligation to make sure an official sponsor's investment is successful. The obligation lies with sponsors and event owners to remove or minimize ambushing opportunities.

AMBUSH STRATEGIES

As long as ambushers do not use logos, imagery, or phrases protected by intellectual property law their activities are legal. Hence, their ambush strategies are carefully and cleverly designed to circumvent the use of these prohibited items. Eight potential ambush strategies are discussed in this section: Sponsorship of the broadcast of the event; purchase of advertising time in and around the event broadcast; sponsoring entities other than the organizing body; presence in and around the event venue; advertising and allusion in the thematic space; capitalizing on an enduring memory; creation of a counter attraction; and authenticity ambushing. These serve as a checklist from which competitors select elements for their ambush and sponsoring companies review in order to develop strategies for defending against ambush. Often some combination of all of them will be used in an ambush campaign.

Sponsorship of the broadcast of the event occurs when television rights holders create and offer to nonsponsors the right to be "a proud sponsor of the (say) NCAA Final Four Championship broadcast." The sponsor pays a rights fee to the broadcast company, not to the NCAA, which is likely to cost much less than sponsoring the event itself. The sponsor's expectation is that the general public will not recognize this distinction. Most major property owners have sought to close down this strategy by including clauses in their contracts with broadcasters prohibiting competitors of official sponsors to sponsor the broadcasting events. However, new technologies, and especially the emergence of social media, make this a dynamic environment that is likely to offer new opportunities for ambushers.

Purchasing advertising time in and around the event broadcasts is perhaps the most common and most effective ambushing strategy used at major events. An experienced sponsorship manager labeled the broadcasters' approach "a very unpleasant form of extortion" (p. 84).[11] Title sponsors typically are required to purchase 15%–25% of commercial advertising time associated with the event in order for the media to recognize their title sponsorship, so the announcers will use the company name and the cameras include it in their shots. This leaves 75%–85% of this time available for competitors. If most or all of it was purchased by a competitor the saturation effect could overwhelm and negate association with the official sponsor. Unless their agreement with the event or the sponsor specifically prohibits them from doing so, the media are likely to aggressively solicit competitors and point out the ambush potential of the opportunity. One experienced sponsor commented: "Presumably since your competitors haven't already spent many millions of dollars to be the official sponsor, they'll have the cash to buy in. And the truth is, the average American on his or her couch lazily watching these competing commercials is unlikely to notice who's "official" and who is not" (p. 85).[11]

There is not much that properties and sponsors can do to counter this, beyond the sponsor buying more of the spare advertising capacity. When properties sell the broadcasting rights inevitably they lose some control over advertising. Typically, the contracts will specify that official sponsors have "right to first refusal" to purchase advertising so at least they are able to secure the prime spots within the telecast.[4] However, the broadcaster has to be able to make a profit from its investment, so the more restrictions imposed by the property that inhibit the broadcaster's ability to sell the advertising space, the lower the fee it will receive for the rights.

Sponsoring entities other than the organizing body, such as individual teams or individual athletes, is a widely used ambushing strategy. Frequently, individual athletes are sponsored by different companies from those that sponsor their team or the event. When all eyes and cameras are on them on the podium, they have often engaged in ambush activity either by covering the logos on their uniforms or by flashing their equipment for the cameras. This may be done subtly, for example, by draping a national flag over the team uniform so the public perceive it to be an act of patriotism rather than ambushing; or blatantly by, for example, waving distinctively branded running shoes at the cameras and the crowd, or with visible body tattoos.

Exhibit 6.1 describes how Nike used its sponsorship of athletes to ambush adidas at the World Cup Soccer tournament, while Exhibit 6.2 notes the conflict centered around adidas and Nike sponsorships at the London Olympic Games.[12] In the following vignette a company that was rebuffed in its attempt to become an official sponsor, responded by creating its own unofficial sponsorship category:

- Migros is the leading Swiss supermarket retailer with 7 million customers passing through its stores weekly. It was not allowed to be a sponsor of the 2008 European Soccer Tournament. UEFA, the property owner, did not permit retailers to be official sponsors to avoid diluting the exclusivity enjoyed by other partners, whose rivals' products may be stocked and promoted by retailers. Since they couldn't be

---

Exhibit 6.1

Nike Ambushes Adidas at the World Cup

At the 2010 World Cup, adidas was an official sponsor, but Nike was not. However, Nike had sponsorship agreements with many of the players who would star at the soccer tournament. The company launched a "Write the Future" ambush campaign in the three weeks prior to the Cup games starting which featured their players, including a three-minute video. The material was used in television advertisements before the Cup and on YouTube. The video was viewed more than 16 million times during the first month. It contained no marks, symbols, or expressions directly related to the World Cup. However, there was no doubt that Nike was using the world-wide focus on the World Cup at that time to promote its brand.

Nike was the uniform provider to 9 of the 32 teams, while adidas kitted 12 of them. Nike was also a "broadcast sponsor" in some countries e.g., Australia, giving the company preferential placement of its advertisements around the coverage.

The Neilsen Company analyzed on-line blogs, message boards, and the social networking sites and reported that Nike was linked to the 2010 World Cup more frequently than any of the tournament's official sponsors and partners. Almost one-third of the on-line discussion focused on Nike, which was twice as much as adidas, the official sponsor.

Exhibit 6.2

Conflicting Sponsorship Commitments: A Source of Ambushing

Adidas was a TOP sponsor at the London Olympic Games and the company also sponsored the British Olympic Committee which gave it the right to provide the British team's uniforms. Hence, athletes sponsored by Nike were required to perform in adidas uniforms. In the U.S. the situation was reversed. Nike was the official provider of uniforms to the U.S. Olympic Committee (USOC), whose team included scores of adidas sponsored athletes, as well as those sponsored by Reebok, Puma, and other companies.

Under Rule 40 of the Olympic Charter athletes are forbidden from appearing in advertising that clashes with official sponsors during the Games. Under the official team member agreements that athletes are required to sign, they must wear official national uniforms. Footwear is exempt from these rules because it is classified as "equip-

ment." Nevertheless, the USOC attempts to protect its sponsors by insisting that the team's uniform at medal ceremonies includes shoes.

Nike insisted that USOC enforce this rule in London, saying that any athletes wearing adidas (or other companies' shoes) at medal ceremonies would be breaking their team member contract with the USOC and engaging in ambush marketing.

Adidas' position as a TOP sponsor gave it the authority to block non-adidas athletes from appearing in advertising or sponsorship during the Games. However, there were exemptions which Nike exploited. Thus, adidas' rivals who sponsored athletes were allowed to feature them in advertisements during the Games period if the campaigns were "generic" and were in circulation at least six months prior to the Games.

an official sponsor, Migros designated themselves as "official sponsors of the fans." Their campaign focused on providing the fans with the equipment, food, and drink to have a good time while the soccer match was on.[10]

• Similarly, at the Salt Lake City Winter Games, Anheuser-Busch was the official sponsor, but the local Schirf Brewery had its delivery trucks painted with the slogan "Watsutch Beers: The Unofficial Beer—2002 Winter Games."[1]

Presence in and around the event venue. As part of their bidding requirements major properties have insisted that host cities create "clear zones," which remove all advertising material that competes with official sponsors from billboards, banners, etc. from in and around an event's venues. However, this solution is not feasible for contexts other than a small number of major events. Thus, most events are confronted with competitors to their sponsors offering product trials and samples immediately outside the event gates and comprehensive advertising and signage around the external periphery of the venue. In situations where the sponsor and/or sport organization is unable to control access to an event, for example, a marathon race using public thoroughfares, they are particularly vulnerable to this form of ambushing.

It has been noted that "In the early days of ambush marketing, companies would employ blimps and airplanes with trailing banners to ambush a major sporting event, but event organizers long ago closed this ambush opportunity by working closely with the Federal Aviation Authority and with host cities to enact air traffic restrictions during such events." (p. 556)[4] The challenge of breaching an organizer's clear zones has led to increasingly creative ambushes as Bavarian Beer demonstrated at Soccer World Cups (Exhibit 6.3);[10] Li Ning illustrated at the Beijing Olympic Games (Exhibit 6.4);[13,14] and the following vignettes relating to the US Open Tennis Championship, the Torino Winter Olympics, and NASCAR confirm:

- Many guests to the US Open Tennis Championship held at Flushing, N.Y. stayed in Manhattan. PowerAde Zero was not a sponsor of the tournament, but it oper-

Exhibit 6.3

Bavaria Beer Ambushes Budweiser at World Cup Soccer Tournaments

At the 2006 World Cup held in Germany, thousands of Dutch supporters made the relatively short trip to Stuttgart to watch Holland play in a second round match. The Dutch team shirts were orange. Hence, thousands of the fans were dressed in orange lederhosen, emblazoned with the brand of Bavaria Beer (which confusingly is Dutch!), given to them by the brewery. A Bavaria spokesperson (with tongue firmly in cheek) said the lederhosen was intended to honor the host country's heritage.

It was Bavaria's attempt to ambush one of the tournament's biggest sponsors, Anheuser-Busch's Budweiser brand. FIFA officials ordered security staff at the stadium not to admit any fans who were dressed in the lederhosen, because it eroded Budweiser's contractual rights to site exclusivity as an official sponsor. As a result, many of the Dutch fans watched the game in their underwear. The world's media feasted on FIFA's reactions and provided Bavarian Beer with extraordinary world-wide visibility.

Emboldened and elated at its success, the company reprised their ambush actions at the 2010 World Cup in South Africa. It hired two Dutch women to go to South Africa and recruit 34 young women who looked as if they were Dutch. The 36 women were given a block of prominent front row seat tickets the brewery had acquired. They entered the stadium in "regular" clothes, but when the game started, they removed these and all were dressed in identical mini-dresses in Dutch orange given to them by the brewery with a tiny Bavarian Beer logo on them. The press subsequently described the women as "gorgeous," "beautiful," and "stunning."

Their prominent seating, provocative identical outfits and physical attractiveness attracted substantial television coverage during the first half of the game, as well as large numbers of press photographers.

At the start of the second half, FIFA had them arrested and all 36 women were escorted by police from the stadium. Again, the world's media coverage ensured that millions of people who were unaware of Bavaria Beer, now knew of it. The company surely knew after its 2006 experience how FIFA would act and knew it would get huge media attention. By ejecting the women and charging the two Dutch women who recruited them under the Contravention of Merchandise Marks Act that FIFA required the South African government to pass, FIFA gave the company all the media attention it sought. Indeed, it effectively strengthened the link between the ambusher and the event, so in many people's minds, it was likely that Bavaria rather than Budweiser would be identified as the official sponsor. A commentator noted:

This incident highlights the challenges for event organizers in protecting their sponsors at the risk of potentially violating consumers' civil rights and freedom of speech, and thus themselves becoming subject to legal action. For instance, are 15 fans attending an event wearing shirts bearing the logo of their employer (a non-sponsor) cause for refusing their admittance? Or is the threshold 50 fans, or 500 fans? The discretion afforded to event organizers seeking to implement such tactics indeed raises its own set of legal concerns. (p. 565)[4]

ated a free PowerAde Zero ferry service from Manhattan to Flushing. To ride the ferry, it was necessary to register online and reserve seats at the PowerAde Zero website. Riders were given samples of the product when they got on the ferry. The brand sponsored Venus Williams and used images of her on the ferry and on other materials. PowerAde Zero's materials did not mention the "U.S. Open." They merely stated, "Take the ferry to the tennis matches." There was no corporate clutter, the company reinforced their brand in a variety of ways, and the company paid no sponsorship fees.[15]

- Target was neither a TOP nor a USOC sponsor at the Torino Winter Olympics, but it developed a substantial presence by purchasing a large number of advertisements on NBC, the U.S. network for the Olympics, and by being the only advertiser on the exterior of the train cars that shuttled fans to and from Torino and the mountain event locations about an hour away. It had negotiated with Trenitalia,

Exhibit 6.4

Li Ning'a Ambushing of adidas at the Beijing Olympics

China's choice as torchbearer for the 2008 Beijing Games was Li Ning, a former gymnast who won six medals—including three golds—during the 1984 Los Angeles Games, China's first big sortie into the Olympics. Before a packed stadium and a worldwide television audience estimated at 4 billion viewers, Li Nang ran around the inside perimeter of the Bird's Nest arena and was hoisted 75 feet in the air by cables, before lighting the Olympic cauldron. A true hero of the Chinese nation and the most decorated athlete at the Los Angeles Games, Li Ning seemed a natural choice to light the Beijing flame.

Since retiring from gymnastics, he had also become a successful entrepreneur. Capitalizing on his personal brand equity, he founded Li Ning, an athletic apparel company that specialized in clothing and footwear with an annual sales revenue of approximately $1.5 billion. Li Ning, the company, was not an official footwear sponsor of the Beijing Olympic Games; the German firm adidas had purchased those rights.

More than a billion people in China alone saw Li Ning's run across the rafters. It is unlikely that these viewers thought just of the man, and not of his shoes. Li Ning was broadcast on Chinese state television, countless other international channels, and was featured on the front page of every national newspaper in China the following day. Al-

most everyone in China knew that Li Ning owned a sports shoe company; outside of the country, the many hundred of millions who did not know this learned it very quickly. This easily made the event the greatest 2 or 3 minutes of free advertising in history—for Li Ning, but not for adidas.

Some might call the Li Ning coup lucky. Perhaps the choice of Li Ning as the flame lighter was simply serendipitous: local hero is invited by well-intentioned government and Games officials to perform a symbolic duty. He happens to own a sports footwear company, but this does not influence anyone's thinking, and the consequences are not anticipated. The world media, however, saw this in a different light; they viewed it as "the boldest case of Ambush Marketing ever pulled off."

A follow-up study was undertaken comprised of 1331 responses from a Chinese consumer panel in which they were asked to answer "Yes" or "No" as to whether a specific brand was a sponsor of the Games. 62.6% correctly identified adidas as a sponsor, but 67.4% incorrectly identified Li Ning as a sponsor. A scale was used to measure the likelihood of a respondent recommending a particular brand to others. On this measure the non-sponsor Li Ning enjoyed a significantly higher likelihood to recommend than did the sponsor adidas.

the Italian train system, to have its red-and-white bull's-eye logo along with pictures of models in red and white winter ice-skating costumes and luge suits, prominently featured on its trains which were called "Target Express" trains taking spectators to various events. Target employees greeted spectators as they boarded trains and distributed logoed noisemakers and large red and white foam fingers. By teaming with Trenitalia, "Target skirted the [Italian} federal law . . . that makes it a crime to affiliate a nonsponsor with the Olympics." (p. 552)[4]

- Home Depot and Lowe's are the two largest do-it-yourself retailers in the US. They are also major sponsors of two of NASCAR's top drivers and Lowe's is the sponsor of Lowe's Motor Speedway in Charlotte. Home Depot displaced Lowe's as the official home improvement warehouse sponsor of NASCAR. When the Coca-Cola 600 was held at Lowe's Motor Speedway, Home Depot put up a giant billboard that fans saw when they entered the speedway. It featured the driver Home Depot sponsored and the message: "We'll see who really owns the track." Home Depot also gave away about 75,000 orange glow sticks to fans so its corporate color would bathe the stands at dusk. At another meet in Alabama, when the Home Depot driver called the fans "obnoxious," Lowe's put up billboards throughout Alabama that read: "we love all fans." Souvenirs featuring Home Depot's driver in raceway gift shops were removed at the six tracks operated by Speedway Motorsports, Inc., the owner of Lowe's Motor Speedway.[16]

The legally protected logos, phrases, and trademarks associated with an event are not available to nonsponsors, but they cannot be stopped from engaging in *advertising and allusion in the thematic space*. This means it is possible for them to develop promotions and advertising in such a way that it gives the impression of being officially related to the event. Exhibit 6.3 described how Nike used the athletes it sponsored to engage in thematic advertising around the World Cup and Exhibit 6.5 shows how a newspaper used this approach.[17] Similarly, Post-It Notes and RCA designed campaigns to trade on the goodwill of the Olympics, even though they were not sponsors:

> Post-It Notes brand ran newspaper advertising that featured letters "U," "S," and "A," on gold-colored post-it notes, followed by the tagline "Go for the Gold, America." Nonsponsor RCA also capitalized on the Olympics with a promotion, advertised nationally, offering consumers a free USA jacket with the purchase of selected RCA television sets. Given that the letters "USA" are not trademarked, this activity was within RCA's rights, again illustrating the challenges facing the Olympics to thwart companies that are clever and determined to conduct promotional activity during the time of the Olympic Games. (p. 208)[18]

At the 2012 London Olympics, Marks and Spencer, which is perhaps the UK's most well-known department store, was not a sponsor. It used the slogan: "On your marks for a summer to remember" and featured British flags, an egg and spoon race, and an oversized gold medal in its promotions which successfully skirted the legal barriers. Similarly, Paddy Power, which is a British betting company promoted its sponsorship of

Exhibit 6.5

Ambushing the Sponsor of a Bicycle Race

The six-day Redlands Bicycle Classic race began in Redlands, California and drew more than 50,000 spectators. The race's official sponsor was the dominant newspaper in the area, the *San Bernardino County Sun*. Its neighboring rival from Riverside, *The Press Enterprise*, was expanding into San Bernardino County. It had failed in repeated attempts to replace the *Sun* as the race's official sponsor, but viewed such sponsorship as an important promotional vehicle for building its circulation in the new area. Frustrated *Press Enterprise* executives decided to launch an ambush to try and become the public's perceived newspaper sponsor of the event. Among other things *The Press Enterprise*:

- Published editions with special wraparound covers about the race, and had hawkers sell them.

- Expanded race coverage by increasing the sports section with two added full-color pages and a blizzard of race photographs.

- Published a 20-page race guide, and deployed 30 to 40 college students to hand out 4,000 copies of the free guide.

- Rented a lot within sight of the race starting line and parked a big delivery truck with a 28-foot-long ad for the paper in the side facing the crowd.

- Set up a booth at the first turn in the race to give away guides, sell the paper, and sign up subscribers.

The Press Enterprise vice-president for marketing concluded: "We were successful in creating the impression that we were the official newspaper sponsor, which, of course, we weren't."

"the largest athletic event in London this year." It was an egg and a spoon race. LOCOG at first instructed the company that owned the outdoor billboards carrying advertisements for this event to take them down, but then performed what Paddy Power said was a "gold-medal-winning U-turn" and allowed them to stay.[29] Nike joined these pre-London Games ambushers by launching a campaign called "Make It Count" featuring the most prominent British Olympic track and field stars. A survey of Tweeters found that Nike (a nonsponsor) was the brand they most associated with the Games, instead of adidas which was a TOP sponsor.[19]

Retailers sometimes use promotions that are themed to a particular sport event but use generic terms that avoid infringing intellectual property rights. For example:

> A company intent on associating itself with the NCAA Final Four may conduct an in-store promotion offering consumers a free basketball in exchange for proofs-of-purchase or inviting consumers to enter to win "a trip for 2 to the College Hoop Championships." While purposely avoiding the use of any registered trademarks, the displays are intended to lure consumers through an implied association with the NCAA Final Four. Such use of consumer promotions, typically conducted in concert with generic phrasing, continue to pose significant legal hurdles for event organizers in that they do not rise to the level required to bring a legal claim of unfair competition. (p. 557)[4]

Congratulatory messages are sometimes used as an entry into an event's thematic space. This is done by companies creating advertising "congratulating" teams or players on their accomplishments: Many times companies using such advertisements may not even have any contractual relationship with the team. An early example at the Barcelona Olympics featured Pepsi endorser and Basketball Dream Team member Magic Johnson with the message, "From all of us at Pepsi to our friend and partner Earvin Johnson: Go get some Magic."[1] Coca Cola was the official Games sponsor. More recently, the National Dairy Council, although not an official sponsor of the NFL, ran a full-page advertisement in *USA Today* congratulating the two Super Bowl MVPs in their "Got Milk?" moustache campaign.[4]

In Chapter 5, it was noted that when a long-term sponsor is replaced by an incoming company, a residual awareness of the previous relationship often endures, so long-term sponsors continue to benefit after their agreement has ended. This enduring legacy enables former sponsors to *capitalize on an enduring memory* and ambush replacement sponsors by, for example, taking up a lower level sponsorship after having been the title sponsor, or engaging in regular communications that reinforces that past link. These are likely to support recall and reinforce the previous sport property/brand association.[20] This strategy was adopted by the former sponsors of the New Zealand Rugby Team which is known as the "All Blacks":

- The All Blacks have always been one of the world's top teams and are a source of great pride to New Zealanders. The team's official clothing sponsors from 1918 to 1999 were Canterbury International Ltd. (CIL). When they were preempted in 1999 by adidas, CIL developed a range of clothing known as Invincibles which was the name given to a legendary All Black team from a previous era that had worn CIL-made uniforms. The promotional campaign was dominated by photographs featuring members of the original Invincibles team. The allusion CIL attempted to create was that this clothing range was officially sanctioned by the New Zealand Rugby Football Union.[21]

Creation of a counter attraction could serve to mitigate the official sponsor's positive impact:

- During the British Open Golf Championship at the Royal Birkdale course, Bentley set up a row of its luxury cars at the adjacent Hillside Golf Club. They were prominently displayed and Bentley promoted their presence there which detracted attention from Lexus which was the official sponsor.[22]

Authenticity ambushing occurs when a nonsponsor company achieves a prominent position at an event because of the excellence of its products rather than as a result of it paying the property owner for that visibility. For example, at the 2008 Summer Olympics, Speedo received such substantial media attention associated with their technologically advanced swimming suits worn by most of the medal winners that the brand was widely identified as a sponsor by the general public.

A variation of this was introduced by a brand of sporting gel. In this case, the authenticity was not obviously visible to the media and general public, but it achieved ambush status by the company articulating the authenticity of its association with sporting excellence to its target audience:

The makers of GU sports energy gel announced that the Brazilian national soccer team had purchased 200 boxes of the product for use during its World Cup training and matches. The company stated: "Unlike partnerships with past and present sponsors, the teams use of GU product will not involve commercial considerations." The company basically is saying, "While others may pay for a relationship with the team, the team pays us because it believes so much in our product." Thus, the team's use of it is obviously authentic. It offers the appearance of being an "official" team product, but, the company incurs no sponsorship cost.[23]

Emerging Internet Ambush Strategies

The Internet has created a host of new opportunities for ambush marketing. These include: domain names and meta tags, unauthorized alignment with official sites, and the sale of keywords.[1]

Ambush marketers may register *domain names* containing the sport property name, and the proliferation of websites and web pages makes this difficult to monitor. Meta tags are the key words embedded in a website's html code that enable search engines like Google and Yahoo to identify the contents of a website:

> When a person searches the term 'world cup' in a search engine like Google, the search engine will look for websites containing the meta tag 'world cup' for producing the search result. The greater the number of meta tags, the higher will be the order of ranking in the result page. When an ambush marketer creates a webpage, having the meta tag 'world cup' . . . in its html code, it may be shown even above the official website of 'world cup' in the search results page. Since meta tags are not visible to the normal users, they are very difficult to detect (p. 43).[1]

Unauthorized alignment with official sites may occur in several ways. An ambush marketer may create the perception that a sport property's website and content is its own by "framing" the material within the ambusher's site, rather than linking visitors to the official site. Alternatively, links to the official site could be designed in such a way as to make visitors believe that the website is endorsed by the sport property or official sponsors. For example, if an ambush marketer's website shows a prominent link to the FIFA World Cup site, it may convey the impression that FIFA has authorized the link. A third unauthorized alignment strategy involves unauthorized use of information available on a sport property's website. Such information can be used to create an impression that the ambusher is associated with the event.[1]

Companies pay providers like Google to make their advertisements appear when specified *key words* are inserted in the search engine. Thus:

> If a person searches the word 'FIFA World Cup' in Google, a number of unofficial web links will appear on the search result page. Only a careful Internet user will know that these are advertisement links and are not related to FIFA in any manner. Through this route, ambushing companies can associate a non-sponsor with an event (p. 44).[1]

Courtesy of iStockPhoto.com

STRATEGIES TO COUNTER AMBUSHING

By the mid 1990s, ambushing had become widespread, but since that time properties and official sponsors have invested substantial efforts in developing increasingly sophisticated and effective approaches to countering it. They have addressed each of the strategies used by ambushers and either closed the loophole or narrowed its potential for exploitation. The counter strategies have involved both legal and market remedies.

Legal Counter-Strategies

Legal remedies are pursued when it is believed ambushers appropriate property rights that they do not own. For example, if the logo or symbol of a team or event was used without official authorization this would be an infringement of the sport property's intellectual property rights. Similarly, it would be an obvious breach of the law to claim an official relationship with an event when none existed. However, the discussion of ambush strategies in the previous section showed that ambushers rely on implication and allusion rather than directly abrogating the legal rights of properties. The issue then becomes one of degree—how far can they push the allusion before it infringes on an event's property rights?

Few cases have reached the courts because (i) this process is costly and is likely to take years to resolve, so there is incentive to settle disputes privately; and (ii) the courts' decisions typically have favored ambushers, refusing to find a violation of existing law unless there has been a clear "trademark and tradename infringement" and this infringement is part of an overall marketing campaign.[24] Ambushers are aided by the fair use doctrine which permits a word or phrase to be used to describe a sports event even if it is a trademark. Thus, in the *WCVB-TV v Boston Athletic Association* case, the court pointed out that the television station's use of the words "Boston Marathon" during its unauthorized broadcasting of the event was fair. The marathon property had licensed

Channel 4 for a fee to broadcast the event, but Channel 5 (WCVB) also broadcast the event even though it was not licensed to do so by simply placing television cameras in the street along the marathon route. The court ruled that there was no infringement of the trademark "Boston Marathon" since reviewers were likely to perceive the channel as merely showing the marathon, rather than believing the channel had some special approval from the trademark owner to do so:

> There is no persuasive evidence to suggest official sponsorship of Channel 5's broadcasts . . . Nor is there any evidence that Channel 5 might somehow profit from viewers' wrongly thinking that BAA had authorized its broadcasts . . . The words "Boston Marathon" describe the event that Channel 5 will broadcast. Common sense suggests that a viewer who sees these words flash upon the screen will believe simply that Channel 5 will show the marathon, not that Channel 5 has some special approval from the BAA to do so.[25]

Perhaps the most prominent case, which was heard in a Canadian court, is summarized in Exhibit 6.6. The case related to Pepsi-Cola's ambushing of the National Hockey

Exhibit 6.6

NHL VS. PEPSI-COLA CANADA:
Overview of a Sports Ambushing Case

Pepsi-Cola Canada conducted a widely publicized consumer contest called the "Diet Pepsi $4,000,000 Pro Hockey Playoff Pool," whereby fans matching information under bottle caps with actual NHL Playoff results became eligible for prizes. The NHL (probably under pressure from Coca-Cola) filed a lawsuit, alleging that Pepsi-Cola Canada, which had no rights to NHL trademarks, had engaged in misappropriation and unfair competition by using marks "confusingly similar" to those owned by the NHL, had infringed on the NHL's trademarks, and unlawfully interfered with the NHL's business associations.

The Supreme Court of British Columbia ruled against the NHL. The Court found that Pepsi-Cola Canada had used three techniques which effectively defended them from this charge. First, they generically referred to the promotion as the "Pro Playoff Hockey Pool" instead of the NHL Playoff Pool. Second, in all their promotion material relating to the contest they included a disclaimer that the contest "is neither associated with nor sponsored by the National Hockey League." Third, under the bottle caps and scratch cards were city names of NHL playoff participants, not the full trade marketed team names.

Pepsi's commercial spots advertised the promotion during NHL broadcasts and they featured former NHL coach Don Cherry, a regular on the television program "Hockey Night in Canada" who was viewed by many as the voice of the NHL. The NHL argued that the defendant's advertising by using a personality clearly identified with the NHL games and by causing the commercials to appear during and in conjunction with the broadcasting of NHL playoff games was "likely to convey to the public a false impression that the NHL and its member teams approved, authorized, endorsed, or were in some manner associated with the contest, and thereby, Pepsi's products. The NHL states this was "clearly designed to tie into and trade upon the goodwill and regulation of the NHL and to thereby misrepresent or create confusion with the public as to Pepsi-Cola Canada's relationship with the NHL." This argument was rejected by the Court who indicated that by purchasing advertising within the playoff broadcast, Pepsi had a legitimate connection with the games.

League and Coca-Cola, which had paid $2.6 million to be the league's official soft drink sponsor. In effect, the court confirmed Pepsi had the right to associate with professional hockey by using a promotion based upon professional hockey players even though Coca-Cola had purchased exclusive sponsorship rights from the NHL.[24]

The first legal action properties usually take is to write a "cease and desist" letter to perceived ambushers. As long as the threat of successful prosecution exists, this will cause many of them to cease their activity. The Pepsi-Cola case emphasized to sport properties the risk of seeking redress in the courts, because if they lose then it removes a potential threat to ambushers, makes it less likely that cease and desist letters will cause them to stop, and gives ambushers greater freedom to act. Thus the Pepsi vs. NHL case result essentially removed the threat of sport properties being able to successfully challenge ambush marketers using unfair competition and trademark infringement arguments.[24]

The inability of traditional legal measures to prevent ambushing caused the Olympics and FIFA World Cup to lead the way in requiring that, as a condition of being awarded the event, countries pass specific legislation directed at explicitly defending sponsors against ambushing. This approach was pioneered in Australia with a statute entitled, "Sydney 2000 Games (Indicia and Images) Protection Act 1996," which augmented the country's existing intellectual property laws. Among its many provisions it incorporated two lists. List A contained the words 'Olympian' and 'Olympics', while list B contained the words 'Bronze', 'Games', 'Gold', 'Green and Gold', 'Medals', 'Millennium', 'Silver', 'Spirit', 'Sponsor', 'Summer', 'Sydney', 'Two Thousand', and '2000'. Any combination of the words in List A with any word in List B was brought within the ambit of the meaning of Sydney 2000 Olympic Games indicia. This was aimed at preventing the common ambush marketing practice of referring to events in indirect ways.

This Act also provided specific measures to mitigate possible economic losses that the SOCOG, SPOC, or a licensed user might incur from contraventions of the Act by providing that the loss or damage they suffered could be recovered. For example, if American Express tried to ambush Visa during the Sydney Olympics and if VISA could prove that it suffered loss of money due to the ambush marketing of American Express, the courts were empowered to direct American Express to reimburse VISA.[1]

Further, the Act provided for "corrective advertisements" by which the courts could require a company to pay for such advertisements in media and at a frequency of the court's discretion if the court was satisfied that indicia or images were used for commercial purposes without authorization. This was a major threat since corrective advertisements would likely have a substantive negative impact on a company's reputation and brand image.[1]

The Sydney Act pioneered the creation of "clean" zones around the sport venues which prohibit nonsponsors' advertising. Thus, for example, at the following Athens Olympic Games, the host organizers cleared 10,000 billboards from areas in and around Athens, including areas along motorways and bus-side advertising.[4] China authorized a similar act passing "Regulations on the Protection of Olympic Symbols" to protect sponsors at the Beijing Games.

When the British Parliament passed the London Olympic and Paralympic Games

Act for the 2012 Games, it incorporated all the features of the Sydney Act, but extended it so that a breach of the act was not only a civil offence, but it was also a criminal offense. The Act prohibited the use of any representation that suggested to the public an association between goods and services or a person who produces them, with the London Olympics. Under its broad definition, an association could be made by any advert or merchandise with any combination of words, marks, or symbols. The courts were to assess by an overall impression whether an unauthorized association was made. The burden of proof was placed on the defendant to convince the court that an association with the Games had not been made.[26] The comprehensiveness and potential reach of this London Games legislation was extraordinary and was considered by some to be draconian. The following illustrations provide an indication of its scope:

- Pub landlords were prohibited from posting signs which said, "Come and watch the London Olympics on our big screen."
- Athletes were not allowed to tweet about any non-sponsor's food or drinks they might be having at meals during the Games, or post video messages to fans from their rooms in the athletes' village.
- It was an offense to sell a ticket without written authorization from LOCOG which prevented scalping and ambush marketers offering a ticket as part of their strategy.
- As a condition of purchasing tickets, fans were not allowed to upload snippets of the day's action to YouTube, or even to post their pictures from inside the Olympic Village or arenas on Facebook: "A Ticket Holder may not license, broadcast, or publish video and/or sound recordings, including on social networking websites and the Internet."
- All bathrooms were checked at every Olympic venue to ensure manufacture's logos on soap dispensers, wash basins, and toilets were taped over or removed.
- Billboard owners were prohibited from selling signage to nonsponsors since the regulations imposed obligations on "persons who own, occupy, or have responsibility for the management of land, premises, or other property" (p. 578).[4]

The NCAA and NFL have followed this lead and now insist on clean zones at the Final Four and Super Bowl venues, respectively. Inevitably, this is controversial since local businesses regard it as usurping their private property rights.[4] The organizations use the host city bidding process to leverage the issue, making the commitment to pass a local ordinance creating clean zones a key evaluation criterion in the process. The NCAA clean zones, for example, typically include the NCAA headquarters, team hotels, and the arena venue. The following are prohibited within the clean zones: "temporary, non-NCAA authorized banners, flags, inflatables, or other promotional devices; temporary sale or complimentary distribution of food, beverage, literature, or merchandise not authorized by the NCAA, and temporary unauthorized entertainment" (p. 568).[4]

Creation and monitoring of clean zones proximate to venues is complemented by aggressive enforcement within venues to remove any resemblance of ambush activity. Often this is facilitated by terms and conditions printed on the back of tickets. For example, at the World Cup soccer tournament in Germany, on the back of the ticket it stated that "All promotional, commercial, political, or religious items of whatever nature, including but not limited to banners, symbols, and leaflets are prohibited." (p. 572)[4] It was this clause that led to the removal of Dutch supporters' orange pants described in Exhibit 6.3. This type of enforcement has become more rigorous in recent years as the following examples illustrate:

> At a cricket match between Australia and India, a South African businessman who was drinking Coca-Cola and refused to surrender another three unopened Coca-Cola cans was removed from the stadium. Pepsi was an official sponsor of the Cricket World Cup, although the company distanced itself from this unfortunate episode. Similar onsite policing occurred during the Olympic Games in Athens when security guards, seeking to protect the rights of official sponsor Coca-Cola, confiscated cans of Pepsi when patrons tried to go through entrance gates to competition venues . . . Before the Olympic Games in Sydney, the IOC, upon realizing that food service company, Aramark, had supplied 30,000 uniforms to the food service workers with its visible logo on the chest, required patches to be placed over the logos in deference to official marketing partner McDonald's. During the Olympic Winter Games in Turin, the IOC, to protect the exclusive sponsorship rights of computer equipment sponsor Lenovo, required that the Dell logos on news reporters' laptop computers be covered with black electrical tape to conceal the Dell brand name. Even more bizarre, tape was placed over the brand name of the toilets at the curling site in Turin. (p. 566)[4]

A danger associated with zealous enforcement is that it becomes a media story. This may have two adverse consequences. First, a backlash against the sponsor from outraged attendees. There were two examples of this at the London Olympics:

- Visa had exclusive credit card rights at the Games, so non-Visa cards, such as Mastercard and American Express were not accepted on the sites at any of the 40 Olympic venues either by vendors or by cash machines. This led to frustration and outraged indignation, and criticism being directed at Visa by those who were inconvenienced.
- Over 800 food retailers at the 40 Olympic venues were banned from serving chips (French fries), despite the organizers' pledge that traditional British food would be featured. The banning edict said: "Due to sponsorship obligations with McDonald's, LOCOG has instructed other caterers they are not allowed to serve chips in any Olympic venue. The only exception to this is if they are served with fish." Thus, while quintessential British fish and chips was preserved, other favored traditional meals such as sausage and chips, gammon, egg and chips, and chicken and chips were not available. The resultant media and public outcry against the company focused on "McDonald's greed," and criticism of the quality of their chips.[27]

The second potential adverse consequence of zealous enforcement is that it may further the goals of the ambusher. This was vividly illustrated in Exhibit 6.3, which describes the ambush of Budweiser by Bavaria Beer at two World Cub tournaments. Another high-visibility example occurred at the UEFA European Soccer championship tournament in 2012:

- Paddy Power is a large international betting company. It was not a sponsor of the Euro 2012 tournament. When Nicklas Bendtner scored his second goal for Denmark in their match against Poland, as part of his celebration he lowered the top of his shorts a couple of inches to reveal the elastic top of his green underpants which were emblazoned with the words "Paddy Power." The live television broadcast focused on this, and photographs of his audacious action appeared in hundreds of newspapers throughout Europe. It was a flagrant breach of UEFA's rule Law 4 which states: "Players must not reveal undershirts which contain slogans or advertising. A player removing his jersey to reveal slogans will be sanctioned by the competition organizer." Accordingly UEFA fined Bendtner $125,000 and banned him from playing in the next competitive tournament match. Paddy Power responded by paying the fine and stated (with tongue firmly in cheek?) "We pride ourselves on listening to our customers and what we heard loud and clear yesterday was that Nicklas Bendtner should not suffer as a result of UEFA's double standards. We don't believe that Nicklas should be penalized for nothing more serious than wearing his lucky underpants which in fairness was only a bit of fun."[28]

It is likely that many people will smile at the ingenuity and "cheekiness" of Bavaria Beer and Paddy Power and will associate it with the World Cups and European Championships, respectively, long after the events are over. Indeed, the relationships are likely to endure much longer than the official sponsors' association with the tournaments which the properties were trying to protect with their legal tools. It has been pointed out that rather than protecting sponsors, extreme enforcement measures hurt them: "Each time the brand police tape over the logo of a non-sponsor, or warn the public about wearing a Pepsi t-shirt to the Games, or insist policeman carry their snacks in unbranded plastic bags, they drag down the brands of the sponsors."[29] These actions demean sponsors, causing them to be perceived as "small-minded," miserly, and petty; obsessed with their corporate bottom-line rather than with the quality of attendees' experiences; and lacking in tolerance and good humor.

In the U.S., the government does not provide any funds for either the Olympic movement or its athletes. It is perhaps unique in the world in this respect. To enable the USOC to fulfill this funding role, in 1998 the Olympic and Amateur Sports Act of 1978 was amended. It authorized the USOC to grant exclusive rights to the Olympic marks and symbols that enables it to attract sponsors, suppliers, and licensees who provide these funds. It entitles the USOC to sue companies that create even the appearance of an Olympic sponsorship. The express language in the Act lessens the USOC's burden of proof by prohibiting any combination of the specified words "*tending* to cause confusion or mistake, to deceive, or to falsely suggest a connection with the corporation or any Olympic, Paralympic, or Pan-American Games activity" (p. 558).[4] The effectiveness of the Act's provisions was evident in the very limited ambush activity that occurred at the 2002 Salt-Lake City Winter Olympics. However these wide embracing protections are confined only to the Olympics and are not available to any other sport property so events like the Super Bowl, Final Four, World Series, etc. are much more prone to ambushing.

Market Counter-Strategies

As long as ambushers do not use logos, images, or phrases protected by intellectual property rights, their activities are legal. Hence, the legal framework will never be sufficient to fully protect against ambushing. For the most part, properties have to rely on market remedies to protect their sponsors.

Four types of market remedies are available. The first is *comprehensive leveraging*, especially activation, of the platform the event provides which was discussed in Chapter 5. The more creative, distinctive, and prominent the activation activity is, the stronger will be the linkages in customers' minds, making it more difficult to effectively ambush the sponsor. If activation is pursued for an extended period both before and after the event, then the potential impact of an ambusher will be minimized. Longevity of a sponsorship similarly offers ambush protection because the brand linkage becomes more firmly embedded in the public consciousness: "The difficulty for any sponsor in taking on the London Tennis Championship at Queens Club, for example, would be to follow Stella Artois at an event that is widely known as "the Stella" (p. 66).[30]

The second preventive tool for combating ambushing is *pre-event education and public relations initiatives*. Production and dissemination of video news releases designed to generate stories about the event owner's intellectual property rights and protection programs may be distributed to the media. Letters may be sent to both local and national constituencies that may influence ambushing, apprising them of an owner's rights. Thus, for example, the NCAA for its Final Four Basketball Championships sends letters to local businesses urging them not to engage in ambush activities and alerting them to rules and restrictions relating to NCAA copyrighted logos and marks such as "Final Four," "March Madness," "The Big Dance," etc.; temporary signage, special events and promotions, and "clean zone" requirements. A second letter from the NCAA is sent to national media, advertising agencies, and major corporations asking "that you refrain from any direct or indirect usage of NCAA championships, tickets, or marks/logos without written consent of the NCAA" (p. 563).[4] These letters may discourage local businesses from inadvertently engaging in ambush activities, but they seem unlikely to be a deterrent to serious ambushers.

Another tactic is to place advertisements in trade journals and newspapers designed to educate the industry on the rights of official sponsors. An advertisement placed by the NCAA titled "How to avoid a blocked shot" was intended to discourage advertisers from ambushing the Final Four:

> If you're thinking of scoring marketing points through the use of NCAA references please remember that the unauthorized association with the championship of use of NCAA trademarks and tickets are violations of the NCAA's property rights. Only official NCAA corporate partners have the right to use NCAA marks,

logos, references, and championship game tickets in advertising, marketing, and promotions. (p. 564)[4]

It has been pointed out that these education and public relations efforts are unlikely to have much impact because (i) "they are premised on a pliant and cooperative media that typically has little if any vested interest in protecting the sponsorship rights of event organizers" (p. 565);[4] (ii) the public is disinterested in the ambush marketing issue and most do not consider it unethical; and (iii) sophisticated ambushers already understand the legal parameters and use subtle, ingenius, and creative approaches to work around them, so their behavior will not be influenced.[4]

A third pre-emptive tool is *the contract*. Many of the previous loopholes that enabled ambushing have been closed through more tightly specified contracts. Athletes who are personally sponsored by companies other than the official team sponsor may now be prohibited from covering their uniform logos or waving their shoes at the cameras during medal ceremonies. Major properties have addressed this by requiring athletes to sign "Team Member Agreements" that prohibit them from giving non-official sponsors publicity during the event. The IOC have extended this in Rule 40 of the Olympic Charter so athletes and other participants in the Games are prohibited from promoting their individual sponsors if they are not TOP or, in the US, USOC sponsors for a month before, during, and after the Games. This is proving to be controversial:

> The idea that Olympians who give up full-time occupations to train are unable to capitalize on their own efforts during the time they are most marketable is unpalatable to millions of people. This means that for the first time, the IOC's marketing restrictions have the real potential to damage the Olympic brand, turning people away from its positive attributes of excellence and achievement and toward describing it as greedy, uncaring, and unfair.[31]

Some major sponsors have indicated a desire to relax these stringent requirements because they want to avoid being perceived as "greedy and unfair."

Properties in their contracts now often prohibit nonsponsors from purchasing large blocks of event tickets by specifying more tightly how tickets are to be distributed and they similarly restrict nonsponsor access to hospitality opportunities.[3] In the early days of ambushing, nonsponsors used event tickets as prizes in promotions, thus implying they were sponsors. However, this is now illegal since their distribution is specified in the contract. Thus, for example, only NFL sponsors can use Super Bowl tickets as a prize in contests or promotions, while only MLB sponsors can give away tickets to the MLB All Star Game or the World Series.

The ability of competitors to ambush official sponsors by becoming "official broadcast sponsors" has been removed by property owners including in their contracts with broadcasters clauses prohibiting competitors of official sponsors to sponsor the screening of events. However, the ambush battleground has moved from broadcast media to social media, where the law has more grey areas that are unrestricted and which is harder to police.

As the head of a social media agency observed: "There's a bigger opportunity now than there ever has been to hijack the conversation. There are no brick walls on the Internet." Similarly, the head of Coco-Cola's global partnerships noted that new technologies mean "intellectual property and content is going to be hard for the IOC to divide up, saying this is the sponsors' piece and this is the broadcasters' piece." The IOC concurred responding: "The links between what is a broadcaster and what is a sponsor may blur."[32] Clearly, this issue will be challenging for sport properties to manage and resolve, and it opens additional opportunities for ambushers.

If all else fails, a final strategy to forestall ambushing is to "name and shame" the ambushers. This involves publicizing the ambush and embarrassing the competitor. The thinking undergirding this strategy was explained in the discussion of attribution theory in Chapter 2. It pointed out that the effectiveness of a sponsor in building brand equity will be influenced by a target market's perceptions of a company's motives for investing in the sponsorship. If it is viewed as the "cause du jour" and lacking genuine sincerity toward the well-being of the sport property, then consumers are likely to be cynical and ignore it.[33] The stronger their attribution of a selfish interest to the sponsorship that blatantly exploits the relationship, the less likely they are to be positively influenced by it. The following example illustrates this effect:

- Opel Ireland (General Motors) were the long-time major sponsors of the Irish National soccer team. They had initiated the sponsorship at a time when the team was not doing well. Some years later the team's fortunes changed. They succeeded on a world stage and the players were feted as national celebrities. At that point, a financial services company tried to ambush Opel using sponsorship of the players as its platform. Opel responded with an advertising campaign featuring the first team they had sponsored many years earlier, with the caption line "We sponsored the band before the bandwagon." The financial services company was chastised by committed Irish soccer fans who expressed unbridled hostility towards it terming it a "bandwagon supporter." As a result of the outcry, the company quickly ceased its involvement with Irish soccer.[5]

The US Olympic Committee threatens to "name and shame" ambushers with campaigns which would consist of half- or full-page advertisements in many of the country's major newspapers featuring a photograph of an ambushing company's CEO under the headline, "Thief!" It is possible that other entities especially the NCAA or individual colleges could mount a "Don't hurt our Athletes" campaign against ambushers which might persuade them to "cease and desist."[34]

SUMMARY

Ambushing occurs when a company that has no formal rights as an official sponsor makes a planned effort to associate itself indirectly with an event in order to gain at least some of the recognition and benefits that are associated with being an official sponsor. There is widespread recognition that ambushing is effective. Perhaps the most convincing evidence that it works is that it has persisted for 30 years.

Discussions of the ethics of ambushing predictably reflect the self-interest of the debaters. Invariably it is perceived as being unethical by official sponsors. However, most now accept that competitors have no ethical obligation to make sure an official sponsor's investment is successful. On the contrary, they have a moral obligation to their stockholders to pursue all legal avenues to enhance a company's profitability.

Ambush strategies are carefully designed to avoid using logos, imagery, or phrases relating to the event that are protected by intellectual property law. Eight ambush strategies may be used: (i) sponsorship of the broadcast of the event; (ii) purchase of advertising time in and around the event broadcast; (iii) sponsoring entities other than the organizing body; (iv) presence in and around the event venues; (v) advertising and allusion in the thematic space; (vi) capitalizing on an enduring memory; (vii) creation of a counter attraction; and (viii) authenticity ambushing. Often some combination of these strategies will be used in an ambush campaign.

Sport properties and official sponsors have developed counter strategies to either remove those ambush opportunities or to narrow their potential for exploitation. The counter strategies embrace both legal and market remedies. Major sport properties now insist in their bidding documents that prospective event hosts create "clean zones" both in external areas proximate to venues and within the facilities. However, zealous enforcement of such measures risks a backlash both from attendees and from media stories reporting on those actions. Rather than protecting sponsors, these actions may result in them being perceived as small-minded, miserly, and petty. While some legal protections may be provided for the Olympic Games or similar mega-events, for the most part the counter strategies have to rely on market remedies.

Four market remedies are available. The first is longevity of sponsorship together with comprehensive leveraging and especially creative activation of the platform the event provides. Second, is pre-event education and public relations initiatives designed to generate media stories about the event owner's intellectual property rights and protection programs and to discourage local businesses from engaging in ambush activities. The strongest defense mechanism is tightly specified contracts. These can remove the "official broadcast sponsor" option in contracts with broadcasters; require athletes to sign "team member agreements" that prohibit them from giving nonofficial sponsors publicity during the event; tightly control how tickets are distributed; and restrict non-sponsor access to hospitality opportunities. Finally, if all else fails then a property may elect to "name and shame" the ambushers.

Endnotes

1. Scaria, A. G. (2008). *Ambush marketing: Game within a game*. Oxford, England: Oxford University Press.

2. Sandler, D. M., & Shani, D. (1989). Olympic sponsorship vs. ambush marketing: Who gets the gold. *Journal of Advertising Research, 29*(4), 9–14.

3. Sauar, A. D. (2002). Ambush marketing steals the show. *Brandchannel*. Retrieved from www.brandchannel.org

4. McKelvey, S., & Grady, J. (2008). Sponsorship program protection strategies for special sport events: Are event organizers outmaneu-

vering ambush marketers? *Journal of Sport Management, 22*, 550–586.

5. Meehaghan, T. (1998). Ambush marketing: Corporate strategy and consumer reaction. *Psychology & Marketing, 15*(4), 305–322.

6. Pruess, H. (2004). *Economics of staging the Olympic Games: A comparison of the Games 1972–2008*. Cheltenham, UK: Edward Elgar.

7. O'Sullivan, P., & Murphy, P. (1998). Ambush marketing: The ethical issues. *Psychology and Marketing, 15*(4), 349–366.

8. Payne, M. (1991, 1998). Cited by Haek, J.

(2005). Ambush marketing: Research and management implications. In J. Amis and T. B. Cornwell. (Eds.). *Global Support Sponsorship* (pp. 207–224). New York, NY: Berg.

9. Welsh, J. (2002). In defense of ambush marketing. *Sponsorship Report, 21*(11), 1, 4–5.

10. McCullagh, K. (2008, July). Enemies at the gate. *SportBusiness International*, pp. 16–18.

11. D'Alessandro, D. F. (2001). *Brand warfare.* New York, NY: McGraw-Hill.

12. Kelso, P. (2012, March 7). London 2012 Olympics: Games caught in the middle of bitter battle between sportswear giants adidas and Nike. *Daily Telegraph.* Retrieved from http://www.telegraph.co.uk

13. Pitt, L., Parent, M., Berthon, P., & Steyn, P. G. (2010). Event sponsorship and ambush marketing: Lessons from the Beijing Olympics. *Business Horizons, 53,* 281–290.

14. Balfour, F. (2008, August 10). Li Ning pulls off Olympic-sized marketing ambush. *Business Week.* Retrieved from http://www.businessweek.com/globalbiz/blog/eyeonasia/archives/2008/08/li_ning_pulls_o.html

15. Kapraun, C. U. (2009, September 11). Sponsorship thoughts on my first US Open experience. *IEG Sponsorship Blogs.* Retrieved from http://www.sponsorship.com

16. Markiewiez, D. A. (2003, January 23). Dueling sponsors. *Bryan-College Station Eagle,* C2.

17. Nicholson, J. (2000, October 2). Guerilla promos in the Golden State. *Editor & Publisher, 133*(40), 38–39.

18. McKelvey, S., & Grady, J. (2004). An analysis of the ongoing global efforts to combat ambush marketing: Will corporate marketers "take" the gold in Greece. *Journal of Legal Aspects of Sports, 14*(2), 190–220.

19. Addley, E. (2012, April 13). Olympics 2012: Branding 'police' to protect sponsors' exclusive rights. *The Guardian.* Retrieved from http://www.guardian.co.uk/sport/2012/apr/13/olympics-2012-branding-police-sponsors

20. McAlister, A. R., Kelly, S. J., Humphreys, M. S., & Cornwell, T. B. (2012). Change in a sponsorship alliance and the communication implications of spontaneous recovery. *Journal of Advertising, 41*(1), 5–16.

21. Haek, J., & Gendall, P. (2002, December/January). When do ex-sponsors become ambush marketers? *International Journal of Sports Marketing & Sponsorship,* pp. 383–401.

22. O'Brien, C. (2012, March). Why ambush marketing could be an Olympic event at London 2012. *Birmingham Post,* p. 31.

23. Andrews, J. (2010, June 1). A new twist on ambush marketing and other interesting events. *IEG Sponsorship Report.* Retrieved from http://www.sponsorship.com/IEGSR/2010/06/01/A-New-Twist-On-Ambush-Marketing-AndOther-Interest.aspx

24. McKelvey, S. (1992, Fall). NHL v. Pepsi-Cola Canada, Uh-huh! Legal parameters of sports ambush marketing. *The Entertainment and Sports Lawyer,* pp. 5–17.

25. WCVB TV v Boston Athletic Association. (1991). #90-1315. U.S. Court of Appeals, First Circuit.

26. Soldner, A. (2010). *Ambush marketing vs. sponsorship values at the London Olympic Games.* Ashurt, Germany: IMR Management Report.

27. Clark, E. (2012, July 13). McDonald's force Olympic bosses to ban all other restaurants from selling chips . . . unless they are served with fish. *Daily Mail.* Retrieved from http://www.dailymail.co.uk/news/article-2172168/London-Olympics-2012-McDonalds-force-Olympics-bosses-ban-restaurants-selling-chips-unless-FISH.html

28. Telegraph Sport. (2012, June 18). Euro 2012: Nicklas Bendtner banned and fined £80,000 by Uefa after exposing sponsored underwear. *The Telegraph.* Retrieved from http://www.telegraph.co.uk

29. Ukman, L. (2012, August 13). Non-sponsors take on the Olympics to align their brands with fair play. *IEG Sponsorship Blog.* Retrieved from http://www.sponsorship.com

30. Masterman, G. (2007). *Sponsorship for a return on investment.* Boston, MA: Elsevier.

31. Andrews, J. (2012, August 9). Will the Olympic movement change its marketing rules? (It better). *IEG Sponsorship Blog.* Retrieved from http://www.sponsorship.com

32. Kortekaas, V. (2012, May 21). Olympic chiefs aim to light up sponsorship. *Financial Times.*

33. Dean, D. H. (2002). Associating the corporation with a charitable asset through sponsorship: Measuring the effects on corporate community relations. *Journal of Advertising, 31*(4), 77–87.

34. McKelvey, S. (2002, April 22–28). Ambush threat the real madness in March. *SportsBusiness Journal.* Retrieved from http://m.sportsbusinessdaily.com/Journal/Issues/2002/04/20020422/Opinion/Ambush-Threat-The-Real-Madness-In-March.aspx

7

Potential Negative Outcomes from Sponsorship for a Sport Property

When sport organizations accept sponsors' resources, they may implicitly be giving up some control over their event. This may result in negative outcomes to the property that were not anticipated when the agreement was signed. This chapter reviews the potential negative outcomes that may occur to a sport organization from a sponsorship agreement, while the following chapter discusses risks that companies may experience. An awareness and consideration of the risks to both parties by both parties reduces the probability of subsequent conflict between them.

Four types of potential risks for sport properties are identified: changes in a sport's format or rules; undue influence by sponsors on organizations or events; erosion of "fan equity" caused by over-commercialization; and negative connotations or controversies associated with sponsors that may impugn the reputation of the sport property.

CHANGES IN A SPORT'S FORMAT OR RULES

In return for their support, sponsors may insist on changing the sporting event so the very nature of the sport is altered. There is a well-known aphorism that says those who pay the piper call the tune! Changes may be implemented to make a sporting event more exciting, entertaining, and attractive to television, or to better fit the media's programming format so the sponsors' audiences are expanded. Tennis is an example of this type of influence. The method of scoring was changed by the introduction of sudden death tie breakers to shorten matches and make them more interesting, while the traditional white apparel was replaced by multi-colored outfits for the same reason.

The growth of one-day and half-day cricket matches in national and international competitions occurred primarily to accommodate the demands of television audiences who wanted to see an immediate and definite outcome, rather than waiting for up to five days for a result which, even then, is not guaranteed to produce a winner. Thus, the majestic, traditional, international format which consists of a series of five games each lasting five days that is beloved by hard-core cricket enthusiasts, "stands at a precipice" according to the 149th annual edition of *Wisden*—the bible of cricket.[1] There is a real possibility the traditional format will become a historical relic, usurped by the "quickie" game and its adapted rules to meet the instant gratification needs of broadcast audiences.

In amateur sport, field hockey has experienced a number of rule changes aimed at making the game faster and therefore more attractive to spectators and to sponsors. The sport of lacrosse witnessed another form of development through the formation of the National Indoor Lacrosse League in the North America. In order to increase goal-scoring opportunities, the net was widened by six inches and the number of penalties reduced, as compared to traditional box style lacrosse.[2]

UNDUE INFLUENCE BY SPONSORS

Consider the following examples of sponsor influence:

- When Nike invested $160 million in a five-year sponsorship of the Brazil national football team, which many consider the leading national soccer team in the world, the company was allowed to specify where, when, and against whom the national team would play twice per year.[2]
- Andretti Autosports' car failed to qualify for the Indy 500 so it negotiated with AJ Foyt Racing. It was agreed that Andretti would pay Foyt $200,000 for its driver and sponsors to take over one of Foyt's cars that did qualify. This was legal under INDYCAR rules which stated that the fastest 35 cars made the race, not the 35 fastest drivers. The arrangement was driven by Andretti's sponsors paying much larger fees than Foyt's sponsors and, hence, having much more to lose by not appearing in the race. There was widespread condemnation of the action with many claiming it impaired the race's integrity.[3]
- Air Canada, a longtime and heavy-spending corporate partner of NHL teams, threatened to withdraw its sponsorships if the NHL did not immediately address the frequency of headshots and resulting injuries.[4]
- Capital One, a NCAA Corporate Champion sponsor, launched the Capital One Cup, given to the university that best demonstrates overall athletic excellence. Organizers opted to weight football and basketball heavier in their algorithm for determining the award winner. Many athletic directors and other influencers verbalized their displeasure with the award's formula.[4]

While sponsorship investments buy brands the right to associate with a property, do they also give them the right to influence the property's presentation of the event even if, like the Air Canada vignette, they are motivated by facilitating the "general good" rather than self-interest?

Another dimension of sponsor influence occurs when the needs of a sponsor become more important than the intrinsic merit of the sporting event itself. The Olympic Games are perhaps the forum at which this issue reaches its apogee, but the issue is debated in other contexts at lower levels of sport. The central role of U.S. television companies and sponsors in financing the Olympic Games has resulted in the schedule of track and field events sometimes being arranged so they can be shown live on prime-time television in the United States. Thus, on occasions, for example, marathoners have been required to race during the hottest part of the day. In such cases, the welfare of the athletes and the focus on the event become subservient to commercial interests. Consider the following examples of the influence of television at the Sydney Olympics:

- NBC's requirement that the overhead power lines and forty-eight electrical towers at Homebush Bay be removed and the cables put underground in order to improve television images; the New South Wales government contributed $20m toward what state leaders called "a luxury we can't afford"
- The positioning of the running track at the Olympic stadium resulting in winds that seriously impeded athletes' performances, simply because television cameras needed a shadow-free main area, not facing the afternoon sun
- NBC's decision to protect its $1.2 billion purchase of television rights by delaying all telecasts until evening prime time (since most of the network's viewing audience lived in a time zone twelve to fifteen hours behind Sydney time).[5]

It has been alleged that as commercial forces have become more prevalent, the pressure on athletes to perform more often and to participate even when they are hurt has increased.[6] For example, cricket used to be a seasonal game. However, the large amount of sponsorship and broadcast revenues that have flowed into the sport have transformed it into a year-round global game with few breaks for international caliber players. Predictably, the increased physical and mental stresses have led to players participating when injured and shorter professional careers.

OVER-COMMERCIALIZATION

There is a concern among some that the pervasiveness of sponsorship in elite sport and the commercialization that accompanies it may over the long term erode the fan base upon which it depends. In the case of soccer, for example, it has been argued:

> The drive for profit that underpins the embrace of sponsorship encourages the club to erode the emotional bond between club and the traditional supporter. This 'fan equity' is the traditional economic basis of the club because the passion shown by the spectators at the ground is what produces the spectacle that makes football a televisual product. However, fans lured by the televised product, which sponsorship demands, see the game as entertainment not as emotional attachment. The net effect of sponsor-driven televised sport may then be to destroy "fan equity" by driving them from the grounds to which they may never subsequently return. (p. 281)[6]

The likelihood of an over-commercialization backlash is most prominent at the grade school level. The following vignette illustrates the issue:

- Fila USA and Footlocker invested $1.5 million over 3 years to remove or refurbish dilapidated basketball backboards in 825 New York City elementary and junior high school playgrounds, and to maintain them. In exchange the companies' logos appeared on the backboards above a motivational message such as "Stay in school." A segment of the community protested vigorously at the "corporate take-over of classrooms, gyms, and arenas to sell kids products they don't need or can't afford."[7]

In an attempt to ameliorate the charges of over-commercialization many sport governing bodies, including the NCAA, NFL, and NBA, have imposed rules limiting the size of corporate logos than can be displayed on team uniforms. For example, the NCAA's uniform rules limit the size and number of manufacturers' logos on game jerseys to "a single manufacturer's logo not to exceed 2¼ inches square." A similar limitation is imposed on socks, headbands, and wristbands.

NEGATIVE CONNOTATIONS OR CONTROVERSIES ASSOCIATED WITH SPONSORS

There is an aphorism that says: People are judged by the company they keep. Sport organizations are increasingly expected to be responsive to social concerns as well as their own financial well-being. Thus, they have to be concerned about partnering with companies that could damage their reputation. In some instances, the negative connotations associated with a company may be public perceptions based on a distorted view of the actual facts. Nevertheless, the risk of damage to the sport property's image remains. Dow Chemical's involvement with the London Olympics described in Exhibit 7.1 illustrates how this might occur.[8]

Exhibit 7.1

Dow Chemical and the Olympic Stadium Wrap

Dow Chemical was a TOP sponsor of the London Olympics. They committed $100 million to the IOC over a 10-year period. Dow became a sponsor for three reasons: (i) To facilitate its reach into new markets, including Russia and Brazil where the next two Games after London would be held; (ii) to accelerate its "transformation strategy" of being perceived as a "solutions provider"; and (iii) as a staff motivation tool.

As part of their sponsorship, the company agreed to pay £7 million for a "wrap" of polyester and polyethylene fabric panels which would encirculate the main Olympic stadium. In return, it secured the right to brand the surfaces with its name until the eve of the Games.

In 1999 Dow had bought Union Carbide, another chemical giant, which had come to public attention 15 years earlier when a di-lapidated plant belonging to its Indian subsidiary in Bhopal, a city of 1.7 million people in the central Indian state of Madhya Pradesh, exploded and filled the air with gases, principally methyl isocynate, an ingredient in pesticides. Some 3,000 people were killed in the first few weeks, many more have died in the years since then, and the death total directly attributable to the world's worst industrial disaster now stands at around 11,000 in the most conservative estimate (the true total may be over 20,000).

Dow bought Union Carbide seven years after the Indian subsidiary had been divested by Union Carbide to a third company McLeod Russel India Ltd. Dow's spokesperson said, "We didn't buy the Indian assets or liabilities because Union Carbide had sold them to McLeod Russel. Are we responsible? Legally? No. Morally, ethically? No."

Exhibit 7.1 *(Continued)*

Dow Chemical and the Olympic Stadium Wrap

Despite Dow's claims of severance from the disaster and the Indian government accepting a $470 million payment in final settlement of any obligations, witnesses attested to a continuing tragedy and wanted the London Olympic organizers to sever links with a company that refused, in their view, to meet its moral obligations. A nurse who was then working in Bhopal close to the site reported:

> "The mistake people make is by continuing to say that this is about an explosion in December 1984. It's about contamination that's happening today." Toxic sludge, she explained, was dumped in pits, on top of plastic sheets, in an attempt to cleanse it through evaporation. Instead the chemicals leached into the ground water. The pits and the sludge are still there, and the water is still used for drinking and washing by people for whom government supplies of water are unreliable.
>
> "I've seen horrendous congenital defects in children: gross retardation and stunting, skin and respiratory conditions, endocrinology problems, unusual cancers. People say they know the water tastes funny, they know it isn't doing them any good, but they don't have a choice. And absolutely nothing is being done. All Dow will say, over and over again, is that it's nothing to do with them."

The nurse organized a petition to protest Dow's sponsorship of the wrap, and to try and galvanize public support to persuade Dow, which declared a profit of $2.3 billion in the previous year that it should regard Bhopal as its obligation. She argued this was a chance for the Olympic movement to live up to its humanitarian principles and to make a real difference in the lives of those who continue to suffer the consequences of the tragedy. Her efforts were endorsed by Amnesty International and reinforced by the Indian team threatening initially to boycott the Games if this was allowed: "We feel that

it will be against the basic principles of the Olympics charter to partner with Dow Chemical, which is responsible for the ongoing disaster in Bhopal," the athletes wrote in a petition sent to the Indian government. Later this threat was more limited and confined to boycotting the opening and closing ceremonies.

A spokesperson for Dow said: "It is disappointing and misguided that some people are trying to assign blame and responsibility to Dow. Dow acquired the shares of Union Carbide Corporation more than 16 years after the tragedy and 10 years after the settlement agreement—paid by Union Carbide Corporation and Union Carbide India, Limited—was approved by the Indian Supreme Court."

In the British Parliament, the Shadow Olympics Minister who played a key role in securing the London Olympics when her party was in power and she was a cabinet minister, and who was still on the board of the London Organizing Committee said: "It's better that we have an unwrapped stadium, rather than a stadium wrapped in the continuing controversy over Dow Chemical's sponsorship." Another elected official said, "This is damaging the credibility of London and the Games."

Dow was defiant, with their vice-president for Olympic operations stating: "This issue is not our issue. We're not going to be bullied by activists or politicians." The IOC and the London Organizing Committee for the Olympic Games consistently supported Dow throughout the public debate. The English Prime Minister also sided with Dow saying:

> We have to recognize two points. The first is that Dow was not the owner of Union Carbide at that time, so this is a different company and a different business. Secondly, and most importantly, the sponsorship of Dow for the Olympics is arranged by the IOC [not the London Organizing Committee]. It is their decision-making process and I think they followed perfectly reasonable processes.

Controversial partnerships that might damage a property occur when it appears the property is "selling-out" by allowing the allure of additional revenues to prevail over the values that sport is alleged to represent, and personal or community well-being. Most of these controversies focus on sponsors in the tobacco, alcohol, gambling, and products high in fat, salt, or sugar (HFSS) sectors. Traditionally, companies in these industries have been major sponsors of sport events, but the debate over the appropriateness of partnering with such businesses is becoming increasingly prominent.

Some people believe the sport industry is compromising its virtue for revenue by helping companies market products that are potentially harmful to public health.[9] It is incongruous to them that sport which exemplifies a healthy fit lifestyle should be used as a promotional vehicle for products that appear to be the antithesis of this. In short, these linkages which are consummated for financial purposes seem to defeat the broader *raison d'être* for sport.

Some sport managers have chosen to remain indifferent to this incongruity because they believe their sports would not be financially viable without sponsorship from companies in these sectors. They are concerned that loss of these revenues would mean either that events would be eliminated or that ticket prices would be commensurately increased. The former outcome is likely to occur in some contexts, but an economist is likely to argue that the latter outcome is improbable. Both of these outcomes assume that costs would remain fixed if sponsorship revenues declined, but in many instances it is likely that efforts would be made to reduce costs. It is naïve to believe that ticket prices would be increased. Most sport managers are charged with setting ticket prices at a level that will garner maximum revenues for their organization, so the current price of tickets is likely to be the highest price the market will bear. If patrons could pay more, then sport organizations would charge more now. Thus, ticket prices could not be increased if sponsorship was withdrawn. The only way to retain viability or profit margin would be to reduce costs which would involve reducing players' salaries, prize money, administrative overhead, etc.

In response to the public health concerns associated with these products, some professional sports leagues in the US have inserted "morality" clauses in collective bargaining agreements with the players' associations. These clauses prohibit players from endorsing or associating with tobacco, alcohol, or gambling companies.[9]

Tobacco

Tobacco companies had a long history of sponsoring sport. Indeed, before 1998 they ranked second behind the automobile sector as the primary investors in sport.[9] During the 1990s, opposition to their sponsorship reached a crescendo. It revolved around three issues. First, through sport sponsorship the product could be associated with the vibrant health of athletes instead of the horrors of emphysema, lung cancer, and the host of other illnesses exacerbated by tobacco products. Second, was the belief that the sport linkage enabled tobacco companies to penetrate the youth market, and more than 90% of people who will ever smoke on a regular basis do so prior to the age of nine-

teen.[10] Third, was the contention that such sponsorship circumvented the ban of cigarette advertising and promotion in broadcast media that was enacted in the US in 1971.

In 1998, the angst with tobacco companies, and the extraordinary costs they imposed on states' health care systems through people's use of the product, resulted in The
Master Settlement Agreement (MSA). In this, 11 tobacco companies executed a legal
settlement with 46 states, the District of Colombia, and five commonwealths and terri-
tories, agreeing to pay these entities $246 billion over 25 years. In addition, the settle-
ment agreement contained a number of important public health provisions, including
several resulting in the severe curtailment of sponsorship investment by the companies.

There were loopholes in the MSA that enabled some limited tobacco sponsorship to
continue. However, these were closed by the Family Smoking Prevention and Tobacco
Control Act passed by Congress in 2009. This gave the Federal Drug Administration
(FDA) the power to regulate the tobacco industry. In June 2010, the FDA issued regulations closing the existing loopholes. They applied to all tobacco companies and all
states, not only to those that signed the earlier MSA, and banned all sponsorship. The
rules stated:

> Manufacturers, distributors, and retailers of tobacco products MUST not sponsor
> any athletic, musical, artistic, or other social or cultural event, or any entry or
> team in an event, in the brand, name, logo, symbol, motto, selling message, rec-
> ognizable color or pattern of colors, or any other indicia of product identification,
> identical or similar to, or identifiable with, those used for any brand of cigarettes
> or smokeless tobacco (21C.F.B. 1140.34c)

The prohibition of tobacco company sponsorship in the US is consistent with actions
taken in many other countries throughout the world. For example, a European Union
Directive prohibited tobacco advertising and sponsorship in its 27 member countries in
2005. The demise of tobacco sponsorship in a short 15-year period is remarkable (and
perhaps a salutary exemplar for other potentially harmful products) given the industry's
aggressive opposition to such legislation and its formidable expenditures on lobbying
and influencing political processes.

Alcohol

The nexus between alcohol, sport, and males has a long cultural history. By no later
than the sixteenth century in the UK "the ale house was the main arena for staging
sports events . . . with fields, greens, courts, rings, and the like arranged in close proximity to the grounds. Here came much cockfighting, boxing, bowling, rugby, foot-
races, and more. Riding on the tendency of retired sport players to become pub owners,
proprietors became sports promoters and programmed contests that would draw the
largest crowds for the sale of brew" (p. 6).[11]

Alcohol companies are major sponsors of sport. In the US, Anheuser-Busch and
Miller Coors rank third and eighth, respectively, on the list of companies most active in
sport sponsorship (Table 1.1),[12] while Labatt and Molson are similarly active in Canada,

Busch Stadium in St. Louis, MO. Courtesy of BigStockPhoto.com

and Guinness and Heineken in Europe. Several decades ago, the substantial investment by beer companies in sport sponsorship was explained in these terms: "Beer drinkers and sports fans are one and the same—indivisible, inseparable, identical! No one drinks more beer than a sports fan, and no one likes sports better than a beer drinker" (p. 74).[13] The ages of maximum beer consumption and maximum sports involvement are the same, both for men and for women. The peak beer consuming years are from 18 to 29, which are the peak years for sports' participants and spectators. Males in the 18 to 34 age group constitute only 20% of the beer drinking population, but they consume 70% of all beer. Breweries have sought tie-ins with sport because this offers them a "macho" vehicle which appeals to their core young adult male target audience. These heavy users are the most critical market segment for beer companies and it is easy to communicate with them through sport-associated events.

The CEO of Anheuser-Busch identified four priorities in the company's quest to enhance profits by increasing overall consumption and sales: (1) improve the image and desirability of beer; (2) keep beer fun and social; (3) increase beer occasions; and (4) improve retail sales. Sponsorship of sports fits well with all four of these strategies and has become the company's primary tool in most of its markets.[11]

As the magnitude of sport sponsorship by breweries has increased, it has been accompanied by a commensurate increase in criticism from those concerned about alcohol abuse. There has been heightened awareness in recent years that alcohol is a drug with the potential to become addictive. There are approximately 79,000 deaths attributable to alcohol use each year in the U.S., making it the third leading lifestyle-related cause of death for the nation. There are more than 1.6 million hospitalizations; more than 4 million emergency visits for alcohol related conditions,[14] and unmeasurable negative costs such as spouse and child abuse, desertion, emotional problems, and fetal alcohol syndrome. The concern is that beer companies' promotions connote it is natural for this intoxicating drug to be consumed while watching, or after participating in, a sporting activity. The question is: Should sport be at all connected with a drug that is responsible for such problems? Sponsorship and advertising by beer companies promotes the image that beer is not very different from soft drinks, and its negative consequences such as traffic deaths, domestic violence, physical deterioration from cirrhosis, hypertension and stroke, and pregnancy risks are ignored.

Alcohol sponsorship aspires to create positive brand image transfer associated with sport teams and athletes: vitality, fitness, fun, health, endurance, speed, and strength. It has been observed that "beer comes to share the luster of healthy athleticism," and that "It's really paradoxic that alcohol and all it stands for should be associated with excellent athletic performance. You cannot have one and the other at the same time. If you're going to perform as a top-grade athlete, you have to cut out alcohol" (p. 78).[13] The close relationship between beer and sport has caused some "to wonder just what kind of cultural hypocrisy is going on when Americans relentlessly insist on immersing sport—our most wholesome, most admired, even (sometimes) most heroic institution—in a sea of intoxicating drink" (p. 70).[13]

In response to their social critics, beer companies point out that when used in moderation, beer has been shown to have positive effects on health. A cardiologist who undertook an exhaustive review of the empirical literature concluded: "A vast literature supports the notion of health benefits of moderate alcohol consumption." However, he issued a caution, "The recent research clearly shows that while moderate alcohol consumption is beneficial, the benefit is lost at higher levels of consumption" (p. 420).[14a] The US Departments of Agriculture and Health and Human Services carefully reviewed all the scientific literature related to alcohol consumption and health and concluded:

> The consumption of alcohol can have beneficial or harmful effects, depending on the amount consumed, age, and other characteristics of the person consuming alcohol. Alcohol consumption may have beneficial effects when consumed in moderation. Strong evidence from observational studies has shown that moderate alcohol consumption is associated with a lower risk of cardiovascular disease. Moderate alcohol consumption is also associated with reduced risk of all-cause mortality among middle-aged and older adults and may help to keep cognitive function intact with age. However, it is not recommended that anyone begin drinking or drink more frequently on the basis of potential health benefits because moderate alcohol intake is also associated with increased risk of breast cancer, violence, drowning, and injuries from falls and motor vehicle crashes. (p. 31)[15]

The USDA/USHHS define "moderate" as one drink a day for females and two drinks a day for males.

The debate over alcohol sponsorship is especially potent in the context of college sports, since they articulate a different mission from the revenue and profit-maximizing model that characterizes professional sports. In an open latter to Congress, renowned college coaches Dean Smith, John Wooden, Joe Paterno, and Jim Calhoun stated, "Advertising alcoholic beverages during college sports telecasts undermines the best interests of higher education and compromises the efforts of colleges and others to combat epidemic levels of alcohol problems on many campuses today." The Center for Science in the Public Interest sought to convince colleges to sign the College Commitment, which features a prohibition of alcohol advertisement during televised collegiate sports events. The document was signed by officials at more than 250 schools.[16] The evolution of the thinking process among college officials is captured by the following anecdote:

> In the mid-1990s, the director of men's athletics at the University of Minnesota negotiated a contract with Miller Brewing Company worth $150,000. Subsequently, he was promoted to vice-president for student development and intercollegiate athletics of the university system. When the contract expired, a new contract for $225,000 was offered. This time he declined explaining, "Being in a new position, I was able to get a big-picture view of what was happening . . . I felt like we were sending students a mixed message." That big picture had included the need for 14 students from the university to enter alcohol-rehabilitation programs and an increase in alcohol-related assaults on that campus, which constituted part of his new responsibilities.[16]

Nevertheless, bowl games, conferences and some individual colleges still accept alcohol company sponsorships. Ohio State, a major athletic power, rejects it and bars its local media partners from airing alcohol advertisements in game broadcasts. Their athletic director explained: "Colleges cannot work hard to tone down the use of alcohol around games, while cashing checks from beer companies. There's a terrible inconsistency there" (p. B12).[17]

The decision confronting sport managers as to whether of not they should solicit or accept sponsorship from beer companies is more difficult than that associated with tobacco companies because, unlike tobacco, the problem is not consumption of beer, rather it is the abuse of beer. This makes it tempting for sport managers to rationalize that there does not appear to be a strong enough case to ban beer companies from sponsorship opportunities. Certainly, the case for a ban ostensibly appears to be less compelling than the case which was made to ban sponsorship by tobacco companies.

Nevertheless, the alcohol industry is operating in an increasingly restrictive regulatory environment worldwide that is reminiscent of the early ruminations which ultimately led to the ban on tobacco products. Alcohol sponsorship of sport is vulnerable. Every time bad behavior by athletes or fans that is fuelled by alcohol receives media visibility, the negative linkage between sport sponsorship and alcohol abuse is reinforced. Their case is not aided by the insensitive, aggressive use of a sponsorship platform exemplified by the "Boony campaign" described in Exhibit 7.2.[11,18]

Alcohol sponsorship has been banned in several countries, most notably France which prohibited it in 1991. Thus, the Heineken Cup, which is the primary rugby club competition in Europe, has to be called the H Cup in France; when the Scotland Rugby

Exhibit 7.2

The Boony Campaign

Alcohol companies are major sponsors of cricket in Australia. The country's governing body, Cricket Australia, aggressively supports this relationship claiming that "banning alcohol sponsorship would impinge on sport's ability to deliver community programs that had a positive impact on health" and "we're paid in dollars, not in schooners" (p. 254).

Foster's Australia's VB (Victoria Beer) had naming rights for Australia's one-day cricket international series. The campaign, which included television commercials, online, sponsorship, point-of-sale and a range of other promotions—was built around 'Talking Boony', a talking figurine about the same size as a can of beer. Talking Boony was a caricature of David Boon, a former Australian cricketer, who was affectionately known as "Stumpy" or "The Keg on Legs." Boon was described in the trade press as "an Australian icon, partly for being a great Australian athlete, but mostly for looking like he should be sitting in the stands drinking beer, rather than padding up in the middle . . . But it was his effort in drinking 52 beers on a Qantas flight between Sydney and London at the beginning of (another) successful Ashes[a] Tour that truly elevated him to icon status." Indeed, he appeared on the cover of one of Australia's highest circulation weekend newspaper magazines half-dressed in cricket gear in a locker-room, holding a can of beer, with the headline "52 Not Out."

The figurine contained a microchip and a timer that enabled him to 'speak' during the cricket; about an hour before the start of the first match he spoke his first words: "Hey, get me a VB, the cricket is about to start", and throughout the cricket he made many other comments to his 'fans'—some about cricket, but many about beer (such as "Have you got any nachos? I like nachos. They go well with beer").

The Boony campaign was criticized by public health advocates for exploiting Boon's notoriety as a binge drinker, arguing that such a promotion could only have a negative effect on the entrenched drinking culture of cricket clubs. However, the advertising industry applauded—and awarded—the campaign. The agency that created the Boony campaign won a prestigious Yellow Pencil award at the D&AD Global Awards in London in the New Uses of Broadcast category for its 'innovative' campaign for Foster' and it won a Lion at the Cannes International Festival for the Talking Boony promotion. They were equally popular with consumers, with all 200,000 sold and 1,900 sold on eBay, with one going for nearly $230.

Not surprisingly, given the positive response from the industry and increased consumer sales, in the following year's series Foster's Australia announced an extension of the Boony campaign by adding "Talking Beefy" to the promotion modeled on former English cricket captain Ian 'Beefy' Botham, who was both Boon's mate and nemesis on the field. The figurines were available as a pair with promotional VB cartons, and the 'Battle of the Tashes[b]' was billed as VB's biggest ever promotion. The promotional material urged people to "grab cartons of VB and find out how these two hairy lipped legends of the game can go pound for pound, tash for tash, beer for beer, right there in your lounge room." The season's 375,000 pairs of figurines, which used infrared panels to verbally spar with each other, were issued with replaceable batteries "in the hope they'll stay in people's homes long after the Ashes are over."

In the third year of this campaign, Shane Warne, Australia's most renowned cricketer of the past two decades and the world record holder for wicket-taking was featured. He became the "face" of the VB campaign (and the talking doll). Warne is a classic "new lad" who appears regularly on the covers of the "new lad" magazines and has provided a constant stream of material for the Australian and British tabloid media, due to his boorish behavior and extramarital sexual affairs. He is a man who "behaves badly." Once again, the multi-million dollar campaign featured mass media advertising, a website, competitions and promotions, and merchandise—including the VB Warne figurine programmed with phrases including, "Ahhh VB, drinking anything else would be un-Australian."

---

[a]An urn containing the ashes of a cricket wicket was satirically presented to England after they were defeated by Australia in a cricket series in 1882. Ever since, it has become the symbolic trophy for which the two nations compete.

---

[b]'Tash' is a colloquial term for moustache, and both of these former captains sported moustaches.

team play in France they have to cover their sponsor's name on their shirts since Famous Grouse is an alcoholic beverage;[19] and Anheuser-Busch replaces beer/alcohol logos on cars it sponsors in Formula 1 racing with nonalcoholic brands it owns when the competition takes place in France. Actions creating momentum likely to lead to more restrictions or bans on alcohol sponsorship include:

- A report commissioned by the European Union calling for an outright ban on alcohol sponsorship throughout Europe on health grounds.
- An Irish government report, *National Substance Abuse Mission Strategy 2009–2016*, which recommended: "Ban alcohol sponsorships of all sporting and large music, comedy, and theatre events." It states: "The burden of health harms and the social consequences of harmful use of alcohol demand the implementation of further measures . . . to reduce the amount of alcohol we drink.[20]
- Australia, New Zealand, Welsh, and South African governments have all indicated an intent to ban alcohol sponsorship.
- The British Medical Association urged the UK government to pass a law that would include banning all sports and music sponsorships by alcohol companies. The government acted on many facets of their recommendation with multifaceted restrictions on the alcohol industry, but to this point has excluded a sponsorship ban from their regulations.

Gambling

Like tobacco and alcohol, gambling has had a long relationship with sport. A contemporary description of crowds en route to the Circus Maximus in Ancient Rome observed they are "already in a fury of anxiety about their bets,"[21] while a close relationship has been documented between gambling and cricket and baseball in eighteenth-and nineteenth-century Britain and the U.S., respectively.[22] One historian, for example, contended that at the onset of the twentieth century its popularity with gamblers meant that, "baseball was an important nexus between urban machine politics and organized crime, albeit a lesser one than prize fighting or horse racing" (p. 87).[23] There have been many cases of game fixing, including the notorious Chicago White Sox players alleged to have fixed the 1919 World Series for $100,000. All of the major US professional sports leagues over the years have had to address betting scandals.[9]

Given this heritage, it might be expected that sport leagues and properties would be wary of entering into sponsoring agreements with gambling companies. In the US such links are generally prohibited by the sports leagues, although they do allow sponsorships by the state lotteries.[9] Nevertheless, in recent years legal constraints on gambling have been relaxed, so it has become more widespread and expanded the types of gaming activities on offer.

There are two dimensions to the issue of sport sponsorship and gambling. The first dimension is the negative perception of corporate responsibility that the clubs are promoting a potentially risky behavior of addictive gambling that is increasingly recognized as a public health issue. The target groups known to be at highest risk for gambling problems are young males and adolescents who both tend to relate to sports.

The second problematic dimension for sport managers relates to gambling posing a threat by introducing incentives for corruption. In recent years, it has been rampant. For example, in US college basketball most betting revolves around whether a team will "beat the spread," rather than win or lose the game. This means athletes can be on the winning team and, at the same time, engage in corrupt actions that reduce the winning margin. This enables them to profit if they bet against their own team on the spread. Using a "forensics economics" approach, it has been estimated that this "point shaving" occurs in as many as 1% of college games.[24]

The emergence of "proposition bets" in recent years has been especially troublesome. These relate not to the result of a game but to some aspect of it. For example, a retired English Premier League player who made 400 appearances for his team said that players would deliberately manipulate set pieces such as corners and throw-ins: "For a while we did this almost every week. We made a fair bit of money. We could make deals with the opposing captain, for example, betting on the first throw, the first corner, who started with the ball, a yellow card or penalty. Those were the sorts of things we had influence over."[25]

Soccer is the world's most popular sport, but it may also be the world's most corrupt sport. European police investigations identified hundreds of matches, including some involving the World Cup, the European Championships, and the Champions League, that had been fixed by corrupt global betting syndicates, many of which are based in Southeast Asia. The biggest betting companies transact around $2 billion a week, which makes soccer gambling an attractive target for criminals.[25a] The preferred method of fixing the outcome of games or "proposition" bets is by bribing referees, but there are also numerous examples of players and coaches cooperating with criminals to fix outcomes. For example, in international soccer matches involving African teams and a South African promoter, referees were bribed to award multiple penalties to a specified team. When the fix was arranged, organized gangs across southeast Asia employed hundreds of people to place a series of bets up to $3,000—the theory being that smaller bets were less likely to draw suspicion.[25b]

Many of these betting companies are based in Asia and the worldwide reach of the EPL enables them to use their sponsorship as a platform to establish credibility in their home markets. While these partnerships give respectability to the companies, there may be a risk that their pervasiveness and the unsavory connotations associated with gambling in sport may damage the perceived integrity of the teams and the league. Despite these linkages, sponsorship by gambling companies in soccer is flourishing. For example, betting companies are the major shirt sponsors at 7 of the 20 teams in the English Premier League (EPL):

Wolverhampton Wanderers—Sportingbet

Stoke City—bet365

Wigan Athletic—12Bet (who replaced 188Bet)

Tottenham Hotspur—Mansion Casino

Swansea City—32 Red (who formerly sponsored Aston Villa)

Sunderland—Baglesports

Bolton Wanderers—188Bet

The EPL is an obvious vehicle for the betting companies since the people most likely to bet on sports are sport fans. After Bwin signed a three-year agreement with Manchester United to become the club's "official online gaming and betting partner," (one of the club's 33 different sponsors), the company's CEO stated: "As Europe's leading online sports betting operator, football is fundamental to our long-term success, making up approximately half of our total sports betting revenue of 261 million euros ($320 million). Manchester United has 569 million followers outside of Europe, providing us with a great opportunity to offer jointly designed and innovative products in countries that do not yet allow real money online sports betting." This partnership complemented Bwin's existing sponsorship with the Spanish team Real Madrid which competes with Manchester United for the title of world's best known soccer club.[26]

The gambling problem is not confined to college basketball and soccer. For example, a top player on the pro tennis circuit commented, "Everyone knows cheating goes on." In tennis, a favored player can retire from a match by feigning injury and thus gift a win to the underdog.[27]

The issue was highlighted by a scandal in cricket. Betair was the title sponsor of the England vs Australia test match series of five games each lasting five days. This rivalry has a 140-year history and each of the games captivates the attention of the general public in both countries, rather than only hard-core cricket fans. The appropriateness of the sport aligning so closely with a gambling company became an issue of contentious debate in 2011 when three members of the Pakistan Cricket team, including the captain, were sent to prison for facilitating winning "proposition bets" for a betting syndicate.

In this environment, is it appropriate for sport properties to be partners with betting companies? The danger of the sport/ gambling companies relationship was identified by the IOC President who said that betting-related corruption was as big a threat to the integrity of sport as doping: "It is a world problem and it is a very pernicious problem. With the introduction of broadband, you can bet worldwide. The danger is in match fixing and you see more and more attempts to manipulate matches. It is as dangerous as doping for the credibility of sport."[28] It has been suggested that, "The crux of the matter seems to be short-term financial gain versus the long-term outlook concerning the integrity of contests as well as the image of sports organizations" (p. 302).[9]

The dangers of sport associating with gambling were recognized by the European Court of Justice which stated in the *Bwin vs Santa Casa* case there was a possibility that "an operator which sponsors some of the sporting competitions on which it accepts bets and some of the teams taking part in these competitions may be in a position to influence their outcome directly, or indirectly, and thus increase its profits."[29] The court's concern was that commercial gambling providers could use their influential sponsorship position to influence the results of matches or to gain access to insider information. A similar view was taken by the Council of Europe in an Adopted Resolution of 22 September 2010 which stated that, "Betting operators should be banned from funding or sponsoring teams or individual competitors if they manage bets placed on competitions in which they are participating."

Products High in Fat, Salt, or Sugar (HFSS)

The targeting of youth by fast food and sugar drinks companies has become a debatable ethical concern. These HFSS products are being increasingly regulated, albeit at a relatively minor level at this point. For example, in the United Kingdom, television advertisements for these products must not be shown on or around programs that may appeal to children under the age of 16. Given the growing concerns of societies about obesity, it seems more restrictive legislation is likely in the future.

Sport is acknowledged by HFSS businesses as being an effective vehicle for reaching the critical youth market. Asked why McDonald's invests so much in sport, the company's director of worldwide marketing said, "It is important that we build brand loyalty with kids . . . sponsorships are a great way to accomplish this."[30] One expert on food policy commented:

> It is very convenient for fast food and soft drink people to sponsor sport, because by doing so they place all the emphasis on activity as the means of avoiding obesity rather than both activity and diet. There is a similarity between the strategy of the food industry today and the tobacco industry. Both have used sport as a means of reaching young people and both began by denying evidence that their products are harmful to health. There is a horrible familiarity in the way the food companies have behaved; they are trying to buy influence and present a kindly face.[30]

The London Assembly is a 25-member elected body that scrutinizes the activities of the Mayor of London and with a two-thirds majority has the power to amend the Mayor's budget or overturn his strategies. In advance of the London Olympics the Assembly passed a motion "to recommend that the IOC introduces criteria for the selection of future Games that exclude food and drink companies strongly associated with high calorie brands and products linked to childhood obesity and to encourage national organizing committees to adopt similar criteria." The chair of the Assembly who proposed the motion said:

> London won the right to host the 2012 Games with the promise to deliver a legacy of more active, healthier children across the world. Yet the same IOC that awarded the Games to London persists in maintaining sponsorship deals with the purveyors of high calorie junk that contributes to the threat of an obesity epidemic.

The Assembly believed that allowing companies like McDonald's and Coca-Cola to be featured as TOP sponsors contradicted the goal of leaving behind a healthy legacy for children.[31]

The conundrum of selecting between revenue enhancement and health concerns over fast food is particularly prominent in the high school context. When soft drinks companies provide sponsorship money to fund high school sports, the questions arise:

Courtesy of iStockPhoto.com

Does pairing sport and HFSS foods and drinks implicitly communicate that one can eat them and still look and feel like an athlete? Should high school sport events be used to promote consumption of a product that the U.S. Department of Agriculture and all reputable health nutrition texts urge students to avoid? Does it make sense for the school to be teaching avoidance in the classroom and to encourage use on the sports field? There appears to be an ethical issue with schools embracing a set of values they probably should be against:

- The fast food industry is under attack from a growing army of lawyers, doctors, and ordinary citizens. Elected officials are coming under pressure to pass laws limiting the junk food sold in schools and to regulate the marketing of products high in fats, sugar, and salt. "Big Food" is becoming a target of protest just as "Big Tobacco" was in the 1990s. Protestors are campaigning for fast-food companies to put cigarette-style warning labels on their food. Junk-food makers have to appeal to children to sell their products. They need to create their customers to service, but is this something that sport managers should support through accepting sponsorship from such companies? Everyone can get excited at the revenues these sponsors bring to the organization, school, or association, but don't sport managers have an obligation to ask whether these products are good for the people being targeted before accepting them as sponsors?[32]

Other Concerns Relating to Corporate Responsibility

In most of the cases described in this section, the nexus between products and their allegedly detrimental health impacts are highly visible. Many other corporate social responsibility issues are less obvious. For example, McDonald's has been accused of accelerating the destruction of rain forests to make way for cattle ranches; wasteful production and disposal of its packaging; and cruelty to animals.[6] Similarly, as Exhibit 7.3 illustrates, sport properties that have associated with ExxonMobil have been subjected to criticism.[33]

Exhibit 7.3

ExxonMobil and the Washington Nationals

When Washington D.C. built a new stadium for the Washington Nationals to welcome baseball back to the nation's capital, it was the country's first LEED certified green major professional sports stadium. One of the team's sponsors was ExxonMobil, whose signage appeared prominently in the stadium. The sponsorship was activated by the distribution of tip cards and by displaying energy saving ideas on the stadium scoreboard.

Environmentalists were outraged. The Strike Out Exxon group protested that the company's involvement in the park, "bur-nishes the image of the worst environmental company on the planet . . . The more environmental the Nationals make that park seem, the stronger the payday for Exxon." Pointing out that the company had spent $20 million to finance groups that questioned links between human activity and climate change, and that members of Congress and other policy makers frequented the new stadium, Strike Out Exxon suggested, "It's perfect politics. They get to associate their name with the goodness of baseball and environmental generosity."

An ongoing challenge for sport apparel companies is to address allegations that their products are produced in "sweatshops" in underdeveloped countries where workers (predominately women and children) are paid low wages; have minimal safety and environmental standards exposing them to dangerous machines and harmful chemicals; and are required to work long hours at unrealistic speeds with no access to unions. Nike, adidas, Reebok, and others face continual criticism. Nike, for example, owns eleven factories in Indonesia that produce 5.5 million shoes, mostly for the U.S. market. The company's typical response to these allegations is: "Nike believes wages are best set by the local marketplace in which a contract factory competes for its workforce."[34]

Organizations such as United Students Against Sweatshops (USAS) urge these companies' products be boycotted. To this point, the protests appear to have gained little traction among the general population, but this may change as corporate social responsibility emerges as an expectation rather than a discretionary philanthropic behavior. Adidas, a TOP sponsor of the London Olympic Games and the maker of Team GB kit, was the focus of sweatshop protests around the Games. For example, campaigners from War on Want released a 90-second video on YouTube alleging exploitation of workers. Their spokesman stated: "Adidas has 775,000 workers making products in 1,200 factories in 65 countries. What's shocking is at a time they are spending $100 million alone on the sponsorship deal with the Olympics, and the additional deals with the athletes, similar amounts of money are not being spent on real improvements in workers' rights."[35]

Mega events provide a platform which activists and protest groups increasingly use to further their own agendas. The platform has been created at great expense by others and is paid for, at least in part, by sponsors. Activists have become skilled in using it to garner the attention of global media, some of which are likely to be responsive to controversial event related stories. Sporting goods are a high-profile part of the garment industry and activists sometimes are able to suggest the sport companies' practices are contrary to the event's professed ethos of "fair play." For example, the Olympic Charter states, "Olympism seeks to create a way of life based on . . . respect for universal fundamental ethical principles."

The relationship of these issues to sport properties may seem tenuous, but the Dow Chemical case in Exhibit 7.1 illustrates their potential for impugning a property's reputation. Enhanced telecommunications and globalization suggest dilemmas of this type will occur with increasing frequency.

Perhaps the worst scenario for a sport property is when the disreputable behavior of a prominent sponsor partner rises to the level of high profile criminality. The exemplar of this situation was Enron's 30-year, $100 million agreement with the Houston Astros MLB franchise for the naming rights to its new stadium. When the agreement was signed, Enron Corporation was America's seventh largest company. The Enron Field name was on all exterior and interior signage, uniforms worn by game-day staff, cups, plates, napkins, and tickets.

When Enron collapsed as a result of unethical practices, tens of thousands of people experienced financial hardship through the loss of their jobs, pensions, funds, or stock. To the Houston and broader American public Enron quickly became a pariah. The name became synonymous with unethical behavior, shame, and failure. The continued use of the name Enron Field stigmatized the Astros. Their spokesperson noted, "The Enron logo displayed on the stadium wrongly suggests to the public that the Astros are associated with the alleged bad business practices of Enron . . . The current perception of Enron is incompatible with the honesty and integrity embodied in baseball as America's pastime and espoused by the Houston Astros" (p. A5).[36] The trustees acting for Enron's creditors refused to surrender the naming rights because they regarded them as an asset that had value. Ultimately, the Astros paid $2.1 million to Enron to remove the company's name from the stadium.

After legendary Penn State football coach, Joe Paterno, was criticized by the official report into the child abuse conviction of his long-time assistant football coach, Nike removed his name from its child-care center. This was an honorary title without the *quid pro quo* which is associated with naming rights agreements, so unlike the Enron case there was no legal problem in taking action. This was also the case at Villanova University where John E. DuPont gave $5 million to build a recreation center which was named the DuPont Pavilion. However, in a high profile court case some years later, DuPont was convicted of murder.[37] Fortunately for Villanova there was no formal written agreement requiring the school to retain the name and it was able to simply call the center, The Pavilion. The potential of corporate or individual donor partners' names becoming an embarrassment to colleges at some time in the future suggests that contracts should contain a clause that provides a dissociation option if a donor or corporate partner embarrasses a college or franchise. Companies commonly include such clauses in contracts with celebrity endorsers and this appears to be an analogous situation.[38]

Obviously, no sport organization would enter into a partnership knowing that the sponsor would damage its reputation, but there are occasions when this may occur inadvertently. The following vignette illustrates the nuances involved in potential relationships that could result in negative outcomes to a property:

- Women's professional tennis rejected a $10 million offer by Tampax tampons to become the sport's global sponsor because the tour feared the affiliation would adversely affect the image and marketability of women's tennis. Local tournament sponsors didn't want to be associated with a WTA Tour presented by Tampax. The tour spokesman commented, "No doubt it would have been great to work with a top flight company like Tambrands, but whether the offer was $3 million or $10 million, image is image, and we received a tremendous backlash for even considering the proposal." A local tournament director added, "I see complications in it. It didn't make me feel comfortable, and I sensed it might not be perceived as positive by my title sponsors and by the public in general. You could almost hear the Letterman jokes and, if you want to deal with reality, the hecklers" (p. B6).[39]

SUMMARY

While sponsorship funding has become a staple source of revenues for many sport events, there are four potentially negative outcomes for properties that may be associated with it. First, sponsors may insist on changing the rules or format of the event so it is more likely to be attractive to broadcast media. Second, they may exercise undue influence on its content, timing, location, or participants. Third, over-commercialization of an event may erode "fan equity"—the passion of fans who traditionally have supported it. Fourth, increased public sensitivity to the negative health impacts of tobacco, alcohol, gambling, and products that are high in fat, salt, or sugar (HFSS) may make it contentious for a sport property to partner with companies in these product classes. Similar controversy may emerge around issues of corporate social responsibility as expectations grow regarding the impact of a company's actions on society.

Tobacco sponsorship has been banned. Alcohol, gambling, and HFSS companies are all operating in an environment that is more regulated than it was a decade ago and which seems likely to become more restricted in the years ahead, and demand from society for corporate social responsibility is growing. Well-documented social and health problems and costs are associated with all of these industries. The parallels between their current societal status and that of tobacco 15 years ago are striking. It can be anticipated that there will be increasing pressure on sport managers to justify why they are partnering with these industries, given their negative impact on society.

Endnotes

1. Wilson, A. (2012, April 11). Wisden Almanack expresses fear for the future of international cricket. *The Guardian*. Retrieved from http://www.guardian.co.uk/sport/2012/apr/11/wisden-almanack-2012

2. Berrett, T. (1993). The sponsorship of amateur sport—government, national sport organization, and corporate perspectives. *Society and Leisure, 16*(2), 323–246.

3. Andrews, J. (2011, May 31). A reasonable solution to the Indy 500 sponsorship row. *IEG Sponsorship Blog*. Retrieved from http://www.sponsorship.com/iegsr/2011/05/30/A-Reasonable-Solution-To-The-Indy-500-Sponsorship-.aspx

4. Beiferheld, S. (2011, April 1). Fans weigh in on sponsors' influence, relationship with sports. *SportsBusiness Journal*, p. 24.

5. Lenskyj, H. J. (2002). The best Olympics ever? Social impacts of Sydney 2000. Albany, NY: State University of New York Press.

6. Slack, T., & Amis, J. (2004). Money for nothing and your cheques for free? A critical perspective on sport sponsorship. In T. Slack (Ed.).

The commercialization of sport (pp. 269–286). London, England: Routledge .

7. Davis, R. A. (1994). Playground blackboard idea nets advertisers, critics. *Advertising Age, 65*(23), 12.

8. Gibson, O. (2012, March 8). London 2012: Dow Chemical defends Olympic Stadium sponsorship deal. *The Guardian.* Retrieved from http://www.guardian.co.uk/sport/2012/mar/08/dow-chemical-olympic-stadium

9. McDaniel, S. R., Mason, D. S., & Kinney, L. (2004). Spectator sport's strange bedfellows: The commercial sponsorship of sporting events to promote tobacco, alcohol and lotteries. In T. Stack (Ed.), *The commercialization of sport* (pp. 287–305) London, England: Routledge.

10. Koop, C. E., & Kessler, D. A. (1997). *Final report of the Advisory Committee on Tobacco Policy and Public Health.* Washington, DC: Action on Smoking and Health.

11. Wenner, L. A., & Jackson, S. J. (2009). *Sport, beer and gender: Promotional culture and contemporary social life.* New York, NY: Peter Long.

12. IEG. (2012, May 29). Following the money: Sponsorship's top spenders of 2011. *IEG Sponsorship Report.* Retrieved from https://www.sponsorship.com/iegsr/2012/05/28/Following-The-Money--Sponsorships-Top-Spenders-of-.aspx

13. Johnson, W. O. (1988, August 8). Sports and suds. *Sports Illustrated, 69*(6), 68–82.

14. Centers for Disease Control and Prevention. (2011). Alcohol use and health: Fact sheet. Atlanta, GA: CDC.

14a. Kocheril, A. G. (2010). Healthy drinking. In G. Payne, B. Ainsworth, & G. Godbey (Eds.), *Leisure health and wellness: Making the connections* (pp. 413–423). State College, PA: Venture Publishing.

15. USDA &USHHS. (2010). *Dietary guidelines for Americans, 2010, 7th edition.* Washington DC: US Government Printing Office.

16. Naughton, J. (1998, January 9). Colleges eye restrictions on promotions by brewing companies. *The Chronicle of Higher Education,* p. A57.

17. Fatsis, S. (2003, November 12). Beer ads on TV, college sports: Explosive mix? *The Wall Street Journal,* pp. B1, B12.

18. Jones, S. C. (2010, April). When does alcohol sponsorship of sport become sports sponsorship of alcohol? A case study of developments in sport in Australia. *International Journal of Sports Marketing & Sponsorship,* pp. 250–261.

19. Singer, J. (2008, January 18–19). Playing regulatory games. *SportBusiness International.*

20. Holland, K. (2012, March 16). Consumption of alcohol up for second year in a row. *The Irish Times.*

21. Sauer, R. (1998). The economics of wagering markets. *Journal of Economic Literature, 36,* 2021–2064.

22. Munting, R. (1996). *An economic and social history of gambling.* Manchester, England: Manchester University Press.

23. Riass, S. A. (1999). *Touching base: Professional baseball and American culture in the Progressive Era.* Champaign, IL: University of Illinois Press.

24. Wolfers, J. (2002, May). Point shaving corruption in NCAA basketball. *AEA Papers and Proceedings, 96*(2), 279–283.

25. Jackson, J. (2012, July 11). FIFA to investigate Claus Lundekvam's claim of Southampton spot fixing. *The Guardian.* Retrieved by http://www.guardian.co.uk/football/2012/jul/11/fifa-claus-lundekvam-spot-fixing

25a. Tatlow, D. K. (2013, February 7). In worldwide soccer corruption scandal, an Asia tie. *International Herald Tribune.* Retrieved from http://rendezvous.blogs.nytimes.com/2013/02/07/asia-the-heart-of-worldwide-soccer-corruption-investigators-say/

25b. Wilson, J. (2013, January 3). Match fixing scandal in South Africa overshadows Africa Cup of Nations. *The Guardian.* Retrieved from http://www.guardian.co.uk/football/blog/2013/jan/03/match-fixing-scandal-south-africa

26. Chapman, M. (2012, August 17). Bwin sponsors Manchester United for social gaming drive. *Marketing Magazine.* Retrieved from http://www.marketingmagazine.co.uk/article/1145960/bwin-sponsors-manchester-united-social-gaming-drive

27. Doughty, S. (2012, March 23). Does procession of injured players show match-fixing is rife in tennis? *Mail Online.* Retrieved from http://www.dailymail.co.uk/news/article-2121877/Does-procession-injured-players-match-fixing-rife-tennis.html

28. Goodley, S. (2012, March 18). London Olympic organizers and bookmakers to hold betting summit. *The Guardian.* Retrieved from http://www.guardian.co.uk/sport/2012/mar/18/london-olympic-organisers-talks-bookmakers

29. Liga Portuguesa de Futebol Professional, Bwin International Ltd v Departmento de Jogos da Santa Casa de Misericondia de Lisboa, ECJ.

Judgment of 8th September, 2009, case C-47/07

30. Kelso, P. (2004, February 21). Fast food firms accused of using sport to attract children. *The Guardian*. Retrieved from http://www.guardian.co.uk/uk/2004/feb/21/health.healthandwellbeing

31. Telegraph Sport. (2012, June 21). London 2012 Olympics: Assembly calls for ban on junk food sponsors. *The Telegraph*. Retrieved from http://www.telegraph.co.uk/sport/olympics/9347221/London-2012-Olympics-Assembly-calls-for-ban-on-junk-food-sponsors.html

32. Tyre, P. (2002, August). Fighting 'Big Fat.' *Newsweek*, pp. 38–40.

33. Becker, B. (2008, July 27). Baseball team clashes with environmentalists over oil company advertising. *The New York Times*, p. 13.

34. Secrets, lies, and sweatshops. (2006, November 26). *Bloomsburg Businessweek*. Retrieved from http://www.businessweek.com/stories/2006-11-26/secrets-lies-and-sweatshops

35. Bowater, D. (2012, June 21). Olympics sponsor adidas to be targeted by sweatshop protesters. *The Telegraph*. Retrieved from http://www.telegraph.co.uk/sport/olympics/news/9316697/Olympics-sponsor-adidas-to-be-targeted-by-sweatshop-protesters.html

36. Easton, P. (2002, February 8). Astros want Enron name off stadium. Bryan-*College Station Eagle*, pp. A1, A5.

37. Cohen, A. (1999, July). The naming game. *Athletic Business*, pp. 37–43.

38. Blumenstyk, G. (1995). Georgia Tech and McDonald's sign $5.5 million deal. *Chronicle of Higher Education*, *XLI*(21), A44.

39. Finn, R. (1993, March 16). Sensitivity over image sinks a women's tennis sponsor. *The New York Times*, p. B6.

8

Potential Negative Outcomes from Sponsorship for a Company

By linking with a sport event through sponsorship, businesses seek to appropriate or "borrow" the image of the sport property and transfer it to enhance their brands' images with target audiences. This is predicated on the sport property having the positive attributes a company seeks. In the past decade unprecedented scrutiny of sport by the media has resulted in a plethora of negative stories emerging relating to doping, cheating, violence, crime, health risks, and negative messages to youth.[1] Clearly, these stories have the potential for negative image transfer to sponsoring companies and their brands that are associated with these sport properties.

Thus, when companies sign sponsorship agreements with sport organizations, there are risks beyond the company not receiving the benefits it anticipated. Sport events are unscripted and uncontrollable, so unexpected and unpredictable outcomes occur periodically. As a consequence, there are occasions when sponsors are confronted with a calamitous negative situation. Given sport's high profile, such outcomes frequently receive prominent and widespread coverage in the media. In these cases, the sponsorship could worsen a company's existing image and reputation. The effect may be enduring and take years to overcome.

It has been noted that, "to date, sponsorship has paid little attention to issues relating to risk in sponsorship"(p. 46)[1] even though as a director of marketing from a TOP sponsor commented: "Sponsorships are essentially risky. So long as there is a potential halo effect, there is also a potential horn effect. If the person, group, or event you sponsor does something that makes consumers cringe, your brand may also make them cringe by association."[2] All business decision processes require that the downsides of any prospective investments be articulated. Hence, companies will review the risks and potential negative outcomes that could emerge from commitment to a sponsorship. There are eight primary risks that companies are likely to consider: Liability exposure, insensitivity to public sentiment, insensitivity to social mores, stakeholder opposition, poor presentation of the event, poor performance, association with disreputable behavior, and trauma to performers.

Exhibit 8.1

Sponsorship and Negligence Liability: A Sample Case

In the case of *Vogel v. West Mountain Corp.*, 470 N.Y.S.2d 475 (A.D. 3 Dept. 1983), the plaintiff, an experienced recreational skier, was injured when she struck a ski tower during a slalom race. In addition to the ski slope operator, Vogel sued the corporate sponsor (Miller) and local sponsor of the race which had been advertised as the "Miller Ski Club Slalom." In her complaint, Vogel argued "Miller was negligent in failing to properly arrange the race course and in failing to warn of the dangers inherent in slalom ski racing." In particular, Vogel maintained that promotional materials indicating Miller's sponsorship of a race "open to all skiers regardless of ability . . . allayed her apprehension and induced her to enter the race." The specific issue before the court was, therefore, "whether the sponsor of an athletic event, absent control, may be held liable in negligence for an injury to a participant."

As a general principle, the court found that mere sponsorship, absent control, does not render the sponsor of an athletic event legally responsible. According to the court, an important criterion in determining possible liability is "whether the realities of every day experience demonstrate that the party to be made responsible could have pre-

vented the negligent conduct." In particular, the court found a legal duty pre-supposes that the organization sponsoring physical activity programs "had sufficient control over the event to be in a position to prevent the negligence." In this case, the court found Miller was never held to be in control, but was merely advertised as a 'sponsor.' Specifically, the court found the organizers of the race had no direct oral or written communication with Miller concerning the racing series. On the contrary, the court found the design of the slope and supervision and control over the race was handled exclusively by employees of the ski slope.

As a practical matter, the court noted that extending "legal liability over a sponsor of an athletic event would provide an undue expansion of the sponsorship relationship." According to the court, the net result of imposing a legal duty and potential negligence liability on mere sponsors would "discourage further participation" in promoting events. In general, the court noted that "a sponsor benefits by the promotion of its product." The court, however, concluded that "financial gain does not of itself give rise to a legal obligation."

LIABILITY EXPOSURE

Exposure to liability risk resulting from alleged negligence at an event the company is sponsoring may be a concern but, for the most part, this fear is misplaced: "As a general rule, negligence liability presupposes that the responsible individual or agency had control over the condition which caused the injury. Consequently, there is no legal duty and subsequent negligence liability where control is lacking" (p. 25).[3] Typical of the case law in this area is the *Vogel v. West Mountain Corp.* case summarized in Exhibit 8.1.

INSENSITIVITY TO USER SENTIMENT

In Chapter 6, a backlash against Visa at the London Olympics was described to illustrate the dangers of over-zealous enforcement to protest sponsors' rights against ambushers. Visa's actions also abrogated what should be a cardinal principle for guiding the actions of all sponsors: Does this action enhance the experience for our targeted audiences? The intent of sponsorship is to deepen bonds with stakeholders by supporting and enhancing the events and experiences in which they engage. If the experience rather

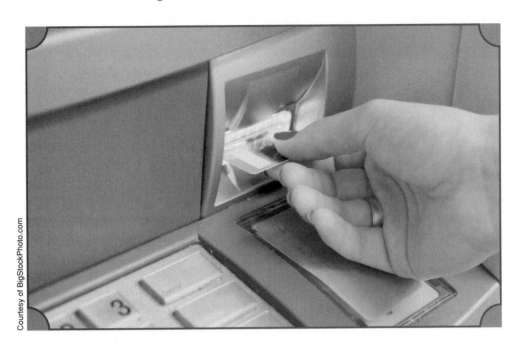

Courtesy of BigStockPhoto.com

than being enhanced is reduced, then the result is likely to be increased alienation, rather than enhanced affection, towards the brand, As one of Visa's many critics observed: "If you want people to like you, give them something. If you want people to hate you, take something away from them."[4]

- At all of the London Games' payment points, the Visa slogan prominently pronounced: "Proud to Accept only VISA." Visa's insistence on enforcing its Olympic payment monopoly resulted in 27 existing ATMs at the main Olympic venues being removed and replaced with just 8 machines that would accept only Visa cards to service the cash needs of up to 800,000 visitors per day. Further, no other credit cards were accepted at any of the venues. Unfortunately for Visa, the IT system failed on two big days. Visitors were, thus, unable to pay for refreshments or souvenirs with their Visa cards, and the shortage of ATMs made the cash option unavailable to many. The frustration resulted in an outpouring of outrage and negative publicity against Visa, exemplified by comments such as: "What did I do wrong to be banned from using my credit card at the largest touristic event in London in the past decade"; "What a terrible thing to be proud of"; and "Great work VISA, now I hate you."[4]

Another concern for companies is reflective of the possible negative outcomes for sport properties discussed in the previous chapter. That is, any wrath the public expresses relating to companies changing a sports format or rules; exercising undue influence on an event; over-commercialization; or using sport to sell products that may be perceived as detrimental to health, may be directed at the companies as well as the sport properties.

Insensitivity to users may take the form of breaching hallowed traditions. The negative backlash from replacing long-established community names on stadiums with cor-

porate sponsor names was discussed in Chapter 4. MLB and Columbia Pictures exhibited similar insensitivity when they sought to break new sponsorship ground in baseball:

> In an effort to exploit its rights as a sponsor of Major League Baseball (MLB), Co-
> lumbia Pictures and Marvel Studios wanted to put logos for its upcoming film
> 'Spider-Man 2' on the bases and on-deck circles in 15 stadiums. Playing surfaces
> had long been considered sacrosanct in US major league sports and as a result
> there was an instant reaction and media coverage that labeled baseball as reaching
> a 'greedy new low.' As a consequence MLB quickly reversed its initial decision to
> provide these rights realizing that it was not considered acceptable (p. 251).[5]

The Wonga case study in Exhibit 8.2[6–10] illustrates two main points. First, the fan base
of a sport team might be morally appalled that their team is sponsored by exploitive
companies apparently lacking a "moral compass," but their long emotional ties to the
team prevent them from withholding their support and money in the form of gate
admissions, season tickets, and merchandise, which is the only action likely to influence
a team owner's business decision.

Second, the fans' ambivalence enables businesses that have a negative image in the
public consciousness to use sponsorship as a vehicle for enhancing that image. Sponsors'
funds are presumed to enhance a team's competitiveness and thus positively align the
company with the team's fans. Indeed, the plethora of companies doing this in the EPL
effectively makes it an "acceptable" norm which ameliorates the moral outrage and potential insensitivity associated with a Wonga-type sponsorship. This point was made by
the Newcastle United manager when he endorsed the arrangement: "You see other
companies whether it is a bank that lends money who are the same type of business as
Wonga, or betting companies sponsoring football clubs and nothing gets said."[10] Consider the following:

- Barclays Bank was the title sponsor of the EPL. Barclays was fined £290 million
  ($453 million) for dishonestly fixing loan and mortgage rates.
- AIG, as the major sponsor of Manchester United, was responsible for the loss of
  billions of dollars of savings of ordinary working people, in the 2008 financial crisis and received a $182 billion bail out from the U.S. government.
- Manchester City, the EPL 2011/2012 champions, are owned by Sheik Mansoud
  of Abu Dhabi, whose family controls the Abu Dhabi government which allegedly
  suppresses civil rights and calls for democracy.

All of this suggests two questions, the answers to which may direct future sport sponsorship partnerships: Should sponsors be subject to similar fit and proper stipulations
that most major sport leagues apply to potential owners? And, is sport as a whole interested in its reputation or its moral wellbeing?[7]

Among the more egregious examples of flouting prevailing social mores have been
sponsorship agreements with brothels. Voukefala, a soccer team in the city of Larissa in
Greece accepted a sponsorship offer from Soula. The team president stated, "We could-
n't afford to turn it down." He pointed out that the brothel was "a legal enterprise val-

Exhibit 8.2

Wonga's Shirt Sponsorship of Newcastle United

Wonga is the UK's highest profile payday leader. It is an online provider of short-term loans which was launched in 2007. It grew exponentially during the Great Recession, for example, in 2011 its revenues tripled to £189 million and it reported profits of £59 million. Wonga provides amounts up to £1000 for a maximum of one month. Its Average Percentage Rate (APR), which is the interest for a whole year on a loan, is 4,214%. These types of exploitative loans are legal in the UK, although they have led to campaigns for national legislation that would cap interest rates as has been done in France (21.6%) and Germany (16%).

Newcastle United is an iconic football team located in the northeast of England. It is one of the most storied and renowned teams in the English Premier League, with a large, passionate fan base. The team negotiated a four-year shirt sponsorship with Wonga at £6 million a year. Wonga already had shirt agreements with Heart of Midlothian, a Scottish Premier League team, and Blackpool, a former EPL team, but these were much lower profile. The Newcastle partnership exposed the Wonga name to a dramatically wider audience.

There was a loud outcry protesting the sponsorship. Newcastle is traditionally a working-class blue collar city leading to charges that "Wonga has chosen to target a region that had comparatively high numbers of people experiencing financial difficulty."[6] It was pointed out that if a supporter took out a Wonga loan to pay for a £49.99 replica Newcastle United shirt, it would cost £71.92 in 30 days time. If it were possible to pay back a Wonga loan in a year, that same shirt would cost £2,107.[7]

Wonga is described by its critics as "immoral and unjust" and "a legal loan shark." The city's leaders were unanimous and outspoken in their condemnation of the sponsorship. The president of the city council called it "disgraceful" saying it "undermines all the work we are doing to crack down on legal loan sharking." The head of the club's fan club described the deal as "shameful" and said "it tarnishes the club's name, image, and reputation." A member of Parliament accused Wonga of "legal loan sharking" and said "It is only through preying on families struggling to make ends meet that Wonga has made enough money to be able to sign this deal with Newcastle."[6] Other characterizations from leaders included: "it is an ugly company"; "a sponsor who blatantly profits from the misery of not having enough money"[7]; and "their enterprise is distasteful and unpleasant . . . exploiting people's desperation."[8]

Wonga were not doing anything illegal. Clearly, the company was seeking image enhancement from its investment. Their head of marketing explained, "Part of our job is to get people to understand that Wonga are good guys."[9] This goal received a boost from the club's respected and high-profile manager who said that he had quizzed Wonga's owner about the business and emerged satisfied with what he heard. "I listened to the owner and their customer satisfaction levels are higher than any other bank or lending facility."[10] By aligning with the large, passionate Newcastle fan base it hoped to counter the widespread popular criticisms of its business; to alleviate the societal pressures for tighter legislation; and to increase awareness of the loan opportunities it offers.

Newcastle United is owned by the proprietor of the UK's biggest sports equipment retailer. He is based 250 miles away in London and has no roots in the Newcastle community. From his perspective, Newcastle United is a business guided by economics and legal rules and regulations, rather than by a "moral compass." Wonga's sponsorship is part of the business' effort to maximize its commercial opportunities. Thus, the team's CEO stated: "We are building a club that can regularly compete for top honours at the highest level. As everyone knows, a strong commercial programme is vital to this goal and I am delighted to welcome Wonga into the fold as our lead commercial partner."[9] Elsewhere, he said, "Wonga's desire to help us invest in our young playing talent, the local community and new fan initiative really impressed us."[6]

ued at 2 million euros ($2.6 million). There were precedents elsewhere. St. Kilda City, a major Australian Rules football club, negotiated a sponsorship deal with a brothel, but bowed to pressure from the league's ruling body and withdrew from the arrangement. However, an Italian soccer team, Trento Calcio 1921, agreed to a sponsorship with an Austrian brothel that the official club website linked through to their sponsor's site, complete with explicit photos of the brothel's employees.[11]

INSENSITIVITY TO SOCIAL MORES

An overarching consideration is the need for companies' sponsorship decisions to be sensitive to the prevailing social and political environments. Disregarding this factor proved painful for Ralph Lauren, an American company that sponsored the American Olympic team at the London Games and created the uniforms worn by the US athletes at the opening and closing ceremonies. The company had similar sponsorship rights for the 2008 and 2010 teams at Beijing and Vancouver, respectively. It had proved to be a lucrative sponsorship for Ralph Lauren which sold versions of the uniform in its stores and online. However, the outfits were made in China. The company had similarly outsourced production of its 2008 and 2010 uniforms, but conditions in 2012 were different. Not only were U.S. unemployment levels high, but it was also an election year. Presidential and Congressional candidates made the creation of jobs in the US the most prominent element in their election platforms and elected officials from both political parties railed against the outsourcing of potential American jobs. In this aroused environment, the outsourcing of production of uniforms to China that the American team would wear in the highest profile showcase event in the world, produced public outrage and "a public-relations nightmare for the company" (p. 4). The majority leader in the US Senate, for example, proclaimed: "I think they should take all the uniforms, put them in a big pile and burn them and start all over again."[12]

Sensitivity/insensitivity to the political environment was exemplified by the insensitive responses to sponsorship involvement of companies that received government tax funds to fend off bankruptcy resulting from the Great Recession. These responses are illustrated in Exhibit 8.3[13] and in the following vignette:

• Northern Rock was a leading British bank with its headquarters in Newcastle. It went bankrupt and had to be bailed out with funds from the British government. Soon after, the company signed a $16 million, four-year sponsorship agreement with Newcastle United, an English Premier League team. [This preceded the Wonga sponsorship described in Exhibit 8.2.] Elected officials and segments of the public were outraged saying the bank should spend its money supporting home mortgage borrowers and business companies rather than the local professional soccer team. A letter writer to the local paper reflected these views: "I lost more than £6,000 by being associated with this bank when it crashed. I find it insulting that they can come up with these sums of cash to support a bunch of overpaid prima donnas."[14]

Exhibit 8.3

A Sponsor's Insensitivity to Public Opinion

RBS is one of the UK's largest banks. It was deemed "too big to fail" and so received substantial government funds to save it from bankruptcy. Thus, it became 82% owned by the British taxpayer. The bank purchased a prime hospitality package at the Wimbledon Tennis Championships for $400,000 and was widely chastised: "Bosses of the bank should be focused on paying taxpayers back as soon as possible, not enjoying centre court and fine dining at Wimbledon" was a typical comment.

As a result the bank withdrew, emailing 500 clients to tell them they were no longer welcome declaring: "It would be inappropri-ate to provide client hospitality at a time when so many customers are experiencing such disruption and are unable to access their accounts, and our top staff need to be available to deal with the computer glitch that has affected up to 17 million customers." This action did not pacify its critics who labeled it a "token gesture that is too little too late." Wimbledon received the funds, but the RBS hospitality suite remained empty. However, the bank's clients did occupy the 48 seats it reserved for each of the first nine days of Wimbledon on Centre Court and #1 Court, and 24 on Centre Court for the last four days which included all the semi-finals and finals.

In contrast to Northern Rock's behavior, many of the large financial institutions in the US that received funds from the federal government's Troubled Asset Relief Program (TARP) engaged in "stealth spending." They sought to hide their sponsorship investments so they would not incur the wrath of government officials or taxpayers:

- Thus at the US Open Golf Tournament, major financial institutions continued their sponsorship, but removed all signage and identification that recognized their involvement. They continued to invite clients to their exclusive hospitality areas, but to non-invitees their involvement remained anonymous. Indeed, even event planners were unaware of whom their clients were. A spokesperson observed: "Symbolism matters" and "it's not that companies don't have the money; they don't want to show they have the money."[15]

When Sheikh Mansour purchased Manchester City of the English Premier League and spent $1.4 billion in the three years immediately after to buy the best soccer players in the world, there was a backlash. Although soccer is highly commercialized, the magnitude and audacity of this expenditure was viewed by many as a step too far. When Manchester City offered Milan $160 million to buy Kaka, a Brazilian player, (the bid was rejected) reasons for the backlash were explained in these terms:

Sheikh Mansour should decide what his purchase of Manchester City is actually about. The Kaka bid, for money beyond sums ever conceived in football before, seemed to point to an identity crisis, between owning a Premier League club to represent enduring values of respect with which the Abu Dhabi ruling family wants to be internationally associated, and a compulsion to throw around unfathomable amounts of money. The dominant reaction among football fans and commentators has been that the proposed £100m for Kaka was "obscene", particularly in an economic environment of mass job losses, bank bail-outs and Woolworths closing down. There has also been some disquiet in Arab opinion at Sheikh Mansour on the back page, throwing £100m and the reported wages of £500,000 a week at Kaka, while on the front page the people of Gaza were being slaughtered and going perilously short of food, water, and medicines. Being dubbed obscene, vulgar, misguided, and ultimately hamfisted was not what Sheikh Mansour and his advisors had in mind when they bought Manchester City.[16]

STAKEHOLDER OPPOSITION

To secure the benefits they seek from a sponsorship, companies want their involvement to be a high profile, very public commitment. The downside of this is that some of its key stakeholder groups, may still view it as philanthropy and not understand its real purpose, and so may be critical. A company's workforce, for example, may loudly decry such an expenditure especially if it coincides with wage negotiations or redundancies. Similarly, shareholders may protest if dividends are below expectation. For this reason, it is easier for companies to invest in in-kind sponsorship because it can be "hidden" from shareholders or employees who may be skeptical of the value of sponsorship. Thus, an executive from Target commenting on his company's sponsorship of the NBA Minnesota Timberwolves' basketball arena observed, "We were concerned about negative reaction from the press, public, and employees. Try telling your employees you can afford to put the company's name on an arena when they are receiving only minimal raises" (p. 4).[17] One of the most widely cited sponsor successes in sport was the Cornhill Insurance Company's sponsorship of England's international cricket games, but one commentator recalls:

> One retains the memory of Cornhill staff pickets parading outside the Oval Cricket Ground in London during a Test [international] match. Their banners pointed out that, while the company was spending £400,000 a year on cricket, it was, so they alleged, being less than generous in current wage negotiations with its own employees. The fact that sponsorship funds, even if diverted into wage packets, would have little effect on them, or that, as part of a marketing campaign, the money is better spent in promoting business and thus underpinning salaries in the long term, is an esoteric argument that cannot compete with emotive banners, especially at a time of rising unemployment (p. 77).[18]

The US Army's sponsorship investments were subjected to such criticisms by Congress which cut funds for this purpose from its budget:

- In budget hearings, the House Appropriations Committee approved an amendment to the defense bill that prohibited the US armed forces from spending any money to sponsor sports. The military spent approximately $60 million on sponsorship, with approximately half of that going to NASCAR teams and properties. The purposes of the sponsorships were to attract qualified recruiting leads on site and to connect with parents, teachers, coaches, and others who influence teen and young-adult career paths, as well as boosting morale among those already in uniform. The military believed it made a dramatic impact when they took a NASCAR or NHRA showcar to a high school to engage with students who could become the technicians, mechanics, and other specialists the military needs. The Congressional representatives did not appear to comprehend how the Army used its relationship with NASCAR driver Ryan Newman, who had an engineering degree, to start conversations with prospective engineers, another targeted specialism the military needs.[19]

These kinds of adverse reactions can only be avoided by potential sponsors engaging key stakeholders and explaining the expected returns from the investment before signing a contract. When this was done before the House floor as a whole voted on the sport sponsorship proposal the motion to reject it failed, because the general in charge of the program emphasized the program's return on investment:

> Last year, we had over 150,000 leads out of the sports marketing program; 46,000 of those—one third—came from NASCAR and the motorsports programs . . . The alternative to this is having a recruiter walk up and down a mall and talk to about 150 people just to get one person to engage with them.[19a]

POOR PRESENTATION OF THE EVENT

The public relations manager of Labatt Brewery, Canada's biggest sponsor of sport events gave an example of this, while another high profile failure reflected badly on Kodak.

- The Labatt Brewery sponsored an ice skating event and paid for advertisements that stated a number of well-known Canadian skaters would appear. Many of the skaters never showed. Not only was the event unsuccessful, the brewery bore the brunt of some hostile consumer reaction. In these instances the backlash was against the major corporation sponsoring the event, not the promoter that nobody ever heard about.[20]
- Kodak sponsored a Kodak Liberty Ride Festival where people in 100 cities were going to pay $23 to ride their bikes, have picnics, and watch a broadcast of a Huey Lewis concert. The problem was that the organization delivered only a tiny fraction of the 500,000 people they promised; weak organization and a poor concept to begin with were at fault. (p. 219)[21]

Golf tournaments and other events featuring individual performers always have an accompanying risk that the top players will not participate or will drop out early (either by losing or by being injured).

Outdoor events are vulnerable to extreme weather conditions such as stifling heat, heavy rain, snow/ice, or severe winds. In some contexts, for example a sailing event, this may add to the authenticity of the experience. Guest VIP participants on the racing boats or spectators on accompanying spectator boats experiencing the miserable, rugged, cold, harsh conditions associated sometimes with sailing may make the experience especially memorable. However, in most contexts the weather can be a spoiler and it is essential to have a back-up contingency plan ready to be implemented if the natural elements do not cooperate.

POOR PERFORMANCE

A major sponsor of English soccer proclaimed, "When football succeeds so does the brand" (p. 72).[22] The failure of the national team to perform well in major tournaments or the sponsors' teams to be successful inevitably limits the return on a sponsorship investment. Risk of poor competitive performance is inherent in sponsorships that focus on teams or individuals within a sport event, rather than the overall event itself, because a central tenet of sports is that there are winners and losers. If a brand or company is associated with a loser, it is unlikely that positive affinity felt by those emotionally engaged with a sport property will be transferred to the sponsor. Indeed, losing may convey connotations of failure and inferiority.

- In the 16 months after Lowe's home improvements chain invested $35 million for the naming rights to Charlotte Motor Speedway, the company became associated with a series of accidents and tragedies that took place at the track. First, during an event at the speedway, debris from a wreck flew into the crowd and killed three fans. Four months later, two Lowe's stores were pipe-bombed in retaliation for the accident. Next, a pedestrian bridge at the speedway collapsed injuring over 100 people, some seriously. Finally, an explosion staged as part of a Memorial Day observance before a major race sent plywood into the crowd and injured four people. Lowe's misfortune caused companies to add clauses to naming rights contracts enabling them to terminate if anything occurs which has a negative impact on the company's image or reputation. One commentator noted, "When you pay to name a facility and then your name and image are part of such negative situations, it's almost like turning lemonade back into lemons" (p. 80).[23]

- A race car or racehorse which consistently finishes "down the field" or crashes/falls hardly projects a winning image. An analyst of Formula 1 motor racing observed, "Coming second, third, or worse can be an embarrassment. There is even a drawback in winning as the only way forward is the same again or down . . . If you are not going to win, you get a bad press. It is a huge risk" (p. C9).[24]
- The world's most famous horse race attracting a global audience of 600 million is the Grand National held in Liverpool, England, annually since 1839. The 4.2 mile course incorporates 30 large and difficult fences. It is viewed as the ultimate test for jockeys and horses. Most of those starting the race fail to finish it. From 1990–2010, 17 horses died, while the 2011 and 2012 races each yielded two deaths. The protests and negative media coverage associated with these deaths caused its long-time sponsor to terminate the agreement.
- The Cartoon Network sponsored a NASCAR Series race car which it termed its "Wacky Racing" car. The intent was to capitalize on the famous loyalty of NASCAR fans to NASCAR brands. The car was variously painted with Scooby-Doo, the Powerpuff Girls, and the Flintstones. However, what would be the impact on the Cartoon Network if children saw their favorite cartoon character on the charred and crumpled hood of a car in which the driver died a violent death?[2]
- Volvo sponsored the Volvo Ocean Race (around the World Yacht Race). Volvo positioned itself as a manufacturer of reliable and safe cars, but on one leg of the race four of the boats in the race failed to complete the leg due to technical problems.[5]
- BMW and Oracle invested over $100 million in sponsoring an America's Cup boat which was eliminated in the preliminary heats before the main event started. BMW's spokesman said, "Sailing stands for high technology dynamism—the same quality BMW wants to communicate in its cars."[25] Since BMW believed this positive association would be advantageous to its brand, does that mean the boat's failure to demonstrate technological superiority resulted in a negative impact on the BMW brand?

Similarly, if a sponsorship is intended to provide a demonstration platform and the demonstration fails, a company suffers public humiliation and negative promotion which is likely to reduce its sales:

IBM's sponsorship of the Atlanta Olympic Games was intended to provide a demonstration platform to showcase its technology to the world. However, glitches appeared in the worst possible places in the IBM system that was supposed to deliver instant information to international newswire services, which would then disseminate it to the world. And, unfortunately, those glitches had an air of absurdity that reporters found irresistible. One boxer was described as being 2 feet tall; another was 21 feet tall. The system failed to yield results for contests that had taken place, but claimed that a Dane and an Australian set new world records in a bicycle race that hadn't yet occurred, while a French fencer was credited with the 400 meters world record. Eventually, IBM was reduced to faxing the results to the media center and running them to the news agencies. High tech had become humiliatingly low tech. And for the estimated $80 million it had spent in Atlanta, IBM got little except a beating in the world press that made every marketer in America wince in sympathy. Fortunately, IBM redeemed itself with its subsequent performance in Nagano at the Winter Olympics, but the lesson is clear: The risks associated with in-kind sponsorship puts your products on a stage in front of the world. If you deliver anything less than perfection, you can injure your brand. (p. 107)[2]

ASSOCIATION WITH DISREPUTABLE BEHAVIOR

If spectators engage in violence, which has frequently occurred among soccer crowds in Europe, or if players use foul language, fight on the field, abuse officials, are caught taking drugs, or whatever, then this disreputable behavior may damage a sponsoring brand's image: "This downside can be huge, especially if you marry your brand to one of pro sports' seemingly endless supply of tabloid-friendly dunces. Make no mistake, consumers will judge your brand by the company it keeps. Yet, incredibly, brand builders still walk straight into dysfunctional relationships with their eyes open." (p. 88)[2]

The array of potential disreputable behaviors is extensive. It includes:

- Doping to improve performance.
- Egregious misbehavior on the field of play.
- Misbehavior off the field of play manifested as irresponsible or criminal acts.
- Misbehavior by fans perhaps most prominently exemplified by the challenges of hooliganism and racial abuse associated with European soccer.
- Corruption by officials or governing bodies.
- Anti-social behavior by players such as social or recreational drug use.
- Cheating on the field of play, for example, using an illegal bat in baseball.
- Betting abuses leading to point shaving, spot betting, bribing referees, and fixing the outcomes of sport events.
- Dysfunctional intrateam relationships among players and coaches.[1]

Elite athletes often have a surfeit of time and many are at a stage in their lives when they are particularly vulnerable to engaging in disputable behaviors. This may be exacerbated by team bonding rituals that push the boundaries of acceptable behaviors. As high profile public figures, they are subjected to intense scrutiny from media seeking sensational copy to sell their product. In addition, advances in technology mean that anyone equipped with a phone and Internet connection can immediately report disreputable events to the world that in past eras would have remained unknown. These conditions make revelations of indiscretions and obnoxious behavior inevitable.[26]

The definition of what constitutes disreputable behavior and hence the potential for negative impact on sponsors varies by sport and context. NASCAR has a long history of teams breaking the rules on car specification to secure an advantage. As one of NASCAR's most famous drivers and team owners said: "I don't particularly tell my guys to cheat, I just tell them not to get caught." The CEO of NASCAR was similarly relaxed about cheating: "We expect everybody to be aggressive with our rules . . . We don't expect somebody to fall into the bad zone too many times." (p. C3). Because of its heritage with moonshine, its roots, and its renegade image, cheating seems to be tolerated and does not arouse the concern of sponsors.[27]

Similarly, when two high profile action sports athletes were featured in *High Times*, a magazine for marijuana users, sponsors did not react negatively since it was consistent with the sports' edgy image. An agent of one of the athletes reported, "Some of his sponsors even called to congratulate him."[28] This is consistent with the suggestion that brands which incorporate image attributes such as "tough" or "rebellious" should embrace disreputable behavior: "If we wanted to market a beer as "rugged, manly, and tough then having sportsmen who fit that mold consuming it, even to excess, helps maintain the message" (p. 218).[26]

Concern with potential negative outcomes from disreputable behavior has caused some sponsors to adopt a policy of supporting events rather than teams or individual athletes. However, property owners may also engage in disreputable behavior as the IOC corruption scandal preceding the Salt Lake City Winter Olympics demonstrated. The revelations threatened to negatively impact sponsors. Exhibit 8.4 describes the incidents and the safeguards that a major sponsor advised others to take so they could extricate themselves from a similar situation.[2]

Exhibit 8.4

The IOC Corruption Scandal

Three years before the Salt Lake City Winter Olympics were held, the world learned that some members of the IOC were "traveling the globe extorting cash, jewelry, tuition fees, you name it" (p. 73) from cities bidding for the Olympics. Despite widespread adverse publicity, the IOC made no effort to enact structural changes that would prevent such a scandal from reoccurring. John Hancock, one of the TOP sponsors, was especially concerned that the absence of reform and the public's distaste for the corruption would corrode the image of the Olympics and devalue the company's sponsorship investment. Their CEO commented, "We believe that if the scandal had gone on too long without a resolution, it might very well have hurt our brand (p. 73)."

The company insisted on structural reforms and threatened to lead a withdrawal of sponsors if the IOC failed to do so. Under pressure, the IOC called a special session and did reform. For an organization steeped in a hundred years of secrecy and self-regard, it reformed to a remarkable degree. It agreed to eliminate its members' visits to bid cities, to require them to regularly stand for reelection, to create financial transparency, and to change the composition of the IOC so that active athletes, national Olympic committees, and international sports federations are all represented on it. Finally, at a later session under continuing pressure the IOC agreed to the "Hancock clause" which was an ethics clause in the Olympic sponsorship agreement that allows sponsors to pull out if it ever again engages in unethical conduct. Now the sponsors, who contribute more than half a billion dollars to the IOC every four years, have half a billion dollars worth of leverage that they didn't have before. The CEO of John Hancock offered the following advice based on this experience:

Make sure that when you give the other players in a sponsorship your marketing dollars, you demand some influence in return. Down the road, because of scandal or overcommercialization, you may find yourself having to protect not just your brand, but also the event itself—and you want to have the power to do that.

Sponsors are not likely to be affected by, or react to disreputable behavior *per se*, rather their response will be dependent on the extent to which the behavior results in outrage and high profile public criticism. This is illustrated by sponsors' reactions to the endemic corruption that pervades the Fèdèration International de Football Association (FIFA) which is the international governing body of soccer. Its membership comprises 209 national soccer associations and it is headquartered in Zurich, Switzerland. The President of FIFA, along with members of the 24 person Executive Committee, and senior officials have all been caught accepting huge bribes and this has been going on for over three decades.[29] Among the more recent revelations are:

- The President and his son-in-law, who was also a member of the Executive Committee, received over $40 million from International Sports Leisure in return for the company receiving worldwide broadcasting rights.
- A member of the Executive Committee was caught reselling soccer World Cup tickets to scalpers for approximately a $1 million profit.
- Bribes were paid to Executive Committee members to secure their votes for a candidate in the election for FIFA President.
- Bribes to Executive Committee members intended to secure their votes for hosting the 2018 and 2022 World Cups.[30]

All of these revelations, and others, received widespread coverage in the media, but there was no public outrage. There was no talk of "let's boycott sponsors' products unless they use their financial muscle to force FIFA to change." The connection between corruption at the highest level of the sport's administration and their local or national team does not appear to have been apparent to fans. Further, because corruption appears endemic and has endured for so long, there may be a sense of resignation among the soccer public cynically accepting that "this is just the way it is." As one commentator asked, "Fans seem to be enjoying themselves, so if a cabal of scheming old men in Zurich happen to be pulling the strings behind the scenes, why should the rest of us worry? . . . So long as the games are good, why does it matter if FIFA is corrupt?"[31]

The lack of outrage enabled FIFA's major sponsors to disregard the corruption and "stay the course." The six major sponsors, who in aggregate invested approximately $1 billion in contracts with the organization, responded to the corruption with blasé statements of mild condemnation. For example:

- Coca-Cola: "The current allegations being raised are distressing and bad for the sport."
- adidas: "The negative tenor of the public debate around FIFA at the moment is neither good for football nor for FIFA and its partners . . . adidas enjoys a long-term, close and successful partnership with the FIFA that we are looking forward to continuing.
- Emirates Airline: "We hope that these issues will be resolved as soon as possible."
- Visa: "The current situation is clearly not good for the game and we ask that FIFA

take all necessary steps to resolve the concerns that have been raised . . . This does not concern or impact our sponsorship rights."

Companies are unlikely to embark on a moral crusade that may destroy a vehicle contributing to their profitability. They will follow, rather than lead, public reaction. Thus, absent a public outcry, disreputable behavior will not discourage sponsors. Their perspective was exemplified by Budweiser's response to the FIFA corruption: "We always take the perspective of the fans and there may have been some rumblings at some point . . . In the end though, fans are focused on one thing, and only one thing, which is the World Cup . . . It is great for the brand essence, it is great for its global scale."[31]

In contrast to the blasé response of sponsors to FIFA's corruption, there was a substantial withdrawal action by sponsors associated with professional cycling as revelations about the use of performance-enhancing drugs made media headlines for a decade or more. The unrelenting visibility of the issue, its widespread global dissemination, and constant criticism outweighed any benefits for many sponsors.

Credit Suisse, an international financial group, terminated its 22-year-old sponsorship with cycling's Tour de Suisse. When asked which sports they believed had a drug problem, 83% of Swiss respondents cited cycling. Only 19% believed that companies should support the race so Credit Suisse withdrew. The bank explained its reasons for withdrawing in a press release: "Internal studies have shown that cycle racing is losing support among some sectors of the population and among Credit Suisse target customer groups in particular, not least because of the doping debate. Credit Suisse therefore takes the view that there is no longer a sufficient basis for continuing the sponsoring commitment."[32] The wisdom of Credit Suisse withdrawing was exemplified by the subsequent experience of Deutsche Telecom, the German telecommunications giant which sponsored a professional cycling team that was embroiled in a doping scandal. It was front page news for several weeks in Germany and received prolonged international media attention as its full ramifications were incrementally exposed.

Finally, the revelation of pervasive, endemic use of performance-enhancing drugs in professional cycling over a period of several decades by the US Anti-Doping Agency, focused on Lance Armstrong, resulted in widespread public condemnation and disgust. As a result, major sponsors withdrew from the sport. The Dutch banking group Rabobank was prominent among them. The Netherlands is one of the most enthusiastic cycling nations in the world and more than half of the Rabobank 27-strong men's team were Dutch. The bank was investing over $20 million a year in the team and had been involved continually for 25 years. The bank's CEO recognized, "Cycling is a beautiful sport, which millions of Dutch people enjoy and a large number of those Dutch people are clients of Rabobank." Nevertheless, he went on to say, "We are no longer convinced that the international professional world of cycling can make this a clean and fair sport."[33]

Most sponsorship contracts include a provision banning the use of performance-enhancing drugs, so it may be technically feasible for sponsors to get money back from athletes or teams that violate these contract terms. However, such an action is likely to be legally contested and result in more negative publicity linking a sponsor to the property, so invariably companies cut their losses and simply terminate the agreement.

TRAUMA TO PERFORMERS

There is inherent risk of serious injury or even death to performers in some high-risk sports such as motor racing, boxing, martial arts, mountain climbing, skateboarding, skiing, ice-hockey, and extreme sports. The negative impact on sponsoring companies from such traumatic events may be financial, whereby they incur a loss of investment, or reputational with damage to their brand. The negative financial impact is illustrated in the following vignette:

- Kanatek was a Canadian independent systems integrator. The company sponsored Sean Egan's attempt to be the second oldest individual at 63 years of age to reach the summit of Mount Everest. Egan had been a champion boxer, marathon runner, and fitness guru who trained diligently for the effort. The Kanatek Expedition to Mount Everest involved the company investing $50,000 for title sponsorship and a further $250,000 to leverage this commitment with a strong series of activation events. Unfortunately, Egan died on the mountain. Consequently, most of the planned leveraging activities had to be cancelled, so much of the return on Kanatek's investment was not realized.[1]

American Football and CTE

Football has a grip on the collective US psyche. A central ingredient in its appeal is its gladiatorial violence. This was recognized long ago. In the 1890s, for example, an image in the *New York World* depicted a skeleton wearing a banner labeled "Death" and was titled "The Twelfth Player in Every Football Game"[34] while the December 1905 edition of the *Cincinnati Commercial Tribune* showed a cartoon of the grim reaper balanced on the crossbar of goalposts, looking down on bodies on the field dramatizing the "ghastly total of 25 killed and 168 injured in football" (p. 292).[34] In the same year, newspapers around the country widely reprinted a statement made by the dean of the divinity school at the University of Chicago who called football, "a social obsession—a boy killing, education-prostituting, gladiatorial sport" (p. 293).[34] In 1897, campaigns in Chicago and Georgia sought to outlaw the sport, while in 1905 Teddy Roosevelt, whose son was then a freshman football player at Harvard, summoned coaches to the White House to discuss reforming the sport before public opinion turned too far against it. Eighteen people had died on the field that year. Despite his efforts, the devastation continued. Another 11 died in 1906. Eleven more in 1907 and 13 in 1908. The number shot up to 26 in 1909, dropped to 14 the following year, then stayed in double digits each year until the eve of America's entry into World War I.[34]

Chronic traumatic encephalopathy (CTE) was first described in 1928. It emanated from studies of the clinical deterioration of boxers so was medically termed "dementia pugilisca" and popularly described as "punch drunk." The name was changed to CTE after it was recognized to be associated with a broader array of activities including American football, hockey, wrestling, and rugby.[35]

CTE is a progressive neurodegenerative disease similar to Alzheimer's in its symptoms—memory loss, irritability, mood changes—but with its own distinct pathology. The leading medical research team investigating its causes define it thus:

> CTE is clinically associated with symptoms of irritability, impulsivity, aggression, depression, short-term memory loss, and heightened suicidality that usually begin 8–10 years after experiencing repetitive mild traumatic brain injury. With advancing disease, more severe neurological changes develop that include dementia, gait and speech abnormalities, and parkinsonism. In late stages, CTE may be clinically mistaken for Alzheimer's disease. (p. 2)[35]

Initially it was believed that CTE was primarily caused by concussions sustained from major collisions and "the big hit." Contrary to popular belief, a concussion is not a bruise to the brain caused by hitting a hard surface. Indeed, no physical swelling or bleeding is usually seen on radiological scans. The injury generally occurs when the head either accelerates rapidly and then is stopped, or is spun rapidly. This violent shaking causes the brain cells to become depolarized and fire all their neurotransmitters at once in an unhealthy cascade, flooding the brain with chemicals and deadening certain receptors linked to learning and memory. The results often include confusion, blurred vision, memory loss, nausea, and, sometimes, unconsciousness. Neurologists say once players suffer a concussion, they are as much as four times more likely to sustain a second one. Moreover, after several concussions, it takes less of a blow to cause the injury and requires more time to recover.[36]

While concussions are associated with CTE, perhaps the most substantive finding of recent medical studies is that they are not the major source. Rather, it is the cumulative impact of thousands of little hits, termed "subconcussive blows," that cause most of the damage. Their ubiquity was highlighted by a six-year veteran of the NFL in an op-ed column in the *New York Times*:

> The truth is that NFL players have been using their heads as weapons since they first donned pads as children. It's the nature of the sport. Sure, coaches tell you to wrap up an opponent with your arms, to keep your head up, to see what you hit. But when a player is moving forward, his knees are bent and his body is leaning forward. The head leads no matter what . . . There are six or seven helmet-to-helmet hits on every play in the NFL . . . Before the 1950s, when they wore soft helmets without face masks, players didn't lead with their heads. They dived at opponents' legs and corralled them with their arms. Leading with the head meant facial disfigurement and lots of stitches. But once leather was replaced by hard plastic, enclosing the head in protective armor, all bets were off. Couple that with the size of today's players and the speed of the modern game, and you have a recipe for cerebellum custard.[37]

The first studies of the brain tissues of deceased NFL players showing that they had CTE were published in 2005. Others have followed and the number will increase as more players dedicate their brains after death for this purpose. These pioneering medical studies of CTE have shown "that for some athletes there may be severe and devastating long-term consequences of repetitive brain trauma that have traditionally been considered only mild" (p. 20).[35] The behavior and personality changes associated with CTE are most likely to occur when former players are in their forties. However, the incidence or prevalence of CTE among those who play American football remains unknown, and it is likely to be many years before sufficient cases have been studied that reasonable estimates of the magnitude of risk can be made. Further, it remains to be determined if some are more predisposed to CTE, and among those who sustain it if some are more resistant to its progress than others.

Many times concussions can be identified by skilled physicians and trainers when they occur. This has enabled rules to be developed by governing sport bodies that specify protocols which have to be adopted in response to concussions. The recent medical evidence suggesting that CTE is caused by sub-concussive blows is much more challenging for the medical community to address. This is because there are no overt signs which cue medical personnel that it is occurring during the time period when players are engaged in the game. Overt signs of CTE, which resemble Alzheimer's disease, are not likely to appear until a decade or so after players have quit playing football. Hence, there are no immediate actions that medical personnel can take to ameliorate the damage. The only definitive diagnosis confirming sub-concussive blows have led to CTE occurs from examining brains of the deceased.

The situation has been exacerbated by two factors in addition to the hard helmets referenced in the *New York Times* op-ed column. First, the increasing size of players has meant the physical damage they can inflict on each other in tackles is more severe. The author reviewed player profiles in a game program for the University of Illinois team of 1967, which was the first football game he ever attended. He found that of the 68 players on the roster, two (3%) weighed more than 230 lbs, while 36 (53%) weighed less than 200 lbs of whom 15 (22%) weighed less than 180 lbs. These players were substantially smaller than would be found on contemporary major college football teams. Second, in the past much of football's action was "three yards and a cloud of dust." This reduced the number of big hits, because there was not much space between players. Today's wide-open passing game means there is more space for gathering speed and momentum between players, so there are more opportunities for major collisions.

In addition to the recent medical evidence and the consequent media coverage, public consciousness of this issue is being awakened by HD television whose remarkable clarity offers views of collisions that were not previously available; and by modern replay technology that occupies more television time than the live action, where the elasticity of the human neck is on repeated display.[38]

Implications for Football and Sponsors

In the manner of Elizabeth Kübler Ross, the NFL has passed through four stages in its reaction to the reality of brain damage. Its first reaction to the published studies was fervent and repeated denial that the results had anything to do with the league or its players. This active resistance shifted to passive resistance, then to passive acceptance and finally by 2012 to active acceptance.[38] This major cultural change was strongly influenced by a study commissioned by the NFL in 2009 which surveyed retired players and reported that Alzheimer's disease, or something very similar, was being diagnosed in former NFL players nineteen times more often than in the national population among men aged 30 to 49. One commentator observed, "It was like Big Tobacco ordering a study that ended up showing that smokers get cancer."[39]

As a result of the evidence confirming football as a cause of CTE, more than 4,500 former players sued the NFL, alleging that not enough was done to inform them of the dangers of concussions in the past, or to take care of them today. The NFL settled the lawsuit by agreeing to pay $765 million to all retired players (not only the plaintiffs). Half was to be paid in the first three years, and the balance over the next 17 years to those retired players with neurological disorders. The NFL made no admission of guilt; resolved all lawsuits from former players; pre-empted any future lawsuits, since players could no longer claim they were unaware of the risks of CTE; avoided the prolonged negative publicity that would have accompanied a lawsuit that could have dragged on for perhaps five years; and avoided the discovery and deposition process that may have suggested culpability in not disclosing earlier any knowledge of the CTE risk which the NFL may have had.

It was noted in Chapter 2 that image is a multidimensional construct so the challenge for sponsors is to capture *only* those meanings they wish to obtain from the sport property.[40] In the NFL's case, the property and sponsors have been effective in facilitating image transfer by exploiting the NFL's macho, gladiatorial dimensions, while discarding the trauma consequences of football's inherent violence.

Sponsors may have concern about potential damage to a brand's reputation from being associated with a sport that substantially enhances the risk of players incurring permanent brain trauma. It has long been recognized that football exacts a physical, orthopedic, and arthritic toll, and those participating in it are aware of those consequences. The emerging question for sponsors is: Is CTE of a different order of magnitude of risk which is sufficient to cause them to desert it? Cigarette companies were prominent sponsors of sport two decades ago but now operate in an environment where their product is seen as dangerous; will the NFL be similarly perceived in 10 or 20 years time? As a result of the 2009 study, Congress held a hearing on the issue before the House Judiciary Committee at which the NFL Commissioner appeared. Several members of Congress portrayed the Commissioner and the league as impeding proper player care, obfuscating the long-term effects of concussions, and compared the league to the tobacco industry.[41]

Given the lack of symptoms associated with sub-concussive blows, the only pre-emptive action available to sport authorities is to ensure all players, and in the case of minors, their parents, are fully informed of the emerging scientific findings. If this "duty of care" is fulfilled, then young men can make an informed decision on whether the benefits they receive from playing football are worth the potential long-term risks that may occur.

It is likely to be many years before science will be able to make meaningful estimates about the incidence of CTE in football. Nevertheless, there may be public reaction in the interim:

> Even if football eludes these threats, the accretive damage might already be done. Ominous headlines, frowning scientists, addled Hall of Famers, the whole slowly unfolding buzzkill can't help but have a suppressive effect on parents. Since parents are the first owners, agents, coaches, and GMs of future athletes, they might already be steering their charges toward other sports. That exodus might soon become a stampede as the latest bad news becomes more widely known.[42]

Will the spectating and general interest public continue to remain indifferent to the trauma and accept with casual distain that getting "your bell rung" or getting "a little dinged up" is an acceptable part of the sport and is evidence of a player's "character?" Will sponsors of the NFL and college football continue their relationship as this issue moves from the shadows to center stage in the media? Will they be concerned about being involved with a sport where the news cycle between games is dominated by questions surrounding which players are "probable," "questionable," and "out of commission" as a result of the previous week's mayhem?[38] Will they want to be associated with the pathetic sight of helpless, brain damaged former players? Will there be negative brand image transfer resulting from a section of the public holding the brands and companies partially accountable for promoting, embracing, or condoning the activity that caused this suffering? Will there be contagion with companies also re-evaluating their associations with sports like ice-hockey where concussions are similarly frequent?

If public indifference persists, it is unlikely that medical evidence will be sufficient to change the culture and format of football, or of its sponsors. Boxing perhaps offers a precedent. The American Medical Association has lobbied to ban boxing to no avail since 1983, although boxing has been reduced to a fringe niche sport, whereas it was once near the center of American sporting life. However, boxing features individuals. It lacks the communal collegiate and civic pride element which is at the core of support for football. Hence, it seems more likely that any change in the attitude of sponsors towards football will be driven by lawyers and insurance companies than by public outrage. With new medical evidence is likely to come new legal risk and liability, which means recalibrated insurance premiums for high schools and colleges that do not have the revenue resources of the NFL.[38] Thus, it seems more likely that high school and college athletic administrators and coaches will have to inform and educate potential football players and, in the case of high schools the players' parents, on the relatively high risk of football players later suffering from CTE in order to safeguard their institutions from future negligence suits.

SUMMARY

From the perspective of businesses, there are eight potential negative outcomes from sponsorship to be considered. Three can be controlled relatively easily by a company. There is unlikely to be any risk of exposure to liability suits from being an event sponsor, and companies can avoid public angst that may be associated with the negative out-comes caused by insensitivity to user sentiments or to the prevailing social and political environments. Also, it may be possible to mitigate potential adverse reaction from stake-holders by engaging with them to explain the expected returns from the investment be-fore signing a contract.

Companies have less control over the other four potential negative outcomes. Poor presentation of the event may result from its poor production, the failure of star indi-vidual performers to appear, or adverse weather. The risk of poor performance is inher-ent in sports, because there are winners and losers. If a brand or company is associated with a loser, it may convey connotations of failure and inferiority. If spectators engage in violence, or if players use foul language, fight on the field, abuse officials, or are caught taking drugs, then these disreputable behaviors may damage a sponsoring brand's image. Finally, there may be adverse financial or reputational consequences from being associated with high-risk sports in which serious injury or death are inherent.

Endnotes

1. O'Reilly, N., & Foster, G. (2008, October). Risk management in sports sponsorship: Ap-plication to human mortality risk. *International Journal of Sports Marketing & Sponsor-ship*, pp. 45–62.

2. D'Alessandro, D. F. (2001). *Brand warfare*. New York, NY: McGraw-Hill.

3. Kozlowski, J. C. (1995, December). Mere pro-gram sponsorship promoting physical activity insufficient control to trigger liability. *Parks and Recreation*, pp. 24–29.

4. Ukman, L. (2012, August 10). Visa and the Olympics: Sponsorship in need of an update. *IEG Sponsorship Blog*. Retrieved from http://www.sponsorship.com

5. Masterman, G. (2007). *Sponsorship for a re-turn on investment*. Boston, MA: Elsevier.

6. Conn, D. (2012, October 9). Newcastle United risks damaging their reputation with Wonga deal. *The Guardian*. Retrieved from http://www.guardian.co.uk/football/david-conn-inside-sport-blog/2012/oct/09/newcastle-united-won ga-deal

7. Gibbs, T. (2012, October 9). Newcastle United's Wonga sponsorship speaks volumes about football, and Mike Ashley. *The Telegraph*. Retrieved from http://www.telegraph.co.uk

8. Edwards, L. (2012, October 9). Newcastle United's new shirt deal with Wonga leaves a bitter taste, but it will be swallowed in the name of progress. *The Telegraph*. Retrieved from http://www.telegraph.co.uk

9. Gentleman, A. (2012, March 1). Wonga: The real cost of a payday loan. *The Guardian*. Re-trieved from http://www.guardian.co.uk/busi ness/2012/mar/01/wonga-real-cost-payday-loan

10. Taylor, L. (2012, October 10). Alan Pardew: Wonga can propel Newcastle into Premier League top four. *The Guardian*. Retrieved from http://www.guardian.co.uk/football/2012/oct/ 10/alan-pardew-wonga-newcastle

11. Leather, J. (2012, September 27). Struggling Greek football team signs sponsorship deal with a brothel. *Metro*. Retrieved from http://metro .co.uk/2012/09/27/struggling-greek-football -team-signs-sponsorship-deal-with-a-brothel-587212/

12. Wilson, E. (2012, July 15). Made where? *New York Times*, p. 4.

13. Ward, V. (2012, June 27). Wimbledon 2012: RBS criticized for 'token gesture.' *The Telegraph*. Retrieved from http://www.telegraph.co.uk /sport/tennis/wimbledon/9360339/Wimbledon -2012-RBS-criticised-for-token-gesture.html

14. Inman, P. (2010, January 18). Northern Rock's £10 million sponsorship of Newcastle United under fire. *The Guardian*. Retrieved from http:// www.guardian.co.uk/business/2010/jan/18/nor thern-rock-newcastle-united-sponsorship

15. Wayne, L. (2009, August 12). Shh! We're cor-porate hosts, but don't tell. *The New York Times*, p. B1.

16. Conn, D. (2009, January 1). Kaka snub must prompt Sheikh Mansour to re-evaluate his pri-orities for City. *The Guardian*. Retrieved from http://www.guardian.co.uk/sport/blog/2009/j an/20/kaka-manchester-city-david-conn

17. Eaton, R. (1991). Inside Target store's spon-

sorship philosophy. *Special Events Report*, *10*(17), 4–5.

18. Head, V. (1981). *Sponsorship: The newest marketing skill.* Maidenhead, England: Woodhead-Faulker.

19. Andrews, J. (2012, May 18). U.S. Congress launches another misguided attack on sponsorship. *IEG Sponsorship Blog.* Retrieved from http://www.sponsorship.com/About-IEG/Sponsorship-Blogs/Jim-Andrews/May-2012/U-S-Congress-Launches-another-Misguided-Attack-on.aspx

19a. Bernstein, V. (2011, February 19). House votes to continue Army sponsorships in NASCAR. *The New York Times.* Retrieved from http://www.nytimes.com/2011/02/19/sports/autoracing/19nascar.html?_r=0

20. IEG. (1986). Brewery forms event production company. *Special Events Report, 5*(11), 7.

21. Aaker, D. A., & Joechimsthaler, E. (2000). *Brand leadership.* New York, NY: The Free Press.

22. Wenner, L. A., & Jackson, S. J. (2009). *Sport, beer and gender: Promotional culture and contemporary social life.* New York, NY: Peter Long.

23. Fleming, D. (2000, June 22). Lowe's can't catch a break. *Sports Illustrated,* p. 80.

24. Steiner, R. (2001, July 15). Corporate fear that drives the F1 circus. *The Sunday Times,* C9.

25. Ewing, J. (2007, June 7). Sport sponsorships: A risky game. *Bloomberg Businessweek.* Retrieved from http://www.businessweek.com/stories/2007–06-07/sports-sponsorship-a-risky-gamebusinessweek-business-news-stock-market-and-financial-advice

26. Connor, J. M., & Mazanov, J. (2010, April). The inevitability of scandal: Lessons for sponsors and administrators. *International Journal of Sports Marketing & Sponsorship,* pp. 212–220.

27. Bernstein, V. (2006, February 21). NASCAR bumps fenders with a scofflaw culture. *The New York Times,* p. C3.

28. SBD. (2003, May 5). Is there concern marijuana is infiltrating action sports? *SportsBusiness Daily.* Retrieved from http://www.sportsbusinessdaily.com/Daily/Issues/2003/05/Issue-153/Sponsorships-Advertising-Marketing.aspx

29. Phillips, B. (2011, August 14). Corruption, murder and the beautiful game. *Grantland.* Retrieved from http://www.grantland.com/story/_/id/6861161/corruption-murder-beautiful-game

30. Conn, D. (2012, July 12). Sepp Blatter faces call to step down at FIFA over 'bribery cover-up.' *The Guardian.* Retrieved from http://www.guardian.co.uk/football/2012/jul/12/sepp-blatter-joao-havelange-fifa

31. Casert, R. (2011, October 25). Budweiser to continue as World Cup sponsor. *The Washington Times.* Retrieved from http://www.washingtontimes.com/news/2011/oct/25/budweiser-to-continue-as-world-cup-sponsor/?page=all

32. IEG. (2000). Assertions. *Sponsorship Report, 19*(21), 2.

33. Walker, P. (2012, October 19). Rabobank ends sponsorship over concerns cycling is not 'clean and fair.' *The Guardian.* Retrieved from http://www.guardian.co.uk/business/2012/oct/19/rabobank-ends-cycling-sponsorship-doping

34. Walterson, J. S. (2000). The gridiron crisis of 1905: Was it really a crisis? *Journal of Sport History, 27*(2), 291–298.

35. McKee, A. C., Stein, T. D., Nowinski, C. J., Stern, R. A., Daneshvar, D. H., Alvarez, V. E., . . . Cantu, R. C. (2012, October). The spectrum of disease in chronic traumatic encephalopathy. *Brain: A Journal of Neurology,* pp. 1–22.

36. McKinley, J.C. (2000, May, 12). Invisible injury: A special report; A perplexing foe takes an awful toll. *New York Times.*

37. Jackson, N. (2010, October 23). The N.F.L.'s head cases. *The New York Times.* Retrieved from http://www.nytimes.com/2010/10/24/opinion/24jackson.html

38. McGrath, B. (2012, November 12). Does football have a future? The NFL and the concussion crisis. *The New Yorker.* Retrieved from http://www.newyorker.com/reporting/2011/01/31/110131fa_fact_mcgrath

39. Laskas, J. M. (2011, March). The people v. football. *GQ.* Retrieved from http://www.gq.com/news-politics/big-issues/201102/jeanne-marie-laskas-nfl-concussions-fred-mcneill

40. McCrocken, G. (1989). Who is the celebrity endorser? Cultural foundations of the endorsement press. *Journal of Consumer Research, 16,* 310–321.

41. Hearings before the House Committee on the Judiciary, House of Representatives (testimony of Roger Goodell), October 28, 2009, and January 4, 2010. Washington DC: US Government Printing Office.

42. Moehringer, J. R. (2012, August 3). Football is dead. Long live football. *ESPN The Magazine.* Retrieved from http://espn.go.com/nfl/story/_/page/Mag15footballisdead/jr-moehringer-120-reasons-why-football-last-forever-espn-magazine

9

The Process of Soliciting Corporate Sponsorships

Because the demand from sport properties seeking sponsors is usually much greater than the demand from sponsors seeking sport properties, the process for arranging a partnership is usually initiated by the property. The efficiency and effectiveness of a property's efforts to solicit corporate sponsorship are likely to be a function of (i) the philosophy that underlies its approach; and (ii) the extent to which the approach is systematically organized. A marketing approach to solicitation involves carefully targeting specific companies or types of companies, identifying their reasons for investing, and customizing sponsorship programs that will bring about mutually satisfying benefits over an extended period of time. Sport managers who accept this philosophy and use it to guide their actions are likely to view themselves as brokers concerned with furthering the profitability of the potential sponsor companies, offering vehicles that will enable their marketing objectives to be met. They seek situations which will advance the goals of both the sponsor and sport event.

The marketing approach requires that a sport organization identify what a company is likely to want in return for investing its resources. This information forms the basis for a discussion with, and development of a proposal for, each prospect. Too often, sport organizations spend too much time thinking about their own needs and not enough time considering what their prospect, the potential investor, is likely to seek from a partnership.

A primary reason for sponsors rejecting what appear to be good investment opportunities relates to budget cycles and amount of lead-time. Budgets are planning documents that operationalize what a company is committed to doing for the next 12 months. Most of the sponsorship budget will be allocated to projects in that budget. However, it is usual to leave a small amount (typically 20–25%) unallocated, which gives companies some flexibility both to shift their sponsorship focus during a year to reflect changes in their competitive environments, and to take advantage of unusually desirable sponsorship opportunities that may emerge during the year. Nevertheless, if a sponsorship is not included in the annual budget, then it is more difficult for a company to invest in it. This means it is critical for sport organizations to be familiar with their target companies' budget cycles and to bring a sponsorship opportunity to a company's attention before the budget is formulated. A lead time of 18 months is not unusual if an event is scheduled for the end of a company's budget year. This allows 3 to 4 months for approaching the company and negotiating terms of a sponsorship; 3 to 4 months during which a provisional budget is reviewed and amended by various managerial and policy levels within the company; and the 10 to 12 months of the budget year that elapses before the scheduled event takes place.

There are other constraints that reinforce the need for a long lead-time. In Chapter 5, it was noted that a sponsorship provides a platform from which a company launches leveraging activities and the cost of these also must be included in its budget. Implementing a leveraged approach will require company manpower that has to be planned and allocated so it is available at the time it is needed. Advertising may be influential in determining lead-time due to the time required to prepare and reserve space in the media. For these reasons, it is unlikely that companies will consider sponsorship proposals that are not part of their regular budgetary planning process.

It has been suggested that the process of courting a sponsor is somewhat analogous to courting a marriage partner:

- Attraction—chemical, physical, emotional, rational.
- The Approach—someone needs to make the first move.
- Courtship—get to know each other and exchange vital statistics.
- Engagement—it could take six weeks, six months, or even six years . . . but do not rush into this.
- Marriage—provided engagement has gone according to plan, the big day is when everything is signed, sealed, and delivered to the satisfaction of all sides. Now the hard work begins. As in marriage, it takes effort to make sponsorship work—and lots of effort from both sides.

  Where the sponsorship breaks down and ends in divorce, it is usually attributable to the lack of communication between the parties, failure to manage expectations, promises made and then broken, or 'infidelity,' where a better offer came along and broke the relationship (p. 27).[1]

This chapter commences with a discussion of how to organize to solicit sponsorships and how to identify and nurture a set of companies whose images and target markets are compatible with the sport event. The criteria used by companies to screen and evaluate proposals are described. Before approaching targeted companies, a property has to inventory its assets, and ascertain the rights it wants to offer, research the needs of potential sponsors and develop a 1–2 page proposal. Communicating the proposal involves finding out who in a company should be contacted, and securing a meeting to discuss the initial proposal. This will lead to the packaging and pricing of rights that meet the sponsor's objectives. The chapter concludes with a discussion of the contract, ways of fostering a close working relationship between a sport organization and its sponsors, and follow-up actions to be taken when an event is completed.

ORGANIZING TO SELL SPONSORSHIPS[2]

The effectiveness of a sport organization's sponsorship effort in formulating, evaluating and implementing partnerships will depend on its willingness to invest resources in developing an organizational structure and acquiring the specialist skills and expertise the task requires. The extent of the structure will depend on the projected scale of sponsorship being sought. There are three broad organizational options for acquiring this expertise: (i) forming an internal marketing team; (ii) hiring an external marketing agency to broker partnerships; or (iii) a hybrid approach in which internal staff have some specified responsibilities, but an outside agency is hired to assist with specific tasks. Irrespective of which organizational model is used, there are four critical elements that it must embrace.[2]

Expertise is gained only with experience. Creating space in the job descriptions of existing staff with no experience in sponsorship resulting in on-the-job training will inhibit the likelihood of success. There must be *internal coordination* because sponsorships often impact multiple divisions within an organization, each of which will have its priorities and concerns as to how the partnership will complement their existing efforts. In addition, personnel in these divisions presumably already have full work loads so something new, even if it will enhance their mission, may be resented, viewed simply as extra work, and not embraced with enthusiasm.

The organizational structure should facilitate *timely response times*. Property owners invariably are in differentt stages of solicitation, negotiation and implementation with multople sponsors. Companies and their brands operate in a dynamic marketplace and need to respond quickly to changes in it. If decsions or actions are delayed by the sport organization, then companies will be reluctant to engage and become cautious when approached with future opportunities.

The *sales team* has to pursue large initiatives such as naming rights where nurturing interested prospects is challenging, and negotiations are likely to be complex and take a long time to conclude. However, in the short term the team has to simultaneously consumate more modest sponsorships. Sometimes the trust nurtured with partners in the modest, short-term investments is a pre-requisite for subsequent larger initiatives.

Forming an Internal Marketing Team

The initial challenge is to announce to potential sponsors that the organization is "open for business" by hiring staff with sponsorship expertise. After they have been hired, their first task is to develop the processes and procedures across divisions and with senior management associated with such tasks as inventorying assests, program elements, and contract negotiations. Clearly, a major downside of this internal model is the substantial up-front investment needed to hire this staff. It is probably not justifiable if sponsorship revenues are a relatively small proportion of an event's funding. Alternatively, if they are central to an event's viability, then investing in internal resources is likely to be beneficial in the long term.

Typically, a sponsorship sales team would have an incentive-based salary structure to encourage the persistent outreach needed for success. The incentive structure would differ for major and modest sponsorships, and there are two ways it can be achieved:

> First, the compensation can be structured so that a larger commission percentage is earned from the sales packages below a certain threshold (e.g., 5% on deals larger than $150,000 and 7.5% on deals below this threshold). Alternatively the commissions of the entire sales team could be pooled so that the team as a whole is motivated to pursue the entire realm of sponsorship opportunities (p. 33).[2]

Hiring an External Agency

An external marketing agency would serve as the sport organization's agent on developing and soliciting sponsorships, negotiating contracts, and activating the sponsorship. However, the sport organization's staff charged with liasing with the agency will remain responsible for ensuring internal coordination and timely response times. The agency would be responsible for the following:

- Developing programs and ideas that meet the goals of the initiative;
- Managing the outreach and solicitation of potential corporate marketing partners by the sales group;
- Serving as the sport organization's agent in negotiations with potential partners— lead negotiations on behalf of the sport organization in determining the business terms of agreements with marketing partners;
- Supervising the implementation and activation of every deal;
- Assissting and advising divisions regarding partnership activities;
- Reviewing and developing partnership agreements as requested, and;
- Tracking and reporting partnerships and the initiative overall. (p. 34)[2]

An agency's cost will be a transparent line-item in a budget. It may appear to be either high or low depending on the internal structure against which it measured. If compared against the cost of assigning the responsibility to existing staff, then it will likely seem high because internal overhead and time opportunity costs associated with internal staff are likely to be underestimated or ignored. Althernatively, if the comparison basis is the cost of hiring a new internal sponsorship team, then in the short-term the agency's retainer fee is likely to be perceived as relatively low.

The agency brings added value through its network of relationships and previous working with corporate sponsors. For example, it may be able to sell a sponsorship to one of its existing client sponsors. Remuneration to the agency is likely to be some combination of monthly retainer and commission:

> There is the possibility that a firm may work on a commission only basis; however, because it would be assuming all of the risk, commission percentages to the agency would be higher than if the agency was also being compensated in part by a monthly retainer. Average commissions typically range from 15% to 20%. If working on commission only, those percentages could increase to 35% or 40%. The

main drawback to this approach is that the sport organization will have to pay a monthly management fee to the agency regardless of how often partnerships are secured . . . The size of the monthly retainer will vary depending on how much is asked of the agency. The sport organization could expect to pay a monthly retainer of $5,000 to $7,500 if the agency is tasked with handling all aspects of this initiative. If only asked to sell opportunities that have been previously built and approved, the monthly retainer could be much lower, $1,000 to $2,000 (p. 36).[2]

Sport properties that are in the strong position of being highly valued by sponsors may outsource sponsorship recruitment and seek a guaranteed minimum revenue from the selected agency. In such cases, agencies need to bid a guaranteed revenue to the property owner, while ensuring their own profit margin:

International Management Group (IMG) has made a success of this approach and achieved significant sponsorship programs for, amongst others, the Association of Tennis Professionals (ATP) Tour and the US and European Golf Tours. There have been failures however, with ISL, for example, going bankrupt in 2001 and not producing its contracted revenues to FIFA for the 2002 and 2006 World Cups or fulfilling its 10-year, $1.2 billion marketing agreement with the ATP Tour. As with all bidding processes, there is a fine line between realistic and non-realistic revenue guarantees (p. 164).[3]

Conflict of interest in likely to be a concern when an external agency is involved. For example, a property will need to ensure that their representation receives sufficient attention and focus, given that the agency is likely also to represent other properties. The potential for egregious conflict of interest increases when an agency represents both property owners and sponsors.[3]

A Hybrid Approach

This model recognizes that there are multiple tasks involved in consumating and managing a sponsorship partnership, so it is possible a sport organization may have in-house capacity to do some of them. For example, it may be able to manage a sponsorship's activation elements, or if an internal sales team is hired an agency may be recruited to package, price, and prepare proposals so the sales team can focus exclusively on selling. The primary potential disadvantage of the hybrid model is the increased likelihood of conflict that arises when multiple organizations work together for a common goal. This can be minimized by ensuring there is clear delineation of roles and responsibilities.

INVENTORY

The starting point for a sport property in soliciting sponsorships is to audit its assets and produce an inventory of rights which it wants to make available to sponsors. Its major assets are likely to include the following[4]:

Intellectual Property: The logos, registered trademarks, images or phrases associated with the event.

Category Exclusivity guaranteeing companies that their competitors will have no official association with the property, so a company's leveraging activities using the property's intellectual property cannot be duplicated.

Media rights for broadcast, print, social media, and Internet outlets.

Tickets and Hospitality for customer entertaining and internal incentive programs.

Venue Signage the pricing of which will depend on size, location, television exposure, attendance, etc. Most major sport properties now use digital signs that span the length of the sidelines in football stadiums or envelop the arena in basketball facilities. Rather than having numerous different static signs, digital signs promote one sponsor at a time. This focuses the audience's attention, removes clutter and enables messages to be changed each game to perhaps address different promotions, so it is more valuable to a sponsor.

Sponsor Identification incorporating a sponsor's name or logo on such items as vehicles, ticket backs, fan givaways, scoreboards, drink cups, official uniforms, letterhead, team publications, and team websites.

Leveraging Events that are experiential in nature and activate the sponsor's investment.

In-Game Promotions which entertain the crowd whenever there is a break in the action. This may include pre-game, half-time, and time-out breaks which sponsors can use to communicate something positive about their brands, which the property will insist is fun, entertaining, and usually interactive.

Pass-Through Rights which allows sponsors to involve business partners in the sponsorship by passing the sponsorship rights through to them. Many retailers and manufacturers seek these rights which enable them to sell them to third parties to defray cost of the sponsorship. Thus, for example, there are thousands of brands in grocery stores competing for shelf space. The most desired spaces are located at the end of aisles at the front of stores. In return for defraying part of the cost of a retailer's sponsorship, a manufacturer often receives the coveted end-aisle slot for a given period of time and the right to some recognition on these point-of-sale shelves of its role as a secondary sponsor of the sport event.

Direct Marketing and Use of a Property's Database recognizes that companies make extensive use of email and mail to customize messages to potential customers. Properties have contact information on their attendees from ticket sales, fan clubs, on-line merchandise sales, and on-line contests. Since the property's customers are likely to be the sponsor's customers, these databases are valuable resources to a sponsor.

DEVELOPING A SET OF POTENTIAL COMPANY INVESTORS

Before any selling takes place, a set of companies whose customers have demographic/lifestyle profiles consistent with those of the event audience/participants, and whose function and/or image is compatible with that of the event have to be identified. The Internet makes sponsorship prospecting relatively efficient, since from websites it is possible to find out information on a company's brands, its mission and goals, location, target markets, whether it sponsors other sport events, and so on. Indeed, many companies now make their sponsorship policy available on the Internet, indicating what events they will and will not support and the kind of information they need for this decision.[5]

In developing the list of prospects, a sport organization should first review the companies with which it does business. If expenditures are made in a category that does not currently have a sponsor, then those purchases should be used as an entré for conversations about sponsorship. Most companies are likely to listen when a property is offering to spend money on their products.[4]

The geographic scope of a property's audience, including any media audience, will dictate whether the search for sponsors (i) should be limited to companies located within a community; (ii) should be extended to regional companies and regional offices of larger companies; or (iii) should embrace national or international companies. Geographic location may be important, even at events seeking national level sponsors. If major companies are headquartered in the host community, they are likely to be prime prospects because the event provides a particularly strong platform that could facilitate client visits to the headquarters and interaction with multiple company personnel; demonstrate the companies' support for the community; and facilitate extensive employee access and involvement with the event. The geographic scope decision guides the types of reference sources that will be used to develop an initial list of prospective sponsors.

Some logical targets for developing a strong list of prospects include the following:

- Active sponsors—companies that are consistent leaders in sponsoring many properties on a local, regional, or national basis;
- Companies from which one's audience purchases or would be likely to purchase;
- Sponsors of similar properties to the one being represented;
- Sponsors of other properties in the same geographical area;
- Companies that are based in, or have a large employee presence in, the market(s) where the property is located;
- Competitor companies of all of the above.[6]

To test the efficacy of the initial set of prospect companies, sport managers should put themselves in the shoes of those companies' managers. If they cannot see why the sponsor's representative would become excited about being a partner in the event, then they should discard the company from the list of prospects. If "the shoe doesn't fit," the sport organization might succeed in attracting a sponsor the first year, but the sponsor is then likely to withdraw with some level of bad feeling and the organization will have to replicate the effort to attract another company in the subsequent year.

A sport property may enlist its Board of Directors or major supporters to assist in soliciting sponsorships. For example:

The University of California's athletic department developed a marketing committee composed of marketing and advertising professionals in the Bay Area, who were also involved in the "Bear Backers" donor/alumni organization. All of these people had strong contacts in the Bay Area and a deep and sincere love for Cal athletics—a perfect combination for opening doors for athletic department marketing staff and developing new sponsorship business . . . Members of the committee are asked to "claim" potential sponsors each year. They are matched with marketing staff and team together with them to sell the sponsorship (p. 122).[7]

Another source of potential new sponsors is existing sponsors who should be asked if they have businesses relationships with companies that they think might benefit from a partnership with the sport property. Because these prospects come from existing partners, it increases their buy-in for an event. Approaching a new prospect with an existing sponsor means there will be trusted personal testimony supporting a proposal. Additionally, established business relationships between companies frequently facilitates cross-selling opportunities for them around their sponsorship of the sport event.[7]

The effective development and nurturing of sponsors requires that a system is established to facilitate networking and scheduling with the set of prospect companies. The system should enable an agency to scan corporate interests and characteristics so it can quickly compile a list of likely prospective corporations for a particular event. Thus, the agency can make the right contact with the right potential sponsor at the right time. The system will be customized to meet the particular needs of a sport property, but the generic approach is shown in Exhibit 9.1.

Each potential sponsor is issued an account code of 0 through 6 using the following classification:

0: fewer than 100 employees
1: from 101 to 250 employees
2: from 251 to 500 employees
3: from 501 to 1,000 employees
4: more than 1,000 employees
5: Civic, social, and service organizations

Each record contains the account number, the company name, address, telephone number, contact person and title, type of company product or service provided, promotion budget, budget cycle, and space to record any sponsorship investments that a company has made. The budget cycle for each company's promotion budget is identified. Each week the organization prints out a list of corporations whose internal budget cycle is due to begin in three months time. This three-month lead period gives staff time to re-establish contact with the corporation's decision makers, have an initial discussion with them, and to prepare a proposal for possible inclusion in next year's budget.

A follow-up file maintains a record of all contacts made with prospective sponsors or contributors by telephone, email, or in person (Exhibit 9.2). Each record contains the company name, the person contacted, and the project with which the contact was concerned. Files are provided for the dates and descriptions of contacts, their decisions to accept or decline a proposition, and comments they make about the association that might be helpful at a later date. In this file, a log of the companies to which a proposal

Exhibit 9.1

A Sample Generic Sponsorship Tracking System

Account type:	4
Prospect corporation:	Jones Manufacturing
Mailing address:	P.O. Box 1000
Mailing city:	Kansas City
Mailing state:	Missouri
Mailing zip code:	64141
Location:	31st and Southwest Trafficway
Location city:	Kansas City
Location state:	Missouri
Location zip:	64141
Telephone:	(816) 968-1234
I. Contact and title:	Frank Jones, chief executive officer
II. Contact and title:	Bill East, president
Type of Company:	Headquarters of building systems manufacturing
Number of Employees:	500
Product service:	1) Engineering, manufacturing, marketing of building systems for nonresidential construction, grain-storage bins, and farm buildings and 2) under-the-floor electrical distribution systems, agricultural products, and energy-management systems.
Budget month:	October
Advertising budget:	$3,000,000
Advertising media:	Newspapers, consumer magazines, business publications, direct mail to customers and business establishments, and network and spot radio.
Investment A:	
Date A:	00/00/0000
Project A:	
Investment B:	
Date B:	00/00/0000
Project B:	
Investment C:	
Date C:	00/00/0000
Project C:	
Reason declined:	

Exhibit 9.2	
A Sample Follow-Up File	
Company:	Jones Manufacturing
Contact:	Bill East
Project:	Sponsorship of temporary building for hospitality purposes at LPGA Golf Tournament
Date:	07/09/14
Explain:	Mailed plans and schematics
Date:	07/17/14
Explain:	Received letter asking to set up time for a presentation. Set meeting for August 1, 9:00 AM
Date:	08/01/2014
Explain:	Had meeting with Mr. East and Mr. Jones. Explained the project and the concepts. They will be in touch with us after they make a decision.
Date:	09/01/14
Explain:	Mr. Smith telephoned. Jones Manufacturing accepted our proposal.
Conclusion:	Will construct structure on site.

was sent is kept, the date it was mailed, and all follow-up contacts concerning that project. This type of system is valuable in preventing duplication, so companies are not invited by different people from the sport organization to support different programs without internal coordination of these requests.

CRITERIA USED BY COMPANIES TO SCREEN PROPOSALS

The number of sponsorship opportunities offered to some companies is overwhelming. As sponsorship has grown, companies have developed approaches for evaluating multiple opportunities that they are offered to identify the most attractive among them that are likely to yield the highest return on their investment. The criteria and screening procedures that they use are intended to ensure that the benefits specified in a company's sponsorship objectives are delivered.

A number of digital screening programs are available which analyze proposals against a company's sponsorship goals. Even when companies have similar goals, they place different weightings on their importance. These are incorporated into a digital system so it is customized for each sponsor. These weighted criteria provide the sponsorship template against which all incoming proposals are evaluated. Many companies adopt a policy by which they will only consider proposals that have been through the system. By analyzing a proposal's offer against the numerically weighted criteria, a points score is produced. This identifies whether the proposal has potential or not for the sponsor to pursue it further.[10c]

Exhibit 9.3

Screening Criteria Used by Business Organizations to Determine Which Sport Sponsorship Opportunities Will Be Supported

1. Customer Audience
- Is the demographic, attitude, and lifestyle profile of the target audience congruent with the product's target market?
- What is the on-site audience?
- Is sponsorship of this sport the best way to communicate about the product to this target audience?

2. Exposure Reach
- What is the inherent news value of the event?
- What extended print and broadcast coverage of the sponsorship is likely?
- Will the extended coverage be local, regional, or national? Is the geographical scope of this media audience consistent with the product's sales area?
- Can the event be tied into other media advertising?
- Can the sponsorship be used to create consumer and trade promotions?
- Will concession areas at the event cooperate in selling the company's product and brand-logoed items?
- What opportunity does the event offer for a sustained presence? That is, what is its future growth potential? How long is the sponsorship usable before and after the event?
- Are banners and signage included in the sponsorship? How many? What size? Where placed? Will they be visible during telecasts?
- Will the product's name or logo be identified on promotional materials for the activity?
  - ○ Event posters? How many?
  - ○ Press releases? How many?
  - ○ On tickets or ticket order forms? How many?
  - ○ Point-of-purchase displays? Where?
  - ○ Television advertisements? How many spots? Which stations?
  - ○ Radio advertisements? How many? Which stations?
  - ○ Print advertisements? How many? Which publications?

- Where will the product name appear in the event program? On the front or back cover? How many and size of program advertisements? Number of programs to be printed?
- Will the product's name be mentioned on the Public Address system? How many times?
- Can the sponsor have display booths? Where will they be located? Will they be visible during telecasts?

3. Distribution Channel Support
- Are the sponsorship's advantages apparent to wholesalers, retailers, or franchisees? Will they participate in promotions associated with the sponsorship?

4. Competitive Advantage
- Is the event unique or distinctive?
- Has the event previously had sponsors? If so, how successful has it been in delivering desired benefits to them? Is it strongly associated with other sponsors? Will "clutter" be a problem?
- Does the event need co-sponsors? Are other sponsors of the event compatible with the company's product? Does the company want to be associated with them? Will the product stand out and be recognized among them?
- If there is co-sponsorship, will the product have category and advertising exclusivity?
- Will competitors have access to signage, hospitality, or event advertising? Will competition be allowed to sell its product on site?
- If the company does not sponsor the event, is it likely that a competitor will? Is that of concern to the company?

5. Level of Resource Investment Required
- How much is the total sponsorship cost, including such items as related promotional investments, activation, staff time and administrative and implementation

(Exhibit continues on next page)

Exhibit 9.3 *(Continued)*

Screening Criteria Used by Business Organizations to Determine Which Sport Sponsorship Opportunities Will Be Supported

effort, and in-kind resources as well as the sponsorship fee?
- Will it be unwieldy and difficult to manage the sponsorship investment?
- What are the levels of barter, in-kind, and cash investments?
- Does the sport organization guarantee a minimum level of benefits to the company?

6. Sport Organization's Reputation
- Does the sport organization have a proven track record in staging this or comparable events? Does it have the expertise to help the product achieve its sponsorship goals?
- Does the organization have a reputation and image with which the company desires to be associated?
- Does it have a history of honoring its obligations?
- Has the company worked with this sport organization before? Was it a positive experience?
- Does the sport organization have undisputed authority and control over the activities it sanctions?
- How close to its initial projections have the sport organization's previous performances been in delivering benefits to sponsors?
- How responsive is the organization's staff to sponsors' requests? Are they readily accessible?

- Is there insurance and what are the company's potential liabilities?

7. Event Characteristics
- What is the perceived stature of the event? Is it the best of its kind? Is it prestigious? Will involvement with it enhance the product's image?
- Does it have a "clean" image? Is there any probability it will be controversial?
- Does it have continuity or is it a one-off?

8. Entertainment or Hospitality Opportunities
- Are there opportunities for direct sales of product and related merchandise, or for inducing product trial?
- Will celebrities be available to serve as spokespeople for the product? Will they make personal appearances on its behalf at the event, in other markets, or in the media? At what cost?
- Are tickets to the event included in the sponsorship? How many? Which games? Where are the seats located?
- Will there be access to VIP hospitality areas for the company's guests? How many will be authorized? Will athletes appear?
- Will there be clinics, parties, or playing opportunities at which the company's guests will be able to interact with the athletes?

The evaluation criteria can be summarized under eight headings from which the mnemonic acronym CEDAR SEE is derived: customer audience, exposure reach, distribution channel support, advantage over competitors, resource investment level required, sport organization's reputation, entertainment and hospitality, and event's characteristics. A set of screening criteria that operationalize these eight major concerns is shown in Exhibit 9.3.

A company is unlikely to consider all of the criteria listed in Exhibit 9.3 in its evaluation process. To do so would create an unwieldy and unmanageable system that would defeat the objective of simplifying the process. Further, a common set is unlikely to be appropriate for all companies because the benefits sought from sponsorship are different. Rather, each company is likely to select from this comprehensive list the 12 to 15 criteria that are deemed to be most salient to its objectives.

CUSTOMIZING PROPOSALS

Traditionally, sport properties adopted an "off-the-shelf" approach to soliciting sponsorships, by which they offered different levels of fixed packages of rights benefits. This approach meant that a wide range of investment opportunities were made available, but they reflected only the sport property's needs and were not tailored to the sponsors' needs. Thus, sponsors were required to fit their platforms around the packages being offered, rather than having a customized package of rights that was specifically designed to facilitate the benefits they sought.

One of the principles pioneered at the Los Angeles Olympic Games was categorization of sponsorships. Purchasing exclusive rights within a product category means that a company has an association not available to its competitors which it can use to strengthen its brand. Usually, exclusivity is viewed as being key to sponsorships since it is used to build an image that is different from competitors. However, exclusivity is likely to be expensive and in some situations a company can accomplish its goals without exclusivity:

> For example, if a company was only interested in obtaining one-half inning of behind-home-plate signage from a MLB team to drive awareness of its brand in a new market and have a suite for the season to entertain new and potential customers, it might not be interested in signing an exclusive deal. The property is looking to generate as much revenue as possible from each category, while at the same time developing relationships that can last for a long period of time. It's much easier to renew a current sponsor than find a new one. An exclusive deal forces the property to maximize revenue from one company, whereas a non-exclusive deal leaves options open for other revenue. For example, assume a MLB team has targeted $1 million of revenue from the banking category. If Washington Mutual Bank is willing to make a non-exclusive deal for $600 thousand, the team might accept this if there are other banks interested in sponsorship to make up the $400 thousand shortfall. (p. 90)[4]

Typically, packages were tiered so each level incorporated different magnitudes of rights benefits which were priced accordingly. The terminology of the tiers varied widely, but they were named to reflect the hierarchal status of sponsors. This hierarchal packaging still prevails, especially among major sport properties, but it is now usually recognized to be a conceptual framework that can be negotiated and amended to best fit a sponsor's objectives rather than a fixed set of benefits. The number of levels is likely to vary with the size of the event. Many smaller properties may eschew the tiering approach and adopt what has been termed "solus sponsorship," (p. 83)[3] whereby a single sponsor receives exclusive use of all the rights to an event that are on offer.

The Olympic Games has five levels of sponsorship which are described in Exhibit 9.4, but its scale is unique.[8] The most common structure consists of four categories: title sponsor, sector or presenting sponsor, official or preferred sponsor, and official supplier status. Each higher level of sponsorship builds on the benefits package offered at

Exhibit 9.4

Levels of Sponsorship at the Olympic Games

The Olympic Games has five levels of sponsorship: TOP, Partner, Sponsor, Provider/Supporter/Supplier, and Licensee.

TOP (The Olympic Program)

TOP sponsors have exclusive global marketing rights and opportunities within a designated product or service category. This includes partnerships with the IOC, all active NOCs and their Olympic teams, and the two OCOGs and the Games of each quadrenium.

Partner

Partner sponsors are managed by the OCOG within the host country under the direction of the IOC. These sponsors support the operations of the OCOG, the planning and staging of the Games, the host country NOC and the host country Olympic team. They have marketing rights within the host country. OCOG's garner more revenues from their Partners, than from the allocation they receive from TOP (Exhibit 1.3). Partners have the same rights as TOP sponsors, but they are confined to the host country.

Sponsors

Sponsors' rights are restricted to NOCs. Their exclusive rights in a product or service category enable them to claim the title "Official . . ." In the host country, they are subordinate to TOP sponsors and Partners. In countries which do not host the Games, the Sponsors of the NOCs are subordinate only to TOP sponsors. To protect the exclusiveness of sponsors the IOC has defined about 100 categories and has reserved 25 for itself for possible TOP sponsors. If a category remains free, the NOC can negotiate to get this category for a national sponsor for that respective Olympiad.

Provider/Supporter/Supplier

This level is designed to provide the IOC, OCOGs, and NOCs with key support and products required for operations. These companies receive limited marketing rights and generally provide in-kind rather than cash support to the entity with which they are partnering.

Licensees

These companies' rights are limited to merchandising. They are authorized to use the Olympic or National Team emblems and mascots. The IOC states they are "designed to promote the Olympic Image and convey the culture of the host region within a controlled commerical environment." Typically, the companies pay a fee of between 10 and 15% for use of the emblems. The merchandise is usually novelty or commemorative items such as t-shirts, caps, mugs and pins. The OCOGs authorize companies to produce Olympic souvenirs, while the NOCs authorize specific souvenirs related to their national teams. The IOC itself operates a limited licensing program around the world which focuses primarily on videos, videogames, and other multimedia products.

the previous level. While there is a general pattern that distinguishes the four sponsorship categories from each other, there is no established list of rights for each of the categories. The categories are simply conceptual frameworks and have no legal meaning other than what is agreed upon when a contract is signed. Thus, the following descriptions of these four categories should be regarded only as illustrative templates which may serve as starting points for negotiations with potential sponsors. They will then be customized to accommodate each sponsor's needs.

Title sponsorship means that the sponsor's name becomes integrated into the event title or team name. This is the highest form of association with an event and offers a sponsor maximum leverage for enhancing brand equity. The title sponsor is likely to insist on the right to veto unsuitable co-sponsors, and to have substantive input into how the event is managed and organized. A title sponsor for major events that are broadcast is likely to be required to commit to a minimum expenditure with the broadcast network. It has been observed:

> The most successful title sponsorships from a naming standpoint are those in which the corporate name and the event are inextricably linked. One of the best examples is the McDonald's All-American High Scool Basketball Game. This game played each spring involves the top-rated high school basketball players in the country. In most cases, these players will be stars at the collegiate level and many will also play in the NBA. Whenever you hear about a top high school player, they're referred to as "McDonald's All-Americans." That's brand equity and title sponsorship at its best! (p. 36)[4]

Sector or Presenting sponsors of a sport event typically pay about one-half to one-fourth of the title sponsor's investment. They are given exclusive rights to associate with an event within a product category or sector. Thus, a company may be the only life insurance, automobile, soft drink, or shoe company associated with the event. Companies are using increasingly creative "presenting sponsor" tag lines that reflect the company's business: "ESPN College GameDay *Built by* The Home Depot," "NCAA Hoop City *Refreshed by* Coca-Cola," and "ESPN GameDay *Driven by* State Farm." (p. 37)[4]

A sponsor is likely to want to define a category as broadly as possible, but the more money a sport organization seeks to raise from sponsorships, the more narrowly it is tempted to define these categories to allow it to sell to more sponsors in different categories. The greater the number of categories that are created, the more difficult it will be, especially for lower level sponsors, to establish their association with a property in the minds of their target audiences. In these cluttered contexts it is likely that when consumers are asked whether a sponsoring brand or a non-sponsoring competitor is associated with a property, they will rely on a default mechanism reflecting which of the brands is most prominent in their memory, regardless of any association with the property.

An Olympic official observed, "The more pressure there is for us to make money, the thinner we slice the apple" (p. 80).[9] Thus, an exclusive category may be defined as "soft

drinks" or as "carbonated soft drinks." This latter, more narrow definition enables the organization to sell another exclusive category sponsorship to a non-carbonated soft drink brand. However, the added "clutter" is likely to mean the price that can be charged for each category will be lower. The conundrum is illustrated by the following scenario:

> A beverage company like Coca-Cola or Pepsi-Cola manufactures and sells more than just soft drinks. Therefore, when they negotiate category exclusivity, they will include all the beverages they currently sell (fruit juice, isotonic, bottled water, coffee drinks, etc.) as well as ones that have yet to be developed. A soft drink company's ultimate goal would be exclusivity of all beverages. Both sides work backwards from the total beverage category until they find common ground that works for both parties. (p. 89)[4]

In major event sponsorship agreements, these categories are carefully negotiated and meticulously defined. This is illustrated in Table 9.1, which defines the scope of the exclusive product category negotiated by the Mars brand in its sponsorship of the World Cup Soccer competition.

Official or preferred sponsors typically are charged about 10% of the title fee. Their benefit package is substantially smaller than that of presentation sponsors. They will only be authorized to invest in product categories that have not been reserved by presenting sponsors. This level offers smaller companies an opportunity to associate with relatively little financial risk but, given the commensurably small benefit package, they are likely to have to work hard to obtain their marketing objectives.

The brands of *official suppliers* generally are not directly linked to the sport event itself and have little obvious connection to it. They offer in-kind goods or services rather than cash, to the sport organization staging it, or to the participants or spectators who are part of it. Typical of such sponsors would be food and beverage suppliers, credit card companies, and equipment suppliers.

For properties that have international audiences, a single category is likely to have different sponsors in different countries. For example, in its Financial Services category Manchester United (MU) sponsors include the following corporations:

- Aon: MU home, car and travel insurance in the UK, Australia, Hong Kong and Indonesia.
- Danaman: MU credit and debit cards in Indonesia.

Table 9.1. Categories Reserved by Mars as an Official Sponsor of the World Cup Soccer Tournament

Candy & confections	Potato chips	Pretzels
Block chocolate, cocoa	Tortilla chips	Popcorn
Chocolate covered snack bars, bisquits, mints	Corn chips	Puffs, curls, balls
Chocolate covered granola snacks, hard candies	Nuts	

- DenizBank: MU credit card in Turkey.
- Krungsri Bank: MU credit card in Thailand.
- Maybank: MU credit and debit cards in Singapore.
- MBNA: MU credit card in the UK.
- Santander Consumer Bank: MU credit card in Norway.
- Shinhan: MU credit card in South Korea.
- Shinsei Bank: MU credit card in Japan.

Typically, to activate their sponsorships, the companies offer signed Manchester United memorabilia, team merchandise at a discounted rate, and the chance to win hospitality tickets to watch the team play at their home stadium in Manchester.

As sponsorship has matured and expertise in exploiting its potential has developed among both sport properties and companies, there has been a movement away from fixed packaging towards tailoring a set of rights that best meets sponsors' objectives. An alternative to starting with a tiered conceptual framework which may better facilitate customization would be for a sports property to identify the rights it was offering and invite an expression of interest from potential sponsors. After evaluating these, the property would meet with each of the companies it deemed to be of most interest and after consulting with them, develop packages to fit each company's objectives. These would be "points of departure" for further refining and negotiating an agreement. Clearly, the more a package is customized, the more likely it is that a company's sponsorship objectives will be met and, thus, an on-going partnership established.

PREPARATION OF A PROPOSAL

The initial proposal should be limited to 1–2 pages. It has to arouse the interest of potential sponsors in the property. Its goal is to secure a meeting, and serve as a focus for that meeting. Company managers are unlikely to review anything extensive initially. They are more likely to scan quickly rather than to read the material, so the first two paragraphs are particularly critical. The most common complaint from company managers is that sponsorship proposals are too long, too descriptive, too generic and bland, and not tailored to their needs. A typical comment is, "Most of the requests that I get are too descriptive and do not outline the key features of the proposal, particularly the benefit that the request can provide to our company" (p. 196).[10] Companies that receive large numbers of approaches are especially likely to disregard those that do not demonstrate a match with their target market and suggest some awareness of a company's likely sponsorship objectives. Thus, before developing a proposal, a property should engage in front-end research to learn about the company, its marketing challenges, and other information that can be used to arouse interest in the sponsorship.

At this stage, the property's mission is to make the potential sponsor aware of what it has to offer and why it is likely to be of benefit to the company. The central concern should be to specify the potential benefits to the company. Too often, proposals make the mistake of describing the merits of a program, its level of excellence, or its economic impact. Sponsors do not buy programs; they buy the expectation of benefits. They buy platforms that help them sell products or services. Hence, proposals should address the sponsor's need, not those of the sport property.

When the initial proposal has been prepared, then the key questions to address are, "Who in the company should be contacted?" and "What is their role?" In companies that are extensively involved in sponsorship, it is likely to be the responsibility of a specialist executive in a sponsorship department, or an external agency working for them. In other companies, however, sponsorship decisions may be made by the chief executive if the business is relatively small, or by individuals with titles such as marketing, sales, or advertising vice-president, or by the public relations department. In large companies with multiple brands, if brand rather than corporate sponsorship is being solicited, then it is likely that brand managers rather than senior corporate officials will be the relevant contact. Finally, sales managers of regional offices should not be overlooked since an increasing number of companies are decentralizing marketing functions and funds.

The worst sort of approach is to send the initial proposal to the Vice-President of Marketing or to the Chief Executive Officer. It should be addressed personally to the contact person. The relevant individual can be tracked by checking the company's website or by phoning the company's public relations or press office, the company's receptionist, or the secretary or assistant of the vice-president of marketing.

In a cover letter, the sport manager should indicate an intention to call in a week to ten days to see if the company is interested and, if so, to arrange a meeting. This resolves the problem of companies taking weeks to respond and means that, if the response is negative, the organization can focus its efforts on other prospects.

Proposals should be directed at the highest level to which the property can gain access. This recognizes the adage that top level managers are paid to say yes, while middle-managers are paid to say no. Too often there is a mistaken tendency to contact employees at a lower level and hope that the request will filter up to the key decision-makers because sport managers feel less intimidated and more comfortable with them. Despite all that has been said about companies objectively evaluating proposals, it was noted in Chapter 1 that there are still instances when the egos and personal interests of senior executives or marketing directors may be a consideration in the decision.

PREPARATION FOR THE INITIAL MEETING

If a company sees merit in the initial proposal, then it is likely to seek a meeting with the property's managers to explore the opportunity further. At this point, it is useful to identify the individuals who will represent the company at the meeting and their position, status and role in the decision process. Several corporate actors probably play a role in the decision process, and they fall into three categories: gatekeepers, influencers, and decision makers. However, one person may fill more than one of the roles.

It is most probable that the contact person in a large company will be a *gatekeeper*. This person may simply report the outcome of the initial meeting and forward the report to others who make the decisions. Alternatively, the gatekeeper may be assigned the role of a "first screener" who evaluates whether a proposal is consistent with the company's objectives. The magnitude of requests received has resulted in some companies now hiring external firms to perform the gatekeeping role. They are given guidelines on the company's needs, and then serve as advisors on content and format of properties' submissions, screen them, and perhaps work with properties to develop some of them further.

The gatekeeper is likely to eliminate some proposals and forward a selective list of others to the decision-makers. A rule of thumb is that a gatekeeper can say no, but he or she cannot say yes. The manner in which a gatekeeper passes along a request may be critical. If he or she is not personally supportive, the information may be relayed less favorably and with fairly evident disapproval. Thus, gatekeepers are key people in determining the success of a proposal and their support must be secured. Sport managers should try and persuade gatekeepers to permit them to present their case directly to the decision-makers. This will ensure the proposal is presented in its best light and that there is an opportunity to answer any questions or objections the decision makers may have.

An *influencer* is a person whose views or advice help shape the attitudes of decision-makers and who, thus, exerts some influence on the final decisions. The third type of actor is the *decision-maker*, who decides whether to support the proposal. In this preparation stage, it is important to identify who will have final decision authority.

An important adage in soliciting sponsorships is that people invest in people first and organizations second. This is true of corporate executives. A valid aphorism in soliciting sponsorship is, "It is not what you know, but who you know." Sport managers are not only selling sponsorship investments, they are also selling relationships. Success is as likely to be attributable to positive personal chemistry as to the worthiness of the investment. The optimum scenario for a sport manager is to have a well-known track record of successful sponsorship partnerships, and a network that enables him or her to personally call the decision-maker in a targeted company, brief the individual on the proposal, and then follow-up with a proposal.

The importance of personal chemistry makes it imperative that a sport organization search for linkages between its personnel and the gatekeepers, influencers, and decision makers in a targeted company. The key questions are, "Who in the organization knows any of the key corporate actors," and "Who can we enlist as an ally?" The best type of linkages are personal acquaintances, but if these links are weak it becomes important to seek referrals. Are there any mutual contacts who could introduce organization personnel to key company officials?

The property's task is to learn as much as possible about the individuals who are gatekeepers, influencers, and decision-makers. Sites such as Facebook and LinkedIn may provide useful profiles. Whenever possible it is desirable to match their backgrounds with senior personnel from the sport organization who have similar backgrounds. A substantial body of empirical research demonstrates that positive interaction between the potential sponsor and property representatives is likely to be greatly facilitated if their backgrounds, personalities, interests, and lifestyles are compatible. Greater perceived similarities result in stronger mutual attraction and affinity. This matching process necessitates finding out background information relating to interests, hobbies, families, and goals. The contact person's secretary or receptionist may be willing to give this type of information.

FACILITATING DISCUSSION

If visual aids are to be used at the initial meeting, the contact at the company should be informed in advance and asked if it will be possible and convenient. A short DVD (2–3 minutes), for example, may be useful to demonstrate the context of the available rights, and to give a "feel" for the event's ambiance. However, this should not exceed five minutes in length. An effective overview presentation explains the property's proposition as it relates to the benefits it is anticipated may be sought by the prospective sponsor. The first minute of a presentation can be the most critical part of it even though it represents only a minuscule percentage of the total presentation time, because it often determines receptivity in the mind of the potential sponsor to the central substance of the proposal. The goal at this initial meeting is to gather information, not to make a sale. This means encouraging the sponsor's representatives to be active participants in the discussion. This can best be accomplished not by focusing on selling pre-determined fixed packages, but rather by framing key questions that will provide the sport property with sufficient information to prepare a customized package of rights that will meet the prospect's objectives. Rather than talking to the prospective sponsors, the challenge is to enter into a dialog with them.

This approach begins by exploring the company's needs: What benefits do you want to see from a sponsorship in which you invest? What criteria are most important in your evaluation of sponsorship proposals? What has worked well and not so well in previous sponsorships with other properties? The primary task of the sport manager during this stage is to listen and to suppress premature tendencies to talk about what the organization has to offer. The goal is to acquire the information necessary to build a comprehensive proposal around the company's priorities, which means asking questions to derive this information and not guessing. When the company personnel hear a summation of the discussion at the end of the meeting, they should believe that they are listening to an echo of their views. During the listening phase, the sport manager should be considering the features, advantages, and benefits of the property's event that are relevant to the potential sponsor's needs.

If discussion is to generate valuable feedback useful to developing a desired package, then it is necessary to draw out any negative reactions the company's representatives may have. These should not be dreaded; they should be welcomed. They provide valuable feedback and are the prospect's way of communicating how to make a sponsorship successful. Responding to negative reactions removes barriers, and the objections provide clues as to how best to meet the company's needs. Guidelines for dealing with negative reactions include the following:

- Never argue
- Respond with facts
- Avoid inflating the objection (i.e., if it is weak, try to ignore it)
- Show respect for honest objections
- Find some common ground (e.g., "I know what you mean. I agree.")

- Turn the objection into a reason for investing (e.g., "Actually, this is exactly why this investment will work for you.")
- Address it as a positive addition to the dialog (e.g., "I'm glad you brought that up.")
- Remember, the prospective investor is always right.[1]

Quiet prospects who hold questions and reservations in their minds and give few clues about their inward resistances are likely to be least influenced by the presentation. If no negative reactions are raised, then it suggests either that the company representatives were prepared to respond positively at the start, or that they were not sufficiently interested to raise an objection. In the preparation stage, someone in the sport property team should play devil's advocate in a rehearsal meeting to try and predict awkward questions or objections that may arise, so responses can be planned.

Over a period of time a sport manager is likely to hear all of the various objections that can be raised and will not be surprised by them. The manager should "keep track of flack" by documenting the objections received and determining the best way to handle them so he or she is prepared to respond when they arise again in the future.

After the company's representatives have explained their needs, the sport manager is in a position to show how the event is able to meet them. While it is likely that there is a general fit between the sport property and sponsor, it is unlikely that an initial proposal will perfectly meet the sponsor's needs since many of their specific requirements cannot be known in advance. The property's challenge, therefore, is to provide the specific results a company seeks which may involve making changes, within parameters the property sets, to the event. As part of this exercise, at this point the company must reveal a budget it is willing to spend, since it is not possible to design a package without that information.

At the same time, the property should be prepared to provide a detailed budget of the event's costs. This allows companies to understand the role of their investments in the context of the total budget, and to reassure them that the event is adequately funded. Sponsors may also be able to identify areas where they can help reduce costs. For example, companies can often obtain better prices on printing, advertising, or other items than can sport organizations.

The proposal should be careful not to promise more than can be delivered. In the interests of developing a long-term, on-going relationship with a company, it is always better to under-promise and deliver more. Indeed, if it becomes apparent after listening to the company's expectations that the event cannot deliver them, then in the interest of a long-term relationship the sport manager should articulate that view and gracefully withdraw.

Using the features, advantages, and solutions approach, the sport manager's summation should review the property's distinctive features; address ways in which the opportunity is superior to other investment options available to the company; and translate features and advantages into solutions that address the central question of how the event can help the company achieve its objectives. For example, if the company's primary aim is to increase sales in a market that the event can reach, then the summation may concentrate on packaging trade incentives that can be presented to dealers, retailers, franchises, or wholesalers to encourage them to sell more products. Alternatively, if awareness is the major objective, then the summation will identify ways that the event could extend the brand's audience reach, gain more publicity, or link with a media co-sponsor.

By the end of the meeting, company executives must feel comfortable with the sport manager's attitude toward the proposed arrangement and with the property as a partner. They must believe that the property is willing and able to fulfill its commitments, that it has an understanding of the company's commercial objectives, and that it is committed to working with the company to help it meet those objectives.

PRICING SPONSORSHIPS

Whatever approach is used to develop a sponsorship package, it is likely there will be a hierarchical structure of benefits and associated prices. The use of different levels allows companies that might not otherwise be able to afford the investment being solicited by a property to choose a lower level of sponsorship. If this is not done, a sport manager may offer a $100,000 proposal to a company that has only $40,000 to invest and, therefore, may lose the opportunity to secure $40,000 of support. However, an organization should probably start by presenting a conceptualization of a premium top-level package that contains all of the benefit rights discussed in the initial meeting, while also letting the prospect know that smaller packages can be negotiated. If the sport manager starts at a low level, it is rare for the sponsor to suggest increasing it. The pricing structure usually becomes less important once the prospective sponsor is convinced that the project is right for them strategically and they can clearly see the "big picture."[6]

Developing, soliciting, and implementing sponsorships involves expense to a sport organization in the form of staff time, opportunity cost, and financial cost. Hence, the starting point for ascertaining a price for a package of sponsorship benefits is to list these expenses to ensure sponsorship agreements generate more revenue than they cost to implement. A typical sheet for explicating these costs is shown in Table 9.2.[1] Staff time is notoriously difficult to calculate, but often it is the major cost center. For example, assume "Evaluation research" involves developing measures, collecting data, analyzing them, and producing a report, and that it takes two staff members a month to do this. If their annual salary and benefit package costs the company $60,000 for each of them, then the cost of staff time on this item is $10,000 [($120,000÷12)]. Accurate measurement of staff time requires staff to keep time diaries.

In addition to staff time, costs listed on the cost sheet should include the face value of tickets, marketing costs (including advertising) associated with promoting the sponsor's involvement, the value of media time, the costs associated with organizing the hospitality opportunities, and so on. The total costs shown at the foot of Table 9.2 constitute the minimum sale price of a sponsorship. If it is sold for less than this amount, then the sport organization will lose money on the agreement.

The value of a sponsorship is dependent upon: (i) the popularity, success (media ratings, wins and losses, etc.) and location of the sport property; (ii) the competitiveness of

Table 9.2. Cost Sheet for the Sport Manager Seeking Sponsorship	
Tickets	$
Hospitality, food, beverages	$
VIP parking passes	$
Event programs	$
Additional printing	$
Signage printing	$
Signage production	$
Signage erection	$
Support advertising	$
Apparel for competitors, officials, media, etc. featuring the sponsor	$
Evaluation research	$
Media monitoring	$
Faxes, phone calls, e-mails, Internet	$
Public relations support	$
Marketing costs	$
Advertising costs	$
Legal and accountancy costs	$
(Other items)	$
Cost of selling sponsorship staff time and expenses based on x hours at $ per hour multiplied by 1.5 for salary plus benefits	$
Cost of servicing sponsorship in staff time based on x hours over the season $ multiplied by 1.5 for salary plus benefits	$
Total costs	$

the business category (greater competition in a category raises the price); and (iii) extent of rights included in the sponsorship package.[4] It is important that the deal works for both sides, because if the sponsor feels that too high a price was paid, then there will be no renewal of the contract.

Acceptance of a sponsorship price will be influenced by opportunities available in the marketplace. An event's price will be compared by companies to that of other events of similar stature and incrementally increased or decreased according to how well it is perceived to compare. An indication of the prices of comparable events can be gleaned from publications such as *IEG Sponsorship Report* and *SportsBusiness Journal*, which report on these issues. However, the most important factor in setting a price is likely to be the market knowledge and experience of a sport property's team and their networks of peers who can provide information on comparable prices at other properties. This expertise is a primary reason for properties engaging agencies to assist and advise them. It has been observed that:

> In many businesses, competition drives the price down—not in the sponsorship world. The more active a category (meaning that there are several companies or more in the category that are involved in sponsorships—some of the most active are soft drinks, auto manufacturers, telecommunications, and beer) the higher the rights fees will be. Some properties that have heavy competition for their rights, such as the Vancouver 2010 Olympic Games Organizing Committee, have relied on bid processes to determine winning sponsors. In effect, these properties are turning the tables on the potential sponsor(s) by asking the interested corporations to submit detailed proposals that include financial and marketing commitments to the property. After receiving all the proposals, the property will select the company in each category that best fits its needs (financial and marketing commitments, etc.) (p. 22).[4]

A package of benefits should be priced as a holistic entity. A single price should not be attached to each component in a package. If components of packages are individually priced, then a sponsor is likely to look for items to cut. If sponsors want to negotiate certain elements to reduce the price, then they will raise the issue. The sport manager should not invite this action by individually pricing components in the proposal. An alternative approach to determining price is for a company to specify its budget and sponsorship objectives at the initial meeting, and for the sport property to negotiate a customized set of benefits that best fits these parameters.

Notwithstanding avoidance of pricing individual components, it is important that activation activities are specified at the outset and a budget allocated for each of them. Chapter 5 pointed out that activation is central to a sponsorship's success, but without a budgetary commitment to those activities they may not come to fruition.

The bulk of a sponsorship fee (at least 65%) should be paid when contracts are signed because costs associated with obligations to the sponsor, such as exposure in promotional materials, are likely to be incurred for a period of time before the event takes place. Discounts should be offered for multi-year commitments because they save time, labor, and legal fees compared to negotiating an equivalent number of one-year contracts. Properties typically add new activation opportunities or assets each year, since this enables them to raise the price of their sponsorships.

An emerging trend is performance incentive pricing. Typically in these instances part of the sponsorship payment will be a fee which is based on an anticipated return to the sponsor. If the property's performace is lower than expected, then the sponsor's price is reduced. Thus, when the French soccer team underperformed at the 2010 World Cup, the French Football Federation had to return almost $6 million to each of its top sponsors to compensate them for the underperformance.[11]

However, if the return to sponsors in terms of increased sales, media exposure, sampling trials, or whatever is exceeded, then the sport property receives additional payments. This provides the property with incentive to be fully involved and to "go the extra mile" to assist the sponsor. In essence, this is a profit sharing approach. The NFL, for example, negotiates such clauses in some of its sponsorship agreements:

- Sirius Satellite Radio has over 20 million subscribers. Its 12-year agreement with the NFL gave it the right to broadcast every NFL game live, nationwide, from pre-season action through the Super Bowl. In addition to paying a fee for those rights, Sirius gave the NFL the right to purchase shares in the company at a fixed rate. The number of shares the NFL could purchase was "50 times the number of new (individual) subscribers to the company's radio service who in the previous quarter have been directly tracked by the company to an incentive program implemented by an NFL member club." Hence, as the number of subscribers (and hence revenues) grew, the Sirius share price was likely to rise. Since the NFL contributed to these increases, it was remunerated by being able to purchase the higher-valued share at the lower rate fixed in the contract.

- When First Tennessee Bank negotiated a 10-year naming rights agreement with a 10-field baseball complex outside of Memphis, it used performance incentives to hedge the risk associated with the uncertainty of how a new property is going to perform. Looking at a new facility with an unknown number of prospective attendees, the bank structured the contract so that its rights fee was based on the number of teams that played in the complex, which was called First Tennessee Fields. Their spokesman observed: "You never know how a new venue will take. It doesn't have a pro sports team as a tenant, so it's not a case of 'if you build it, they will come.'" The bank paid a flat fee during the first three years of the partnership. In the fourth year, First Tennessee calculated a rolling average of the number of people who either used or frequented the venue during the previous three years. The bank then compared the three-year average to a baseline attendance number it determined at the beginning of the relationship. It increased or decreased its annual rights fee based on how the two numbers compared. A three-year average was used to ensure that an unexpected spike or decrease in annual attendance did not unfairly factor in.[12]

It seems likely that performance-based pricing agreements will become more prevalent within sponsorship. It means that a sport property can enhance its price by delivering enhanced bottom-line benefits to sponsors.

Many companies prefer to support an event with in-kind services rather than cash, and this is equally valuable if the services are budget relieving. In-kind may include providing personnel, materials, technology, specialist skills or access to marketing assets such as databases, communications or introductions to other potential sponsors.[12a]

In-kind should be valued the same as cash if it substitutes for line items in a budget. For example, if there is no need for a car, then an auto company should not be allowed to offset its cash payment by offering a car. However, if air travel is required, the airline should be treated as a cash sponsor. Perhaps the company has an advertising budget that could be used to assist the property in promoting the event in return for a hospitality package, or perhaps they have hundreds of retail outlets that could be used to sell property merchandise. The possibilities for in-kind assistance offering creative partnership opportunities are likely to be numerous.[13]

Valuing in-kind contributions is challenging and often contentious. The issue revolves around agreeing which value should be used. If a company provides computing systems software and advice, in-house printing, hotel rooms, airline tickets, or carrier service, how is the value of these services determined? Should it be retail cost, wholesale cost, published price, commonly negotiated discount price, or price during a sale? The most common practice is to use retail cost. In-kind contributions valued at retail cost can result in both parties benefitting. Consider the following example:

> Let's say the Yankees must purchase $250,000 of grass seed and lawn maintenance items each year to keep the field in prime playing condition throughout the season. If the Yankees enter into a sponsorship deal with Scott's and receive all necessary product as part of the deal, it essentially saves the Yankees $250,000 out of their annual budget. From Scott's standpoint, the company will realize a savings as well because it might cost them $125,000 (wholesale cost—true cost to the manufacturer) to provide the Yankees $250,000 (retail cost) in lawn care items. (p. 85)[4]

Given the substantial costs involved in sponsorship, there is a growing trend for major sponsors to seek to self-liquidate the cost of their sponsorship by involving their suppliers in the event. This might be achieved by a title sponsor sub-contracting product category rights to product manufacturers or distributors with which it has close ties, through direct merchandising sales, or through the sale of television rights fees. For example, a sport manager may approach a grocery chain and offer it title sponsorship of a golf tournament for $90,000. The organization may suggest to the chain that it offer $5,000-per-hole packages to 18 of its vendors. In return for their sponsorship, the vendors may be offered special in-store promotions and the highly sought-after end-aisle location for a given period of time. Each hole on the course would have the sponsor's banner on it. This enables the grocery chain to receive all the visibility, image, and goodwill benefits associated with title sponsorship at no direct cost to itself:

- Mervyn's is a mid-market department store chain in California. To change its staid image to a place where younger shoppers find hip, relevant fashions, it sponsored Beach Bash at California's Hermosa Beach, which included AVP-sanctioned men's and women's pro beach volleyball, inline skating, skateboarding, stunt cycling, and alternative bands. Its lead sponsorship gave it the rights to sell cosponsorship to vendors. The company sold cosponsorships to several of its vendors including Side Out, a maker of volleyball apparel, and Lee Company's Pipes line, geared for bikers and skateboarders. Vendors received on-site benefits, identification in Mervyn's ad campaign, and an enhanced, event-themed presence in its stores. These cosponsorships enabled Mervyn's to come close to liquidating its rights fee. In addition, by partnering with brands already relevant to youths, Mervyn's reduced the risk that it would seem out of place at the youth-oriented event—i.e., it borrowed its cosponsors' images as well as the event's image.[14]

- The Fiesta Bowl produced a hot air balloon race in Phoenix. The title sponsor was Fry's Food Store. The store's buyers went to 50 of their vendors and sold sponsorships to each of them for $1,500. Fry's used its leveraging power derived from shelf space positioning and end aisle displays to persuade the vendors to participate.[6]

From a sport property's perspective, the downside of allowing a sponsor these "pass-through rights" is that they may include product categories which the property could potentially sell on its own. This is particularly true of grocery retailers where most active sponsorship categories are sold such as beer, soft drinks, snack foods and cereal. Thus, in these situations, the property and company have to agree on which categories will be included in the pass-through list.[3]

HANDLING REJECTIONS

Sponsorship may be conceptualized as a program that an organization is selling. From this perspective, it is reasonable to anticipate that the development of sponsorship may follow a typical program life-cycle curve that progresses from introduction through take-off and maturation to saturation. The introduction stage may last two or three years before the sponsorship program gathers momentum and enters the take-off stage. During this period, a sport property may experience a large number of rejections to its proposals.

The success or failure of initial interactions with a prospect should not be viewed in the immediate context of whether support was forthcoming. Rather, the contact should be regarded as the beginning of a long-term relationship. A period of time may be needed to consolidate a relationship that has been established before sponsorship support emerges. Early efforts may yield relatively little, but there may be a future return on them as personal relationships and confidence in the sport property are nurtured.

When a targeted company rejects a sponsorship proposal, there should always be an effort to find out why. This involves asking questions, such as: "Was the package wrong?", "Did we fail to deliver enough benefits?", "Was the return on the company's projected investment inadequate?", "Did we ask for too much of an investment?", "Did we misread the company's target market?", "Did we send the wrong person?", and "Was the presentation ineffective?"

It is essential to follow-up. The objective is not to challenge the decision, but rather to ascertain why the proposal was not accepted and if the company would be interested in working with the sport organization in the future. When proposals are turned down, it is often not because a business cannot benefit from them, but rather because the timing was not right for the company. Polite persistence pays off. Thus, immediately after an unsuccessful effort, a letter of thanks should be sent to let a prospect know that the time spent visiting with the organization's representatives was appreciated. Contact should be maintained with the targeted company on the assumption that it may be a prime prospect for support in the future.

THE CONTRACT

The notion of an exchange relationship, which was discussed in Chapter 1, is the conceptual underpinning of all marketing transactions. However, in the context of sponsorship, a fluent exchange is especially challenging to transact because it involves a business relationship between, at best, organizations with widely different aims, and, at worst, a commercial company well-versed in sponsorships and an inexperienced sport property with different needs and expectations.[13] The two parties often operate in different environments, do not understand each others' businesses, have dissimilar reasons for their involvement, and seek different ends from the arrangement.

For these reasons, once general agreement has been reached with a company, some form of written document should be developed to ensure that both sides' interests are protected. Initially, this should be drafted by representatives from both sides without input from lawyers so that the issues are freely discussed. If both sides' lawyers are involved from the outset, there is some liklihood that they will be concerned with giving their respective clients "an edge" and become focused on legal technicalities prematurely. This could poison the chemistry between both parties. When a draft has been completed, then legal advisers may be used to ensure that the intent is expressed accurately.

Agreements may be documented by a letter of confirmation, a letter of agreement, or a formal contract. The magnitude of resources being exchanged and the expectations of the sponsor will guide the appropriate format. A confirming letter is not a contract per se, since it is not signed by both parties. The letter agreement is a contract signed by both parties but is less formal, less expensive, and often less intimidating than a standard contract. The formal contract is no more enforceable than a letter of agreement, but it does commit the parties to giving greater attention to the details involved. It has been observed that:

> Misunderstandings usually arise when the parties to the agreement have different views as to who will do what to exploit the sponsorship. The way to avoid this is to go through every possible element of the project beforehand and agree to the areas of responsibility. These details should be included in the contract so that in the event of any disagreements the original arrangement can be referred to. (p. 191)[13]

Exhibit 9.5 illustrates, in the context of a MLB team sponsorship agreement, the details with which assets are described in a contract.[15]

A comprehensive list of the types of issues to be covered in contract agreement discussions is shown in Exhibit 9.6.[16] However, given the element of unpredictability associated with sporting events (e.g., weather, injury, etc.) and the large number of facets involved in a sponsorship partnership, both parties should recognize the need for some degree of flexibility in interpreting their contractual agreement.

WORKING TOGETHER TO MAKE IT HAPPEN

Exhibit 9.7 offers a framework of fundamental stages which are central for a company to optimize its return from a sponsorship investment.[16a] While their implementation is

Exhibit 9.5

An Illustration of the Level of Detail With Which Asset Rights Are Specified in an MLB Contract

Term of Deal: Five years from date of agreement
Total Payment: $4.75 million cash
Payment Schedule: $950,000 per year

Package:

Stadium Signs
- One 24-by-24 foot exterior scoreboard sign, on south side of stadium
- One corporate ID on fascia under lower suite level
- One 60-by-42 foot tower facts mural
- Two 22-by-26 foot tension panels
- Two 6-by-12 foot signs above main concourse concession stands
- Two 5-by-12 foot signs above upper concourse concession stands
- Two 4-by-10 foot wall signs on main concourse and upper concourse
- Four 6-by-4 foot wall signs on ramps
- One 16-by-40 foot mural in main concourse
- Two 5-by-4 foot signs flanking concession areas and restrooms
- Videoboard advertising
- One identification per quarter with sponsored vignettes, replays or commercials on stadium rodeo replay scoreboard

Advertising
- One full-page, four-color ad in *NFL Insider*
- Periodic mentions in team's Newsletter, no less than once per year
- Presence on team's Internet page, including linking to sponsor's site
- Three 30-second commercials on the team's Radio Network during games. Option to purchase same number of spots for post-season games
- One 30-second commercial for pre-season game locally broadcast on the team's television affiliate

Suite
- Ability to upgrade location of current suite with capacity for 18 people at no cost, subject to terms and conditions of the luxury suite agreement. Suite will be located approximately on the 30-yard line on west side.

Season Tickets
- 16 tickets for all home games: 10 in the general admission section and 6 in the club section

Super Bowl Tickets
- Ten tickets for the next Super Bowl
- Six tickets for all other Super Bowls during the term of the agreement

Hospitality
- Four parking passes
- Tailgate party for 100 guests at one game each season
- VIP Day for 20 guests at one practice session each season
- One away-game trip per season for four guests
- One non-catered function each season

Appearances
Team shall use best efforts to make following persons available for appearances:
- Two player appearances each year
- Two appearances of the team's dance team each year
- Two appearances of the team mascot each year

Miscellaneous
- Jointly create community outreach programs designed to make an impact in the community and reach mutually beneficial promotional objectives. Annual allocation of approximately $50,000
- Create special events, marketing and advertising programs. Annual allocation not to exceed $25,000
- Distribute a giveaway to each fan at one home game each season. Team will allocate $50,000 to produce the giveaway. Additional cost will be at sponsor's expense
- Access to team mailing list twice a year for sponsor's direct mailing purposes

Exhibit 9.6

Issues to Address in a Sponsorship Agreement

Official status:
What is the sponsorship category? Are there veto rights with this category? That is, does a sponsor in this category have a say in who else can be a sponsor? Does the sponsorship extend to other sites or related events?

Sponsorship fee:
What is the fee? How and when is the fee to be paid? Is the fee refundable for any reason? Secured by letter of credit or escrow (e.g., if television ratings or other performance indicators are poor)?

Title rights:
Will the sponsor's name appear in the title? How will trophies be named? Who will present the trophy or prizes?

Television exposure:
Who owns and controls TV rights? Does the sponsor have rights of first refusal on television advertising spots? Is there a ratings guarantee? Will there be a rebate if ratings fall below this guarantee? Can the sponsor use TV video footage in its regular advertising? Does the sponsor need to obtain permission prior to using video clips for commercial reasons? Who is responsible for negotiating television time? Is a portion of the sponsorship fee credited to the TV coverage? Will the property obtain all the rights necessary from participants to allow use of clips in commercials without further compensation?

Public relations and media exposure:
Will key athletes mention the sponsor's name when being interviewed by the media? Will the sponsor's name be included in media releases? Who is responsible for media releases? Can the sponsor develop its own media marketing campaign?

Logo use:
Under what conditions can the sponsor use the organization's logos or trademarks? If special logos are deveoped, who owns them? Can the sponsor use the logo to promote its own image and products? Does the sponsor have merchandising rights? That is, can it make and sell souvenir items?

Signage:
How many banners, athlete patches, placards, arena boards, or flags can the sponsor use? What size? Where can banners be placed and what can appear on them? Who is responsible for making and paying for signage? Who is responsible for placing the signage on-site? Distance from others' signs? Signs on vehicles? Any conflicts with existing permanent signage at the venue?

Advertising rights:
In what manner can the sponsor use the organization or event for advertising purposes? Will the sponsor's name be on stationary or in the program? On television billboards? On merchandise? Where will it be placed? Can the sponsor use photographs related to the sponsorship for product promotion and advertising? Who is responsible for individual consent to use the photographs in advertising? What limitations are placed on the use of photographs?

Athlete use:
Will athletes make personal appearances on behalf of the sponsor? Will key athletes or coaches attend pre- or post-competition parties? Will athletes wear the sponsor's name during competition?

Hospitality rights:
Does the sponsor have the right to a hospitality tent? Does the sponsor get free tickets for tie-in contests, to give to key clients, or for other use?

Point of sale promotion:
Can the sponsor's products be on-site? What type: cigarettes, alcohol? Can the sponsor run on-site or off-site promotions associated with the sponsorship? Can the sponsor team up with other companies to form cooperative promotions? Who receives the profits from merchandising?

Direct mail lists:
Will mailing lists of ticket holders or athletes be made available to the sponsor? What form of promotions can the sponsor undertake with these mailing lists?

Product sampling:
Will a place be made available for product display and sampling? What types of products can be made available for sampling? Will you accept cigarettes and beer?

Legal liabilities:
Who is responsible for injuries to spectators, participants, or officials? For infringement of trademarks? What if it rains or there are problems with television transmissions? Who pays existing expenses?

Future options:
How many years does the sponsorship last? Does the sponsor have renewal options? How many years does the option last? How are sponsorship fee increases to be determined next year? After that?

Exhibit 9.7
Fundamental Steps for Optimizing Return From a Sponsorship Investment

Step 1. Work backwards.

Start with the end in mind. If you don't know what you want to get out of your sponsirship *before* you get into it, your sponsorship is doomed to fail. Answer these two basic but critical questions.
  1. Whom do you want to reach?
  2. What do you want to communicate to them about your brand?
     • functional advantages?
     • image advantages?
     • emotional associations?

Step 2. Check the fit.

Check the fit between the sponsored property and your marketing objectives.
  • Are the fans in your target? How many of your target members are fans?
  • Can you create a sponsorship premise that leads to the desired inferences?
  • How successful have other sponsors been with this property? How have they used this property to their advantage?

Step 3. Start early.

Don't wait until the event begins if you want to fully mine the value of your sponsorship.

Step 4. Forge a link.

Forge a link in the fans' minds between your brand and the sponsorship.
  • Invest to build a link between your brand and the property.
  • Use every communication opportunity available.
  • Develop an activation program.

Step 5. Define the meaning for your target.

Define for your target the meaning of your sponsorship in every possible message.
  • Don't leave it up to their imagination. Tell them what conclusion they should draw from your sponsorship.

Step 6. Remember—One sponsorship with impact is better than ten without.

  • One sponsorship that consumers notice, remember, and properly interpret is far more valuable than ten that are unnoticed, unremembered, or meaningless.

primarily the sponsor's responsibility, the sport property's managers should be fully engaged as partners in the effort.

When a partnership agreement is reached, this should not be regarded as the terminal consummation of a relationship. From a company's perspective, it may be a trial offer only from which the company will withdraw if returns are not satisfactory. The sport organization also should view it from this perspective and recognize that the agreement is a tentative initial step. Sometimes all efforts are directed to securing a sponsorship and little thought is given to servicing it. A long-term association requires building trust with sponsors by demonstrating commitment to accomplishing a company's objectives.

The marketing adage: Your best customers are your best prospects, suggests that if companies are pleased with the results accruing from their expenditure, then they are likely to be receptive to continuing the relationship. They are also likely to be valuable sources of testimonials and referrals to others. It is much less costly in time and effort to sustain an existing sponsorship arrangement than it is to find a new partner. This means that if a sport property adopts the short-term perspective that it needs the checks from sponsors so it can go about its business, then it is likely to be costly in the long term.

A fundamental tenet of working together is that properties should provide business for their sponsors whenever there is an opportunity to do so.[4] Thus, for example, a sponsor in the credit card category should expect that all of the property's employees will use that card for both organizational and personal purchases. The top sponsorship executive for the Bank of America stated: "When [we are] the sponsor as an official bank, we really want to be the offical bank of the property. We want their corporate banking, investment, payroll, retirement, financing and wealth management business. We want to develop a universal relationship as part of our investment."[17] When it is making a purchase, the property's starting point should be, "Can this purchase be made from one of our sponsors?" When a property requires computer or telecommunications equipment, airline tickets, or whatever, it should first think, "How can the money be spent with one of our sponsors?"

Many teams will provide an annual gift to their season ticket holders and sponsors. If the team is going to spend the money anyway, it makes sense for them to spend it with one of their sponsors (restaurant gift card, retail gift card, electronic item, etc.) If a sponsor doesn't already exist in the category where the spending will occur, it provides the property a reason to talk to companies in that category. As the business of sponsorship has become more sophisticated over the years, most companies will listen when a property is offering to spend money on its products or services, particularly if the spend is guaranteed. (p. 86)[4]

A key to nurturing a close working relationship and to building goodwill is constant communication between the parties and a total commitment to meeting the company's needs. Coordinating interactions with media is particularly important to ensure that both sponsors and sport property are communicating consistent and complementary messages. If a sport organization does not have the level of expertise in media relationships that is available to its major sponsor, then it should consider inviting the sponsor to coordinate this function.

An effective and enduring sponsorship relationship requires that it be viewed "through an alliance lense—as a comarketing alliance where both parties invest assets (financial, human, intellectual) and play a role in the strategic goal setting. In contrast to a unidirectional coperative agreement, in a sponsorship alliance both parties would seek to achieve goals linked to the strategic direction of the firm." (p. 333)[18] A property should embrace a sponsor's priorities and make them their own by offering suggestions on how the sponsor's rights can be exploited and leveraged. This can best be accomplished by creating a project team, comprised of representatives from both entities, which will stay with the project for the duration of the partnership. This encourages a sense of involvement and can pre-empt the emergence of serious problems. For a major sponsorship that serves as a comprehensive marketing platform, a company is likely to involve personnel from marketing, public relations, advertising, sales promotions, finance and management, and the sport property team should be similarly comprehensive. Among such a group some divergence of views is inevitable, but constructive criticism and debate often is a key element for a successful outcome.

Courtesy of iStockPhoto.com

The sport property should designate a project leader for each sponsor who serves as the focal contact liaison and is the conduit for all communications. This individual should be positioned as an advocate within the organization, charged with seeking to further the sponsor's goals. However, even when a project leader is appointed frustrations can still arise. While project leaders may identify additional benefits to a property from more active collaboration with sponsors, they have to convince those to whom they report and persuade them to release the necessary resources. The issue of investing additional resources creates a conundrum for sport managers as one of them explained:

> Should we explore their business plans, their industry data, try to make sense of another industry, or multiple industries given we have several sponsor partners? If we do it for one sponsor do we need to do it for all, have we got the people or resources required to do this, what level of risk are we prepared to assume given the greater strategic input that would invariably follow? (p. 329)[18]

However, the evolving role of companies' use of sponsorship means that much of the rights fee paid is premised on leveraging opportunities the platform provides, not merely association with a sport property *per se*. If properties fail to commit resources to participate in the leveraging process, then presumably this will be reflected in lower rights fees than would otherwise be paid.[18]

If multiple sponsors are involved with a property, then regularly scheduled meetings that all attend will facilitate an interchange of promotional ideas and make sponsors feel part of the event. Many organizers are nervous about bringing sponsors together and avoid it because they believe it might raise conflicts. This concern is misplaced. Since the business categories and goals of each sponsor are likely to be different there need be no conflict among them and there are many cross-sponsorship promotions that can be done when all parties share their interests, investments, and leveraging plans. Indeed, one of the strong assets a property can offer a sponsor is its company and business networks. The organizers of the Olympic Festival in Minneapolis called their sponsors a Patron Advisory Group. The group met regularly to good effect:

> The Patron Advisory meetings were a selling point for some smaller companies who wanted to get next to the big guys. Company representatives really looked forward to networking among themselves, to be able to create new business. We used the meetings to invite potential sponsors and show them how many sponsors were already on board and to show that this was a real live event. Also, it was a chance to tell all the sponsors the same thing at the same time. It gave them the perception that everyone was getting equal treatment and were on an equal level.
>
> The advisory meetings were also a way for the partners to gain publicity and to show off to each other. Many of the meetings were held at the corporate headquarters of the respective hosts. 3M gave out its corporate pin and Post-it Notes that announced its association with the Festival during one of the first meetings. That set the stage for the other sponsors. Some got really carried away and took it to the extremes. Dayton's and Target held an elaborate ceremony in the Metrodome where they set-up Greek architecture and had chariots riding around.[19]

These types of meetings can facilitate development of cross-promotion opportunities. These are cooperative arrangements among sponsors that enable the companies involved to obtain greater leverage—either from the sponsorship or from other business arrangements that evolve out of the sponsorship. Sport managers can facilitate them by asking companies which of the other property sponsors they would like to meet and hosting one-on-one meetings with the two partners to initiate the dialog. Effective cross-promotions will extend both sponsors' visibility, but the main value they offer is either taking the partner into a new, nontraditional distributional channel, or using the partner's merchandise in sweepstakes and incentive programs to create new business. The following illustrations of cross-promotion were designed to accomplish these respective goals:

- Subaru of America leveraged its presenting status of the Down & Dirty National Mud and Obstacle Series with Merrell shoes. Subaru activated their sponsorship by offering a $100 Merrell gift certificate to customers who took a test drive. Their spokesperson reported: "We were able to drive traffic to our dealerships while introducing customers to the Merrell brand. It was a win for us, a win for Merrell and a win for the consumers who took advantage of the offer." Cross promotions should be low-hanging fruit for properties. Even if a cross-promotion doesn't happen for a particular event, sponsors will always appreciate an introduction to brands that share similar customers.[20]
- New York City Marathon signed a sponsorship agreement with Food Emporium Inc. This created a new promotional platform for several of the race's other sponsors including Barilla, Coors Light, Emerald Nuts, Gatorade, *The New York Times*, and Poland Spring. The retail chain promoted the platform through circulars and end-aisle displays. The race spokesperson said: "By striking the partnership with

Food Emporium, we were able to offer each partner the opportunity to be part of a cross-promotion that lets them gain more exposure, tap into a bigger audience, and ultimately sell more units."[21]

- American Express cross-promoted with fellow sponsor Polo Ralph Lauren at the USTA US Open Tennis Championships. AmEx offered a $50 gift card for Polo to consumers who spent $100 on their cards at the tournament. Their spokesperson explained: "It was a win-win. Consumers spent money on their AmEx card, they went to a Polo retail store to use the gift card, and hopefully they spend more than the $50 and put it on their AmEx card."[22]
- At the FIFA World Cup, Scottish & Newcastle UK (S&N), one of Europe's largest beer sellers, linked with Ladbrokes.com, a large betting company. Consumers buying promotional multipacks of S&N beer brands such as Foster's, Kronenbourg 1664, John Smith's Extra Smooth, or Strongbow could claim a free $8 bet by using a code number to open an account at Ladbrokes.
- Each year the Kentucky Derby race in Louisville has a different fragrance sponsor. The event works with a major retailer, which in turn goes to Giorgio Armani, Estée Lauder, Ralph Lauren, or others to design a special perfume for the festival. It works well because the retailer has exclusivity to the perfume's introduction, although it may be sold elsewhere after the event, while the fragrance company has substantial promotional dollars to support it. The Kentucky Derby's role is to present the official fragrance and to provide sampling opportunities on site and in the Derby packages they put together for hotels.[7]

The more that executives and employees of a sponsoring business can be involved and can feel ownership in planning and implementing the sport event, the more likely they are to make a long-term commitment. As part of this process, key decision makers should be given access to celebrity sports people, behind-the-scenes areas where ordinary spectators are not permitted, and excellent seats from which to view the event. If there is extensive involvement by multiple company managers, then when companies restructure or go through mergers it reduces the chance that changes in personnel may leave a sport property without its company advocates. "If you have a program with a company whose employees actively support your cause, if a new branch manager or CEO comes in, it's hard to throw the program away without angering a lot of people" (p. 225).[1]

POST-EVENT FOLLOW-UP

The way in which the follow-up is addressed will influence the likelihood of receiving future support from investing companies. The intent in the follow-up stage is to enhance relationships that have been established. A prime objective should be to make the individual in the company who made the decision to invest look good to senior management and throughout the entire organization. Also, most in the company will not be aware of the sponsorship's merits and if there is turnover of the sponsor's liaison staff then the partnership may be vulnerable. Thus, evaluation reports are insurance against this occurrence. The follow-up should consist of three actions. Evaluation of the extent to which a sponsor's objectives were achieved is likely to be primarily the sponsor's responsibility. Measures used to accomplish this are discussed in Chapter 10. However, at the time of the initial agreement, event organizers should check with the sponsor to see what inputs the property can provide that will assist in the evaluation, rather than guessing their needs.

The second and main task of a property is to provide each sponsor with a recap or fulfillment report. The report should be customized and written so it addresses the sponsor's objectives and priorities. Again, at the beginning of the partnership, sponsors should be asked what they want to see in the fulfillment report. The template shown in Exhibit 9.8 offers a starting point to focus this discussion. The more thorough and comprehensive the wrap-up report, the better armed the sponsor's representatives are to acquire funds to continue it in the future. Increasingly sponsors are requesting interim reports on how their investment is performing so they can monitor it, as well as the comprehensive wrap-up. As one sponsor of NFL teams explained: "If an issue comes up in a post-event report, there is nothing we can do about it because it's the end of the

Exhibit 9.8

A Template for Reporting Tangible Outcomes Sponsors Received from their Investment

- Number of participants/attendees, demographics, lifestyle information, purchasing habits and trends
- Local/regional/national/international news media print coverage and trends
- Television viewership, ratings, and demographics where possible and a digital copy of the telecast, plus clips of local affiliates' coverage of the event
- Radio coverage with a broadcast signal overlay on the sponsors' sales areas (number of ads, promotional spots and on-air mentions—compared to the stations' rate cards so value of exposure can be estimated)
- Complete list of associate sponsors/hospitality suite customers and trends
- Information on merchandising, product displays, sampling, and signage with photographs
- On-site sampling and merchandising report (number of coupons redeemed or number of people sampled)
- Samples of coupons generated by all sponsors and the event itself
- Clip book of advertisements and property-generated promotional activities relating to the event
- Clip book of news releases and news clips tracking back to event public relations
- Public-address system announcement log with sponsor scripts
- A copy of the event program and posters
- Samples of tickets, especially if the tickets included the sponsors' marks
- Samples of media sponsor promotional tie-ins with comments on their effectiveness
- A personal letter of thanks to the sponsor signed jointly by the property's senior managers

season. We are challenging our partners to be timelier in sharing information that will help what we are trying to accomplish."[23]

Properties should provide examples of how they went beyond the terms of the contract to provide additional sponsorship benefits. However, they should be sure not to inflate or over-interpret information. The report should be written from the disinterested perspective of an independent consultant stressing failures and weaknesses as well as successes, with suggestions on how to remedy them in the future. To be seen as a trusted partner, properties must be honest in recognizing their own shortcomings and clarify how they will be rectified. To enhance the probability of a sponsor using the report so it is read and shared with others, rather than merely filing it, a property should ask each of its partners which format and delivery methods they prefer—hard copy, disk, PowerPoint, email, etc.

The fulfillment report provides a *bona fide* reason to meet and review the sponsorship. It is an entré for the third post-event follow-up action which is initiating discussions about future investments in the event. These will be guided by the timespan and arrangements for renewing or canceling that were included in the contract. The discussions should be held soon after the event is completed so that maximum time is available to make changes in future extensions of the partnership, or to find other sponsors if necessary. To facilitate this discussion, it is advantageous for a property to personally deliver the fulfillment report and go through it in a presentation to the sponsor.

SUMMARY

Adopting a marketing approach is key to successfully soliciting corporate sponsorship. This requires that proposals focus on the potential for delivering what companies are likely to want in return for investing their resources. Sport managers should perceive themselves as brokers who are concerned with furthering the business objectives of potential sponsor companies by offering opportunities from which both they and the organization benefit. A primary reason why companies reject proposals is because they are submitted too late to be included in the annual budget. This implies that a 15–18 month lead time may be needed if proposals are to receive consideration.

There are four critical elements that a sport property must embrace to optimize its sponsorship efforts: expertise, which is gained only from experience; internal coordination of the platform's activation across multiple divisions within the property and integration with their existing efforts; a process that expedites decision-making to ensure that decisions are timely; and a sales team equipped with the talent to pursue both short-term and more complex long-term sponsorships. These critical elements may be acquired by forming an internal marketing team, hiring an external agency, or using a hybrid model by which the property is responsible for some elements of the sponsorship effort, but hires an external agency to do others.

The starting point for a sport property in soliciting sponsorships is to audit its assets and produce an inventory of rights which it wants to make available to sponsors. Before any selling takes place a set of companies in the appropriate geographic area should be identified whose customers have demographic/lifestyle profiles consistent with those of the sport property's audience/participants, and whose function and/or image is compatible with that of the event. Using these guidelines, a list of potential sponsors and a profile of each company on the list can be developed and entered into an information retrieval system.

As recognition of the effectiveness of sponsorship has grown, companies have developed criteria and evaluation procedures for sifting through the multiple opportunities they are offered. They tend to focus on eight factors in their evaluation: customer audience, exposure reach, distribution channel audience, advantage over competitors, resource investment level required, sport organization's reputation, event's characteristics, and entertainment and hospitality opportunities.

Traditionally, sport properties adopted an "off-the-shelf" approach to soliciting sponsorships, by which they offered different hierarchal tiers of fixed rights packages so a wide range of investment opportunities could be presented. Hierarchal packaging still prevails, especially among major sport properties, but is now usually recognized to be a conceptual framework within which rights packages are customized to best fit a sponsor's objectives. The number of levels varies but the four categories structure that is commonly used comprises: title sponsors, sector or presenting sponsors, official or preferred sponsors, and official suppliers.

The initial 1–2 page proposal should be customized to arouse the interest of a potential sponsor by demonstrating a match between the property's and company's likely sponsorship objectives, and including tentative suggestions of how the property might meet those objectives. The proposal should be addressed personally to the most senior corporate executive who is responsible for sponsorship. Its goal is to secure a follow-up meeting.

In preparation for a meeting with the company it is useful to identify the individuals from it who will be present and their positions, status, and roles in the decision process. There are three categories of roles: gatekeepers, influencers, and decision-makers, but one person may fill more than one of the roles. Since personal chemistry is critical in business relationships, the sport organization should search for linkages that any of its personnel may have with a company's decision-makers; and also search for background information on the company representatives' interests, families, and lifestyles, which will help facilitate personal interaction at a meeting.

The goal at an initial meeting is to encourage the company's representatives to provide guidance on what they seek from the sponsorship, so the property can acquire the information necessary to build a comprehensive proposal around the company's priorities. It is especially important that any negative reactions or reservations about the proposal be articulated, so there is an opportunity to address and reverse them.

The pricing of a bundle of rights starts with listing the property's costs that will be incurred in implementing them. This ensures the sponsorship generates more revenue than it costs. Beyond this basic step, price will be set according to those charged by other properties and adjusted to reflect perceptions of the property's value compared to others. Thus, the most important factor in establishing price is likely to be the market knowledge and experience of a sport property's team and their networks of peers who can provide information on comparable prices at other properties. Many companies prefer to support an event with in-kind services rather than cash, and this should be valued the same as cash if it substitutes for line items in a budget.

When a sponsorship proposal is rejected, reasons for the negative outcome should be identified. If these can be rectified in the future, then the initial rejection may constitute the beginning of a long-term relationship. When a proposal is accepted, a written contractual document should be developed to ensure that both sides' interests are protected. To nurture a long-term relationship, the sport organization has to view the sponsor as a partner and work to help the company realize its objectives. This may be achieved by nominating a staff person to be a liaison with the company and to be its advocate within the sport property. If multiple sponsors are involved, facilitating interaction and networking among them is likely to be productive. Follow-up actions involve helping the key decision makers in the company evaluate the extent to which their objectives were met, providing a fulfillment report, and initiating discussions about future investments in the event.

Endnotes

1. Kolah, A. (2001). *How to develop an effective sponsorship programme*. London, England: Sport Business Group.
2. Octagon Inc. & Civic Entertainment Group. (2010). *Fairfax County Park Authority sponsorship marketing plan*, Fairfax, VA: *Fairfax County Park Authority*.
3. Masterman, G. (2007). *Sponsorship for a return on investment*. Boston, MA: Elsevier.
4. Lynde, T. (2007). *Sponsorship 101*. Mableton, GA: Lynde and Associates.
5. Cornwell, T. B. (2008). State of the art and science in sponsorship-linked marketing. *Journal of Advertising. 37*(3), 41–55.
6. Torfa, D. J. (2008). Strategies for sales of corporate sponsorship programmes to the corporate community. *Journal of Sponsorship, 2*(1), 57–66.
7. Skinner, B. E., & Rukavina, V. (2003). *Event sponsorship*. New York, NY: John Wiley.
8. Preus, H. (2004). *The economics of staging the Olympics: A comparison of the Games 1972–2008*. Cheltenham, UK: Edward Elgar.
9. D'Alesandro, D. F. (2001). *Brand warfare*. New York, NY: McGraw-Hill.
10. Aguillar-Manjarrez, R., Thwaites, D., & Maule, J. (1999). Insights into the roles adopted by the recipients of unsolicited sort sponsorship requests. *International Journal of Sports Marketing & Sponsorship 1*(2), 185–205.
11. Kandar, J. (2010, September 29). Is "pay for performance" the newest sponsorship trend? *IEG Sponsorship Blog*. Retrieved from http:// www.sponsorship.com/About-IEG/Sponsorship -Blogs/Jon-Kander/September-2010/Is--Pay -for-Performance--the-Newest-Sponsorship -Tr.aspx
12. IEG. (2012). The rising impact of performance-based agreements and other alternative deal structures. *IEG Sponsorship Report*, May 3.
12a. Fenton, W. C., & Collett, P. (2011). *The sponsorship handbook*. Hoboken, NJ: Jossey-Bass.
13. Sleight, S. (1989). *Sponsorship: What it is and how to use it*. Maidenhead, Berkshire, England: McGraw-Hill.
14. IEG. (1999, April 26). Retailer takes beach event tie to "hippify" its image. *Sponsorship Report*, pp. 1–2.
15. Greenburg, M. J. (2000). *The stadium game*. Milwaulkee, WI: Marquette University, National Sports Law Institute.
16. Brooks, C. (1990, December). *Athletic Business*, pp. 61–62.
16a. Crimmins, J. R., & Horn, M. (1994). Sponsorship: From management ego trip to marketing success. *Journal of Advertising Research, 36*(4), 11–21.
17. IEG. (2006, July 10). Tracking ROI becomes Bank of America's top sponsorship priority. *IEG Sponsorship Report*. Retrieved from http:// www.sponsorship.com/iegsr/2006/07/10/Trac king-ROI-Becomes-Bank-Of-America-s-Top -Sponsor.aspx
18. Farrelly, F. (2010). Not playing the game: Why sport sponsorship relationships break down. *Journal of Sport Management, 24*, 319–337.

19. McCally, J. F. (1990, May). Corporate sponsorship and the U.S. Olympic Festival '90: A mutually beneficial marketing arrangement. Unpublished paper, Department of Marketing Mankato State University.

20. IEG. (2009, April 27). Ten ways properties can add value to their sponsorship efforts. *IEG Sponsorship Report*. Retrieved from http://www.sponsorship.com/iegsr/2009/04/27/Ten-Ways-Properties-Can-Add-Value-To-Their-Sponsor.aspx

21. IEG. (2012, January 30). The importance of sponsor cross-promotions. *IEG Sponsorship Report*. Retrieved from http://www.sponsorship.com/iegsr/2012/01/30/The-Importance-Of-Sponsor-Cross-Promotions.aspx

22. IEG. (2010, January 18). Why cross-promotions with co-sponsors should be top priority for properties, sponsors. *IEG Sponsorship Report*. Retrieved from http://www.sponsorship.com/iegsr/2010/01/18/Why-Cross-promotions-With-Cosponsors-Should-Be-Top.aspx

23. IEG. (2010, April 2). Sponsors call for more and better sponsorship reporting. *IEG Sponsorship Report*. Retrieved from http://www.sponsorship.com/iegsr/2010/04/05/Sponsors-Call-For-More-And-Better-Sponsorship-Repo.aspx

10

Measuring the Impact of Sponsorships

E
valuation answers the question: What did the sponsoring company achieve in relation to what it wanted to accomplish? From the perspective of a sport manager, evaluation has two purposes. First, it provides a measure of the extent to which a sponsorship met its objectives. Sponsorships sometimes are terminated not because they have failed to deliver value, but because nobody measured their impact. The second purpose is that evaluation provides sport managers with results which they can use subsequently in sales presentations to future potential sponsors.

A RELUCTANCE TO EVALUATE

Despite extensive lip service being given to the importance of evaluation, it has been widely observed that performance measurement remains underused, underdeveloped, and embryonic: "There is too little evaluation and too few reliable and valid techniques available" (p. 239).[1] Thus, 28% of 200 sponsorship decision-makers in major companies reported spending nothing on research to measure the impact of their investments, while an additional 44% reported spending 1% or less of their sponsorship budget on outcome evaluation. The researchers concluded these results showed, "A familiar picture of a medium that recognizes the importance of measuring return on investment and return on objectives, but continues to struggle with finding the resources to do so and determining what the right things to measure are."[2]

There appear to be three reasons for the generally low effort committed to evaluating the extent to which a sponsorship investment meets its objectives: The proprietary nature of such research; fear of the consequences; and the complexity and difficulty of measuring the impact of a sponsorship.

Substantial expense may be incurred in developing research methods, techniques, and tools. Thus, companies are reluctant to publicly reveal either findings from their research or the protocols they adopt. They want to exclusively preserve the benefits from their research expenditure, regarding such information as being proprietary, and believing that revealing it would be advantageous to competitors.

Some of the resistance to developing meaningful measures of performance may be attributable to a lack of confidence by a property in its ability to deliver good value. There may be fear this would give sponsors leverage to negotiate lower rights fees, more concessions, or a reason not to renew the sponsorship. As one experienced company sponsorship manager observed: "We believe that if you can't prove that a sponsorship is working for your brand, it probably isn't, and you should get out" (p. 109).[3] However, the counterpoints to these concerns are that an evaluation may save an under-performing sponsorship program by demonstrating how it can be improved, and if results exceed expectations then higher rights fees can be negotiated. From a sponsor's perspective, this latter result would appear to be the only negative outcome associated with evaluation.

Sponsorship is an unusually complex phenomenon to measure. Multiple dimensions combine to create the complexity Typically, sponsorship is used as a platform for an array of other marketing tools. This makes it difficult to isolate the independent contribution of the sponsorship. Even if other tools are not being used simultaneously, there is likely to be some carry-over effect from their previous use.

Different brand categories and different companies within categories are likely to have different objectives. Further, the complexity of measuring impact is compounded as the number of target audiences expands. For example, with global sponsorships the objectives for different cultures and audiences are likely to differ, reflecting brands being at different points in their life cycles; variations in the exposure and popularity of the sport property (for example, soccer in the US and UK markets), and differences in the image connotations of a sport property among cultures (for example, rugby in Italy compared to New Zealand).[4]

The evolution of both increased activation and social and digital media have added to the measurement challenge. Finally, there is asymmetry in the time frames. Enhanced brand equity among consumers may take years to accomplish, so the full impact on a company's bottom line may not occur until long after the sponsorship investment has been made.

STAGES IN THE EVALUATION PROCESS

The process of evaluating a sponsorship has three stages: (i) set objectives; (ii) identify benchmarks against which success will be measured; and (iii) identify who will lead the evaluation effort, which includes specifying responsibilities for the analyses to be undertaken, data collection, interpretation of the data, and the report deliverables.

In Chapter 5, the importance of using S.M.A.R.T. (specific, measurable, achievable, result-oriented, and time-bounded) objectives was discussed. Properties cannot be expected to assist their partners' efforts if they do not understand the sponsors' priorities. Further, there is no point in spending funds on evaluation that is not tied to a metric that operationalizes a sponsor's objectives and/or is not actionable (i.e., does not offer guidance on which elements in the sponsorship's leveraging program are weak/strong and how they might be enhanced).

The success of a sponsorship cannot be measured unless it is known what it is intended to achieve. In some contexts, there is resistance to doing this:

This is easier than it sounds. A lot of organizations don't like to be tied down to specific objectives because it gives them less room for maneuver after the event. If your objectives are vague, you can claim any improved measure as a success. But it's never easy to go back to the board and explain why certain stated targets weren't achieved, particularly if the choice of sponsorship was their idea. (p. 20)[5]

Assuming there is a commitment to develop S.M.A.R.T. objectives, the second question then becomes: What outcome should they be specifying? There are two options. The optimum outcome measure is the return on investment (ROI) that a sponsorship delivers. That is, for every $1 invested, how many dollars does the sponsorship deliver in return. The ROI is calculated by the following formula:[6]

$$\frac{(\text{incremental sales} \times \text{profit margin}) - \text{investment}}{\text{investment}} = \% \text{ ROI}$$

The following illustrative numbers operationalize the formula:

- Investment: . . . . $1 m
- Incremental sales tied to the sponsorship: . . . . . $3 m
- Profit margin over sponsorship period: 40%

$$\frac{(3{,}000{,}000 \times .40)}{1{,}000{,}000} = \frac{(1{,}200{,}000) - (1{,}000{,}000)}{1{,}000{,}000} = 20\% \text{ ROI}$$

However, the complexity of measuring sponsorship makes it very expensive so only a few major corporations develop the sophisticated econometric models needed to accomplish an ROI evaluation. Such models are likely to incorporate a brand's historical sales data, as well as information on historical spending related to the brand on advertising, sales promotion, price discounting, and other factors. By controlling such variables, it may be possible to calibrate a model which predicts, for example, an x% increase in brand equity will result in a y% increase in sales or profits.

In addition to the complexity and expense issues, other limitations of the ROI outcome are that it focuses on short-term sales rather than on long-term relationships with consumers, and it ignores the impact of "experiential" or "engagement" marketing which refers to making a connection with consumers in a favorable environment. There are a multiplicity of objectives that may be desired outcomes from a sponsorship, many of which do not have direct financial returns, and ROI fails to embrace them. Consider the following example relating to the sponsorship objectives of a professional services firm:

The firm's objectives are about relationship building and so their measurements in terms of achieving those objectives, and therefore their returns, are focused on how many relationships they have built, the manner in which they were built, and their relative strength, using the sponsorship program as a platform. They even have a score for how people inside the organization rate each relationship on a scale of 1 to 5. The effectiveness of the sponsorship is therefore calculated on how strongly it has contributed to increasing these relationship measurement metrics. The firm does not value their returns in cash at all. In fact, in cash terms they see investment in sponsorship as the equivalent of a retailer's 'loss leader'—as money spent to attract people in rather than make a direct contribution to the bottom line (p. 102).[7]

All of these factors make the ROI outcome non-feasible for most sponsors and property owners. Instead, many of them have opted for return on objectives (ROO) as an alternative outcome to measure, regarding it as both useful and "doable." This evaluates a sponsorship on how well it accomplishes a sponsor's *a priori* objectives. ROO is a multidimensional approach to evaluating sponsorship since its measures may address the impact of sponsorship on brand equity, intention to purchase, increasing consumer traffic, sales, employee morale or any other objective at which a sponsorship may be directed. However, it has been observed: "There's no point measuring more than four or five. Otherwise evaluation becomes too elaborate and expensive. This can be a particular problem in big multinational organizations—where local and international objectives overlap with each other. Analyzing minor details can distract you from your main goals." (p. 20)[5]

The second stage in the sponsorship evaluation process is identifying benchmarks against which success will be measured. Too often, companies wait until the sponsorship program is underway before they think about measurement issues. When it is relegated to the status of an afterthought, the opportunity to establish benchmarks at the outset is missed. Benchmarks make it possible to identify any shift in the objective of interest pre- and post-sponsorship, and to measure for how long a shift endures after the event is over.

Three types of benchmarks should be established. First, identify the level of current performance immediately before the sponsorship is launched. If, for example, an objective is to use the hospitality component of a sponsorship to achieve more widespread distribution among retailers in a given target market, then research undertaken may reveal that 28% of retailers in the target area carry the brand. This provides a basis both for establishing a reasonable objective, such as increasing the distribution network to 40% of retailers, and for assessing the sponsorship's success.

If the 40% objective has been met by the end of the sponsorship, then the question becomes: Was the 12% increase all attributable to hospitality activation associated with the sponsorship, or was at least some of it attributable to other factors, for example, a general improvement in economic conditions? The second type of benchmark is designed to address this question. It requires establishing a comparative group who were not exposed to the hospitality experience. Thus, if the brand's distribution among that group of retailers expanded by 3%, then 9% of the 12% improvement among those who were hosted could reasonably be attributed to the hospitality experience.

A third type of benchmark is for the comparative group to be comprised of competitive brands. Again, only increments of a shift beyond those achieved by the other brands would be attributed to the sponsorship. If these types of benchmarks are not established, then the real effect of a sponsorship will remain unknown. In their absence, there is likely to be a post-event "fudging" and a rationalization of what the data show, which may be grossly misleading.

The third stage in evaluation planning is to address the question: Whose job is evaluation? Both sponsor and sport property partners will have a role, but there needs to be clarity on what analyses will be undertaken; who will collect the data needed to do them; who will interpret the data; and what deliverables in terms of reports will be produced.

Since corporate sponsors presumably have rich insights into the nuances of their business objectives which a sport property cannot possess, it is reasonable to expect companies to take responsibility for leading the evaluation effort. However, frequently this does not occur and companies look to the sport property for leadership. The optimal strategy for a property may be to include funds for evaluation as a line-item in its proposal for a third-party to lead the effort.

There are two reasons for involving a third party when a sponsor does not take the lead. First, it is a specialist task which a sport property may be ill-equipped to handle. Second, it distances the property from any allegations or suspicions of producing biased results or interpretations that favor its position. Writers of a report can interpret the data in ways that accentuate any case they want to make with either internal or external audiences. Consider the following example of biased interpretation of data in the context of a sponsorship partnership between MLB and Taco Bell.

- If MLB was writing the report and submitting it to Taco Bell, it might conclude: "Taco Bell was recognized by more than 9% of avid MLB fans and 7% of casual MLB fans as the official quick-service restaurant (QSR) of Major League Baseball. Given that Taco Bell ranks No. 6 in *QSR* magazine's top 50 in 2009, they should be ecstatic from the boost MLB is providing."

  However, if Taco Bell were writing a report interpreting the same data to MLB it might state: "Taco Bell was only the third-most recognized QSR brand among MLB fans, and 44% of avid MLB fans could not even offer a guess as to the official *QSR* sponsor. How is the MLB relationship benefiting this brand?" (p. 10)[8]

MEASURES OF SPONSORSHIP OUTCOMES

Three types of sponsorship outcomes may be measured: Cognitive, affective, and behavioral. Cognitive measures address exposure and awareness. Affective measures are concerned with level of emotional connection and consider such outcomes as image transfer, attitude change, loyalty, relationship building, and preference. Behavioral measures evaluate; sales leads, propensity to purchase, customer traffic generation, sampling and product trial, sales, and impact on stock price. These are summarized in Figure 10.1.

Cognitive Measures

Cognitive measures are the weakest approach to evaluating a sponsorship's effectiveness. The two widely used cognitive measures are exposure and awareness. The heroic assumption justifying the use of exposure measures is that amount of exposure is related to knowledge of a brand's association with a sport property among a target market. Awareness is a more legitimate measure of effectiveness since it evaluates the extent to which a

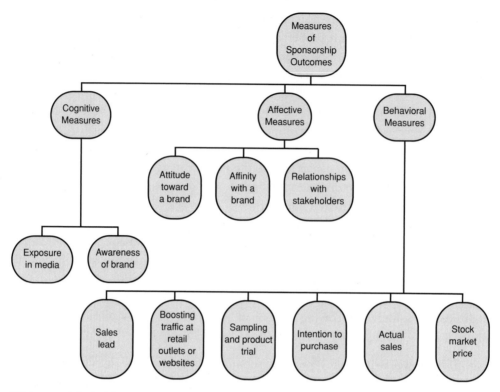

Figure 10.1. Measures of Sponsorship Outcomes.

target market has knowledge of the brand/sport property relationship. Because there is no affective emotional bond, customers for whom linkage exists only at the cognition level are highly vulnerable to counter-arguments and promotional efforts made by competing brands.

Exposure

Exposure is the most primitive, least useful, but most frequently used measure of sponsorship effectiveness. It has been consistently criticized as being conceptually flawed; its limitations have been repeatedly exposed; and its failings universally acknowledged. Nevertheless, throughout the short three-decade history of modern sponsorship, it has remained the most widely used measure.

Its widespread popularity is attributable to three factors. First, the measure is easy for managers to understand. Second, the data are relatively easy to collect. Indeed, media exposure is the only evaluative measure sport managers can undertake without intruding into the business of an event's sponsors. Other measures requiring, for example, pre- and post-tests of awareness levels of a sponsor's product or sales performance, require sponsors to reveal information they are likely to consider as being proprietary. The practicability of exposure measures has been expressed in the following terms: "In an environment where uncertainty regarding the ability to measure sponsorships' effects still exists and where adequate budgets for research are not always available, the popularity of this approach lies in its practicability, i.e. it is something that [both sponsors and sport property managers] can do" (p. 263).[4]

Third, exposure measures offer quantifiable statistics which give the [false] appearance that sponsorship decisions are based on objective data. In a field of measurement uncertainty, such results ostensibly provide a tangible indication of benefit. Further, the numbers generated are invariably very large. Even though they are spurious, they offer comfort and peace of mind to those responsible for, and who have to justify, investment decisions.

The Measurement Process

Exposure measures are comprised of three elements. First, all media coverage that mentions a brand's sponsorship of an event is tracked and identified. If it is a mega event this may be overwhelming, so sometimes samples are used which are then scaled up. The media monitored will include broadcast, social, digital, and print.

Second, the aggregate amount of time or space coverage that occurs in each medium will be measured. This may consist of the seconds and minutes a picture of the brand and verbal reference to it occur in a broadcast; the number of hits recorded at a sponsor-related website or in social media; and the number of column inches mentioning a sponsor's brand in the print media. Image recognition technologies have now largely replaced manual measurements of media coverage. These are programmed to report such details as a logo's position on a screen, its size, degree of clutter, and the duration and legibility of its appearance. So, for example, a logo's appearance in the corner of a cluttered screen is differentiated from contexts in which it is large and central on an uncluttered screen.

Despite the technological advances, two factors have made it increasingly difficult to obtain accurate measures of exposure. First, the emergence of digital video recorders (DVRs) has resulted in time-shifting, whereby people record programs for later viewing rather than watching them live, and the DVRs skip the advertising. The second factor is the challenge of tracking fragmented audiences since people watch television on countless websites and on multiple devices.

The third stage is to assign a dollar value to this coverage. This is done by applying the cost of an equivalent amount of advertising time or space to it. For example, if a 30-second advertising slot in a NASCAR broadcast sold for $100,000 and a brand received 2 minutes aggregate screen time and verbal mentions, then the reported exposure value would be $400,000.

However, most companies apply some form of weightings to the advertising equivalency rates. These may be of two types. First, companies have widely different views about the relative effectiveness of sponsorship exposure and advertising. Some enhance advertising equivalency rates by up to 300%,[4] rationalizing that sponsorship coverage qualifies as news or editorial content. They believe that this has more credibility and is not subject to the skepticism which is inherent in many people's response to paid advertising. More commonly, others deeply discount the advertising equivalency rate, sometimes by as much as 90%, because they believe that multiple fleeting logo images or mentions have much less impact on an audience than focused advertising.

The second form of weighting may reflect the relative quality of media coverage, rather than only its amount. Quality is likely to embrace three elements. First, the degree of a brand's match with a medium's audience demographic and lifestyle profile. Second, extent of clutter. This is expressed as media coverage achieved by the sponsor brand as a percentage of exposure attained by all sponsor brands. If this percentage is relatively high, then a brand is deemed more likely to emerge from the clutter of other sponsors and make an impact. Thus, it is given a higher weighting. A third element in quality weightings relates to prominence and position. For example, a favorable editorial mention may be considered to be of greater value than mentions in a sports column, or a name in a headline or photograph may be given higher value than a mention of a brand in the body of a story. Some companies assign different weightings to different media. Thus, Cartier International assigned points to its print exposure by type of publication—upscale readership carried more weight than wide-circulation—and by type of mention, so the company's name in a headline or photograph rated higher than in text.[9]

Exhibit 10.1 illustrates how exposure values may be measured and reported.[9a] The large dollar values which exposure studies invariably report are comforting and reassuring to all concerned among both sponsor and sport property managers. Consider the following report and reaction:

- Izod took title sponsorship of the Izod Indy Car Series. The company reported it generated billions of digital impressions, delivering more than 25 million on Facebook and Twitter alone. Based on these data, Izod executives concluded the title sponsorship delivered a 350% return on the first year of its sponsorship. The company's executive vice-president for corporate marketing commented, "Return on investment is off the charts. It is amazing" (p. 11).[10]

Courtesy of BigStockPhoto.com

The Failings of Exposure Measures

Few who are knowledgeable about sponsorship evaluation would share this executive's enthusiasm, because exposure measures have two fundamental conceptual flaws. First, exposure is a supply-based measure reflecting how effective a company has been in disseminating information through the media. It measures only how many people had the opportunity to see or hear a logo or sign. It fails to report an audience's response to the exposure—even whether it was noticed or not:

Exhibit 10.1

Measuring Exposure Value to Sponsors of Cars in the NASCAR Sprint Cup Races

There were 36 races in the NASCAR series. The exposure study analyzed 717 primary and secondary car and driver partners that had participated in the series, along with all race venues' signs and on-screen graphics and audio mentions from the races' TV broadcasts. Eighty-five sponsored locations were measured in areas ranging from leaderboard graphics that viewers see on their TV screens to exposure a sponsor may have received by having its logo on a trophy.

Video feeds from each race were broken down and evaluated for all brand detections that occurred on screen and were clear and in focus for at least one full second. Each of those individual detections was then evaluated based on its duration, average size, location, and relative isolation (or lack thereof) from competing brands: Was the logo a featured image on the screen or was it shown among other sponsors?

Because location and clarity significantly affected the measured value of each detection, quantity did not always translate into increased value. Also, for the purpose of summary calculations, each audio mention was assigned a duration of five seconds.

The following table shows the dollar value assigned to the leading brands for their exposure when the weighted media equivalency costs were applied, together with the shift in value from the previous year.

Negative shifts from the previous year reflected both a reduction in television airtime for the race series, and a reduction in the prices paid for advertisements during the race broadcasts so the equivalency dollar value was lower.

Rank (Previous Year Rank)	Brand	Value (Change from Previous Year)
1 (1)	Sprint	$272,155,764 (−15.8%)
2 (2)	Chevrolet	$121,329,942 (−2.2%)
3 (3)	Toyota	$77,990,935 (−9.8%)
4 (6)	Ford	$64,845,387 (+1.0%)
5 (5)	Lowe's	$52,796,613 (−24%)
6 (9)	Budweiser	$51,614,847 (+30.2%)
7 (7)	AT&T	$46,569,518 (−3.4%)
8 (30)	DirecTV	$36,142,367 (+145.5%)
9 (11)	FedEx	$35,934,179 (+12.2%)
10 (29)	Nationwide	$35,044,151 (+132.9%)

Measuring "visibility" leaves the real questions unanswered. Does anybody notice the logo in the background? What message about the brand is communicated by the logo on the scorer's table? The brand is paying a high price to be seen in this particular environment. Is being seen on the scorer's table at the NBA All Star game really worth any more than being seen on the side of a building somewhere? Does anyone know that the brand is a sponsor of this event? Does anyone care? These questions aren't about visibility. These questions are about impact (p. 12).[11]

Exposure is not an outcome measure that is relevant to most companies' objectives, since they are likely to focus on how potential customers' relationships with a brand have changed. It is the *impact* on consumers that is of interest. Hence, it makes no sense to measure something that is not an objective of the sponsorship. When Eurocar, a Paris based car-rental company, invested in title sponsorship of a cycling team in the Tour de France, a representative reported that the company was "calculating every second that our logo is seen on the screen" and "there is no doubt this Tour has paid for itself." A commentator responded:

> All that means is the company's logo was on the screen (along with dozens of other corporate logos) during the broadcasts. Did any of the TV viewers even notice the logos? Do they feel any better about Eurocar because they sponsor the team? How much does the sponsorship influence their decision about which company they will use the next time they rent a car?[12]

For exposure to influence customers in a desired way, members of the target market have to notice a logo or message and absorb it. There is a substantial probability this will not occur, because individuals are exposed to many more communications than they can possibly accept or decode. Selective perception and retention means that people become aware of, and retain, only a small portion of the information to which they are exposed. They tend to select that which is of interest and is consistent with their existing feelings and beliefs, and ignore the rest. If a name, picture, cue, logo, banner, or other signage does not appeal, or if there seems to be no good reason why it should be noted, then an individual is unlikely to open his or her senses to it, and, therefore, it will not be received. This explains the results Coca-Cola obtained from exit interviews undertaken at a NASCAR event called the Coca-Cola 600. For seven hours, people in the stands watched cars race 600 miles around a huge Coca-Cola logo. Yet 60% of them could not name the title sponsor afterwards.[13] Communication is not a one-way process from the sponsor's brand to its target market, which the media exposure measure implies. Rather, it is a two-way process that depends on the intended recipients being sufficiently interested to interpret and absorb the communication.

The second conceptual flaw in using media-equivalence exposure measures stems from the discussion in Chapter 1 on the evolution of sponsorship. While it was initially perceived to be a communication vehicle, it has evolved far beyond that role. Now it is viewed as a platform for strategically positioning brands to differentiate them from competitors, and as a mechanism for activating unique consumer experiences. It is a qualitatively different vehicle from advertising, designed to accomplish different outcomes. Thus, using advertising equivalency costs as a measure of its effectiveness makes no sense.

In addition to these conceptual flaws, there are multiple pragmatic problems with advertising equivalency exposure measures. Three sources of error in their calculation invariably result in substantially inflated values being guaranteed. First, article length is measured and equated with advertising space, even though the sponsor's name may only be mentioned a couple of times in the article. Second, typically, the maximal rate card value is assumed when quantifying the cost of equivalent advertising space, and few companies in fact pay these full rates. Third, the assumption that two seconds here and four seconds there of background signage or logo, when summated are equal to a television spot that gives an advertiser 30 seconds in which to sell is fallacious. Experiments on the recall of visibility of signs at sports arenas compared to advertising for the same brand led one group of researchers to conclude that individuals needed 10 times more exposure to signage than to a commercial advertisement to approximate a similar recall impact, because of the subtle nature of the background signage exposure.[13] It was noted earlier that this lack of equivalency is sometimes addressed by discounted weightings, and that the weightings varied widely among companies. The weightings may be assumed by some to be scientifically derived, but in fact they are entirely arbitrary and not defensible.

Finally, exposure measures assume that additional exposure will always add substantive value to a brand. This ignores the phenomenon of a saturation curve showing decreasing increments of value from exposure over time. For example, Coca-Cola has an unaided recall of around 95%, so additional increments of exposure are likely to be of little value to that brand.

The only minor utility of an exposure measure is that a sponsor can consistently compare the amount of media exposure a brand receives from one event to another, from one season to another, or compared to other brands. This may indicate whether media coverage of the sponsored event is growing or contracting.

All of these failings of media-equivalency exposure measures led one experienced evaluation specialist to state:

> It is incredibly frustrating when clients and agencies defend the outdated cluttered scrum of media-measurement models. The "media value" default has only two key uses. It is great for property owners to negotiate a better deal with brand partners. And it is always the last-gasp tool of a desperate agency or marketing director looking to post-rationalize why they have splashed out millions (p. 123).[14]

Awareness

Awareness indicates the extent to which a target audience recognized a brand's association with a particular sport property. It is a more useful measure than exposure since it evaluates a dimension of customer response, rather than merely the amount of media visibility generated. In Chapter 2, three situations were identified in which companies were likely to establish enhanced awareness of a brand as a primary sponsorship objective: launching a new brand in the market place; expanding an existing brand into new markets; and multinational companies replacing national or regional brands they have acquired with their own international brand. In addition, Figure 2.1 illustrated that awareness was a prerequisite base condition without which image transfer and other affective objectives could not be accomplished. There are two types of awareness measures: recognition and recall.

Recognition evaluations use prompts or aided memory cues. These may take the form of dichotomous questions: Is brand X a sponsor of property Y? Or, I am going to tell you some of brand X's current or recent sponsorships, for each one tell me whether you were aware of brand X sponsoring that event before today.[15] Alternatively, the questions may present respondents with multiple choices some of which will be fictitious: Which of the following brands is a sponsor of property Y? Responses indicate the percentage who correctly identify the sponsor brand after being given the prompt.

Recall is unaided response. It measures how many respondents can name a sponsor without a prompt. Three sponsorship recall protocols are widely used:[15]

- *Sport property protocol*: When you think of property A, which sponsors come to mind? Or, Name all the brands that sponsor the Dallas Cowboys.
- *Brand sponsor protocol*: When you think of brand B, what sponsorships come to mind? Or, Can you identify sponsorships with which brand B is involved?
- *Category sponsor protocol*: When you think of category C, (say banking or insurance), what sponsorships come to mind? Or, I am going to read you a list of products. For each one, tell me if there is any brand that is a sponsor of the Dallas Cowboys.

The different approaches will produce different estimates of recall. This has two complications for evaluation. First, to make comparisons it is imperative that the questions are asked in the same way. Second, multiple approaches should be used to assess trend results to ensure they are reliable and not merely a function of the question's format. Because they are prompted, recognition questions will invariably result in much higher proportions reporting awareness than if recall measures are used.

Tracking awareness over time enables a company to ascertain whether its linkage with an event is increasing at a satisfying rate. For example, CGU Insurance sponsored the National Cricket League in the UK. Its market surveys asked the question: Have you heard of a company called CGU? The surveys were undertaken during five months in its first year of the sponsorship. Figure 10.2 shows awareness during this period increased from 5% to 42% among the middle- and upper-class males who constituted its target market[1]

Tracking also enables sponsors to identify if awareness levels have plateaued or reached saturation level. At that point, additional investment is likely to yield such small increments of enhanced awareness that it is no longer a prudent investment:

- Cannon made a commitment of $5 million to sponsor the English Premier League. In a three-year period, awareness of Cannon went from below 20% to more than 80%. The company decided reaching the last 15% or 20% would not be cost effective, so it withdrew from its soccer sponsorship. However, Cannon did this in a very positive way. It invited all the journalists who covered the original announcement three years earlier to a press conference and explained how successful the sponsorship had been. Coverage of its withdrawal was very upbeat and the league was able to find a new sponsor without any problem.[16]

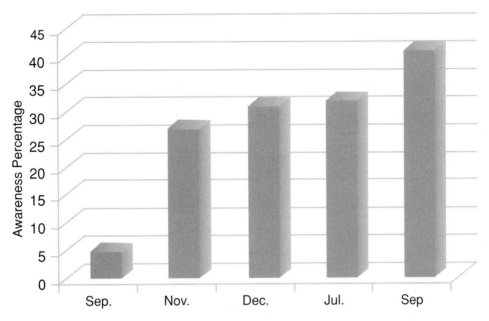

Figure 10.2. Brand Awareness Tracking Evaluation for CGU Insurance.

For a sponsor to gain a competitive advantage from the investment, its association with the sport property must be shown to be stronger than that of its competitors. This is measured by "exclusive awareness" which is defined as the percent of the target market who recognize the links between the brand and property, minus the highest percent who mistakenly believe there is a link between a non-sponsoring competitor and the property. The pioneers of this approach define a successful awareness link as a recognition score that is 10 percentage points higher than that of the nearest competitors. They offered the following example:

- Coca-Cola was the long-time official soft drink sponsor of the NFL. Fans of NFL football were asked to pick out the NFL sponsors from a list of over 80 brands, presented not by category but in a completely random order. Thirty-five percent of football fans who regularly consumed soft drinks named Coke as a sponsor of the NFL. However, 34% mistakenly identified Pepsi as a NFL sponsor. The authors commented, "It does Coke little good to be recognized as the sponsor of the NFL by 35% of NFL fans who are soft drink users, when 34% mistakenly believe Pepsi is the sponsor" (p. 13).[11]

This example has a further measurement implication. It suggests, for example, if a market leader generated 60% recall from its sponsorship, attributed recall might have been 20 or 30% even without the sponsorship. Hence, the recall measure would overestimate the effect of the sponsorship. The example also illustrates the potential error inherent in awareness studies. Recognition and recall are notoriously faulty. One way to gauge their accuracy is to ask respondents how confident they are in their answers. This could provide an estimate of how much of a response is attributable to an heuristic or to educated guessing rather than actual memory.[17] When this issue was discussed in Chapter 2, it was pointed out that selective perception screens out much of that to which people are exposed, so it is not encoded and transmitted to memory:

- In a two-week period after the European Championship Soccer Tournament was completed, sponsorship awareness questioning revealed that 50% of the fans who reported watching or attending at least three of the games were unable to name any of the sponsors involved. Only 2 out of 10 identified McDonald's and 1 out of 10, Coca-Cola and Pringles in an unprompted/top of the mind awareness approach. A prompted recall approach achieved a higher awareness with 85% of fans identifying Umbro, the England team kit sponsor, while 75% identified Carlsberg another England, UK television coverage, and tournament sponsor. The research also showed that Carling, a non-sponsor, achieved nearly as much recall at 69% and another non-sponsor, Nike, achieved 71% which was ahead of tournament sponsor adidas (70%). (p. 231)[1]

People frequently use the two heuristics of relatedness or congruity and prominence to infer a sponsor and construct a response to awareness questions as substitutes for actual recollection of a sponsor's link with an event.[17] The more natural the image fit is between a brand and the event, the more likely a brand is to be identified as a sponsor of the event. The prominence and familiarity with a brand heuristic suggests that if people use a brand or if it is a market leader, then they are likely to identify it as a sponsor. These heuristics are favored because brands that meet these criteria are more cognitively accessible to people. For example, one study reported that only 6% of people used their actual memory of the sponsorship when asked to recall event sponsors; 40% of them recalled sponsors based on "relatedness" (that is, congruence of the property with the brand's image) and 21% tended to assume that a market leader in a product category was the company affiliated with the event; the remaining 31% of responses were based on random guesses.[18] Another study reported that people recalled seeing the brands they used, irrespective of whether those brands were involved in sponsorship.[18]

Heuristics are especially prone to be used if a sport property has many sponsors. The greater the amount of clutter, the more challenging it is for a particular sponsor to be remembered. In these situations, previous cognitive associations are relied upon when people are asked to identify event sponsors. An implication of this heuristic phenomenon is that market leaders and highly related companies are likely to receive some credit for sponsoring whether they actually do so or not. It also suggests that any ambushing strategy these companies initiate is likely to have a high probability of success of consumers' misattributing a sponsorship to a more congruent, prominent, or familiar brand.

Measuring Affect: The Emotional Connection

The cognitive measures of quantity of impressions and enhanced awareness through recognition or recall measures do not necessarily translate into more sales. This was illustrated in the following example:

- A manufacturer and distributor of alcohol sponsored a horse racing classic for 15 years in a bid to achieve a greater awareness of the company's leading brand among cognac drinkers who were followers of this sporting activity. With media coverage exposure showing an annual increase, the company assumed that the brand was achieving significant awareness amongst its target markets [a questionable assumption]. They commissioned a market research study to identify extent of positive attitude change. The findings showed that attitudes to the brand were no more positive among those cognac drinkers who could identify the brand's association with the sponsorship, than among those respondents who were unaware of the brand sponsorship. These findings suggested to the company that the sponsorship investment (which was over $500,000) had no impact on the level of positive attitude to the brand, and thus the company considered withdrawing from it.[19]

In contrast, stronger emotional attachment to a brand is likely to lead to more sales. It is emotion rather than cognition that leads to action. In Chapter 1 it was pointed out that the special attribute of sponsorship is that it can facilitate a deepening and enriched relationship with a brand. This quality has led to sponsorship becoming a primary vehicle for engagement marketing, which is designed to inspire passion, reinforce loyalty, and create a sense of shared values. Thus, one experienced sponsorship manager observed: "Return on Involvement is where the game is going to be played . . . Sponsorships are all about emotion. . . . [and the need is] to measure emotional connectivity" (p. 20).[20]

Sponsors may have two types of emotional connectivity objectives. At the retail level, the focus is on strengthening customers' emotional bonds with a brand. However, in a business-to-business context concern is likely to shift to establishing affective relationships with key stakeholders.

Sponsors invariably seek image transfer from their association with a sport event. Companies recognize that for many people sport is an important part of both their self-identity and their civic pride. They are emotionally invested in "their" teams. Sponsors seek to capture some of that passion so sports fans become advocates for their brands.

If image transfer occurs at the retail level then is should be reflected in two outcome measures. First, there should be positive change in a target market's attitudes, favorable thoughts, preferences, or liking towards a brand. This can be measured before and after the event by use of Likert-type scales such as: "How favorable are you towards buying Brand X?" (extremely unfavorable/extremely favorable) or "How would you describe your attitude towards Brand X?" (very negative/very positive).

Alternatively, a rank ordering process could be used: "List the top 3 brands that you think of when considering the purchase of (a new car, insurance, financial services)"[6]; Or, "Rank order the quality of the following [credit cards]:

American Express
Discover
Master Card
VISA

Or, if the intent is to acquire specific attributes of a sport event, the ranking could relate to those attributes: "Rank order the [trust, "coolness", credibility or whatever] of the following." This ranking approach was used by VISA as part of the company's evaluation of its role as an Olympic Games TOP sponsor:

- Respondents were asked which brand or company offered the best credit card service. Three months before the Games, VISA's advantage over MasterCard was about 15 percentage points. During the games it doubled to 30 points. A month after the Games its superiority was 20 points, still greater than before Games level. This suggested that VISA's sponsorship resulted in a change in its relative position in the market place.[11]

A second method of assessing image transfer is to use affinity measures. These address how closely people feel connected to a brand. There should be a belief that the brand fits well with customers' lifestyles, values, and self-images so there is a sense that "The brand is like me." Degree of affinity can be measured by statements such as, "Brand X is for people like me" or "Brand Y is my type of brand," with respondents reporting their reaction on Likert-type scales anchored by agree/disagree.

Affinity measures were used to evaluate image transfer associated with Toyota FJ Cruiser's sponsorship of three grassroots, off-road trail events.[21] Scores from those who participated in the three sponsored events were compared with responses collected from those at three events that Toyota did not sponsor. The results in Table 10.1 show impressive affinity gains were associated with the sponsorship, while the scores in Table 10.2 indicate that the enhanced affinity translated into strong advocacy for the brand among participants.[21]

The primary vehicle for establishing affective relationships with key stakeholders in a business-to-business context is hospitality. In Chapter 3, it was noted that hospitality associated with sponsorship offers opportunities for "money-can't-buy" experiences. This makes it a potentially strong vehicle for creating or reinforcing an emotional relationship or "good chemistry." The goal is to establish warmth, likeability, trust, and

Table 10.1. Emotional Bonding with the Toyota FJ Cruiser Brand at Sponsored and Non-Sponsored Events

Statements about Toyota and FJ: (agree/disagree scale 1–5)	Non-sponsored Events	Sponsored Events	% Change
Toyota is a brand I trust	3.2	4.0	25
Toyota supports my lifestyle as a . . .	2.7	3.8	41
FJ Cruiser suits my rugged lifestyle	2.6	3.7	42
FJ Cruiser is tough like me	2.4	3.5	46
Toyota enhances experience at events important to me	2.3	3.7	61
FJ Cruiser suits my personality	2.5	3.4	36

Table 10.2. Advocacy For the Toyota FJ Cruiser Brand at Sponsored and Non-Sponsored Events			
Likelihood to act (scale 1–5)	Non-sponsored Events	Sponsored Events	% Change
Recommend any Toyota 4x4 to a friend or relative	2.9	3.8	31
Recommend FJ to a friend of relative	2.4	3.7	54
Attend FJ Cruiser event	2.3	3.4	48
Post positive news about FJ on forum or blog	1.9	3.3	74
Start a conversation about FJ Cruiser	2.3	3.2	39
Start my own FJ Cruiser group or event	1.5	2.1	40

credibility with potential customers, with the expectation that such bonding will lead to future sales. The professional role of the invited guests should be consistent with the sponsorship's objectives. For example, if awareness is an objective, then invitees should include directors of organizations who communicate with the target audience.

The evaluation challenge is how to assess the success of hospitality investments, beyond anecdotal observations. A suggested set of performance indicators is shown in Exhibit 10.2.[22] It is not appropriate to quiz invitees directly about enhanced bonding, but if this has occurred then it should be reflected in the outcome measures shown in Exhibit 10.2. These outcomes are unlikely to occur immediately, so they should be assessed later—(say) six months after the event. They should be measured against a control group comprised of companies whose executives were not entertained. However, since companies' hospitality is most likely to be extended to their best customers and prospects, it is difficult to establish a comparable control group, so the results often have a built-in bias.[22]

Exhibit 10.2

Key Performance Indicators for Corporate Hospitality

Inputs
- Number of companies invited
- Number of contacts invited
- Number of refusals
- Cancellation ratio
- No-show ratio

Outputs
- Number of guests entertained
- Quality of attendees (scoring)
- Level of enjoyment of attendees (market research)

- Stated impact of attendance (market research)

Outcomes
- Sales impact: volume and value
- Increased account profitability
- Reductions in days outstanding (and positive impact on cash-flow management/bank interest charges)
- Number of referrals received

Measuring Behavioral Outcomes

The ultimate goal of sponsorship is to increase sales and profits. However, in many cases it is not feasible to establish this relationship directly because there are too many other factors that could have contributed to sales changes over the period of the sponsorship. These could include: changes in economic conditions; other promotional communications from the company that are in effect over the same time period; increases or decreases in competitors' marketing efforts; and carry-over effects from previous sponsorship or promotion investments. Nevertheless, there are six desirable behavioral outcomes that may be measured: sales leads, boosting traffic to retail outlets, sampling and product trial, intention to purchase, actual sales, and stock price.

Sponsors may acquire *targeted sales leads* from negotiating access to a property's database of patrons, from sign-ups associated with some form of sweepstakes, or from hospitality invitees. By tracking how many of these leads are converted into sales, it is possible to measure their dollar value:

- Ameritech Corp. received $20 to $25 million in new business each year from its title sponsorship of a senior PGA Tour stop. The company entertained 200 CEO-types and 3,000-plus customers during event week. The company surveyed account executives to tally leads and new sales from the event.[23]
- In its first year as a sponsor of California State University, Fresno, California Federal Bank reported that supporters opened more than 2,000 Bulldog checking accounts as a result of the bank having access to the 60,000-member alumni mailing list. It estimated that its six-year sponsorship investment would be a profit center before year two.[25]

Boosting traffic to retail outlets is most frequently done through using a sport property's assets—players and equipment—at retail outlets; sweepstake competitions; or through advertising that leverages the sponsorship platform. NASCAR is a prime exemplar for use of a property's assets:

- DeWalt Industrial Tool co-sponsored a NASCAR team. They displayed the cars and drivers at major retailers such as Home Depot and Lowe's who stocked their products. As a result of the visits, these stores featured the DeWalt products. The company's marketing manager reported this increased visibility typically led to a 30% sales increase during the promotion period. He regarded TV exposure in race broadcasts as "icing on the cake. It is new business from incremental shelf space that justifies the cost of sponsorship."(p. 8)[24]

Sweepstakes to boost traffic were used by PrimeCo, Uniroyal Tires, and Domination Homes:

- PrimeCo Personal Communications L.P. sponsored the MLS Chicago Fire. Traffic was driven to 34 PrimeCo stores by making them the entry point to win one of 14 opportunities to kick a goal at halftime for $1 million. The promotion drew

8,000 entries, and while some people went in strictly for the promotion, the increased traffic generated incremental sales.[25]

- Uniroyal Tires used in-store giveaways such as co-branded soccer balls as part of the activation of its sponsorship of US Youth Soccer. This resulted in over 100,000 people being driven to its independent dealers of whom approximately half became customers.[25]
- Dominion Homes was a sponsor of the NHL Columbus Blue Jackets. The team was a key component of The Great American New Home Give-Away, a sweepstakes designed to drive traffic to Dominion's 35 model home centers in central Ohio. The grand prize was a $175,000 home. The builder reported a 20% increase in visits and 16% year-on-year sales increase, while nationally new home sales rose 7.4%.[25]

Visits to websites put people close to the purchase decision (maybe only a click or two away) making it a desirable behavioral outcome. Thatlook is a referral service for elective cosmetic surgery. It used title sponsorship of a NASCAR race as a promotional platform and reported more than 4 million hits in the three days following the race, whereas national daily traffic averaged under 100,000 hits.[26]

It was noted in Chapter 3 that *product trial or sampling* in some product categories is a key stage in moving people from the interest to the purchase stage in the customer decision making process. For some sponsors, the opportunity to expose sport participants or fans to test drives, new energy bars or drinks, or whatever is a primary sponsorship objective.

Intent to purchase is the closest surrogate measure to actual sales. It is assessed by surveying a target market to ascertain the likelihood of them buying a sponsor's brand. The following examples illustrate results from surveys commissioned by Bassing America and NASCAR:

- Bassing America is a membership organization of 55,000 fishermen. A key to the organization's success in attracting and retaining sponsors is the research which Bassing does each year concerning its members' purchases and intentions to pur-

Courtesy of BigStockPhoto.com

chase: Bassing tries to find out what members own by brand, what they have
purchased by brand, their intent to purchase by brand, and when they anticipate
buying. The information is compared to prior years' results (looking back three or
four years) to determine if sponsor's products are being supported. Findings are
especially helpful when contract renewals are near. The results show sponsors how
involvement with Bassing has increased their sales. For example, one annual survey showed that 15% of members owned a Ranger boat and another 21% said
they intended to purchase one. Four years later, 27% owned, and 43% intended
to buy a Ranger boat.[27]

- It was reported that 72% of NASCAR fans said they would "almost always" purchase a sponsor's brand over that of a closely priced competitor.[25] Forty-two percent annually said they switched brands when a manufacturer became a sponsor.[11]

Intent to buy can be measured by using a Likert-type scale and asking: "How likely is it
that you will try to buy [brand] that sponsors the [Dallas Cowboys] in the next three
months? (very likely/very unlikely).[27] It may be valuable when soliciting sponsors for a
sport property to collect more generic responses relating to intent to purchase such as
"Whenever possible, I try to buy brands that sponsor the [Dallas Cowboys] (strongly
disagree to strongly agree).[28]

Gains in sales are most convincingly tracked when they occur on site concurrent with
an event. Thus, a common feature of beverage sponsorships is an exclusive right to sell
on-site and such sales can easily be tracked. Similarly, service companies such as credit
card issuers and wireless providers are likely to have sales outlets at properties they sponsor. For example PrimeCo's sponsorship of MLS's Chicago Fire enabled them to sign-
up on site an average of 20 new customers for a year-long service plan and phone at
each of the team's 14 home games.[25]

Sometimes, the sponsorship agreement requires a property to purchase services or
equipment in a given category from a sponsor. For example, Delta Airlines' partnership
with the PGA Tour stipulated that if fares and routing were compatible, the PGA's
travel agency would book its players on Delta. The airline used a tracking code to tally
this revenue.[25] Alternatively, the agreement may include cross-marketing commitments
among sponsors. For example, VISA's sponsorship of the United States Postal Service
(USPS) cycling team resulted in dramatic increases in use at USPS stations. A spokesperson reported, "In year one, our business with them grew by 30% to $850 million" while
in year two it escalated by an additional 27%. A contributing factor was an incentive
that if USPS customers used a VISA card, then they would be entered into a sweepstakes to win a trip to the Tour de France.[25]

Two primary approaches are used to track sales gains. The first is to tie sales directly
to the sponsored event by tracking the redemption of coupons or ticket discounts given
with proof of purchase:

- Burroughs Wellcome Company experimented with a women's tennis sponsorship
  to market a new sunscreen lotion. By distributing coupons at the venue and tracking how many were redeemed, the company found that the tennis events effec-

tively reached the target audience of upscale women aged 30 years and older. In the following year, the company expanded its sponsorship to 12 major tournaments based on those results.[29]

- Bell Cellular Inc. co-sponsored events such as the Cadillac Golf Classic. To prompt attendees to subscribe on-site, Bell Cellular offered coupons worth $110 off the first year's bill. In one year, they signed up to 1,675 new subscribers accounting for nearly $1 million.[29]
- Subaru tracked sales of 177 vehicles to three sponsorships, each of which attracted fewer than 10,000 people. The events were a cross-country ski marathon, a canoe and kayak expo, and a sled dog marathon. Subaru created a specific offer around each sponsorship so dealers were able to tie sales back to the event. For example they offered to pay the event registration fee ($100) for the next five years to sled dog customers, and a free canoe to the expo visitors.[25]

The alternative way to measure increases in sales is to compare sales for the two- or three-month period surrounding the sponsorship to sales during a comparable period. The comparable period may be the same months in the previous year, or a similar period at another time of the year if sales of the brand are not seasonal.

- The Guinness company measured the impact of its Rugby World Cup sponsorship by comparing sales figures during the October/November time period when the event was held with sales in the same time period in the previous year. The percentage increases reported included: France 37%, Australia 20%, South Africa 24%, Great Britain 17%, Dubai 71%, and Malaysia 200%.[30]
- When Telecom company Ameritech invests in a sponsorship, it sets a sales goal based on prior sales during the same time period. For instance, if a prior period saw 4,000 phones sold, the company may target an additional 2,000 sales from a sponsorship-related promotion.[23]
- General Nutrition Centers sponsored numerous events connected with their 2,500 stores. Typically in return for sponsorship, they offered a 20% discount on event entry fees and this brought people into the stores. A computerized tracking system at the cash registers of all company-owned stores measured traffic before, during, and after an event, and tracked increases over the same-period, same-store levels from the previous year. For example, General Nutrition Centers provided $2,000 sponsorship to the Los Angeles Marathon Bike Tour. The discount entry opportunity brought in approximately 200 incremental customers, which, given an average purchase for $20 per visit, provided a two-to-one return on investment.[31]
- An axiom in the soft drink business is that if a product goes on the floor, it sells. When Coke plans an event-themed promotion, it estimates the number of incremental cases it will sell, factors in a profit ratio per case, and calculates its return based on actual sales and the amount it spent on rights fees. For example, through its ties with NASCAR, Coke saw incremental sales of 30 million commemorative bottles and placement of 20,000 vending machines and point-of-purchase displays bearing NASCAR themes in retail outlets such as Home Depots and Wal-Marts.[23]

Title sponsorships of major sport properties, especially those with global appeal, are expensive, as are "official product" sponsorship agreements associated with those major properties. Their magnitude invariably results in them receiving widespread media coverage. These large investments are made with the expectation that they will increase the company's profitability. For a publicly traded company, a key effectiveness metric of a sponsorship investment is its *influence on the stock price*. If the marketplace agrees that the company's commitment is wise, then announcements of title of official product sponsorships should be positively associated with changes in stock market prices.

This relationship was confirmed in a study of 53 official product sponsorships for the NFL, MLB, NHL, NBA, and the PGA (Professional Golfers' Association). The mean increase in stock prices around the time of the sponsorships announcements was around $257 million. This reflected an increase in the average sponsor's stock price of about 1.1%.[32] Within these results, two findings were notable. First, investors believed the association with major league teams would have greatest positive impact on sponsoring firms that were relatively small players in their market. Second, sponsorships where the congruency or fit with the sport were strongest received higher acceptance from the stock market.

In contrast to the positive findings relating to official product sponsorships, a study of the share price impacts of 114 title sponsorship agreements concluded that on average they had no impact.[33] However, there were nuances in the overall findings. NASCAR title sponsorships were positively received. The authors suggest, "It may be that the popularity of NASCAR is combined with some rather straightforward sponsorship deliverables, namely attendance and TV viewing and, particularly, a loyal demographic. In the case of golf and tennis, events appear to rely more on hospitality and more opaque relationships to the title event designation."(p. 15)[33] Like the official products sponsorships, this study also found that obvious congruence between the event and the product was an important facet of the stock market's acceptance of a title sponsorship agreement.

SUMMARY

Evaluation from the perspective of a sport manager has two purposes: (i) measuring the extent to which a sponsor's objectives were met, and (ii) providing information that can be used in sales presentations to future potential sponsors. Despite widespread lip service being given to the importance of evaluation, many sport properties and sponsors do not invest in it and many of those who do use inappropriate measures. There are three reasons for this failing: the proprietary nature of such research; a fear of the results of an evaluation by a property stemming from a lack of confidence in its ability to deliver good value; and the complexity and difficulty of measuring the impact of a sponsorship.

There are three stages in the evaluation process. The first is to ensure that SMART objectives are set, since the success of a sponsorship cannot be measured unless it is known what it is intended to achieve. The outcome objectives can relate either to return on investment or to return on objectives. The second stage is identifying benchmarks against which success will be measured. There are three benchmarks that may be used:

level of performance before the sponsorship; comparison of performance changes with a group who were not exposed to the sponsorship; and comparison of performance changes with competitive brands. The third stage is to resolve which evaluation tasks will be the responsibility of the sport property and which will be undertaken by the sponsor.

Cognitive measures are the most frequently used but they are the weakest. There are two of them. Exposure measures track the amount of media coverage a brand receives from a sponsor and use media equivalency values to arrive at a dollar value for the coverage. Frequently, weightings are incorporated to reflect the relative attractiveness of different types of media coverage. The exposure approach is conceptually flawed because (i) it measures only the extent of media output and offers no insight as to whether or not people received, interpreted, or absorbed the message; and (ii) it treats sponsorship as being analogous to advertising when it is a qualitatively different vehicle designed to accomplish different outcomes. Despite its fundamental failings, exposure continues to be the most widely used evaluation technique because the data are easy to collect, they are easy for management to understand, and they are quantitative giving the [false] appearance that sponsorship decisions are based on objective data.

Awareness is a more useful cognitive measure than exposure since it evaluates a dimension of customer response, rather than merely the amount of media visibility generalized. It is measured by either recognition or recall. Recognition uses prompts or aided memory cues, while recall refers to unaided responses. Recognition measures will invariably result in much higher proportions reporting awareness, than recall approaches. Recognition and recall are notoriously faulty. Responses often reflect congruence of a brand's "fit" with an event, level of market leadership, or people's usage level, rather than their actual memory of a brand as an event sponsor.

Affect measures that identify extent of the emotional connection between a brand and its target market are much more useful and valuable than cognitive measures. Image transfer is a widely sought objective of sponsors. If it occurs, then it should be reflected in two outcome measures. There should be positive changes in a target market's attitudes, favorable thoughts, preference or liking towards a brand, and people should feel an affinity connection to a brand. Both of these outcomes can be measured by Likert-type scales. In business-to-business contexts, hospitality is used to build affect with customers—warmth, likeability, trust, and credibility. This can be measured in subsequent sales with hospitality invitees.

There are six behavioral outcomes that can be measured: (i) targeted sales leads; (ii) boosting traffic to retail outlets or to websites; (iii) product trial or sampling; (iv) intent-to-purchase, measured by surveys ascertaining the likelihood of people buying a sponsor's brand; (v) actual gains in sales made on site or by contract with the sport property for its business; and (vi) changes in stock price when an investment in a sponsorship is announced.

Given both the difficulty of isolating the impact of a sponsorship and that many sponsorships have multiple objectives, it is likely most companies committed to serious evaluation will use combinations of the approaches discussed in this chapter.

Endnotes

1. Masterman, G. (2007). *Sponsorship for a return on investment*. Burlington MA: Butterworth-Heinemann.

2. IEG. (2011). Decision-makers survey; Sponsors favor activation budgets in 2011. *IEG Sponsorship Report*, March 14.

3. D'Alesandro, D. F. (2001). Beyond the mother-in-law strategy: Avoiding consumers' indifference. *Sponsorship Report, 20*(6), 1, 4–5.

4. Meenaghan, J. A. (2005). Evaluating sponsorship effects. In J. Amis and B. Cornwell (Eds.). *Global sport sponsorship*. New York: Berg.

5. Fry, A. (2008). Evaluation: Maingoals. *Sport-Business International*, April, p. 20.

6. Madrigal, R. (2012). Personal communication with the author.

7. Collett, P., & Fenton, W. (2011). *The sponsorship handbook*. Hoboken NS: Jossey-Bass.

8. Beiferheld, S. (2010). Is measurement up to sponsors or properties? Answer: Yes. *SportsBusiness Journal*, July 26, p. 10.

9. IEG. (1990). A guide to sponsorship evaluation. *Special Events Report*, September 24, 4–5.

9a. Broughton, D. (2010). Lower ad rates drive down expo sure value. *SportsBusiness Journal*, __ December 20, p. 13.

10. Mickle, T. (2010). Izod: 350% return in first year of IndyCar deal. *SportsBusiness Journal*, November 15, p. 11.

11. Crimmins, J., & Horn, M. (1996). Sponsorship: From management ego trip to marketing success. *Journal of Advertising Research*, July/August, 11–21.

12. Ording, M. (2012). Measuring TV exposure does not capture sponsorship ROI. *IEG Sponsorship Blog*, May 3.

13. Poknyqzynski, J. (2000). Sports sponsors know what they want. *SportsBusiness Journal*, June 5–11, 2.

14. Pearsall, J. (2010). Sponsorship performance: What is the role of sponsorship metrics in proactively managing the sponsor-property relationship? *Journal of Sponsorship, 3*(2), 115–123.

15. Tripodi, J., Hirons, M., Bednall, D., & Sutherland, M. (2003). Cognitive evaluation: Prompts used to measure sponsorship awareness. *International Journal of Market Research*, (4) 435–455.

16. IEG. (1986). Evaluation sponsorships. *Special Events Report*, December 15, 5.

17. Johar, G. V., & Pham, M. T. (1999). Relatedness, prominence, and constructive sponsor identification. *Journal of Marketing Research, 36*(3), 299–312.

18. IEG. (2000). Research on recall rates raises flags for sponsors. *Sponsorship Report, 19*(3), 1,3.

19. Meenaghan, J. A. (1983). Commercial sponsorship. *European Journal of Marketing, 17*(7), 5–73.

20. Gillis, R. (2009). The credibility gap. *Sports-Business International*, March, p. 20.

21. Savary, J. (2008). Advocacy marketing: Toyota's secrets for partnering with trendsetters to create passionate brand advocates. *Journal of Sponsorship, 1*(3), 211–224.

22. Collett, P. (2008). Sponsorship-related hospitality: Planning for measurable success. *Journal of Sponsorship, 1*(3), 286–296.

23. IEG. (1999). ROI: Sponsors share how their deals pay off. *Sponsorship Report, 18*(6), 1, 7.

24. IEG. (2002). DeWalt strategy ensures eight-figure motorsports team title pays for itself. *Sponsorship Report 21*(20), 8.

25. Ukman, L. (2007). *How to measure, justify and maximize your return on sponsorships and partnerships* (5th ed.). Chicago, Illinois: International Event Group.

26. IEG. (2000). Thatlook.com sets sights on more sponsorship. *Sponsorship Report, 19*(15), 3.

27. IEG. (1990). Evaluation: Measuring return on investment. *Special Events Report*, September 7, 3, 6–7.

28. Madrigal, R. (2001). Social identity effects in a belief-attitude-intentions hierarchy: Implications for corporate sponsorship. *Psychology and Marketing, 18*(2), 145–165.

29. Lavelle, B. (1991). How Bell Cellular boosted its return from events. *Special Events Report, 19*(12), 4–5.

30. Rines, S. (2002). Guinness Rugby World Cup sponsorship: A global platform for meeting business objectives. *International Journal of Sports Marketing & Sponsorship*, December/January, 449–464.

31. IEG. (1995). General Nutrition Centers see sales increase, seek deals. *Sponsorship Report, 14*(23), 5.

32. Cornwell, T. B., Pruitt, S. W., & Clark, J. M. (2005). The relationship between major-league sports' official sponsorship announcements and the stock prices of sponsoring firms. *Journal of the Academy of Marketing Sciences, 33*(4), 401–412.

33. Clark, J. M., Cornwell, T. B., & Pruitt, S. W. (2006). The impact of title event sponsorship announcements on shareholder wealth. *Market Letters*.

Index

About the Author

John L. Crompton

John L. Crompton holds the rank of University Distinguished Professor and is both a Regents Professor and a Presidential Professor for Teaching Excellence at Texas A&M University. He received his basic training in England. His undergraduate work was in physical education and geography at Loughborough College. After teaching high school for a year, he attended the University of Illinois, where he completed a MS degree in Recreation and Park Administration in 1968. In 1970, he was awarded another MS degree from Loughborough University of Technology in Recreation Management.

In 1970, he joined Loughborough Recreation Planning Consultants as their first full-time employee. When he left as managing director in 1974, LRPC had developed into the largest consulting firm in the United Kingdom specializing in recreation and tourism, with a full-time staff of 25 which was supplemented by a number of part-time associate consultants.

In 1974, Dr. Crompton came to Texas A&M University. He received his doctorate in Recreation Resources Development in 1977. For some years he taught graduate and undergraduate courses in both the Department of Recreation and Parks and the Department of Marketing at Texas A&M University, but he now teaches exclusively in the Department of Recreation, Park and Tourism Sciences.

Dr. Crompton's primary interests are in the areas of marketing and financing public leisure and tourism services. He is author or co-author of 18 books and a substantial number of articles that have been published in the recreation, tourism, sport and marketing fields. He is the most published scholar in the history of both the parks and recreation, and the tourism fields.

Dr. Crompton has conducted many hundreds of workshops on Marketing and/or Financing Leisure Services. He has lectured or conducted workshops in many foreign countries and has delivered keynote addresses at the World Leisure Congress and at Annual National Park and Recreation Conferences in Australia, Canada, Great Britain, Japan, New Zealand, South Africa, and the United States.

He is a past recipient of the National Park Foundation's Cornelius Amory Pugsley award for outstanding national contributions to parks and conservation; the US Department of Agriculture's Agricultural Colleges National Teacher of the Year Award;

the National Recreation and Park Association's (NRPA) Distinguished Professional award; the NRPA National Literary award; the NRPA Roosevelt award for outstanding research; the Distinguished Colleague and the Distinguished Teaching awards of the Society of Park and Recreation Educators; the Travel and Tourism Research Association's Travel Research award; the U.S. Department of Agriculture National Award for Teaching Excellence; and is a Minnie Stevens Piper Professor for excellent teaching in the state of Texas.

At Texas A&M, he is Cintron University Professor for Excellence in Undergraduate Teaching. He has received the Bush Excellence Award for Public Service (presented personally by President H. W. Bush); the Vice Chancellor's Award for Excellence in Graduate Teaching; the Texas Agricultural Experiment Station's Faculty Fellow and Senior Faculty Fellow Awards for exceptional research contributions; the University Distinguished Achievement Award for Research and the University Distinguished Achievement Award for Teaching.

He was a member of the NRPA's Board of Trustees for nine years; and is a past president of four professional bodies: the Texas Recreation and Parks Society; the American Academy of Park and Recreation Administration; the Society of Park and Recreation Educators; and the Academy of Leisure Sciences. He is a Board member of the National Recreation Foundation.

In 2006, the city of College Station named a new 16-acre neighborhood park, John Crompton Park. Dr. Crompton served four years as a city councilman for College Station from 2007–2011, and was Mayor Pro Tem in 2010–2011. The city's population was 95,000, the annual budget was $260 million, and there were approximately 900 full-time employees. The six council members and the mayor were all elected city wide.